OLD MASTER DRAWINGS

FROM THE COLLECTION OF JOHN AND ALICE STEINER

In memory of John Steiner and for Alice Steiner ■ ■ ■

EXHIBITION ITINERARY

YALE UNIVERSITY ART GALLERY
NEW HAVEN, CONNECTICUT
April 18 – June 8, 1986

SANTA BARBARA MUSEUM OF ART
SANTA BARBARA, CALIFORNIA
August 9 – September 14, 1986

SPRINGFIELD MUSEUM OF FINE ARTS
SPRINGFIELD, MASSACHUSETTS
October 5, 1986 – January 4, 1987

MUSCARELLE MUSEUM OF ART,
COLLEGE OF WILLIAM AND MARY
WILLIAMSBURG, VIRGINIA
February 27 – April 12, 1987

Old Master Drawings from the Collection of John and Alice Steiner

edited by

ALFRED MOIR

assisted by

Carmen Roxanne Robbin
Richard Serros
Hans Van Miegroet

with contributions by

Janice Isemoto, Ann Lenard, Teresa Longyear, Faith Mayo,
Noel Moyer, Robin Thorne Ptacek, Isabel Ronchietto

SANTA BARBARA MUSEUM OF ART
1986

Cover: Titian, ***A Grove of Trees Beside a Pool***

Published by the Santa Barbara Museum of Art
1130 State Street
Santa Barbara, California, 93101

Edited by Alfred Moir
Designed by Deborah Hewitt
Photographed by David Stansbury

Typeset in English Times by Marguerite Graphic Arts Service, Chicopee, Massachusetts & Sir Speedy, Springfield, Massachusetts
Printed in an edition of 1,500 by W. E. Andrews Co., Inc. of Connecticut

Library of Congress Cataloging-in-Publication Data
Moir, Alfred
Old Master Drawings from the Collection of John and Alice Steiner
Bibliography: p.
1. Drawing—Exhibitions. 2. Steiner, John, 1903-1983 Art collection—Exhibitions. 3. Steiner, Alice, 1912- Art collections—Exhibitions. 4. Drawing—Private collections—United States—Exhibitions. I. Moir, Alfred. II. Santa Barbara Museum of Art.
NC31.S74043 1986 741.94'074'049491
85-31793 ISBN 0-89951-060-4

TABLE OF CONTENTS

Chief Curator's Foreword

The field of old master drawings, while not without its rivalries, is distinguished by special qualities of generosity and collegiality among its collectors, scholars and dealers. It is a small kingdom within the larger art world and consequently depends upon the regular exchange of information (even when it differs), and certain kinds of cooperation prove both useful and necessary. Exhibitions based on the collaboration of distinguished collectors, scholars and institutions are typical of this spirit. The Steiners, and many other drawing collectors, make their collections available to scholars and students and most collectors lend regularly to exhibitions. Collectors in turn, have benefited from the guidance of others and have turned to curators, dealers, scholars for advice in the process of forming their collections. While learning themselves, each aids and encourages others interested in old master drawings.

John and Alice Steiner have not been collecting drawings for a long period of time, but they have made up for this in the energy and enthusiasm they have given to building a collection which is extensive, varied, and of extremely high quality considering the relatively short time they have had to accomplish this. To do so, it seems as though they must have spent every spare moment visiting exhibitions, studying catalogues and consulting dealers, so broad is their acquaintance with the sources and the resources within the field. They have made it a point to visit drawing collections wherever they travel and when they appeared at the Museum on their first visit to Santa Barbara, it was an unexpected opportunity to renew an acquaintance begun some years earlier when they loaned a drawing to an exhibition project of mine. That meeting led to further contacts and a growing friendship from which developed the idea for this exhibition. Our Museum—with its excellent collection of modern drawings and growing collection of old master drawings—has a long history of interest in this medium and in the encouragement of drawing collecting, connoisseurship and scholarship. Thus, we consider this collaboration of students, collectors, experts and institution to be a most appropriate enterprise. Furthermore, it is a rare honor for us to be able to sponsor the exhibition of so distinguished a collection. For me, having the responsibility for the coordination of all these resources is the most challenging and at the same time the most rewarding of all curatorial duties, somewhat like conducting a complicated orchestral work.

In preparing this catalogue, the students in Professor Moir's seminar have made a careful evaluation of existing information as well as having the chance to do original research—the responsibility to challenge or substantiate the attributions of the drawings assigned to them. This exercise of the indispensible skills of their discipline provides them with a very special opportunity. Many generations of students will be indebted to the Steiners, as are we, for their willingness to share what they have accomplished. Some collectors might reserve such work to eminent scholars, but it is characteristic of the Steiners that they have twice made their collection available to university students for that purpose. The result may be less homogenous than the work of a single author, but the drawings themselves vary considerably in the kind of information they can yield and they range over many periods and styles. Some will remain enigmatic, others have an impressive concensus of opinion; it is the nature of many old master drawings to be both changeable and/or irresolvable of attribution. Each publication broadens or revises our knowledge; each catalogue—including this one—brings new information and other insights to this complex, fascinating field.

At the core of this endeavor is the collection itself. Great collections are the result of many factors. The means and the desire to acquire works of art are necessary, but they cannot guarantee that an outstanding collection will result. A certain passion, persistence, a trained eye, and luck are all part of the process. Thus, the results differ according to the factors at work. The first and most indefinable of these is the vision of the collector, something formed from the raw materials of his life and focused at the moment he confronts the object of desire. The Steiner collection is the collaborative effort of a husband and wife and, therefore, the interplay is even more involved. The accomplishments of Alice Steiner and the late John Steiner speak very clearly about the two remarkable people who created this collection. The privilege of viewing many of these drawings with John Steiner—as I did in the last months of his life—was a vivid revelation of the joy that he derived from them; it is a cherished memory. And it is good to know that the collecting will be continued by Alice Steiner.

We are indebted to all those who have made this multi-faceted project possible: to the Steiners, John and Alice, for creating and sharing their collection; to Professor Alfred Moir and his students whose scholarly labors make up the contents of this catalog (and all those upon whose earlier work they drew); to the staff of the Santa Barbara Museum of Art who provided innumerable services for the publication and exhibition, especially Barry Heisler, Curator for Collections, and intern Holly Wilson who, in giving careful attention to *every* detail of this catalogue, has made the crooked straight and the rough places smooth; to Richard Mühlberger, Director of the Museum of Fine Arts, Springfield, Massachusetts, and his staff for special help with the catalogue and exhibition details (especially to designer, Debbie Hewitt and photographer, David Stansbury, who have created a publication worthy of its contents); to Richard S. Field, Curator of Prints, Drawings and Photographs, Yale University Art Gallery; and to Mark M. Johnson, Director, Joseph and Margaret Muscarelle Museum of Art.

Robert Henning, Jr.
Chief Curator

COLLECTOR'S FOREWORD

It is with a heavy heart that I am writing a preface to this catalogue for a second exhibition of our drawings. Our first, much smaller exhibition took place in 1977, at the Fogg Art Museum, Harvard University. It was at that time the culmination of our wishes, after having started to collect drawings only six years before. John had set himself a secret deadline for this event: his seventy-fifth birthday. We were a year ahead of schedule and were very proud of the fact that we had managed to acquire so many worthwhile drawings together. At that time I promised myself never again to let so much of our collection leave us at one time.

In May 1983 both Alfred Moir and Robert Henning approached us with the idea of another exhibition, partly to celebrate the newly refurbished Santa Barbara Museum. John said "yes". Neither he nor I knew at that time how ill he was - he died about six weeks after these conversations. I now feel bound to break my promise to myself in order to keep his and, therefore, dedicate this exhibition to his memory.

Even at the time of the Fogg exhibition we had more drawings than could have been exhibited - it was mainly a question of room then. Of course we went on buying and have acquired many more drawings since that time. And I have continued on myself with this activity - John would be surprised to see quite a few drawings here that he never knew about, but which I hope are up to his standard.

What we said at the time of the Fogg exhibition about art providing an oasis for us in these ever more frightening times still holds true and there is really nothing more that I can add. It only remains for me to thank all those who worked so lovingly and diligently on this exhibition and on the beautiful and scholarly catalogue that goes with it.

Alice F. Steiner

EDITOR'S FOREWORD

This exhibition originated in February 1983, when John and Alice Steiner came to spend a month in Santa Barbara. During their visit, they familiarized themselves with the Santa Barbara Museum of Art, its collections, its curatorial staff, and its friends. They met Santa Barbara collectors of art and saw their collections. At the kind suggestion of Konrad Oberhuber, they made contact with me and became aware of the city's other art center, at the University of California in Santa Barbara. They visited the University Museum and its collections, met several of my colleagues, inspected our library, and saw some of the exhibition catalogues that had been prepared by the University faculty and graduate students.

This exhibition and catalogue are not the first instance of cooperation between the University and the Santa Barbara Museum of Art. Several of my colleagues have worked on collaborative projects. This is the fifth exhibit of Old Master drawings that I have curated at the museum, and the second full-scale publication, the other being the catalogue, *European Drawings in the Collection of the Santa Barbara Museum of Art,* prepared in collaboration with a group of University students.

During the Spring of 1983, Robert Henning, Jr., Chief Curator, made tentative arrangements for exhibition here of a selection of drawings from the Steiners' collection. The following June, I visited John and Alice in New York to make the preliminary selection of drawings to be included. Working with a museum, its curatorial staff, and University contributors was not a new experience for the Steiners. In 1977, Konrad Oberhuber and his students at Harvard participated in an exhibition of portions of the Steiners' collection at the Fogg Museum. The catalogue they prepared has proven an indispensable resource for this exhibition and catalogue.

Selection of drawings from the collection was a pleasure, although not without some pain. The pleasure came from the range, variety, and quality of the drawings, the documentation that the Steiners had painstakingly gathered, and the assurance with which most of the attributions could be made. The pain came from the necessity of excluding some beautiful drawings. The original intention was to include no more than one drawing by each artist. However, in the face of the splendid group of sheets by the Tiepolos, my resolve vanished, particularly because none of the Tiepolos had been shown in the 1977 exhibition from the collection. As a glance through this catalogue will show, a few other duplications turned out to be irresistible as well. In keeping with the character of the exhibit as a joint museum-university venture, some choices were determined as much by the historical as by the aesthetic significance of the drawing, particularly when it would introduce a theme or motif that otherwise would be lacking. Fortunately academic interests of this sort could be satisfied without compromising quality.

In going through the collection, I was struck by the ubiquity of the human figure in the drawings and by the frequency with which these figures were given an environment. That is, the draughtsman had not simply sketched the figure — or an arm or a leg or any object — and left it floating on the sheet, but had also created the illusion of a three-dimensional setting, or environment, for it. This recurring characteristic suggested an emphasis on a characteristic of the art of drawing: the opportunity it provides the artist to suggest so much with so little. Many drawings demonstrate the magic of the draughtsman's ability with pen and ink or chalk to conjure up the image of the human figure out of the void of the blank sheet of paper. These works were selected to show his next trick: to create by means of a few lines, an environment with apparent length, depth, height, time, furniture, foliage, weather, or whatever is necessary and appropriate to rescue the figure from the void and to give it a place to put its feet down and be at home.

So the drawings in this exhibit are complete in the sense that they not only include figures but also situate them in some place. This place may be elaborate and detailed as in the della Rovere interior (number 38) or the Goeree piazza (number 75). Or the environment itself may be the real theme of the drawing, as in the Swanevelt (number 87) and other landscapes where the human figures are mere accessories. Or the setting may consist of nothing more than the few lines necessary to suggest clouds or a podium as in the Tiepolos (numbers 42 and 43) or a floor and a wall as in the Ghezzi (number 22). Three drawings in the group may seem exceptions: the

Bibiena (number 7), the Titian (number 46) and the van Uden (number 89), because apparently none of them includes a human figure. But all three are appropriate for human occupation and, in fact, in the Titian a couple of figures are faintly visible; the Bibiena is ready for humans to move in; and the van Uden is waiting for its maker to use it in a peopled painting.

A third of the drawings in this exhibit were included in the 1977 exhibit. Thus, we have been able to include many of the most distinguished drawings from that show without duplicating it. At the same time, in the remaining two-thirds of this show, we have had the opportunity of presenting a number of drawings the Steiners acquired during the intervening years.

Chronologically the exhibit spans three centuries: the earliest artists, Urs Graf, Titian, and Heemskerck, were all born before 1500; the latest, Gian Domenico Tiepolo, Fragonard, and Hubert Robert, all lived into the nineteenth century. Geographically, the travels of the artists covered great distances: south with Beinaschi and Stevens in Naples and north with van Everdingen in Scandinavia and Waterloo in Danzig; from the east with Stevens in Prague to the west with van de Velde and Rowlandson across the English channel. There were few who did not travel great distances, at least during their youths. We discover artists from the Netherlands haunted hardly less by the Alps and the Rhineland than by Italy. Landscapes and religious subjects with either single figures or groups, prevail in the exhibit, but there are also historical and mythological subjects, and a couple of portraits. There are many undercurrents: the role and importance of the artist's atelier; the influence of patrons like Rudolf II or the Medici; the inspiration provided by the theatre and such public events as festivals, royal baptisms and funerals; the importance of printmaking in the Netherlands; the evolution of the Dutch visions of landscape. Ominously there is also an undercurrent of discord: the Sack of Rome that sent Perino del Vaga in flight from the Holy City, the invasions and religious conflict that dislocated so many of Antwerp's artists during the late sixteenth and early seventeenth centuries, and, as if in answer, Huchtenburg's presentation of the excitement of battle. There also are some surprises: the long shadows cast by Raphael, the Carracci, and Rembrandt, are not unexpected; but the frequency with which the influence of Jacques Callot or Roelandt Savery has to be acknowledged may be.

Many of these drawings were made in preparation for prints or paintings, but a surprising number of them seem to have been made as ends in themselves. The media range from simple chalk or monochromatic pen and ink to colorful gouache or watercolor. While these 101 drawings do not give a complete picture of western European draughtsmanship during the three centuries, they do give quite a comprehensive one; the omissions are as much of individuals as of regions or schools.

The preparation of this catalogue was facilitated by the documentation that the Steiners have maintained throughout their years of collecting. They have been assiduous in seeking (and remarkable in heeding!) expert advice. But they also have trained themselves, and they have pursued their collecting with passion. Once they acquired a drawing, they didn't just file it away. They subjected it to intense scrutiny and systematic scholarship. Each drawing has its own page or pages in a notebook, recording not only its physical characteristics, history, subject matter, and related literature but also relevant expert opinions. Mrs. Steiner generously made all of this invaluable documentation available. We have also used, as source material, entries from the 1977 catalogue done for the Fogg Museum show by Konrad Oberhuber and his students at Harvard, adding or revising where necessary. The general conclusions on each drawing in the 1977 exhibit have been summarized, but much of the specific evidence and reasoning leading to those conclusions has been left out. Some of our entries add little more than another point of view to what was written at that time. Other drawings have been given a new interpretation in the light of a number of relevant new publications. And we have made a few discoveries as well.

The process of writing this catalogue began in a seminar at the University during the Autumn quarter of 1984. Each of the students — six graduates and one undergraduate — undertook responsibility for three drawings that had not previously been catalogued, and for updating two that had been included in the 1977 catalogue. During the Winter and Spring quarters, work was continued independently under my direction by two of the graduate students, Roxanne Robbin and Richard Serros, assisted by two undergraduates, under a Fund for the Improvement of Post Secondary Education (FIPSE) grant. Mr. Serros wrote most of the entries on sixteenth century Italians; Ms. Robbin's are on Italians of the seventeenth century. Two other graduate students also participated: Hans van Miegroet did most of the Flemish artists, and Ann Lenard worked on several of the Dutchmen. Finally, I did preparatory research on all of the drawings during four trips to New York and abroad, prepared entries not done by the graduate students, wrote most of the biographies, and served as a ruthless editor, cutting down the student contributions to a manageable length and attempting to give a unity of style to the text. I was assisted at the onset by Kathy MacIver for bibliography.

None of this would have been possible without the cooperation of many individuals to whom special thanks are due. First of all, Alice Steiner who has stripped the walls of her house to loan us the drawings, provided the basic documentation, and has been most generous of her time and hospitality. Second, Konrad Oberhuber, in the latest of many acts of friendship to me, provided the impetus for the exhibit by bringing the Steiners together with us in Santa Barbara and then by encouraging the idea of having the exhibit. He has another responsibility: as a trusted and generous friend of the Steiners whose expert advice they have often sought. In this connection, I should also mention Dr. Ann Zwollo, Professor Egbert Haverkamp Begemann, and Mr. Jacob Bean. While they have no direct connection with either this exhibit or the catalogue, their opinions appear again and again in the Steiners' archives, providing much useful information and many of the attributions.

In Santa Barbara, Robert Henning, Jr., Chief Curator of the Santa Barbara Museum of Art, has been the key to this complex project. He has ably overseen the numerous technical details essential to the project including invaluable editorial advice, leaving all the pleasure of choosing the show and compiling the catalogue to me and my students. Curator of Collections, Barry Heisler, has been ever helpful. Holly Wilson, curatorial intern at the Santa Barbara Museum of Art, has provided invaluable editorial assistance and careful research. As usual the Art Library of the University of California, Santa Barbara, has been indispensable. Particular thanks are due to Dr. Felipe Cervera, head of the Art Exhibition Catalogue collection, Susan Hillery, Melinda Land, and Kathleen MacIntosh in Circulation, and William Treese who oversees it all. Much is owed to the Frick Art Reference Library in New York and the Witt Library in London and to the assistance provided by their staffs. Thanks are due also to Professor Edmond J. Keller, Associate Dean of the Graduate Division of the University and director of the FIPSE project, for support of the students, and to Christine Iriart, FIPSE project manager, for exemplary administration.

Finally I want to thank the students who participated, for their enthusiastic cooperation, diligence, and intelligence.

Alfred Moir
Professor of History of Art
University of California, Santa Barbara

Entries prepared by the students are signed with their initials; unsigned entries are by the editor.

All drawings have been remeasured for this catalogue. The height was measured along the right edge and the width along the bottom. The dimensions given for sheets that are irregular in shape are the longest height and the longest width. Height precedes width.

The description of the medium is based on the present appearance.

No description of paper is given unless it is in some way unusual.

No inscriptions on mounts are given unless they provide important information (i.e. provenance).

In concurrence with the collector's wish, the name of the last previous owner or auction source of each drawing is not included in the provenance. The catalogue of the previous exhibition is listed separately from other references to the literature respecting a drawing, as Oberhuber 1977, preceded by the name of the student-author of the entry. Otherwise, full bibliographic references are given in the appropriate footnotes to works mentioned in respect to one drawing only. Footnote references to sources consulted for more than one drawing are abbreviated to the author's family name, the source's date, and volume, page and illustration number. Full references to these sources are given in the Bibliography of Frequently Consulted Works.

A few periodicals and standard references are consistently abbreviated as follows:

AB: Art Bulletin
Burl: Burlington Magazine
JdPK: Jahrbuch der Preuszischen Kunstsammlungen
L: Frits Lugt, *Les Marques de Collections de Dessins et d'Estampes*
Le Bl: Charles Le Blanc, *Manuel de l'amateur d'estampes . . .*
MD: Master Drawings

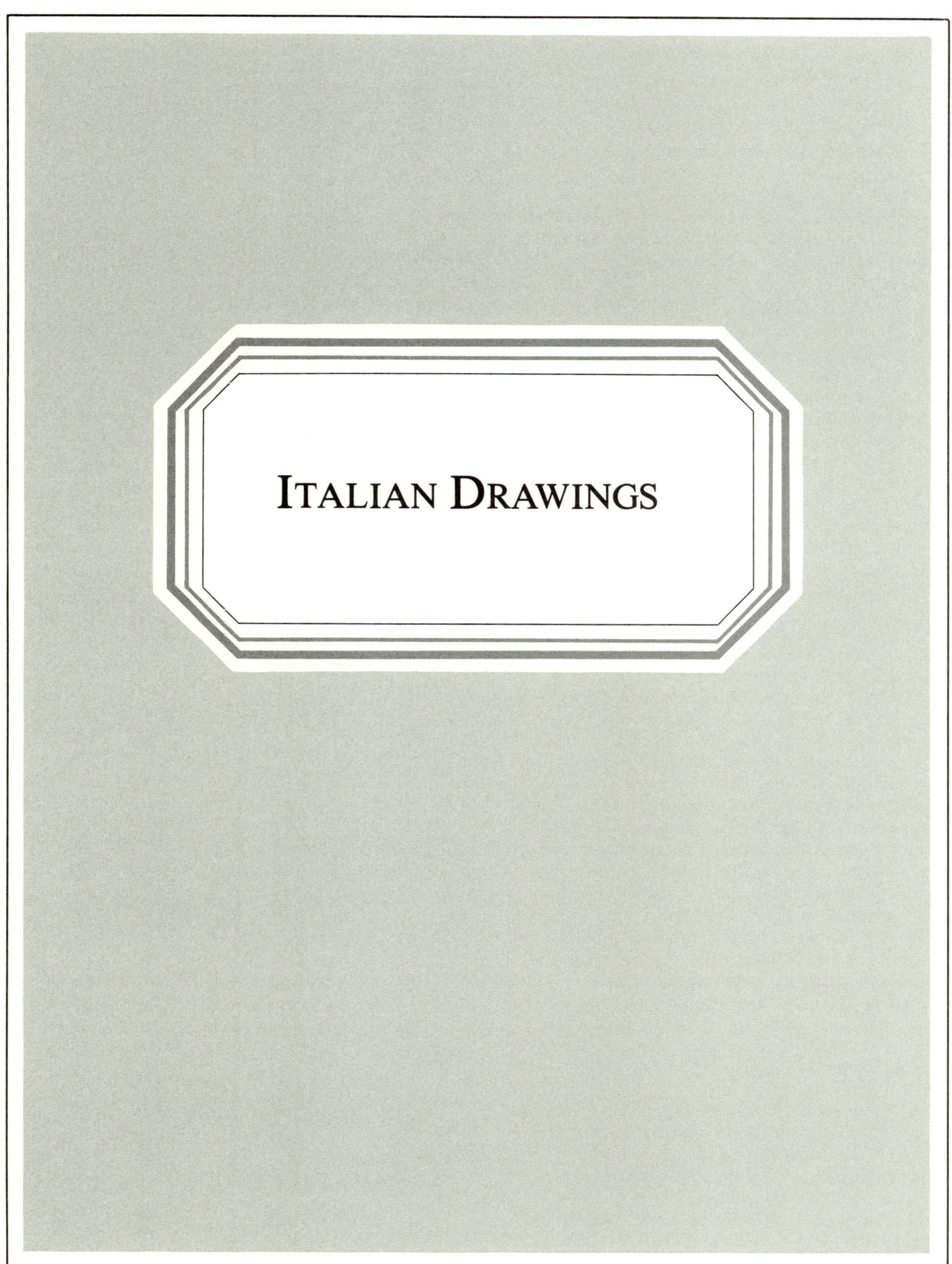

Italian Drawings

1.

FRANCESCO ALLEGRINI OR HIS CIRCLE
(Gubbio 1624-1663 Rome)

Four Figures Looking to the Left

Pen and brown ink with touches of black ink, brown wash; 133 x 108 mm.
Inscription: illegible word, lower left, in pen and ink
Provenance: Sir Joshua Reynolds (L.2364); unidentified collector's mark next to Reynolds' mark: capital B encircled by a corona of small triangles
Acquired 1972

For this puzzling drawing, attributions to Carlo Bonone, Giacomo Cavedone, and Giovanni Baglione have been suggested as well as to Francesco Allegrini. Furthermore, the subject matter is uncertain. Probably the original drawing was larger, and a section on the left, with the event to which these four figures are reacting, has been cut off.

The taut manner of drawing, the physiognomies, and the use of wash to develop the figures' volume, all have affinity to Baglione's draughtsmanship. But this style is more labored; the pen line starts and stops, while Baglione's usual delineation flows without interruption, forming beautiful lines that in themselves create a sense of the figures' corporeality. Allegrini's manner of drawing is closer, as can be seen in his *Lot and His Daughters* in the Metropolitan Museum[1]. There the central figure's face is comprised like the face of the man on the left, of three dots of wash without any drawn contour, and drawn contours are sometimes reinforced by swathes of wash. Closest to this drawing is the *Mounted Horseman*[2] by Allegrini that was in the London art market during 1984[3]. The same mannerisms appear in both drawings: the abbreviated rendering of hands, the pointed triangular feet, and the physiognomies of the equestrian and of the standing woman.

Despite the similarities, the monumentality of the figures differs from Allegrini's customary spasmotic delineation of contours, which seems finicky in comparison. Perhaps these differences can be accounted for by assigning the drawing to some pupil of Allegrini or another member of his family. His father, Flaminio, and his son and daughter, Flaminio Jr. and Angelica, were also artists, and their individual styles have yet to emerge from the shadow of Francesco, the family's best known member[4].

As for the subject matter, it is tempting to suggest the *Calling of St. Matthew* (Matthew ix: 9). The bearded man on the left would then be the saint himself, responding to Christ's summons with the hand gesture made famous by Caravaggio's painting in the church of San Luigi de'Francesi in Rome. Alternatively, the subject might be *Mary Magdalen Washing Christ's Feet* (John xii: 2-6). In this case, Christ and the Magdalen would have been in the left portion of the sheet, and would have cast the two shadows that are seen on the floor. These three men would be disciples and this woman Martha, all dismayed at the Magdalen's use of such an expensive ointment that might better have been sold for the benefit of the poor, as Judas had sensibly suggested. C.R.R.

1. inv. no. 80.3.256; Bean, 1979, p. 17, no. 4.
2. The subject is in fact probably from Torquato Tassi's epic poem *Gerusalemme Liberata,* and the equestrian is probably Clorinda, the Saracen heroine-warrior. Allegrini painted fifteen scenes from the epic in a ceiling in the Palazzo Mattei-Paganica in Rome, now in the Sala dei Capitani in the Palazzo dei Conservatori (Gere and Pouncey, 1983, p. 27).
3. Kate Ganz, *Exhibition Catalogue,* London, Summer 1984, p. 1, fig. 6.
4. Gere and Pouncy, 1983, p. 26.

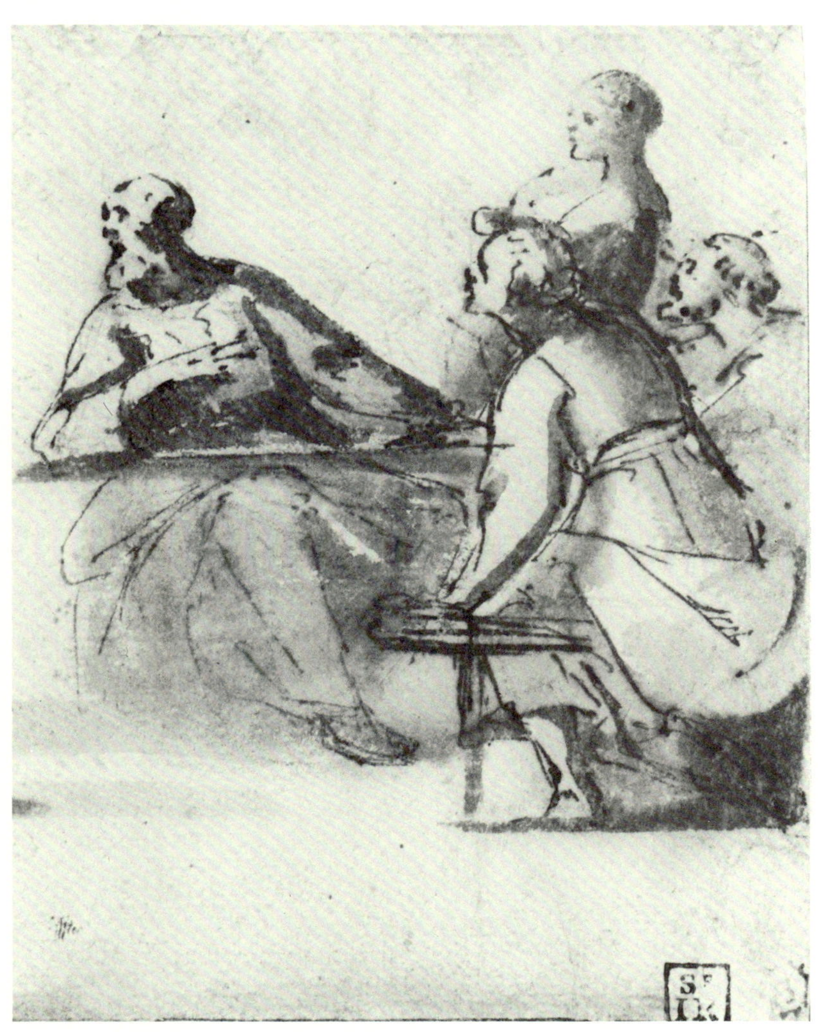

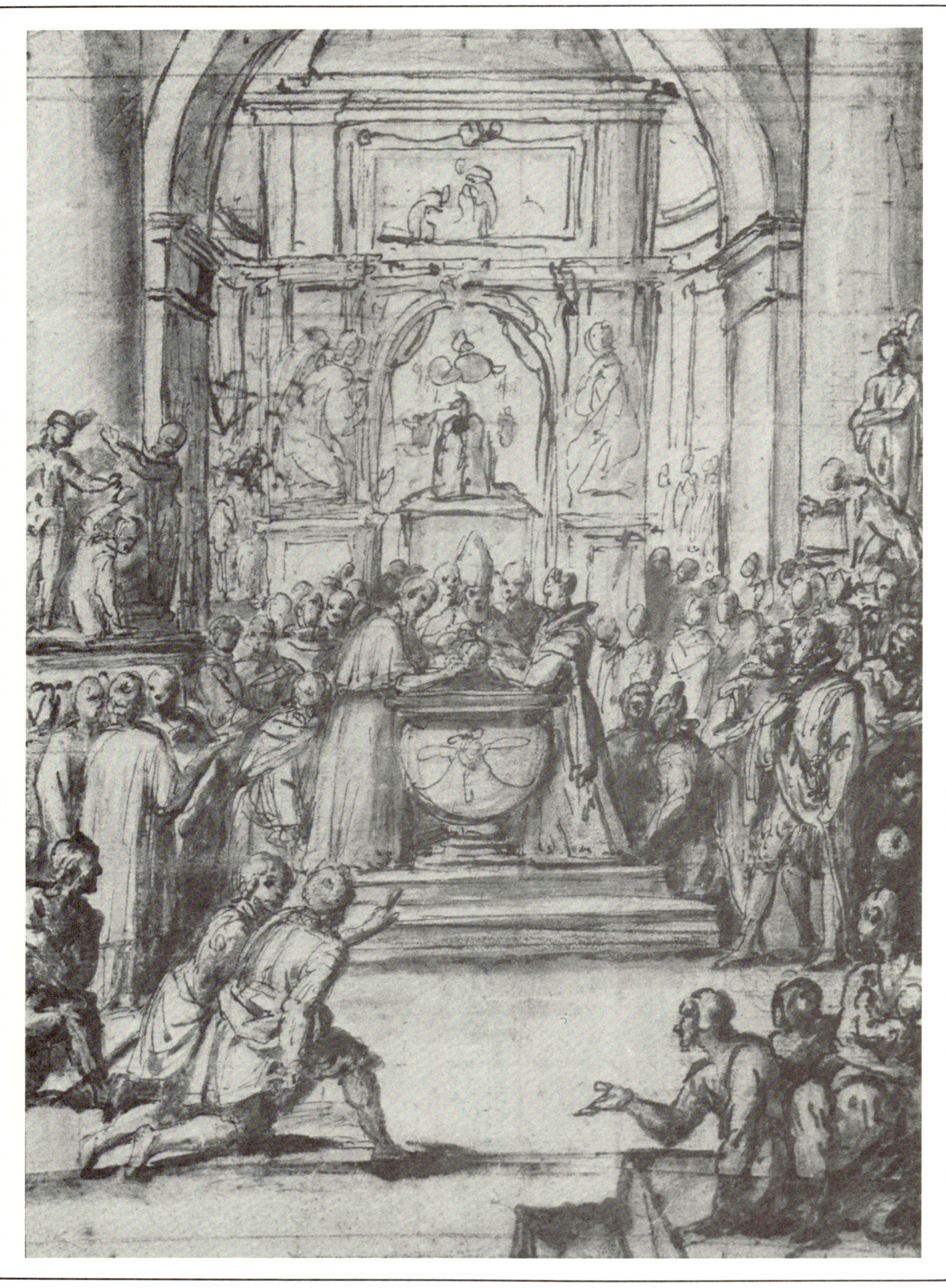

2.

ANONYMOUS TUSCAN
Late Sixteenth or Early Seventeenth Century

A Baptism

Pen and brown ink with touches of black ink, brown wash, squared in black chalk; 252 x 178 mm. including a strip 19 mm. high added across the bottom
Provenance: Christie's, London, 11 Dec. 1979, lot 68 as attributed to Passignano
Acquired 1980

This drawing presents knotty problems both of attribution and of historical signification, which have not as yet been solved. For the attribution, a number of Tuscan artists have been tried — the Florentines Passignano, Cigoli, Jacopo da Empoli (number 19), Giovanni Biliverti, and the Sienese Pietro Sorri — and found wanting, as has also the Tuscan-influenced Belisario Corenzio. Whoever the artist, he was probably Tuscan and in Jacopo da Empoli's circle, which was large and endured for decades after his death.

Because it is squared off, this drawing can be assumed to have been preparatory for some large project — a painting in oil, a fresco, a banner or a tapestry. Most likely, it was preparatory for one of the commemorative scenes included in the lavish painted decorations for the celebration of births, weddings, funerals and distinguished visitors with which Medici history abounds[1].

It must commemorate the baptism of some royal or at least exalted noble person. The infant is surrounded: by the officiant in the center, another cleric on the left, and a lady — the mother or godmother? — on the right. Another lady kneels on the steps behind her, and standing still farther behind is a gentleman in civilian dress with a ceremonial sword, who provides something of a secondary focus. The rest of the crowd includes a number of clerics, two men kneeling and gesturing in the left foreground, at least one of them military, and many anonymous men and women. Their excitement is manifest by some gestures and poses and by three figures in the left middleground who have scaled a column base to gain a better view. A number of these minor spectators are unclothed, as if the draughtsman were still in the process of determining their poses. Obviously the christening was a public occasion.

The architectural setting seems so specific as to be identifiable, either as the apse, a transept, or a large chapel of a church. To the left and right of the tabernacle appear what may be sculptural figures of the Angel Annunciate and the Virgin Mary depicting the *Annunciation.* Overhead is a painting or a bas-relief of two figures, one kneeling and the other standing, perhaps representing the *Baptism of Christ* but conceivably one of several other themes — *Christ Taking Leave of His Mother, Noli me tangere,* or some episode involving the presentation of a scapular (in the hands of the standing figure) to a hooded monk. The presence of the *Annunciation* might place the event in the church of the Annunziata, but what can be seen of the architecture in the drawing contradicts this hypothesis. It is barely conceivable as the interior of the Cathedral Baptistry as it was temporarily remodeled in 1577 for the occasion of the baptism of Filippo de'Medici[2]. The lack of any heraldic device anywhere in the drawing would be disturbing if coats of arms were customarily included in preparatory studies of this sort. Apparently they were not.

Two other drawings supply some clues for this sheet. One, in the Uffizi (inv. no. 9359F)[3], is thought to be a preparatory study from the studio of Jacopo da Empoli for one of the 26 banners representing scenes from the life of Margherita of Austria, the second wife of King Philip III of Spain and the sister-in-law of the Grand Duke Cosimo II. These banners were displayed in the Medici church of San Lorenzo in Florence on the occasion of the funeral of the queen held there 6 February 1611. The second drawing, in the Ashmolean Museum[4], is by Jacopo da Empoli himself, and is a preparatory study for one of the illustrations in the book

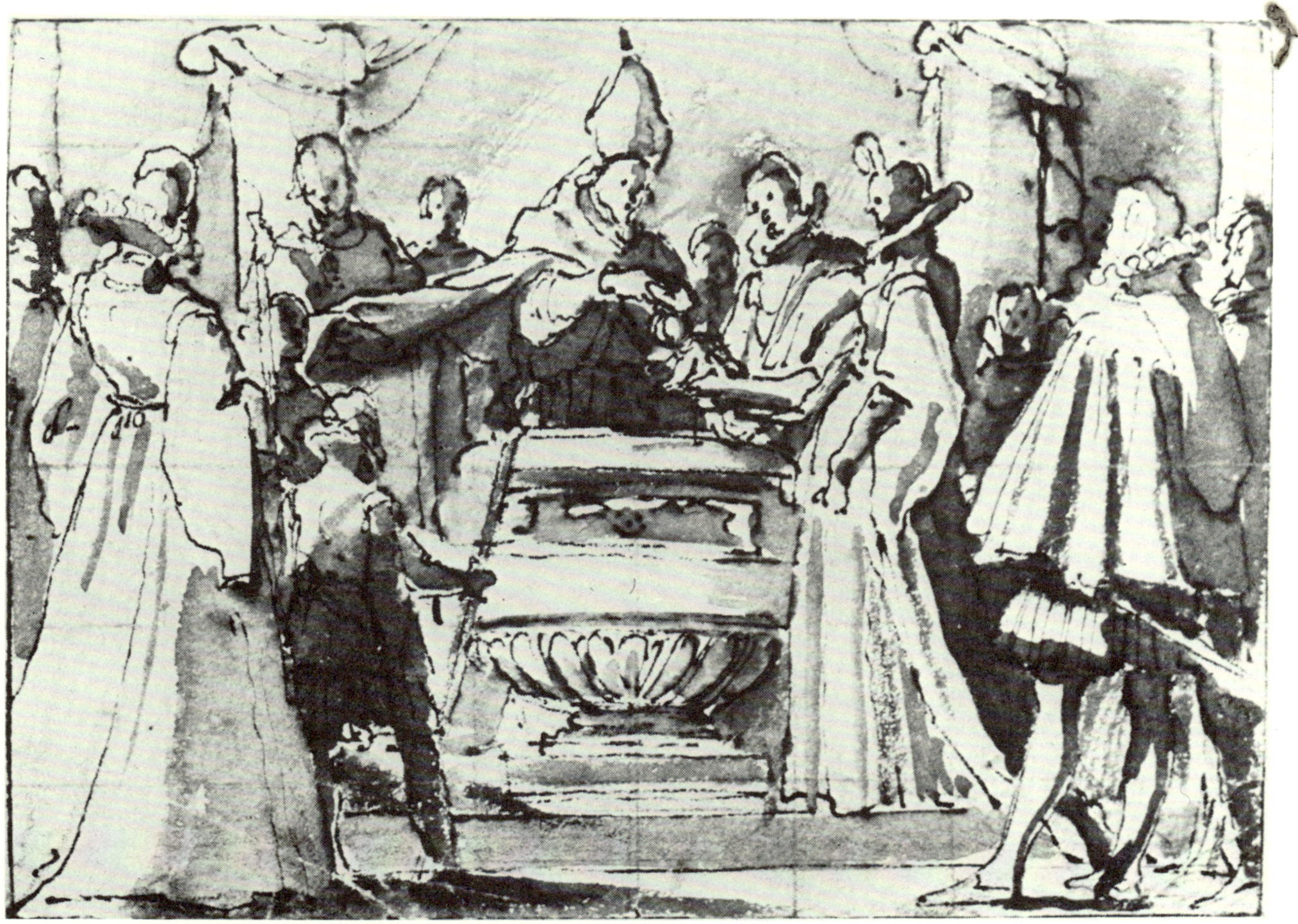

Jacopo da Empoli, *Baptism of the Spanish Prince*, Ashmolean Museum, Oxford

prepared in 1611-12 to commemorate the funeral. Antonio Tempesta (1555-1630) was charged with the responsibility for the twenty-six illustrations to Altoviti's text; indefatigable as he was, he and the other artists in his studio etched only eleven of them, and the remaining fifteen plates were prepared by Jacques Callot (1592/3-1635). One of Callot's plates (Lieure no. 63), from Empoli's pen and wash drawing, represents the baptism of a prince of Spain. Focused only on the rite and the principal participants and without the architectural setting, either the drawing or the print seems likely to have been the source of this composition.

This drawing could be a rejected proposal from Empoli's studio for the original banner or the illustration. An alternative explanation is that it was prepared for some other baptism, even much later. Worth consideration as the possible artist, despite his being active later rather than earlier in the century is Agostino Melissi, a pupil of Biliverti's who is documented in Florence for about half a century beginning in 1631[5]. Melissi was very eclectic and made a practice of copying old masters, so his manner of drawing was like his predecessor's. Furthermore he was a designer for the Medici tapestry works, and did preparatory drawings for a series commemorating the life of Cosimo I, woven during the late 1650's, for which this drawing could have been made. Perhaps Melissi deliberately recreated the earlier style, using Empoli's drawing — or perhaps Callot's print derivative from it — for another baptismal commemoration.

1. See, for example, the register of events that were celebrated between the marriage of Cosimo I in 1539 and the funeral of Cosimo II in 1621, in the exhibition catalogue by Giovanna Gaeta Bertelà and Annamaria Petrioli Tofani, *Feste e Apparati Medici. . .* , Gabinetto Disegni degli Uffizi XXXI, 1969, pp. 195-233.
2. See Eve Borsook, "Art and Politics at the Medici Court II: The Baptism of Filippo de'Medici in 1577," *Mitteilungen des Kunsthistorischen Instituts in Florenz,* XIII, 1967/8, pp. 95-114.
3. Bertelà and Petrioli Tofani, *op. cit.*, no. 89 and pp. 138-141.
4. Anthony Blunt, "A series of Paintings illustrating the History of the Medici Family executed for Marie de Médicis II," *Burl* CIX, 1967, p. 565, fig. 19. Miles Chappell called attention to this article.
5. See Annamaria Petrioli Tofani, "Nota su alcuni disegni di Agostino Melissi," *Paragone* XXX, no. 353, 1979, pp. 99-103.

3.

ANONYMOUS VENETIAN

Page from a Ducale of the Corner Family

Body color over black chalk, gold, on vellum; 218 x 155 mm.; losses from water damage on verso
Acquired 1974

This miniature was probably executed as the frontispiece for a Venetian *ducale,* a book described as "a kind of covenant, which the Doge made with the Venetian people on his election, but in a wider sense . . . other documents such as ducal commissions, congratulatory addresses offered to a Doge, etc[1]." Another source adds that they were "books of local laws especially prepared in the name of the Duke for the new mayors of each of the cities in the Venetian Republic[2]." A number of specimens are in the British Museum, dating from the late 15th century to 1620; there are others in the Museum of Fine Arts in Budapest and in the Hermitage in Leningrad.

The dimensions of this illumination are typical of those found in these *ducali* as is the inscription on the verso. It tells us that the nobleman, Carlo Corner, was appointed commander of the regiments in Udine and received the keys of that city on 13 October 1474, to serve at least until June 1475. The appointment is made in the name of the Doge Pasquale Cicogna, who however did not reign until 1585-95; presumably his name was somehow mistaken by the scribe for that of the Doge Pietro Mocenigo whose reign (1474-77) does correspond to the date on the document. The style of the illumination is certainly that of the later date. The error can probably be explained by recognizing the inscription as not the actual appointment but rather commemorative, commissioned by Carlo Corner's descendents to honor their ancestor. The image of Corner may have been based on a bust: he is shown in three-quarter view, whereas painted portraits of ca. 1475 were normally in profile.

The composition is typical of *ducali* illuminations: within an elaborate frame including the family coat of arms, the subject of the document is shown in a pious pose in the lower right, with his patrons behind him as sponsors, and an overseeing divine figure, in this instance Christ with the orb as *Salvatore Mundi.* Carlo Corner is sponsored by St. Mark, who is made recognizable by his lion attribute, which is also the symbol of Venice. The other figure, wearing a mantle covered with fleur de lys and carrying a crown, has been identified as St. Louis of Toulouse. However, inasmuch as both St. Louis of Toulouse and King St. Louis of France are customarily represented as young and clean-shaven, this grey-bearded elder must be someone else, very possibly Charlemagne, who would be appropriate considering Corner's given name. Corner has his right hand on his chest (over his heart ?) and his left on a book (the Bible ?) as if he were taking an oath.

There are a number of approximately contemporary *ducali* pages that are similar in format. One formerly in the Herbert List Collection in Munich is strikingly similar in format, dimensions, and style[3]. It represents the Madonna and Child with SS. Stephen and Francis, and a procurator of the Loredan family, who could almost be Carlo Corner's brother.

Although many of the *ducali* illuminations are without specific attribution, several are associated with three artists: Alessandro Merli, active in Venice from 1590 to 1615, who is the most frequently mentioned; Giorgio Colonna, who worked at the Basilica of San Marco during the second half of the 16th century; and Gaspero Veronensis, who in 1551 signed and dated a beautiful page now in the Morgan Library (inv. no. M353, fol. IV). The Steiner and List illuminations have both been attributed to Merli. However the two signed examples of Merli's illuminations, the Commission of Giovanni Andrea Venier of 1600 in the Biblioteca Marciana in Venice, and the unfinished and undated page of the Procurator Dinanzi with Madonna and Child and St. Jerome in the Hermitage, contradict the attribution. Their format is about the same, but their style is more linear, without the delicate modeling of the Steiner and List examples. Colonna's work is more spacious than either Merli's or any of the other pages, as if he were a panel painter rather than an illuminator.

Closest to the Steiner and List pages is the horizontally oriented *Procurator Presented by St. Vincent Ferrer to St. Mark* in the National Gallery, Dublin, which Sir Karl Parker attributed to Gaspero Veronensis. The few other illuminations that have been attributed to Gaspero confirm this similarity, particularly the undated *Procurator Presented to St. Mark* in the Staedel Institute in Frankfurt, but they tend consistently to be more spacious. Furthermore, there is a time-lag of more than thirty years between Gaspero's two dated works of 1551 and 1552 and the presumed date of the Steiner page. Therefore, although it is clearly equal in quality to Gaspero's *oeuvre,* it can not be attributed with any certainty to him or any other identified illuminator, and so must, for now at least, remain anonymous.

R.S. and A.M.

1. David Diringer, *The Illustrated Book: Its History and Production,* New York, 1958, pp. 349-50.
2. Kevin Kane in exhibition catalogue, *Selections from the . . . Bick Collection,* Dartmouth College, Hanover, NH, 1971, no. 17.
3. Illustrated as by Giulio Clovio in Colnaghi's catalogue, *Old Master Drawings,* of April–May 1966, no. 75. The dimensions are nearly identical: 222 x 154 mm. In the List collection the illumination was attributed to Alessandro Merli.

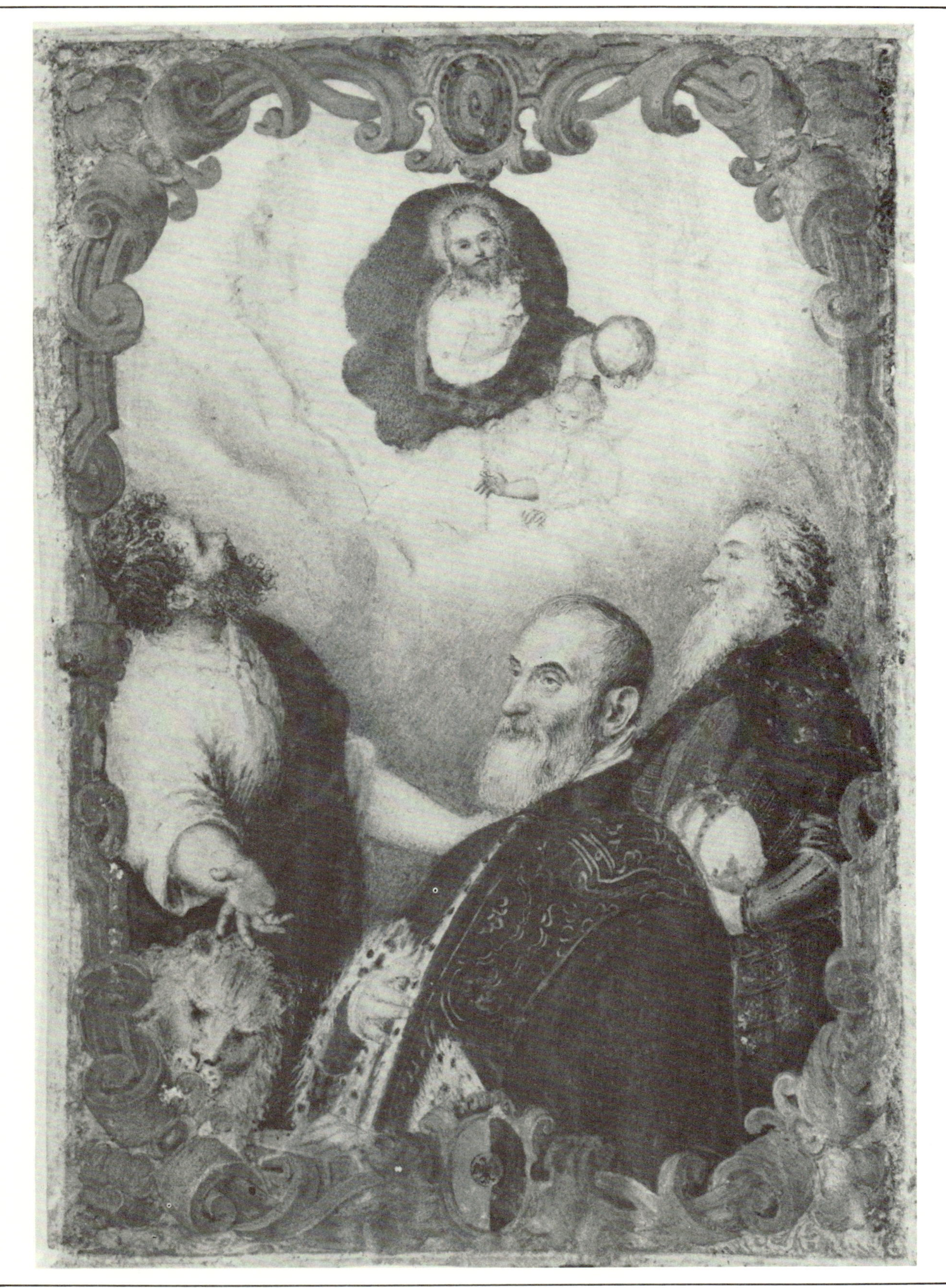

4.

GIROLAMO FRANCESCO MARIA BEDOLI, called IL MAZZOLA
(Viadana ca. 1510 - Parma, Mantua, Modena - 1560 Parma)

Study for a Canephoros Figure

Pen and brown ink, brown wash, over black chalk; 259 x 105 mm.; squared off
Inscribed recto upper left corner in pen and brown ink: *Dionisio/Calvart,* verso in pen and ink: (illegible word) *Dionisio* (illegible word): both inscriptions by old hands
Provenance: Marquis de Chennevières (L.702/3)
Acquired 1982

Bedoli's birthdate is uncertain, but he is described by Vasari as a *"putto e pittore"* with Parmigianino in 1521-22, and therefore presumably he was already in his master's studio while still very young. After marrying Parmigianino's cousin Elena Mazzola in 1529 and appropriating the family name by which the older master was also known, he also consciously emulated his style. When Parmigianino died in 1540, Bedoli inherited his patrons and carried out his unfinished commissions.

This drawing is a preparatory study for the completion of the most famous and admired of those commissions, the elaborate decoration of the east apse and vault ceiling of the church of Santa Maria della Steccata in Parma. Parmigianino had undertaken the project in 1531, but by 1539 the sponsoring confraternity had lost patience and discharged him. Bedoli then took over and was awarded a contract to complete the north and south vaults and apses. A contract was made in 1547 for the vaults, and in 1553 he began the apse frescoes, which were completed in 1568. This drawing, for one of the Canephoros figures on the coffered ceilings on the south vault, must have been done between 1547 and 1553, because the contract called for completion of the vault frescoes before work on the apse commenced.

The scheme of the iconography for the vaults had been worked out by Parmigianino, and Bedoli followed it. The freshness and grace of this drawing are closer to Parmigianino than to Bedoli's frescoed figure, which is heavier, even overworked, with more elaborate drapery folds and jewelry. Another Bedoli drawing for the same figure, in pen and brown ink and wash over black chalk, was recently in the London art market[1]. It is closer to the fresco, and like it, heavier in delineation and also in the forms of the body.

The Canephoroi in Greco-Roman mythology were majestic female figures, wise virgins, who tended the temple of the oracle of Delphi. They carried the sacred water of the prophecy from the fountain of Castalia on Mount Parnassus to Delphi (see number 29). The attributes of the Canephoroi were water jugs, lamps, and keys. Although not apparent in this drawing, there is a chain across the bosom of the figure in the fresco, and this chain is probably a type of chatelaine for keys. Parmigianino depicted his Canephoroi for the church carrying water jugs on their heads. The appropriation for a Christian church of a pagan image of wise virgins guarding the temple would not have seemed inappropriate to a Mannerist. References, unless overtly pagan, could be reinterpreted in a Christian context and thereby display the sophistication and learning of both the artist and the patrons. The wise virgins could be likened to one of the Societies of the Virgin Mary that even today are often responsible for the physical care and decoration of Roman Catholic churches. R.T.P.

1. Sotheby's, London, 4 July 1975, lot 185, ill. p. 35

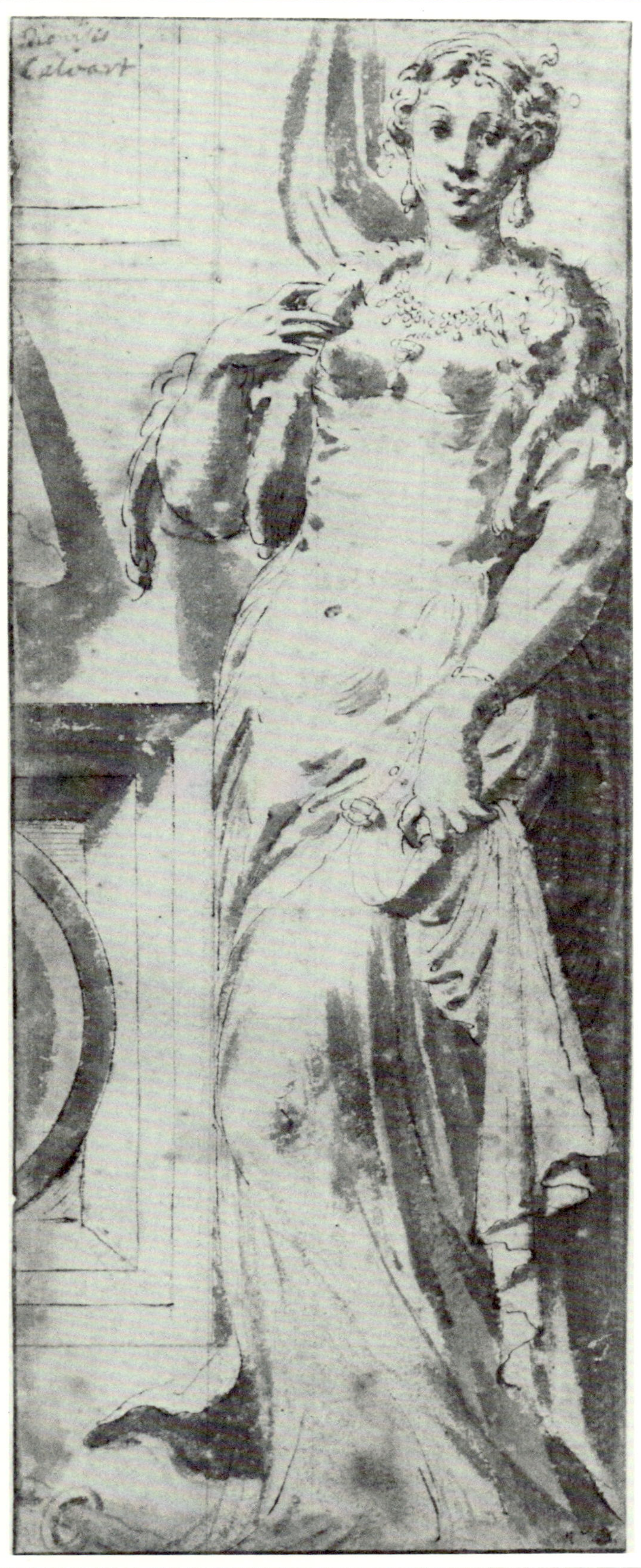

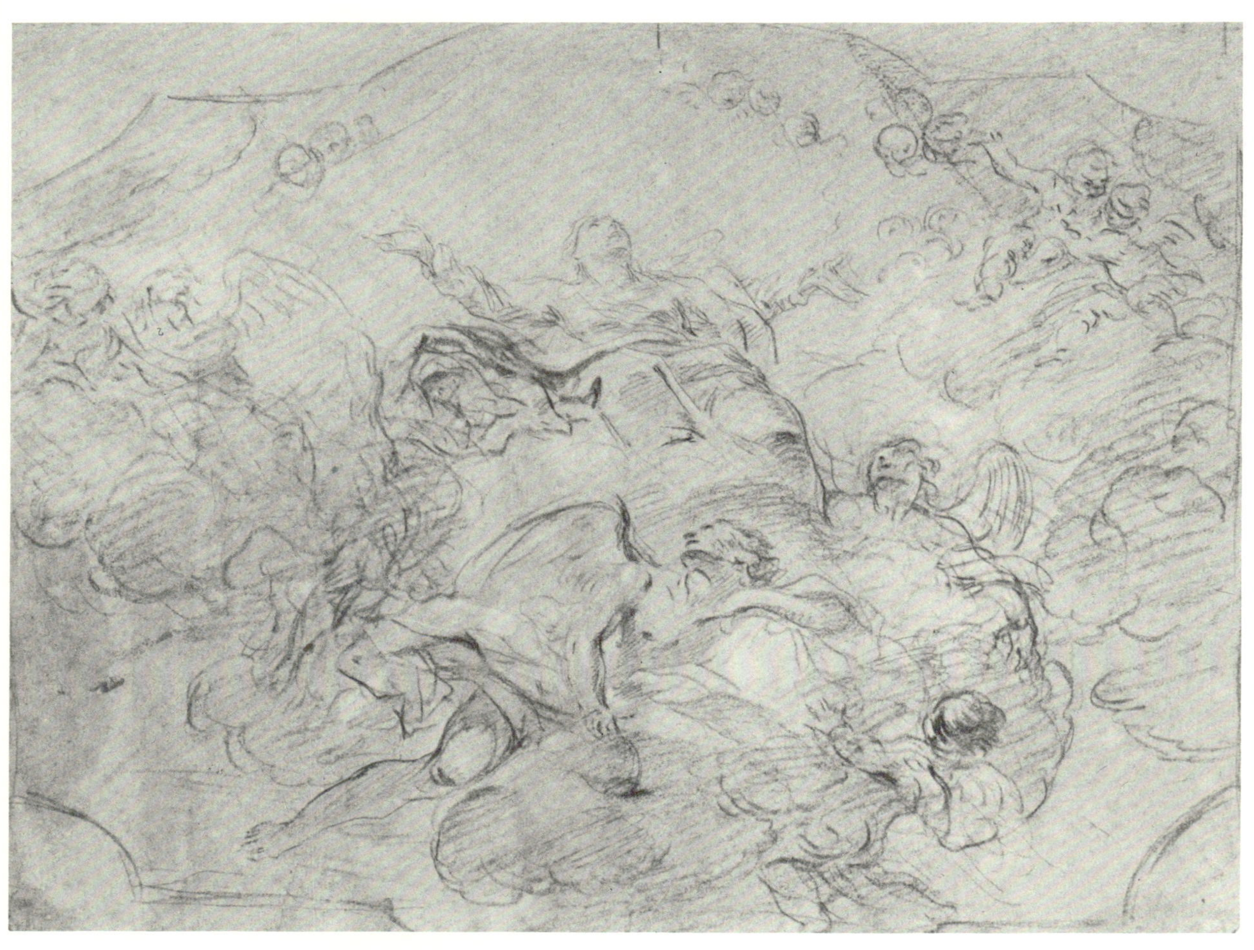

5.

GIOVANNI BATTISTA BEINASCHI
(Fossano [near Cuneo] 1636 – Turin, Rome, Naples – Naples 1688)

The Assumption of the Virgin

Red chalk, 274 x 363 mm. Watermark: heart with cross and letters GB
Acquired 1980

Beinaschi is remembered primarily as a painter of large-scale frescoes in Naples, a contemporary of Luca Giordano (1634-1705) and as prolific an artist. Born in Piedmont, the precocious Beinaschi was first trained in Turin by the Savoyard painter Esprit Grandjean. By 1652 he was already in Rome, a pupil of Pietro del Po from Palermo. It was at this time that Beinaschi discovered the manner of Lanfranco, who had died in 1647. He followed it the rest of his life, reinforced perhaps by a trip to Parma and by the influence of Mattia Preti (1613-99). He went to Naples in 1664 and was highly successful there, busily frescoing acres of walls and ceilings in churches until his death[1].

Beinaschi borrowed from Lanfranco shamelessly and so skillfully that his drawings are often confused with the older master's[2]. Generally his draughtsmanship was looser than Lanfranco's, sometimes to the extreme of near-formlessness. But at his best, as in this drawing, Beinaschi could recreate both the form and spirit of his hero. Comparison of this drawing, however, with the preparatory study in pen and wash[3] made by Lanfranco for the *Assumption* (in the Augsburg Museum) painted in 1631 for the Fugger family, shows the characteristic differences between the two hands. Particularly notable is Lanfranco's unmistakable ability to create a greater effect of plasticity, in both individual figures and groups; by comparison, the Beinaschi drawing seems strangely flat. Correspondingly Lanfranco's figures have more force, as if more passionately motivated, while Beinaschi's seem to gesture politely because it's expected of them.

Beinaschi painted *Assumption* frescoes in the church of Santa Maria del Suffragio in Rome and in the Congregation of the Bianchi della Giustizia in Naples, as well as a number of other Marian scenes. At this time it is not possible to associate this drawing with any painting.

1. The most recent biography of Beinaschi is by Fausta Navarro in the exhibition catalogue *Civiltà del Seicento a Napoli,* Naples, 1985, vol. I, pp. 116-117, 191-192.
2. The attribution of this drawing to Beinaschi was confirmed by Erich Schleier in a letter to Rudolph Joseph dated 23 July 1969.
3. at Windsor, inv. no. 4350.

6.

STEFANO DELLA BELLA
(Florence 1610 - Rome, Paris - 1664 Florence)

Small Figure Studies

Pen and brown ink over graphite; 114 x 168 mm.
Provenance: Giuseppe Vallardi (L.1223); William Mayor (L.2779); Christie's, 4 July 1972, lot 75 (illustrated)
Acquired 1973
Rebecca Zurier in Oberhuber, 1977, number 2, pp. 26-8
Loaned by Lori Steiner

In the preface to a catalogue on Stefano della Bella published in 1772, Jombert described him as "le plus célèbre dessinateur et graveur qui ait existé jusqu'à present"[1]. The extremely fine, supple, and expressive delineation in this drawing is characteristic of his style. Perhaps its origin can be found in della Bella's first training as a goldsmith's apprentice. He then studied painting before turning to printmaking. Baldinucci, the historian of Florentine art, tells us that Stefanino learned his craft by making drawings after the prints of Jacques Callot. He also drew copies of prints by Lucas Van Leyden, Holbein, and Durer. He studied etching from the Florentine Remigio Cantagallina, a colleague of Callot and a designer of court festivals, who was himself a charming draughtsman. In 1633, under the patronage of the Medici, della Bella went to study in Rome. The compositions of miniature figures and the rather stiff delineation of form found in his Roman drawings are strongly reminiscent of Callot. Despite this influence, from the beginning della Bella's use of line was more sensitive, imaginative, and descriptive. He received inspiration from Roman life — in the streets, the countryside, and among the ruins. Returning occasionally to Florence, he found there also Medici theatrical spectacles, equestrian ballets, and wedding celebrations to design and document.

In 1639 della Bella left Rome for Paris, in the entourage of Alessandro del Nero, ambassador of the Grand Duke Ferdinando II to the court of Louis XIII. He must have been overcome by the richly chaotic street life and frequent court activities of Paris because he did not begin to work until months after his arrival in the city. Print publishers such as Langlois (known as Ciartres), Israel Henriet, and Pierre Mariette offered him a variety of lucrative projects. He also received commissions from Cardinals Richelieu and Mazarin. As a result, these years in Paris were his most productive. There he designed fanciful theatre productions, exotic fireworks and even a set of playing cards for young Louis XIV.

Several of the vignettes in this drawing reappear in an elaborate print by della Bella, published in 1646, *Le Pont Neuf à Paris,*[2] a large, panoramic view of the daily street life of Paris. It records such landmarks as the Hôtel de Nevers, the Tour de Nesle and, at the center, the bronze equestrian statue of Henri IV by the Florentine sculptors Giovanni Bologna and Pietro Tacca. Densely populated, the scene is full of street characters and action — gypsies, carriages, vendors and even the extraction of a tooth. The woman walking with a child and an infant in the foreground of this drawing and the woman in the upper right picking up her skirt are echoed in reverse in the print. The woman in the center leaning over a tray with two children appears in the print but not reversed; and now the children are leaving her. And the dandies on the left of the drawing apparently have also strolled into the print. Nor did the characters in this drawing serve only *Le Pont-Neuf.* The peasant on horseback (top right) reappears as a rider in the background of another print[3]. Zurier has also observed that the cavaliers are related, though not as closely, to city and traveling scenes in the two series *Agréable Diversité* de figures[4] and *Diversi Capricci*[5].

The line in della Bella's Parisian drawings is freer, more responsive and undulating than in his earlier work. The figures have become larger. Shading is rarely by means of the mechanical parallel hatching derivative from Callot and characteristic of della Bella's early drawings. The gracefully suggestive delineation and the subtle, tellingly observed scenes of this drawing are characteristic.

In the later 1640's, particularly after a visit to Holland, della Bella was strongly influenced by Rembrandt and the Dutch landscape artists, notably Breenbergh and Jan Both both of whom had visited Rome, and by Swanevelt (number 87), who was resident in Paris during della Bella's stay there. In these later works, della Bella borrowed Dutch etching techniques to enhance the tone and texture of his work. As a result, his drawings and etchings became more painterly. He fled Paris in 1649 to escape the anti-Italianism of the first Fronde and returned to Florence, where, except for brief visits to Rome and Venice, he remained until his death. T.L.

1. Quoted by Antony Blunt, *The Drawings of Giovanni Benedetto Castiglione and Stefano della Bella...at Windsor Castle,* London, 1954, p. 89.
2. De Vesme, *Stefano della Bella, Catalogue Raisonné* (Reprint from La Peintre-Graveur Italien [1906] with an introduction and additions by Phyllis Dearborn Massar), New York, 1971, vol. I, pp. 132-3, no. 850, vol. II, p. 175, ill.
3. De Vesme, *op. cit.,* vol. I, p. 78, no. 195; vol. II, p. 52 ill.
4. De Vesme, *op. cit.,* vol. II, p. 39, nos. 118 and 119.
5. De Vesme, *op. cit.,* vol. II, p. 42, nos. 135 and 137.

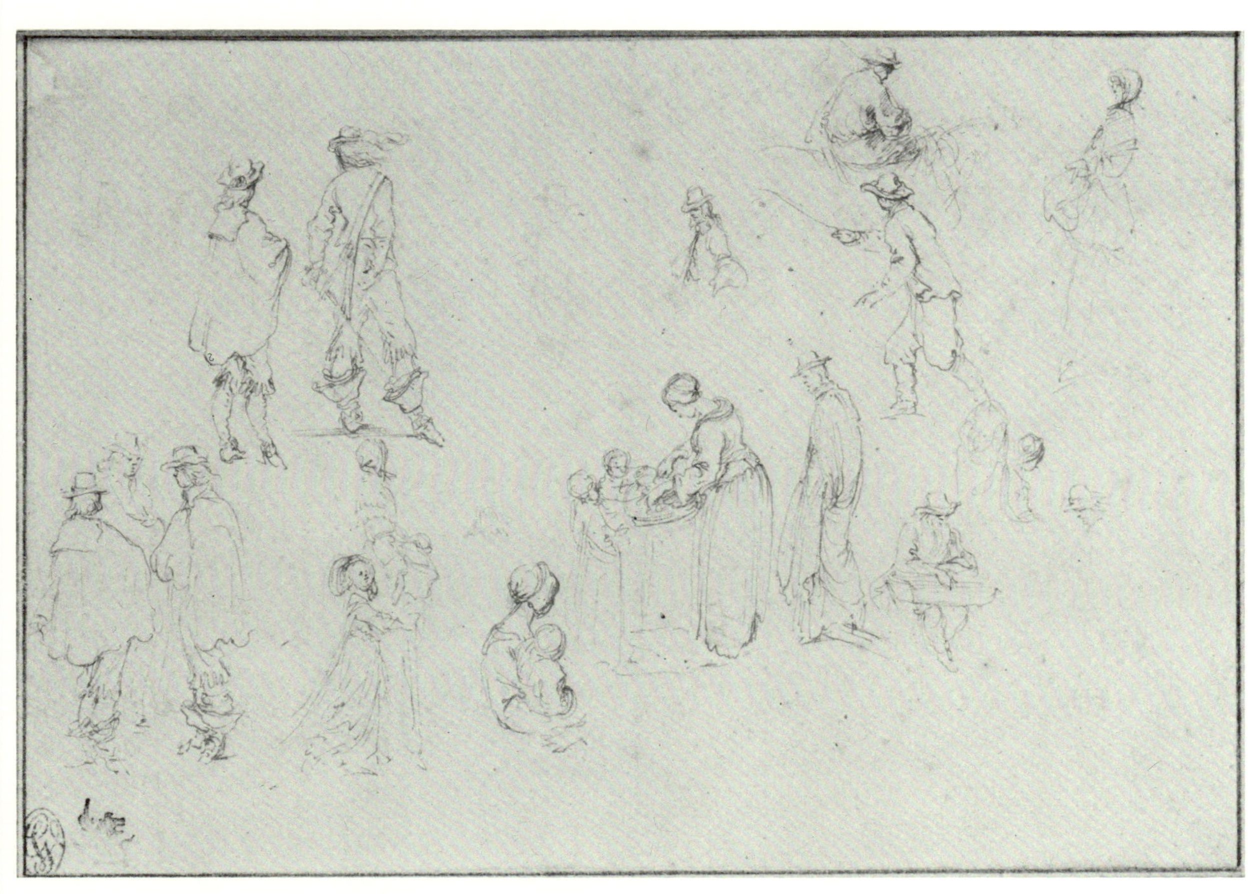

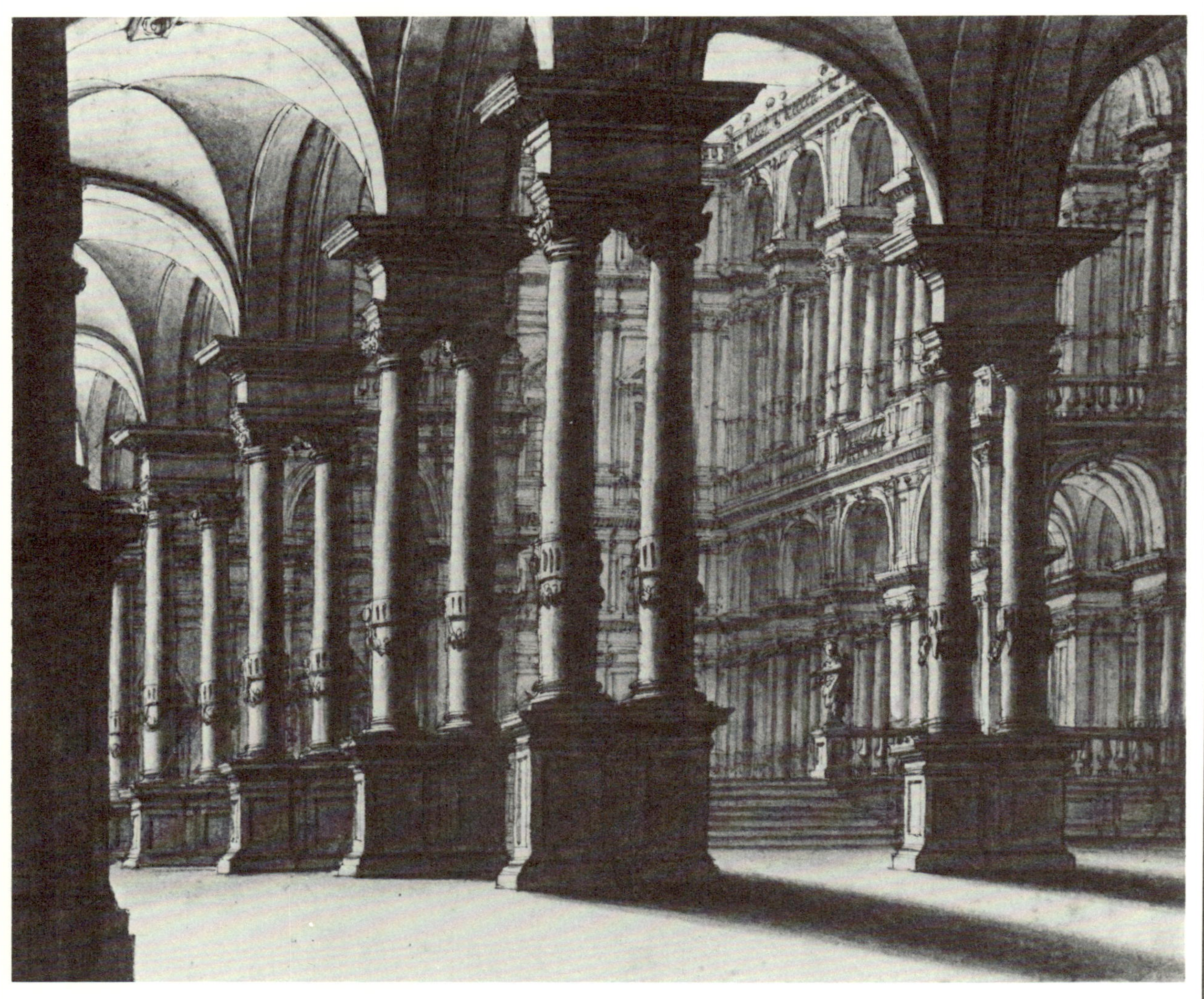

7.

FERDINANDO GALLI BIBIENA
(Bologna 1656/7 - Parma, Barcelona, Vienna - Vienna 1743)

Architectural Fantasy

Pen and brown ink, brown and grey washes over black chalk; 199 x 243 mm. including a 9 mm. strip added across the top
Provenance: Mrs. Mary Brandegee (L.1860)
Acquired 1974

The Bibiena family, through four generations spanning a century and a half, gave Europe its leading stage designers and architectural fantasts. The family name was not Bibiena at all but Galli. The founding member of the family, Giovanni Maria Galli (1618-1665), was born in the Casentina in the town of Bibbiena. When he went to Bologna in 1628 to begin his career, he found another artist named Giovanni Galli already there, so he took the name of his home town, minus a "b," and the name stuck.

Giovanni Maria had two sons, Ferdinando and Francesco (1659-1739), who together with their descendents disseminated the style associated with the family over North Italy, into Spain, and into the countries of the Holy Roman Empire. By the time of the death of Giovanni Maria's great-grandson Carlo Ignazio, in 1778, members of the family not only had built theatres, opera houses and sets from Naples to Berlin, but also had published their imaginative designs extensively. The family style did evolve, particularly in the direction of increasing fantasy, but the members worked so closely together that it is difficult to differentiate one hand from another.

This drawing, formerly attributed to Ferdinando's son Antonio (1697-1774), is probably by Ferdinando himself. Originally trained as a painter, Ferdinando studied architectural and theatrical engineering. Then for two decades he served the Duke of Parma, Ranuccio Farnese, before going to Barcelona in 1708 to stage the wedding of the Hapsburg pretender to the Spanish throne, the so-called Charles III. Charles lost the Spanish throne to the Bourbons; he was then elected Holy Roman Emperor as Charles VI, and in 1712 sent for Ferdinando to come to Vienna, where brother Francesco had already settled in 1700. Henceforth Vienna served as the family headquarters, from which the active members traveled over most of western Europe carrying out their commissions.

There are basically two types of Bibiena architectural drawings: sketched caprices that are clearly imaginative fantasies, and finished studies like this one that are drawn as if they were real views of actual (or at least proposed) buildings. Although belonging to a tradition going back to mid-15th century Italian representations of ideal cities, they derive directly from the perspective stage settings of the 16th century. These stage settings were symmetrical, with a dominant central axis. Ferdinando was famous for his innovation of the angular perspective like this one, where the spectator seems to be passing by and glancing at an angle, usually through some kind of screen, into the open space of the architecture.

This drawing is distinctive because of the sharp contrast between light and dark, the firmness of the delineation and the precision of the details, the clarity of the composition, and the relative simplicity of the architecture. In contrast to many — in fact to most — Bibiena architectural studies, elaborate as this courtyard is, nonetheless it seems conceivable in scale and design, as if some sufficiently extravagant patron might actually have had it built. For this reason, Ferdinando, who was the most architecturally-inclined member of the family, seems likely to have been the draughtsman. Several other drawings attributed to or initialed by Ferdinando appear to confirm this attribution, including several in the Theatre Museum at La Scala in Milan[1], and appropriately enough one in the collection of the architect Philip Johnson[2].

1. Mario Monteverdi, exhibition catalogue, *I Bibiena,* Mantua, 1975, particularly no. 4 p. 22, ill. p. 12.
2. FARL, photo no. 52.854.

8.

AGNOLO DI COSIMO TORI called BRONZINO
(Monticelli near Florence 1503 - Florence, Pesaro, Rome, Pisa - 1572 Florence)

Study of a Male Nude for the Martyrdom of St. Lawrence

Black chalk; 239 x 460 mm.; upper and lower corners made up
Inscribed recto, lower right corner in graphite: *Angelo Bronzino*
Acquired 1975
Exhibited: Cleveland 1979, no. 10
Literature: Charles R. Saumarez-Smith in Oberhuber, 1977, no. 3 pp. 28-30; Olszewski, 1981, no. 10, pp. 34-35

Bronzino studied with Jacopo Pontormo (1494-1556) in Florence and developed into the archetypal Mannerist portraitist. He served Cosimo I (1519-1574), the first Grand Duke of Tuscany, as court painter, producing a series of marvelously haughty, meticulously detailed images of the Medici family.

This drawing is a preparatory study for Bronzino's fresco of the *Martyrdom of Saint Lawrence* commissioned by Cosimo in 1565 for the church of San Lorenzo in Florence and completed in 1569. The painted figure, in the lower right corner of the fresco (as might be assumed from the shape into which the model has been twisted), represents a river god. Saumarez-Smith notes that it is somewhat different from the drawn figure, which has broader shoulders and more simplified rhythms; in the fresco the sphere has been transformed into an urn and moved to the model's lap, so as to make the figure's back correspond more precisely to the vertical edge of the composition. For this reason, he suggests, "this drawing, unlike the other surviving studies[1] is unsquared: Bronzino was still experimenting with the figure's torsion, and was as yet still uncertain in his outline."

The relevance of a river god to the martyrdom of the saint is somewhat tenuous, but presumably it refers to the river Tiber flowing through Rome, the scene of the martyrdom. This obscurity is typical of Bronzino, just as the figure is typically Mannerist in serving primarily a formal rather than a thematic role. Saumarez-Smith aptly quotes Professor Freedberg's description of the fresco as "a beautifully artificial fusion of gymnasium and ballet, played upon an antique stage". This contortionist on the sidelines, the central players, and even the young deacon-saint — whose story would seem to demand pathos — appear to be entirely unmoved, as if they were somnabulants going through the motions of the event, unaware of its import.

Unfeeling as they are, the figures and the whole fresco certainly are grave in mood. Even this drawing seems solemn, as if the finesse of Bronzino's process in making it were a mark of his seriousness. Bronzino had a serious prototype in mind when he conceived of this figure. Its similarity to the back of the *Belvedere Torso* and the unusual placement of the head on the shoulders are too striking to be merely coincidental. Bronzino must have preserved this resemblance, deliberately following Michelangelo who, having been inspired by it in the *ignudi* on the Sistine ceiling and perhaps for the Medici tomb *Day* figure, is reported to have exclaimed, "This is the work of a man who knew more than nature!"[3], a statement that might well have been the Mannerist painter's motto. R.T.P. and A.M.

1. In the Louvre (inv. no. 10900) and in the Uffizi (inv. no. 10220). See Craig Hugh Smyth, *Bronzino as a Draughtsman, an Introduction,* Locust Valley, N.Y., 1971, fig. 40.
2. Sydney J. Freedberg, *Painting in Italy 1500-1600,* Hammondsworth, 1971, p. 315.
3. Quoted from Howard Hibbard, *Michelangelo,* New York 1974, p. 78.

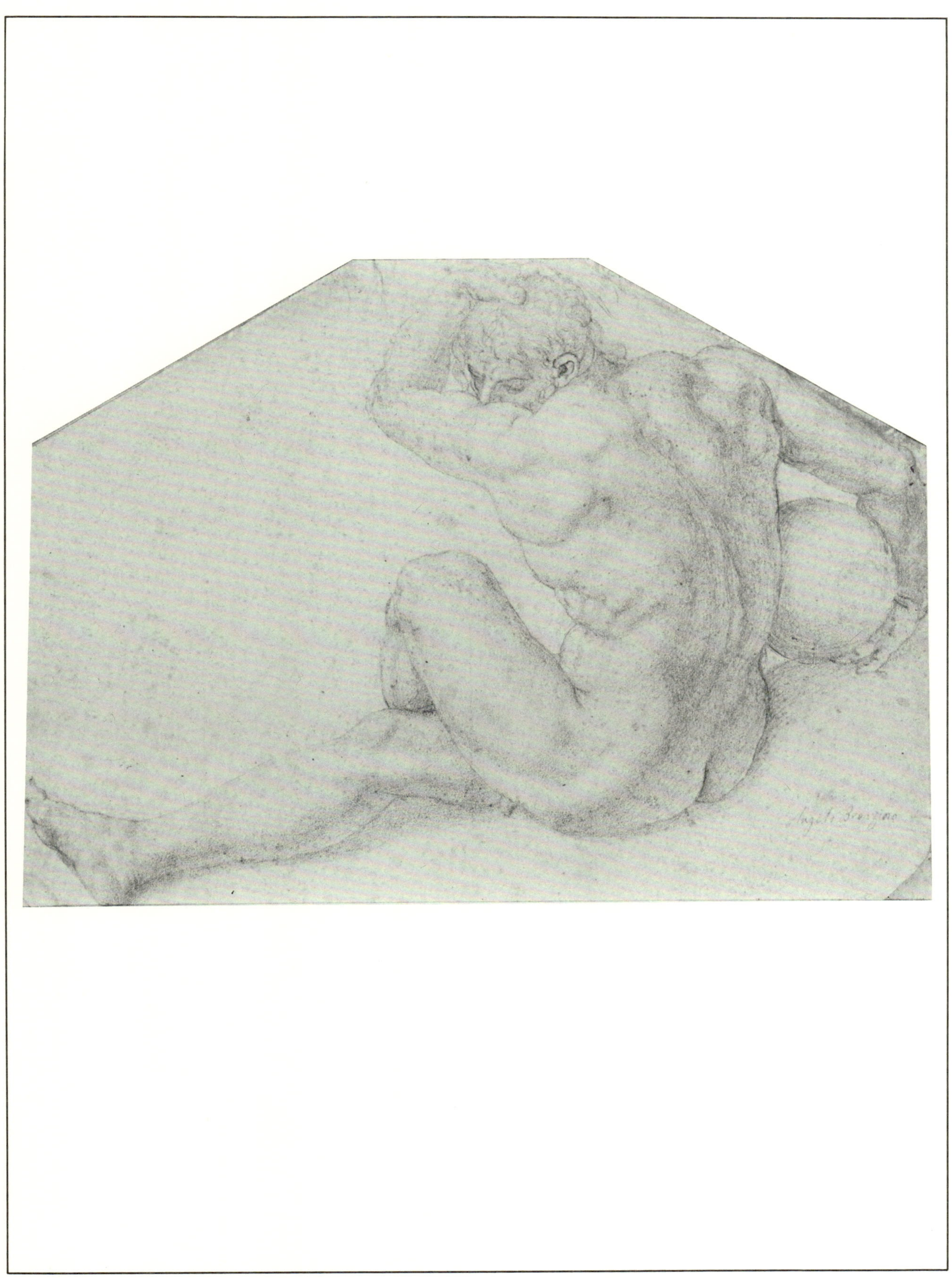

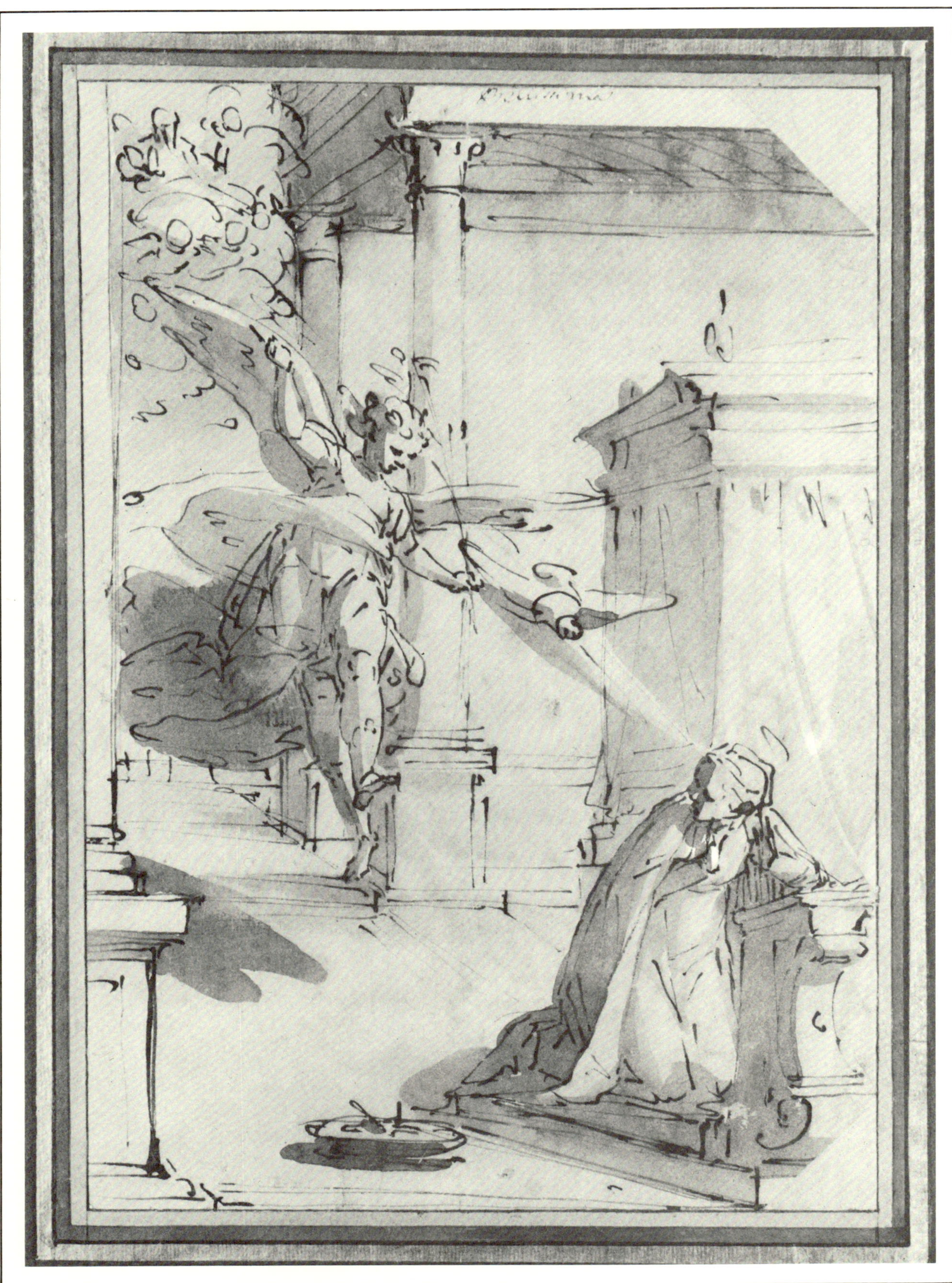

9.

LUCA CAMBIASO

(Moneglia [Liguria] 1527 - Rome, Genoa - 1585 Madrid)

The Annunciation

Pen and brown ink with grey and brown wash; 288 x 204 mm. Upper and lower right corners made up

Inscribed recto top center, in pen and brown ink: *Bellisima*

Provenance: Sotheby's, London, 25 November 1971, lot 146 (ill.)

Acquired 1972

Andrea E. Kaliski in Oberhuber 1977, no. 4, pp. 31-32

Exhibitions: Cambridge (Mass.), 1977, number 4 (ill.), Cleveland Museum of Art, 1979, no. 124

Literature: Nancy Ward Neilson, *Italian Drawings from Midwestern Collections,* exhibition catalogue, St. Louis, 1972, number 10; Olszewski 1981, number 124, pp. 149-151

Loaned by Lillian and Robert Fraker

Cambiaso was trained by his father and after a visit to Rome established himself in Genoa and soon became the city's leading decorative painter. Called to Spain by Philip II, eventually he died there, but his legacy in Genoa, through his students and assistants, and through competent imitators, persisted well into the next century.

The master himself drew a good deal, often repeating the same subject while he was working out his ideas. Copies of his originals were apparently made by his followers in his studio and afterwards. And his impact on Genoese art was so great that reverberations in the form of pseudo-Cambiaso drawings and paintings, often by artists known and recognized in their own right like Ottavio Semino and Giovanni Battista Paggi, continued well into the next century.

No less than fifteen drawn versions of the *Annunciation* are attributed to Cambiaso, but a number of these are either school-pieces or copies. Olszewski, supplementing Kaliski's catalogue entry, has sorted these versions out, reducing the total number of autograph drawings to seven: this sheet and one each in the Louvre (inv. no. 9207), the Palazzo Rosso in Genoa (ex. Durazzo Collection number 1866), the Uffizi (inv. no. 13759), the Cleveland Museum (inv. no. 59-200), Chatsworth, and Christ Church, Oxford (inv. no. 1225). The rest he believes either are by imitators or are copies after known or lost works by Cambiaso. For example, there are actually two Cambiaso *Annunciations* in the Louvre. Only one (inv. no. 9207) is by Cambiaso himself; the other (inv. no. 9208) Olszewski attributes to Ottavio Semino. However, there are also two copies of each of the Louvre drawings: one copy of the Semino imitation is at Chatsworth and another at the Uffizi (inv. no. 13778); and of the authentic Cambiaso sheet, one copy is in the Gabinetto Nazionale delle Stampe in Rome (Fondo Corsini no. 128311) and the other was offered at Sotheby's in London 10 March 1977 as lot 164. Mysteriously, the Louvre original and its two copies all are marred by nearly identical vertical and horizontal folds.

The authenticity of the Steiner sheet is unquestionable, as much because of its peerless quality as for its documentation. It is a study for the painting commissioned in 1568 by Antonio di Franchi in the name of Battista Grimaldi, for the church of the SSma. Annunziata di Portorio in Genoa. Other studies for details of the painting have been published by the Suidas[1] and by Robert Manning[2]. Cambiaso's typically crisp calligraphy has the effect of electrifying the atmosphere, particularly reinforced here as it is by the flash of light suggested by the wash. This wash also serves to emphasize the plasticity of the two principal figures, which is essential to the characterization of their different states of being and personalities: the archangel, giving no thought to the miracle of his exemption from the law of gravity, bursts with supreme self-assurance from his realm into the modestly earthbound privacy of the startled Virgin Mary. Impulsive and dramatic as the action is, nonetheless the composition is brilliantly cohesive: the potentially overpowering diagonal sweep from God the Father through the archangel and the dove of the Holy Ghost to the Virgin is interrupted by the vertical accents of the two figures, countered by the recession into the depth on the left, and anchored by the architectural elements.

Kaliski, noting that the drawing is proportionately a little wider than the painting, suggests that it may have been cut down for its eighteenth century mounts, and notes also that the clipped corners indicate that it was once pasted into an album.

1. Bertina Suida Manning and Wilhelm Suida, *Luca Cambiaso: La Vita e le Opere,* Milan, 1958, pp. 39-40.
2. Robert Manning, exhibition catalogue, *Drawings of Luca Cambiaso,* Finch College Museum of Art, New York, 1968, p. 21.

10.

LUCA CAMBIASO

The Sacrifice to Leto

Pen, brown ink and wash; 203 x 342 mm., including two strips, 29 mm. and 30 mm. wide, added by the draughtsman to the right edge of the sheet
Exhibited: Adolphe Stein, Bury Street Gallery, London, 1981, no. 21, plate 16
Acquired 1981

Leto (Latona in Latin) was a daughter of a Titan, Koios. Her sister Asteris threw herself into the Aegean rather than to succumb to the desires of Zeus. As a reward of sorts, Zeus' jealous wife Hera transformed her into a floating island, Delos. Leto was more cooperative than her sister, so when Zeus became enamoured next of her, she became pregnant with twins. Pursued by Hera, she found refuge on the island, which Zeus then anchored. Hidden in the bosom of her sister, now the island of Delos, Leto gave birth to twins, who grew up to be the major Greek gods Apollo and Artemis.

The people of Delos and of Thebes, which had close ties to Delos, held an annual celebration honoring Leto with a sacrifice and feasting. During one of the sacrifices, the fatally proud Niobe, Queen of Thebes, demanded that they honor her, the mother of seven sons and seven daughters, instead of Leto, who had only the two offspring. When the people abandoned their celebration of Leto in favor of Niobe, Leto was insulted and cried for vengeance. Unfortunately for Niobe, both of Leto's children were expert archers, and they made quick work of Niobe's fourteen children. Mad with grief, her husband the king killed himself, and Niobe was left alone to regret her pride.

This drawing is related to a scene in a cycle of frescoes by Cambiaso in the Palazzo Lercari in Genoa. An old, rich and powerful Genoese naval family, the Lercaris would have been pleased by the moral of the legend of Leto, i.e. not to disturb or overthrow traditionally entrenched powers. The cycle was completed during the 1570's, presumably the *terminus ante quem* for the drawing. In fact, it is reflective of a somewhat earlier phase of Cambiaso's draughtsmanship, when he was first developing his summary proto-cubist style, perhaps in response to his association after 1550 with the architect Giovanni Battista Castello, who had brought with him from his native Bergamo some new German artist's manuals, with similar simplified geometric renderings[1].

Two other versions of this drawing exist, in the Uffizi[2] and at Princeton[3]. Although similar in composition and size, they do display some differences in arrangement of the figures and in details. Most notably, in the Uffizi version a small cross is drawn on the side of the pedestal of Leto's statue. Combined with a stroke of wash, this cross is an efficient means of indicating the interior molding of the base. In the other versions, the cross has lost its structural meaning, as if the original drawing had been misinterpreted. Similarly, in the Uffizi drawing a shadow cast by the sacrificial fire on the altar in front of the pedestal is indicated by wash on the pedestal base. In the other versions, the wash shades the floor between the altar and pedestal but not the pedestal base. In the fresco, the base is not in shadow either. Throughout the Uffizi version, the wash seems to be used more boldly with greater volumetric effect. Thus, the Uffizi drawing is probably the first of the three and the one most certainly from Cambiaso's own hand.

The fresco differs from all three drawings in proportion, its height being less in relation to its width. As a result, the capitals of the engaged columns do not appear, nor do the domical crowns of the niches; and the figures (also rearranged) are taller, larger and more prominent. These differences reveal the purpose of the drawn compositions as working out the staging of the scene, and imply a number of other detailed preparatory drawings intermediate between these compositional studies and the completed fresco. R.T.P.

1. Olszewski, 1981, p. 148.
2. inv. no. 6941S; Anna Forlani Tempesti, exhibition catalogue, *Disegni Italiani della Collezione Santarelli, Sec. XV-XVIII*, Gabinetto Disegni e Stampe degli Uffizi, XXV, 1967, no. 43, fig. 48.
3. Gibbons, 1977, no. 88.

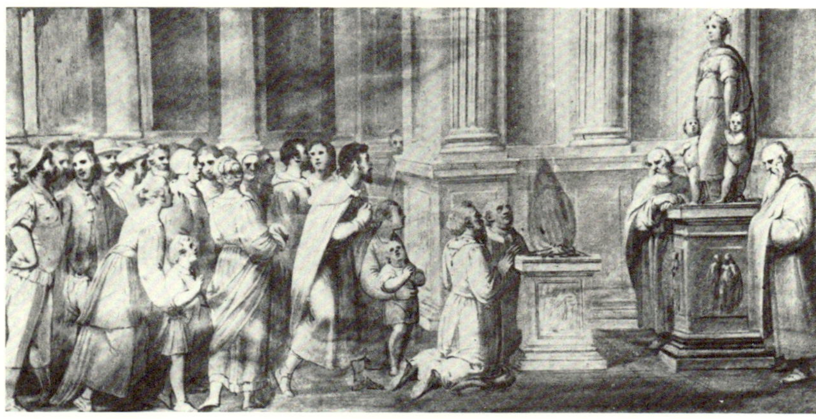

Luca Cambiaso
The Sacrifice to Leto
Palazzo Lercari, Genoa

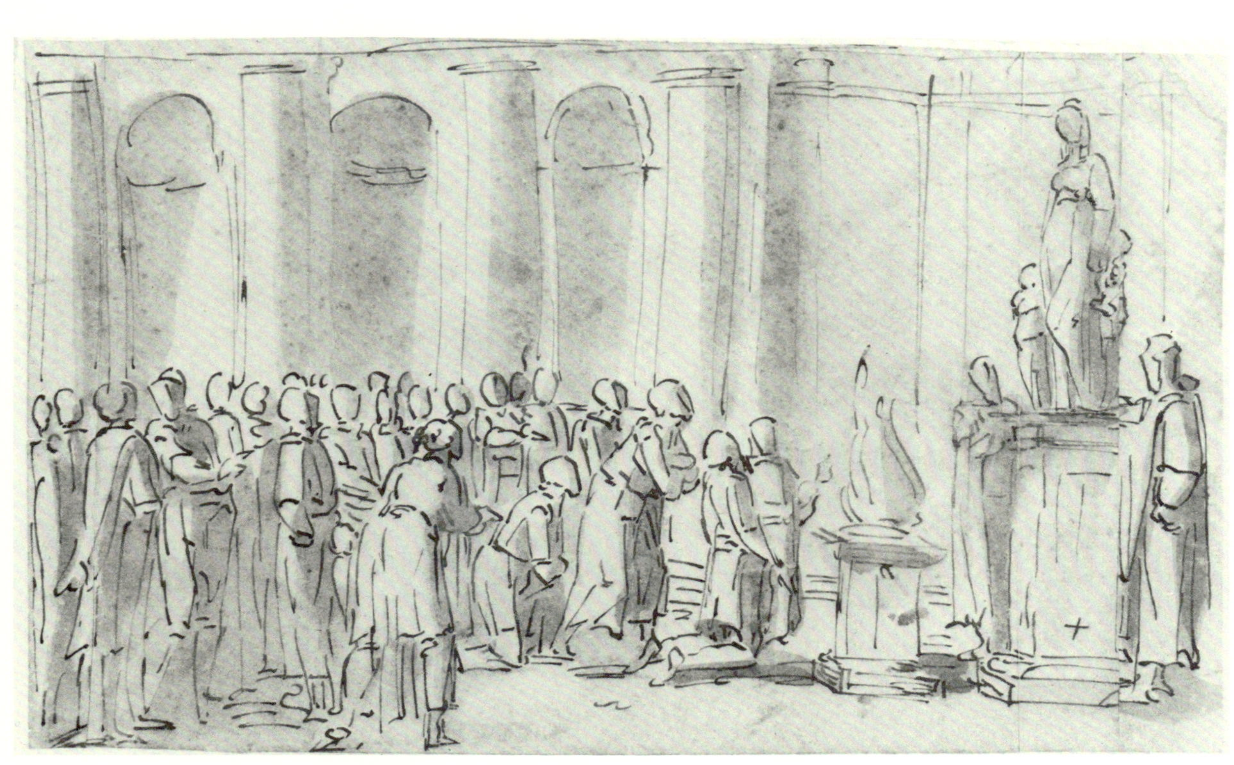

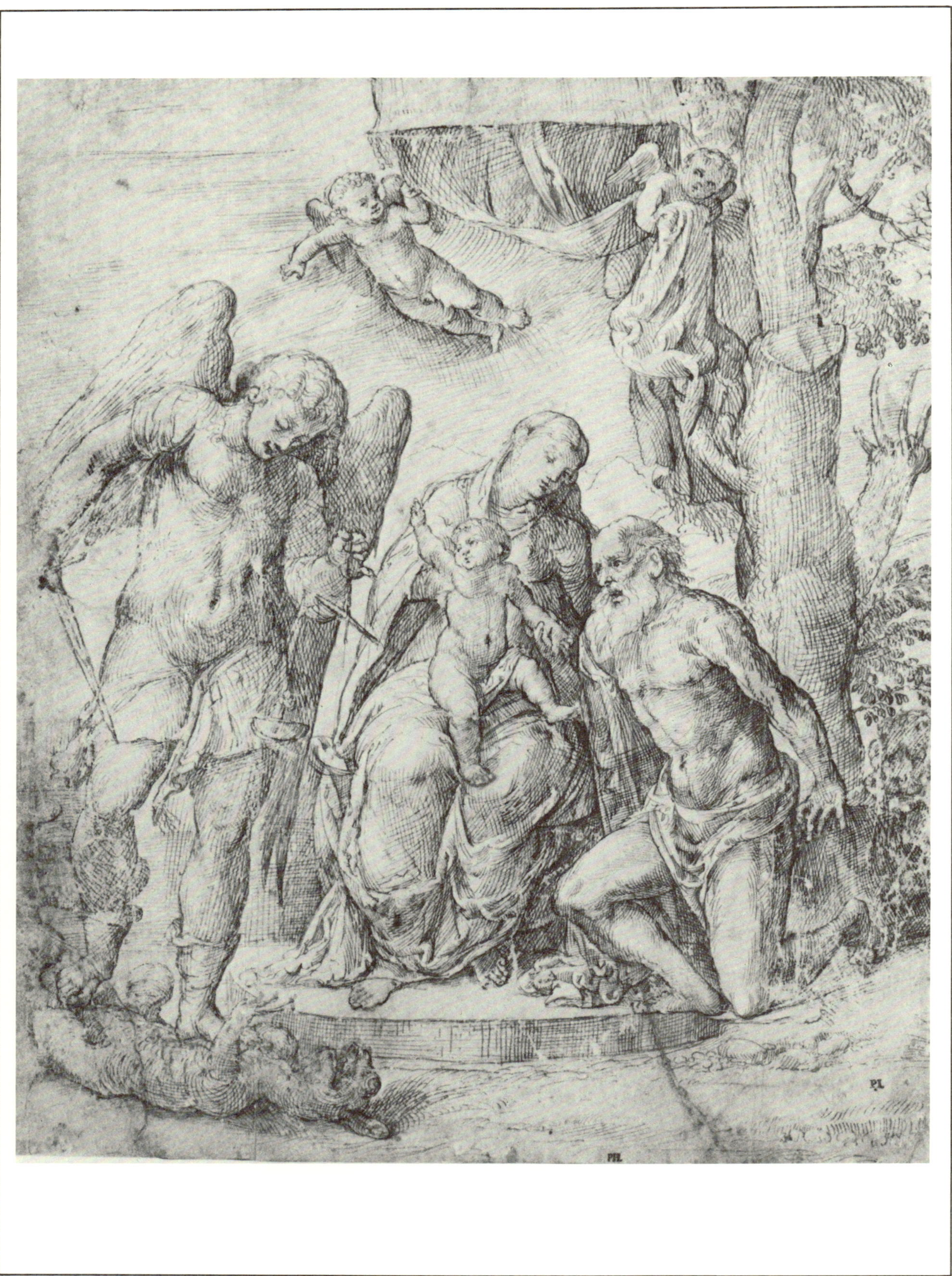

11.

DOMENICO CAMPAGNOLA
(Venice 1500 - Padua 1564)

Madonna and Child with Saints Michael and Jerome

Pen and brown ink over black chalk on brownish paper; 323 x 274 mm.; losses along top and at right corners made up; tears lower left and center repaired
Provenance: Sir Peter Lely (L.2092); Prosper Henry Lankrink (L.2090); Hugh Squire; Sotheby's, London, 4 July 1975 lot 16; P. & D. Colnaghi
Acquired 1976
Oberhuber, 1977, no. 5, pp. 32-34
Literature: Oberhuber, 1976, no. 57

Born in Venice of German parents, Domenico Campagnola was adopted by his first teacher, Giulio Campagnola, whose family name he adopted. Domenico was so precocious that already at seventeen he was producing signed and dated engravings. The great promise that he showed during these years never came to full realization, although he later worked in the studio of Titian and throughout his life he produced good works with some originality. This drawing dates from these early years, and reflects the mind of a young artist who is absorbing the major artistic achievements of this time.

Smiling, and holding the instruments of judgment (the sword and scale), St. Michael looks down at the not very fearsome dragon, which reaches up to him. St. Jerome, with his cardinal's hat and his lion discreetly concealed behind him, watches this judging of the beast, apparently with some dismay. The Christ child waves a signal for St. Michael to carry out the sentence, and the Virgin turns her head away from the execution. The putti overhead seem to be adjusting the royal cloth of honor behind the Virgin and Child.

Oberhuber noted of this drawing that the "composition and style link it closely to his engraving *Virgin and Child with Saints* of 1517." Despite a rather superficial compositional relationship between the two, they are not comparable stylistically, and the print seems to predate the drawing by a few years. The print betrays the uncertain hand of a novice: the flattened stylized leaves above the Virgin; the ill-conceived, poorly drawn heads and hands; the unstructured left leg of the saint (Ursula?) at the left; and the inexpressive drapery of the figures at the right, especially that around the kneeling St. Catherine's legs.

The Steiner drawing on the other hand shows a greater sense of form in the figures, foliage, and drapery, as if the draughtsman had matured and fully absorbed the styles of Giovanni Bellini and Cima da Conegliano, as well as the early Titian's. The St. Jerome, especially his head, is close to the type popularized by Bellini and often used by Cima. Cima's *St. Jerome* in the National Gallery, Washington, of ca. 1495, shows a similar head with sunken cheeks, hooked nose, balding scalp, and projecting beard, as well as a similar body type. These features are quite different from those of St. Jerome in the print. A better comparison might be with an unfinished drawing of *Isaac and Jacob* in the Uffizi of ca. 1525. The more assured hatching and the fuller volumes of those parts that have been brought to completion are closer to the Steiner drawing, as are the old man's face and the folds of his drapery.

The style of this drawing is clearly different from Campagnola's looser late manner, as can be seen in *Christ and St. Peter on the Water* at Chatsworth, from the last decade of his life[1]. Therefore, it seems reasonable to place this drawing in his youthful maturity at about 1520-25, with the possibility that it was executed for a print. R.S.

1. Anna Poniz Santagiustina, "Disegni tardi di Domenico Campagnola, 1552-1564," *Arte Veneta* XXXV, 1981, pp. 67-68.

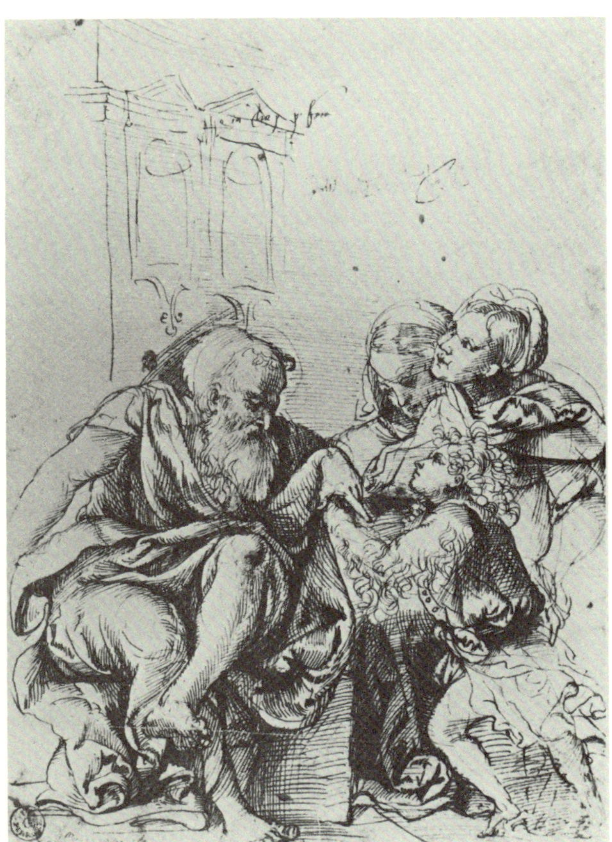

Domenico Campagnola
Isaac and Jacob
Uffizi, Florence

12.

GIOVANNI ANGELO CANINI

(Rome 1617 - Paris - 1666 Rome)

Vision of St. William of Aquitaine

Brown wash heightened with white on brown prepared paper; 472 x 349 mm.; a horizontal fold discernable across the middle; traces of an illegible previous drawing underneath

Provenance: L.Pollack (L.788b)

Acquired 1982

According to the *Vita Sancti Wilhelmi,* composed around 1125 by the monks of Gellone, William (755-812), who was the Duke of Aquitaine before becoming a monk, beheld an angel who took him by the hand and led him to the desolate valley of the Gellone[1]. There he founded a Benedictine monastery, later called Saint Guilhem-du-Desert, remains of which are now in the Cloisters in New York City.

In this drawing William is being struck by the divine light of the apparition. He wears a thick mantle, presumably the black one worn by future Guillemite monks of his order. This cloak hides the chain mail he reputedly wore against his skin for self-mortification. From beneath the cloak's bulk appears a military plated skirt; and he wears sandals that are reminiscent of a Roman soldier's. In a lightly indicated jumble on the ground are a spear and helmet, both of which allude to William's famous battles in southern France against the Saracens for his emperor, Charlemagne.

Above the man floats a barely discernible head, rendered in a few strokes of light wash toward which William's open-mouthed gaze is directed. Part of this celestial epiphany are three *putti* who hover in the clouds above William. The third angel looks up to God for instruction as he dangles an awkward hand to lead William to Gellone.

Nicholas Turner attributes this drawing to Giovanni Angelo Canini, a lesser known artist practicing primarily in Rome in the mid-seventeenth century[2]. In deciphering Canini's drawing style, Turner identifies the anatomical features typical of Canini as a "hard, mask-like face" with "a broad nose and large, staring eyes," and large hands splaying their fingers[3]. Very noticeable in the Steiner drawing are William's long, untapered fingers; his long toes appear also in the study of a foot in Canini's drawing for the figure of St. Paul in the Gabinetto Nazionale delle Stampe in Rome (inv. no. FC 127281), a preparatory study for the *Conversion of St. Paul* (1659), which was painted for the church of S. Giovanni dei Fiorentini in Rome.

Although the Steiner drawing is not a preparatory study for any known work by Canini, his painting of Christ's *Charge to St. Peter* of 1659 in the same church, is similar compositionally. Even more noticeable is the similarity between the Steiner sheet and Canini's undated drawing of *St. Benedict in the Wilderness Receiving Bread from the Crow* in the British Museum, of which Bloemart engraved a variant. In each of these works a solitary saint kneels before an image of Christ against a backdrop of rugged trees framing at least one edge of the scene. Moreover, both St. William and St. Benedict use a rocky outcropping as a *prie-dieu,* and are accompanied by birds fluttering in the upper-right of the drawings.

The history of St. William of Aquitaine had been depicted in Italian art before Canini, but it may be significant that in 1664 Canini accompanied a nephew of Pope Alexander VII, Cardinal Flavio Chigi, to Paris on a mission of atonement to Louis XIV who had humiliated the pope during the preceding years[4]. Conceivably, the Steiner drawing is a pointed reference to Louis who, like St. William, was a ruler, but unlike the saint, refused to submit as a devout Christian to papal authority.

Canini made this trip into France two years before he died, sketching places of interest on the way from Marseilles to Paris[5]. Since, in addition, St. William of Aquitaine is a French saint, it is tempting to try to date the Steiner drawing late in Canini's career. But stylistically such a date is difficult to substantiate. In his study of Canini's preparatory drawings, Turner concluded that the artist had a change of style about 1659 when his figures lost a certain monumentality which was compensated for by their being bathed in a subtler light. St. William's figure type is closer to the fresco of *St. Mark Approving the Construction of the Basilica* of ca. 1653 in the church of S. Marco in Rome[6] than to the figures in two preparatory drawings for the *Conversion of St. Paul* of 1659. In Canini's later style, light defines the contours of the drapery folds in a soft, atmospheric manner, while in the Steiner drawing the effect is less subtle as light glances off the edges of the crisply folded clothing. Nor can the clearly defined hatching on the neck, sleeve and face of St. William be considered subdued. The forehead of the angel reaching down to William is also caught in so strong a light that it breaks up into a geometric abstraction, an effect quite unlike the soft highlights of the late drawings. The problem in dating the Steiner drawing is compounded by the fact that part of the softened light effect in these later preparatory drawings may be due to the chalk technique employed in them, and that the brown wash and white heightening of this drawing, even in its unfinished state, invites the different effect. C.R.R.

1. Bédier, Jopeph, *Les Legendes épiques, recherches sur la formation des chansons de geste,* 3rd edition, Paris, 1926, vol. I, pp. 118-120; L. Schutz and K. G. Kaster, *Lexicon der Christlichen Ikongraphie,* Rome/Vienna, 1976, vol. VIII, cols. 604-5.
2. According to the Steiners' notes on the drawing.
3. Nicholas Turner "Drawings by Giovanni Angelo Canini," *MD,* XVI, 1978, pp. 387-97.
4. Ludwig von Pastor, *The History of the Popes,* 1957, vol. XXXI, pp. 111-112.
5. Turner, *op. cit.,* p. 395, no. 17; von Pastor, 1957, vol. XXXI, p. 111.
6. Turner, *op. cit.,* fig. 3.

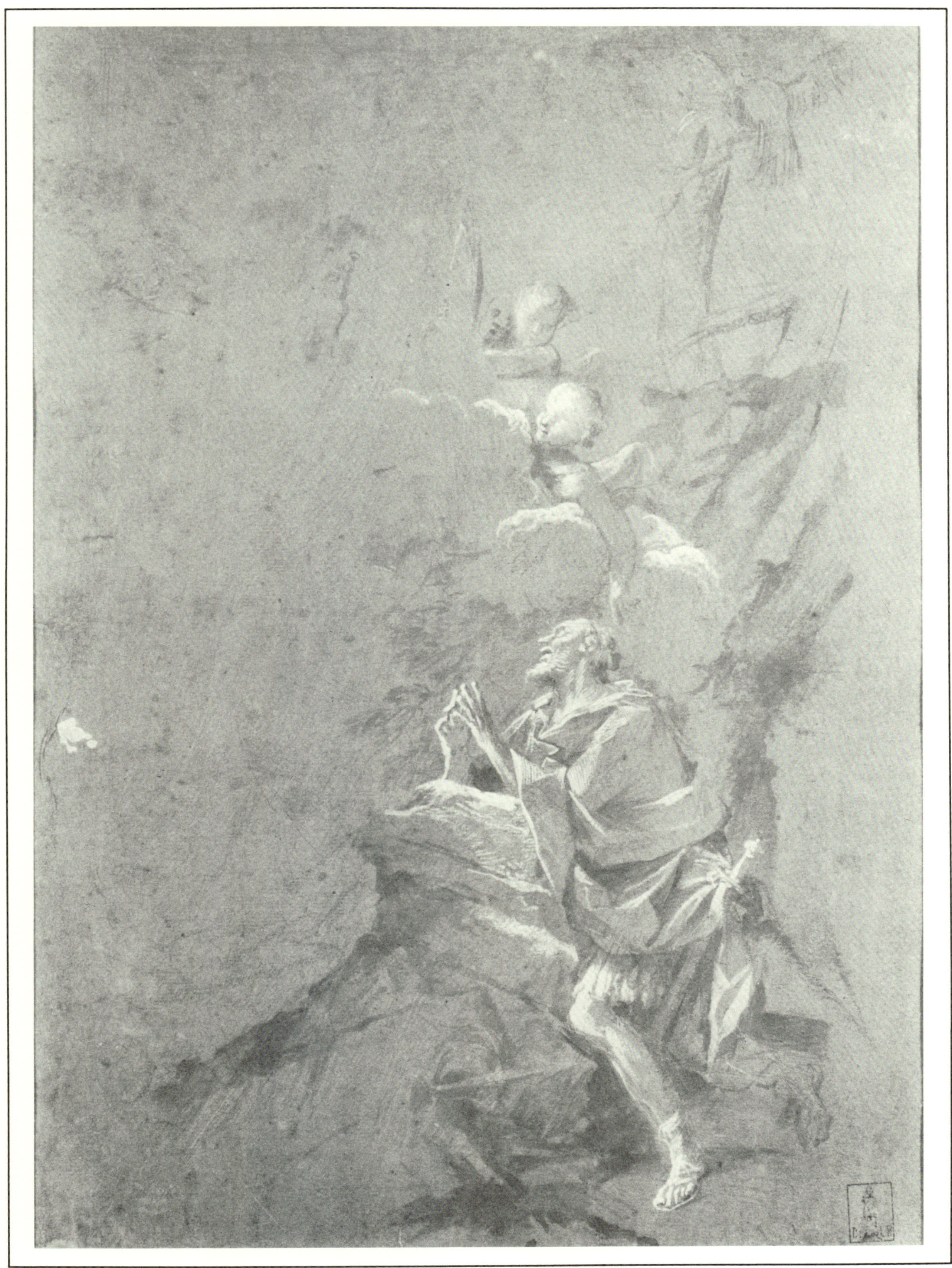

13.

ANNIBALE CARRACCI
(Bologna 1560 - Parma, Venice, Rome - 1609 Rome)

Venus in the Clouds

Black and pinkish chalk, pen and brown ink, brown wash with touches of white and pink gouache, on blue-grey tinted paper; 173 x 230 mm.; upper right corner made up; repairs on left and right sides
Inscribed verso, in graphite *Ann Caracci*
Provenance: J. E. Pryde, Fife, Scotland
Margaret P. Morgan in Oberhuber, 1977, number 7, pp. 37-8
Acquired 1974

Annibale, the most distinguished member of the Bolognese family of artists, was responsive to a variety of influences. Originally a student of Bartolomeo Passarotti (1529-92) and of his cousin Lodovico Carracci (number 14), Annibale traveled extensively in North Italy absorbing much of what he saw in Parma and in Venice into his own art. Collaborating with Lodovico and with his brother Agostino (1557-1602), he carried out commissions in Bologna and established a teaching academy there. In 1595 he was called to Rome to decorate the Camerino in the Palazzo Farnese and when that project was successfully accomplished, he was commissioned the decoration of the famous Gallery. His masterpiece, the Farnese Gallery, inspired successive generations of painters, not only those who assisted him in carrying it out but also those in later years who studied it.

The firm not to say heavy contours of this Venus are unusual in Annibale's *oeuvre,* and the whole sheet is exceptionally colorful. But the delicate modeling of the torso, the truly brilliant graphic characterization of the hair and of the face, and the convincing liberation of this opulent figure from the laws of gravity, betray the hand of the master himself. The outline separates the body from the background rather than imprisoning it, so that it floats graceful and free, simultaneously corporeal and weightless, stately and voluptuous. The delineation of the outline is very deliberate, the parallel hatching abstract and disciplined, and the interior modeling delicate, yet the whole drawing seems quite spontaneous.

Although exceptional in Annibale's oeuvre, this drawing is not unique. Full-bodied female nudes appear throughout his career, more frequently after his move to Rome than before. During 1595-97, his first years there, when he was working on the Camerino Farnese, he was absorbing the classically monumental grandeur of Roman antique and Renaissance art and synthesizing it with the lighter, more emotional art of Bologna. As a result, his figures became more solid as well as more rounded and plastic. He prepared his compositions for the Palazzo Farnese very carefully; there are nearly 300 drawings for the Camerino and about a thousand for the Gallery. Most were done in black chalk, heightened with white on blue-grey paper, but he also made many pen and ink sketches with wash, or without.

Despite its unusually elaborate medium, basically this is a black chalk drawing on blue-grey paper, reinforced by pen and ink and by white highlights. It is very similar in rendering to the *Allegorical Figure Leaning on a Column* in the Louvre, with the same fullness in the hip, rounded abdomen, and soft modeling, especially in the torso; and in both drawings the contours are defined by dark lines. The Louvre drawing is a preparatory study for the figure of *Securitas* in the Camerino. Other preparatory drawings for the Camerino, notably the study for Iole in Besançon (inv. no. D1496) and the study for Circe at Windsor (inv. no. 2066) suggest that the Steiner figure is contemporary — i.e. 1595-97. Several studies for the Galleria also seem comparable; but in general they tend to be more sculptural and monumental.

Although this pose appears in other contexts elsewhere in Annibale's oeuvre, the drawing is unique in having no known specific relation to any other work of his, drawn or painted. The identification of the figure as Venus is based on her beautiful classical head and profile, the mirror in chalk that she holds in her right hand, and most of all on her display of the nude splendor of her body. The face in chalk faintly visible above her right shoulder is inexplicable. The alternate identity it might suggest, of a Jupiter enfolding Io in the clouds comparable to Correggio's painting in Vienna, seems precluded by the mirror. N.M. and A.M.

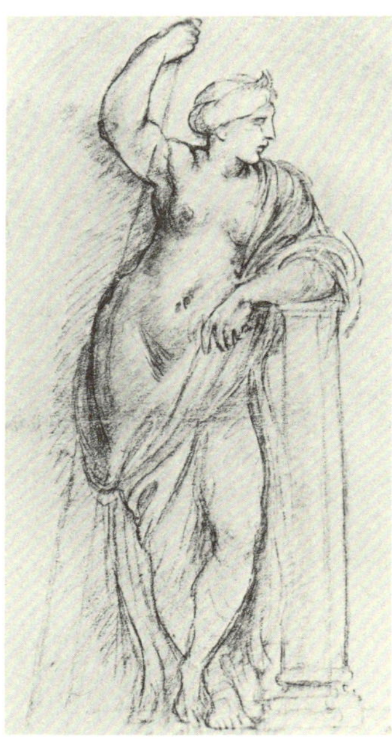

Annibale Carracci
Allegorical Figure Leaning on a Column
Louvre

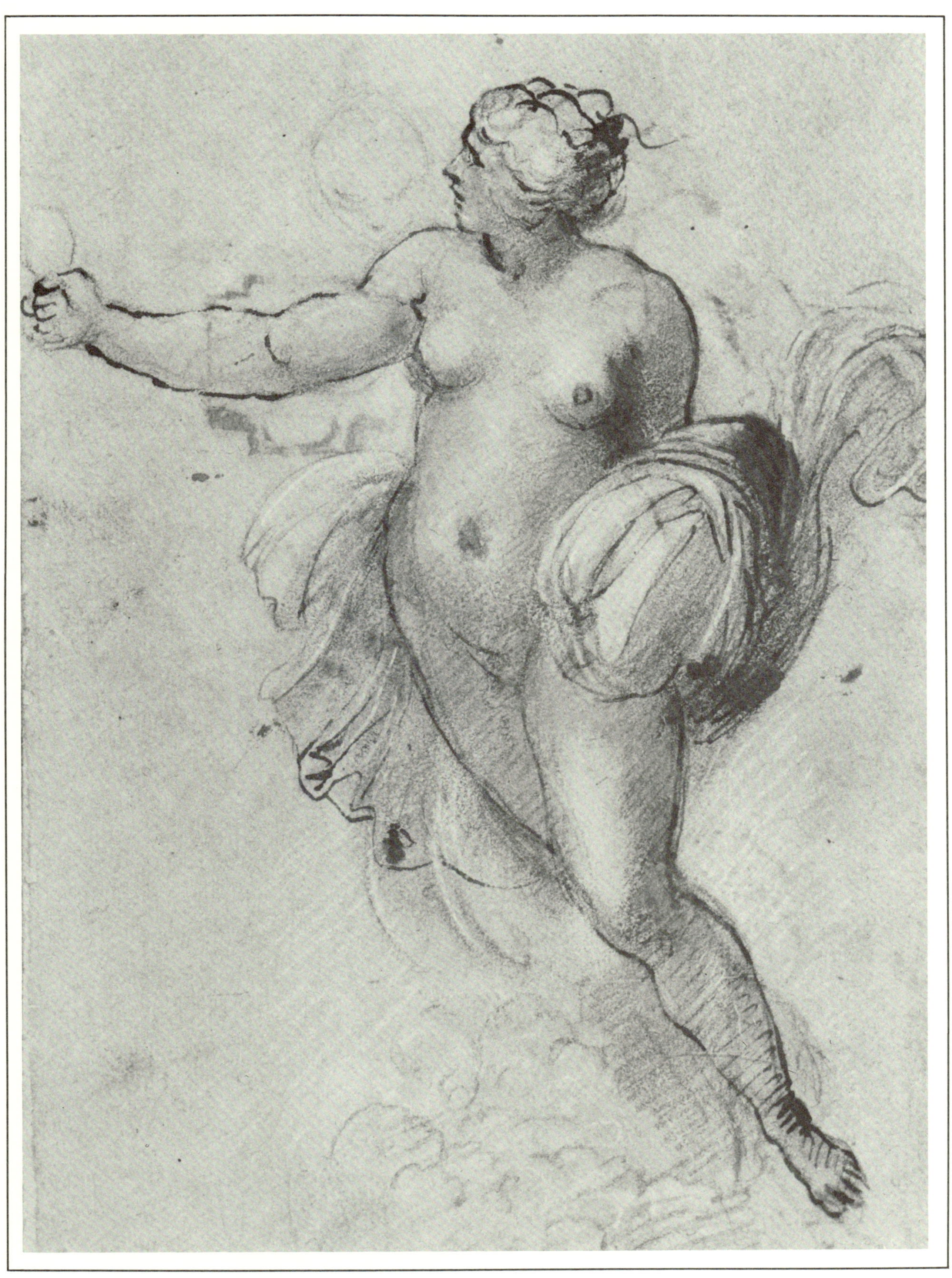

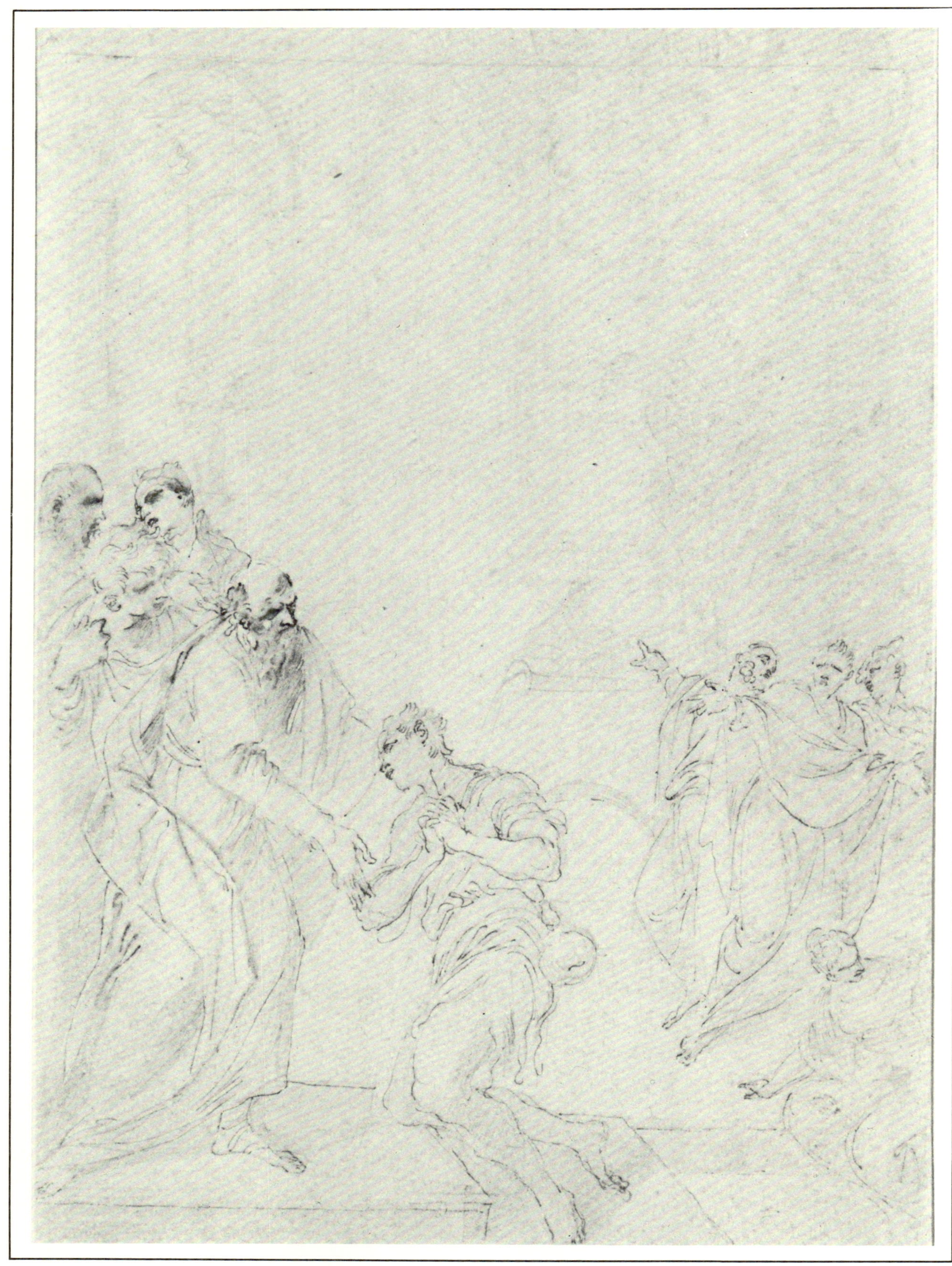

14.

LODOVICO CARRACCI
(Bologna 1555 - Emilia, Venice - 1619 Bologna)

The Return of the Prodigal Son

Pen and brown ink, brown wash, black chalk, on buff paper; 240 x 202 mm.
Susan J. Cooke in Oberhuber, 1977, no. 8, pp. 38-40
Acquired 1974

After youthful travels to Parma and Venice Lodovico, the senior member of the Carracci family, remained in Bologna for the rest of his life, except for a month's visit to Rome in 1602. Thus, unlike his cousins Annibale (number 13) and Agostino, he never experienced the influence of Roman art, and maintained his allegiance to the Emilian-Venetian tradition of Correggio, Titian and Tintoretto. As a result, he like Annibale became a *capo di scuola,* but of a less classicistic sort that inspired the more fluid, colorful, Baroque style of the early Guercino (number 23).

Lodovico and his cousins collaborated not only in founding their school in Bologna but also in the important fresco cycles at the Fava and Magnani palaces. At times, however, they may have competed with each other rather than cooperating. Notably in the early 1590's, perhaps largely as a result of the design that his brother Annibale provided him, Agostino was chosen to paint his famous *Last Communion of St. Jerome* in the Bolognese church of San Girolano della Certosa. Lodovico made a drawing[1] of the same subject, which has led to the supposition that he wanted the commission for himself[2].

Whether cooperating or competing, each member of the family tried his hand at composing the parable of the prodigal son. This drawing provides certain evidence of Lodovico's participation; the only reference to his having painted the subject is a description in 1631 of the Dulcini Gallery in Bologna to a picture otherwise completely unrecorded and therefore suspect in attribution[3]. A painting of the *Prodigal Son's Return* by Annibale, although lost, is well documented. Probably originally in the Lambertini chapel in the church of the Corpus Domini in Bologna, it was in the Palazzo Zambeccari in 1727 when it was sold by Giovanni Pietro Zanotti to the Duc d'Orléans. It was engraved in the famous *Galerie du Duc d'Orléans* (no. 9), an indispensable record of the collection before its dispersal during the French Revolution. Annibale may have painted the subject a second time: a *Prodigal Son* attributed to him is listed in the 1743 inventory of the Palazzo Zambeccari; it may have been either autograph or a copy of the Orleans painting. The only other surviving trace of the Orleans painting, apart from the engraving, is a variant version in the Bologna Pinacoteca by Lucio Massari, a Carracci pupil who assisted Annibale[4].

Judging from a group of his drawings, Agostino Carracci was also involved. A drawing at Windsor[5] is a rough sketch of the whole composition and a study of the father and the son. The composition in another drawing at Windsor[6] attributed in the inventory to Lodovico but given by Wittkower to Agostino, is much further developed, with careful study of the details of the figures rather than of the background, much like the Steiner drawing. Related drawings attributed to Agostino are at Windsor, the Louvre and Chatsworth[7]. The most fully developed compositional study is in the Uffizi[8].

The role of each member of the family in the *Prodigal Son* project, if indeed they were all working together at the same time on a single commission, cannot be determined. The evidence of this and the other drawings suggests that Agostino was most active in the evolution of the composition, apparently in collaboration with his brother and his cousin. That this drawing is Lodovico's seems certain. The graceful, languorous bodies with small heads, the segmented composition, the atmospheric effect, and the combination of firm lines with soft wash, are typical of his draughtsmanship. Comparison with his drawing of the *Last Communion of St. Jerome* at the Metropolitan Museum demonstrates that both are works of the early 1590's, contemporaneous with Lodovico's *Preaching of St. John the Baptist,* which he painted to hang just opposite Agostino's *Last Communion* at San Gerolamo della Certosa.

The parable of the prodigal son appears in the Gospel according to St. Luke (xv: 10-32). In it Christ tells his questioners the story of the younger son who asked his father for his inheritance, spent it foolishly in living high, and then went home, penniless and contrite. Christ's moral, "there is joy in the presence of angels of God over one sinner that repenteth" and "Be glad: for this thy brother was dead, and is alive again," is touchingly conveyed in human terms by the quiet moment being shared by the understanding father and the humble son, particularly in contrast to the fluster of the other figures. J.I.

1. In the Metropolitan Museum, (inv. no. 65:11:1).
2. Bean, 1979, p. 81, no. 108.
3. Heinrich Bodmer, *Lodovico Carraci,* Magdeburg, 1939, p. 39.
4. Donald Posner, *Annibale Carracci,* London, 1971, vol. I, p. 161, no. 2.
5. Rudolf Wittkower, *The Drawings of the Carracci...at Windsor Castle,* London, 1952, no. 96*v*, p. 113, fig. 12.
6. Wittkower, *op. cit.,* no. 52, p. 112, plate 30.
7. Cooke in Oberhuber, 1977, p. 38.
8. Posner, *op. cit.,* vol. I, fig. 54 as by Agostino.

15.

GIOVANNI BENEDETTO CASTIGLIONE
(Genoa 1600/1610 - North Italy, Florence, Rome, Naples, Genoa - Mantua 1663/1665[1])

Crucifixion with the Swooning Virgin, Saints John and Mary Magdalene and God the Father

Oil sketch in brown with touches of blue, red and white on cream paper; 401 x 274 mm. (sight); creased; later gold self-frame
Provenance: Benjamin West (L.419); Private Collection, England
Acquired 1975
Rebecca Zurier in Oberhuber, 1977, no. 10, pp. 43-45
Exhibited: Philadelphia, 1971, no. 54; Edinburgh, 1972, no. 29; Metropolitan Museum, 1976
Literature: Ann Percy, exhibition catalogue, *Giovanni Benedetto Castiglione: Master Draughtsman of the Italian Baroque,* Philadelphia Museum of Art, 1971, no. 54, pp. 90, (ill.); Edinburgh, 1972, no. 29

Castiglione traveled so extensively throughout his career that he might be identified as one of the first national Italian artists (as opposed to his contemporaries who were Venetian or Florentine or Roman or whatever). However, despite the long periods he spent in Rome and Mantua, he is generally considered a Genoese artist. He was trained there, perhaps by Van Dyck, and he involved himself profoundly with the local painters of nature, including the landscapist Cornelis de Wael (number 96). But his travels, mostly during the 1630's, exposed him to a full range of old and new art in Italy. He was notably responsive, to the Bassano family, to Bernini, Poussin and Pietro Testa, and perhaps to the *bamboccianti.* At the same time the originality and intensity of his art, and its technical brilliance, were so striking that its influence was widespread.

His paintings are relatively rare and unknown in the United States[2], although their panache is so great as to force recognition of Castiglione as a great Baroque artist, perhaps as the Rubens of Italian painting. He is better known and greatly admired for his prints and drawings. Castiglione evidently gave much thought to the theme of the Crucifixion. He saw it not only as a central to Christian history and doctrine and therefore quite literally a cosmic event, but apparently also as an opportunity for representation of the most agitated emotions and for evocation of an equally intense response. So he drew many versions of it — Percy lists eight (including the Steiner example) plus a ninth that is lost but known through copies, and a small painting and a monotype as well[3]. These different versions inspired many copies. Most of them are brush drawings like this one, basically small oil paintings on paper[4]. The *fattura* is always rich and loose, and the setting always stormy and wind-swept, as if Castiglione were visualizing . . . about the sixth hour there was a darkness all over the earth . . . And the sun was darkened . . ." (Luke xxiii: 44-45). Otherwise, no original composition is the same as any other: the only constant presence is the crucified Christ's, and His position is changed in each drawing, as are the identities of his companions.

The Steiner drawing seems the most experimental of all Castiglione's versions of the subject, less for the inclusion of God the Father with angels than for the unique placement of the cross so that He and Christ are seen from three-quarters behind. Zurier suggests this device to be Castiglione's own invention, although she notes a possible prototype by Van Dyck. Castiglione may also have recalled Veronese's *Crucifixion* which he would have seen in the Church of San Nicolo della Lattuga ai Frari in Venice (now in the Accademia) or one of its variants[5], where the good thief is in almost the same position. It is an effective device to engage the viewer in the pathos and drama of the image, and it is very Baroque.

The date of this and the other *Crucifixion* drawings has been subject to some debate, summarized by Zurier. Her suggestion of ca. 1651 seems reasonable, particularly because of the documented presence of Castiglione in Rome between 1647 and 1651. Thus he coincided there with the completion of Bernini's *Ecstasy of Saint Theresa* in the church of Santa Maria della Vittoria, which Zurier convincingly proposes as a source for Castiglione's swooning Virgin. C.R.R. and A.M.

1. For a discussion of Castiglione's birth and death dates, see Percy, *op. cit.*, p. 47, note 1.
2. There are few of his paintings in the United States. Burton Fredericksen and Federico Zeri, *census of pre-nineteenth-century Italian paintings in North American public collections,* Cambridge (MA), 1972, list only eight, plus two by followers.
3. Percy, *op. cit.*, pp. 42, 89-90, 152; fig. 32 and numbers 51-54 and M7.
4. For a description of Castiglione's technique of painting in oil on paper, see Ann Sievers in Deborah J. Johnson, 1983, p. 42: "Castiglione chose coarsely-ground pigments without a binding medium and mixed them on his palette with varying amounts of oil according to the paint opacity he desired."
5. The closest is the small canvas, formerly in the Gemaldegalerie in Dresden (inv. no. 232), where the good thief's pose is identical (see Terisio Pignatti, *Veronese,* Venice, 1976, no. A71, fig. 784).

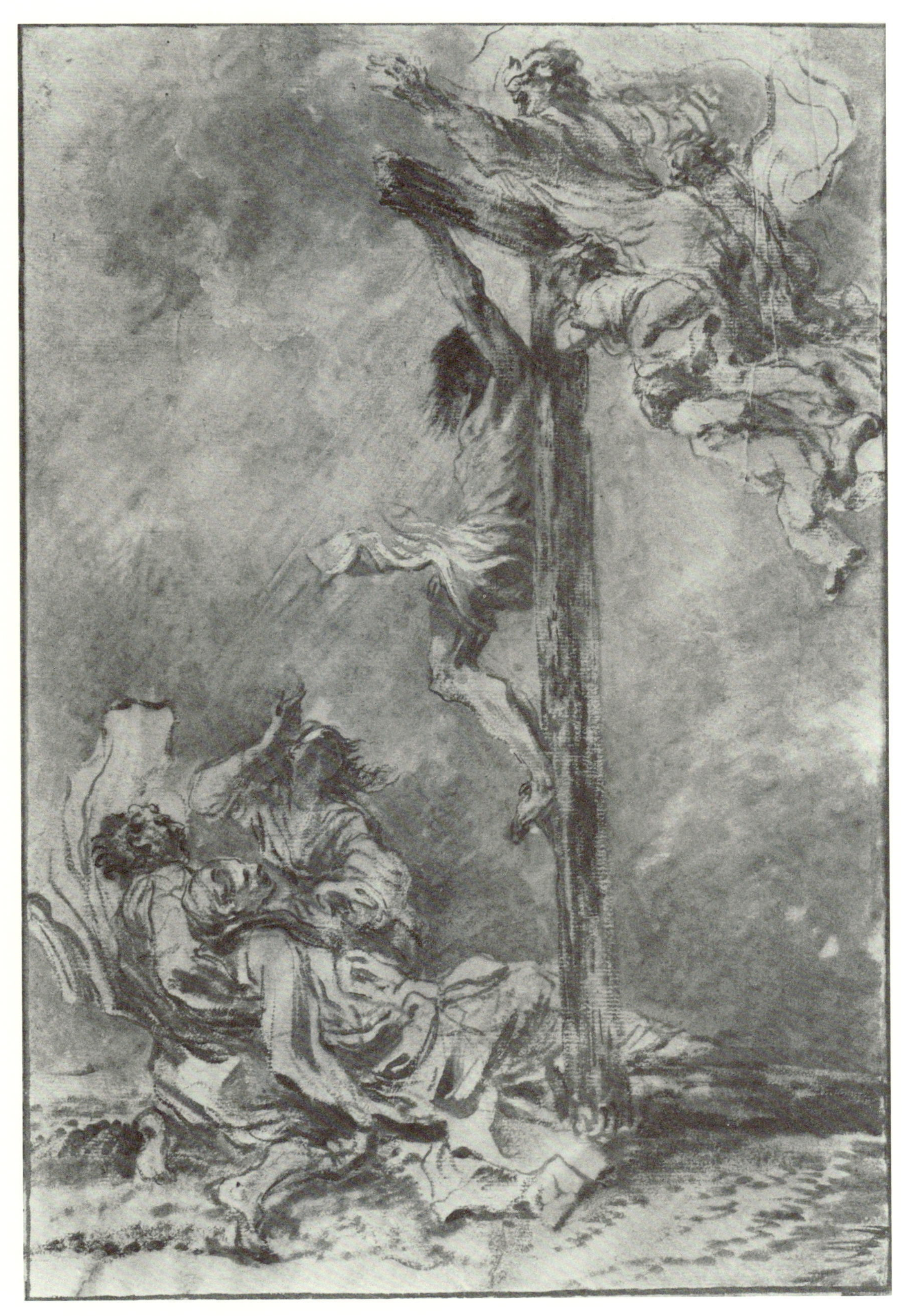

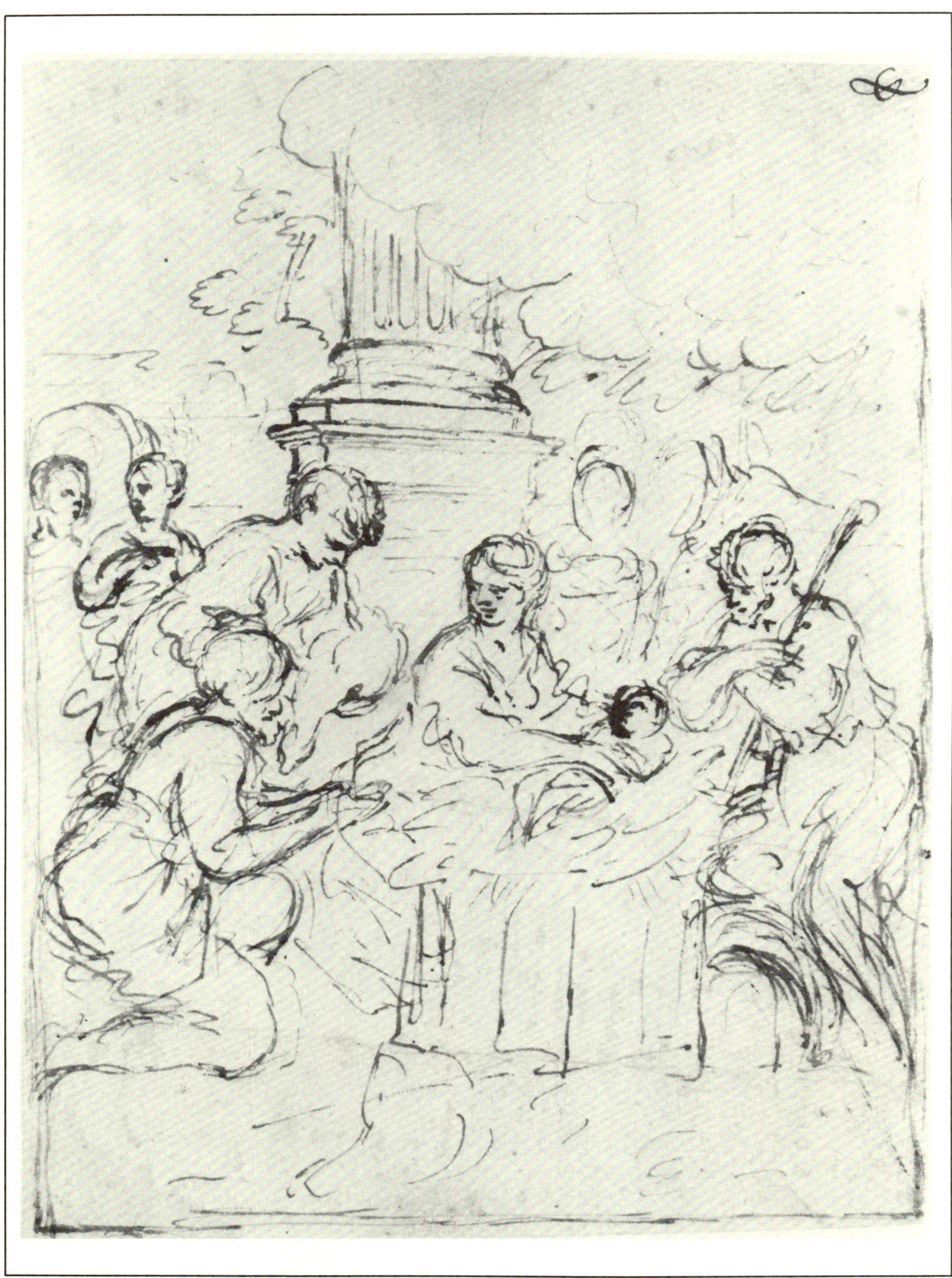

16.

PIETRO BERRETTINI called PIETRO DA CORTONA
(Cortona 1596 - Rome, Florence - 1669 Rome)

Adoration of the Shepherds

Pen and brown ink, 203 x 156 mm.; repaired horizontal tear about 1/3 up from the bottom
Inscribed verso in pen and ink: *Pietro da Cortona;* on backing recto in 17th century hand: *Pietro da Cortona inv. e fece*
Provenance: unidentified collector's mark (?) upper right corner; Pietro Scarpa, 1978
Acquired 1985
Exhibitions: Grand Palais, Paris, 1978
Literature: Pietro Scarpa, ed., exhibition catalogue, *Dessins Anciens,* Grand Palais, Paris, 1978, no. 35

Pietro Berrettini, born in Cortona, was first trained in Florence by the painter Andrea Commodi with whom he went to Rome in 1612-13. There he was a pupil of another Florentine, Baccio Ciarpi, who is otherwise scarcely remembered, and made profound studies of the antique and the Renaissance. Cortona's success began with his meeting his first great patrons, the rich and cultivated Sacchetti brothers, the Marchese Marcello and Monsignor Giulio, who was soon to become a cardinal. The Marchese commissioned of Cortona a series of frescoes to decorate the family villa (now the Villa Chigi) at Castel Fusano near Ostia. He also introduced Cortona to the Pope, Urban VIII Barberini (reigned 1623-44), whose closest friend the Marchese was. Under the auspices of the Sacchetti and the Barberini families, Cortona's brilliant career got under way. He had numerous important church and palace commissions in Rome and trained many artists, including his chief assistant, Ciro Ferri (number 20). During most of the 1640's, Cortona worked primarily in Florence on the splendid frescoes in the Pitti Palace for the Grand Duke of Tuscany, Ferdinando II de' Medici. His vast and joyful decorative cycles in Rome and Florence affected 17th century Roman and Florentine art profoundly, and established him as the leading decorative painter of his time in Italy. He was also an architect, and though his architectural commissions were less numerous than his paintings, they were hardly less inventive.

During the late 1620's, Cortona painted two *Adorations of the Shepherds,* an altarpiece in oil in the Roman church of San Salvatore in Lauro (1628-30) and another in fresco in the chapel at the Villa Sacchetti[1]. This drawing is comparable stylistically to Cortona's preparatory studies for the Villa Sacchetti frescoes. For example, in his drawing[2] for the *Triumph of Ceres* fresco in the gallery in the villa, the delineation is similarly rapid and energetic. However, in the Steiner drawing the contours are firmer and less discontinuous as if Cortona had been so anxious to record his thoughts quickly that he almost scribbled them with numerous short strokes. He seems to have been more concerned with the placement of the figures, their relationship to each other and their general shapes, than with elegant delineation of fine details. Notably, the depiction of hands and feet is summary, although the faces are defined in more detail.

The vigor of this draughtsmanship appears in a study[3] for the *Offering to Pomona,* another fresco in the gallery of the villa. Small, scratchy and jagged strokes of the pen define Pomona's drapery so that she seems almost to vibrate, and outlines throughout the drawing are more cursory yet strong. More attention is given to details in the Pomona than in the Steiner drawing and it is somewhat more finished, but in both the artist has made a spontaneous short-hand summary of the scene, so that his corrections and changes are insignificant in the context of the overall composition.

The Steiner drawing not only is in the style of the preparatory studies for the Villa Sacchetti frescoes, it also has the same number of figures as the chapel altarpiece. They are somewhat rearranged in composition but in a similarly shallow space, so they must be contemporaneous. Cortona was already making use of assistants at the Villa Sacchetti, and this drawing can probably be explained as his first thought for the altarpiece, while he was still working out the composition in his own mind. T.L. and A.M.

1. Briganti, 1962, nos. 29 and 23, respectively.
2. Briganti, *op. cit.,* fig. 79.
3. Felice Stampfle and Jacob Bean, exhibition catalogue, *The Seventeenth Century in Italy. Drawings from New York Collections,* New York, 1967, fig. 54.

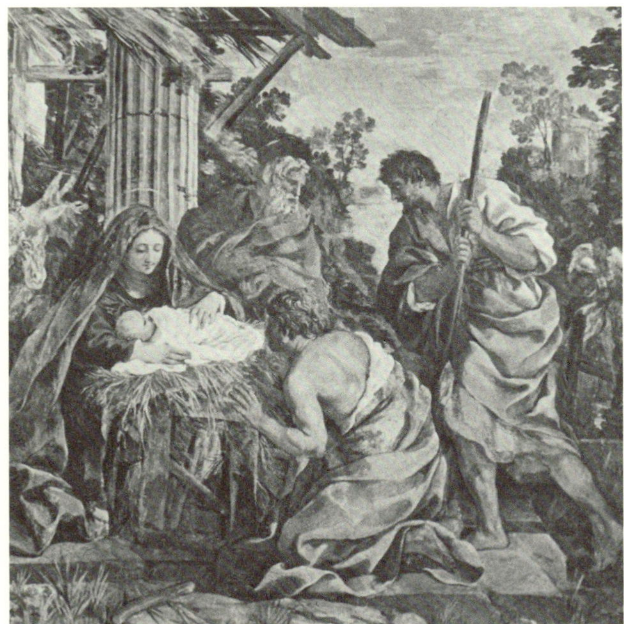

Pietro da Cortona
Adoration of the Shepherds
Villa Chigi, Castel Fusano, Ostia

17.

DONATO CRETI
(Cremona 1671-1749 Bologna)

Madonna and Child with Saints Ignatius of Loyola and Petronius

Pen and brown ink; 230 x 185 mm.
Acquired 1972
Loaned by the J. Pierpont Morgan Library, New York

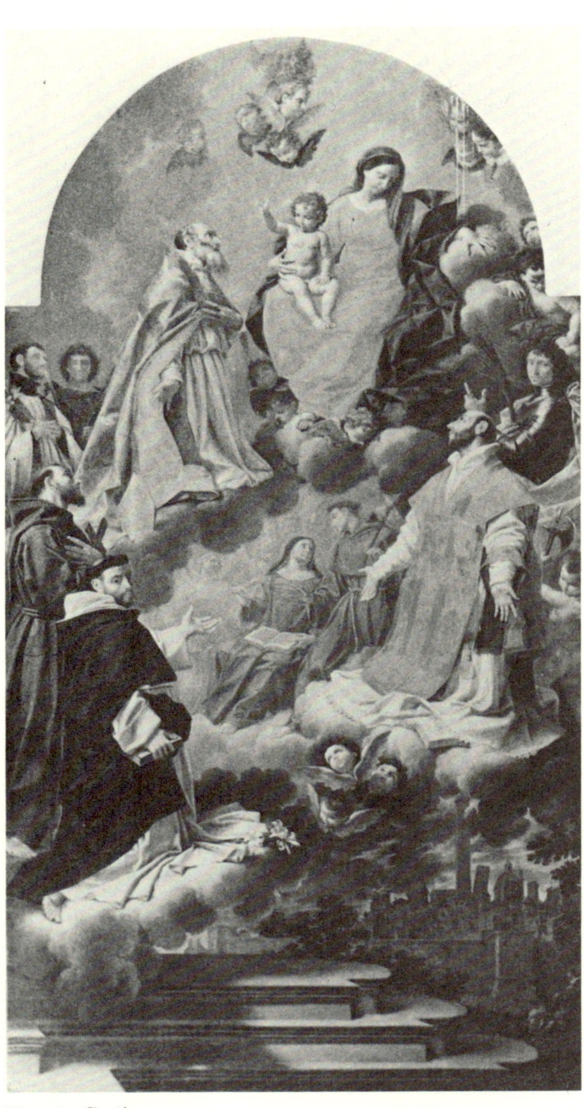

Donato Creti
Madonna in Glory with Saints
Sanctuario della Beata Vergino, di San Luca, Villani

The predominant figures in this drawing are the Virgin enthroned in clouds, and Christ, who is balanced on His mother's right knee. Mary gazes down at St. Petronius (Bishop of Bologna, 432-449, and patron saint of the city), while Christ looks toward the founder of the Society of Jesus, St. Ignatius of Loyola, His right hand poised in benediction. This extended arm is echoed by Mary's which rests on a cloud. The resulting configuration of limbs can be read as a cross. Two other clearly defined figures in the drawing are the angels behind St. Ignatius, one strumming a lute, the other playing a flute.

Donato Creti was a student of Pasinelli, continuing the long Bolognese classical-idealist tradition which began with the Carracci family and evolved under Francesco Albani and Guido Reni[1]. Two altarpieces by Creti in Bologna, clearly derived from Reni, are related to the Steiner drawing. The first, the *Madonna and Child in Glory with St. Ignatius,* in the church of San Pietro[2], was completed by 1737, and the second, the *Madonna in Glory with Saints* in the Sanctuario della Beata Vergine di San Luca is dated 1746[3]. The drawing's resemblance to the San Pietro altarpiece begins with the similar pose of St. Ignatius and his juxtaposition with the Virgin and Christ Child. St. Ignatius' features in both the drawing and the altarpiece are close to Guido Reni's representation of the saint in his altarpiece of the *Madonna and Child in Glory with Patron-Saints* (1631), now in the Bologna Pinacoteca[4]. This in turn is very close to Sanchez Coello's portrait of the saint, based on his death mask[5]. Finally, the two musical angels behind St. Ignatius in the drawing are a variant of those in the lower right corner of the San Pietro altarpiece.

Despite these affinities, the drawing seems to have been preparatory, not for this altarpiece, but for the later altarpiece, at the Sanctuario della Beata Vergine. The most prominent saints in this painting are Ignatius and Petronius, who have exchanged their positions before the Virgin and Child. St. Petronius now occupies the honored position closer to the Madonna and Child, while St. Ignatius is on a lower cloud, the mirror image of his previous pose and with the same attributes. The lute-playing angel reappears as one of the faint background figures in the central vignette but now seated with his head turned in the opposite direction. With minor differences, the poses of the Madonna and Child are

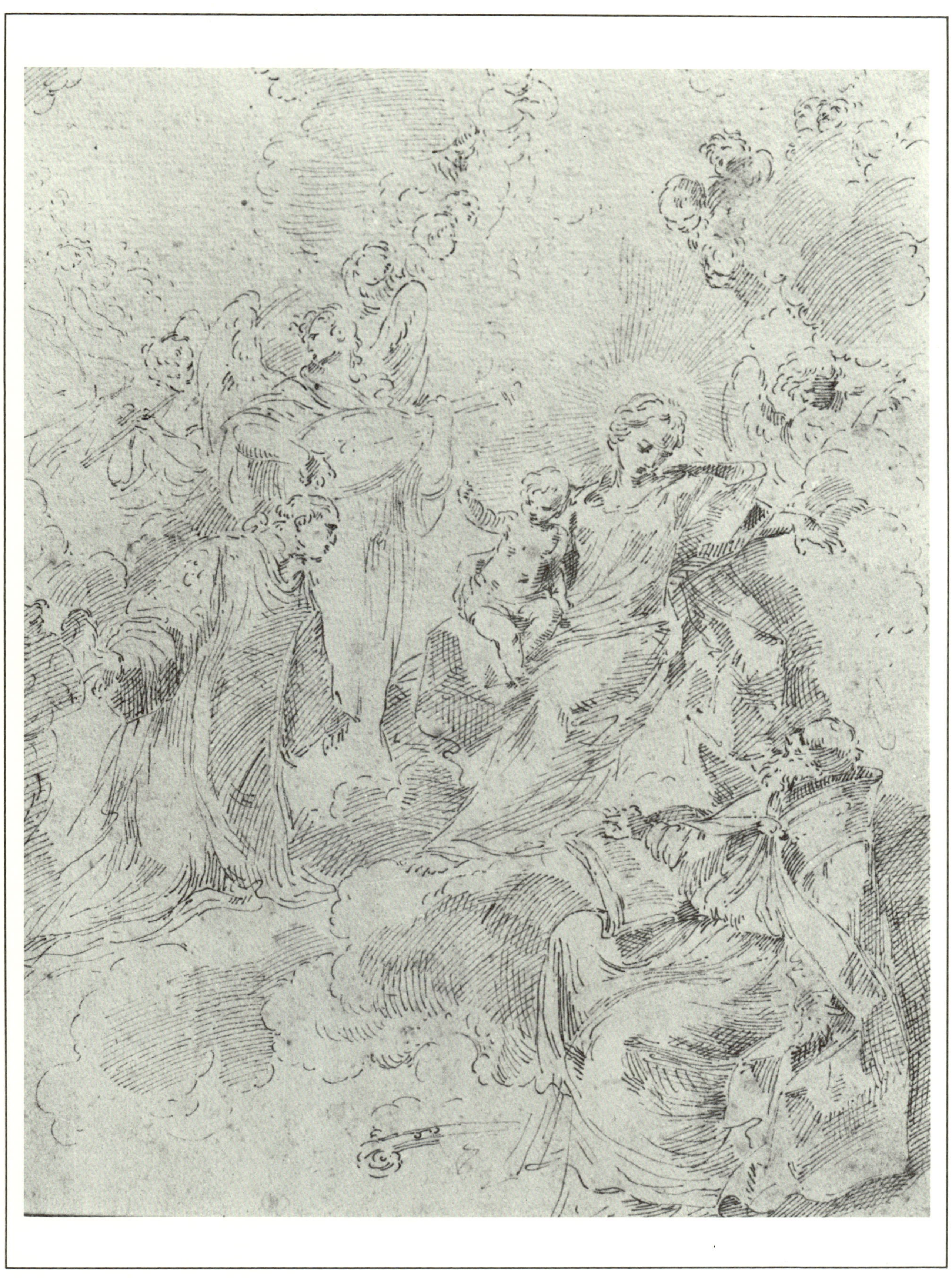

almost identical in the drawing and the 1746 altarpiece.

Roli[5] relates another drawing of the *Madonna and Child with St. Petronius* (in the British Museum, inv. no. 1946-7-L3-852), to the 1746 altarpiece. It shows St. Petronius sinking to his knees before the Virgin and Christ. The poses of this Madonna and Child are different from those in both the altarpiece and the Steiner drawing; but St. Petronius' pose, including his hand upon his heart, is close to that of the bishop in the altarpiece.

The changes in the attributes of the saint within the three works are noteworthy. The book which in the Steiner drawing is situated on St. Petronius' thigh, is held aloft by the cherub in the London drawing, and has disappeared in the final painting. The crozier and halo in the Steiner drawing are not present in the London drawing where Creti places a miter on the head of the bishop; in the altarpiece, the miter is removed from the saint's head and floats at his side. Because the Steiner drawing seems linked in many ways to the San Pietro painting but is clearly a study for his later Sanctuario altarpiece, it provides an important clue as to how Creti adapted successful earlier compositions to new commissions. The drawing must have been done a little before 1746, the date of the altarpiece of the Sanctuario della Beata Vergine in San Luca. Another drawing by Creti of the *Madonna and Child in Glory with Saints and Angels* in the Ambrosiana in Milan (Cod. F 283 inf., no. 26), confirms this dating. In publishing it, Ruggieri describes it as *"neoreniano"* (i.e., "Reni revived") and dates it as ca. 1746[6]. C.R.R.

1. Dwight C. Miller, "Donato Creti" (review of Roli's book), *Burl* CXI, 1969, pp. 306-7.
2. Roli, *Donato Creti,* Milan, 1967, p. 90 figs. 85, 87, 89.
3. Roli, "Drawings by Donato Creti: A Chronology," *MD* XI, 1973, p. 30 fig. 2.
4. Cesare Gnudi and Gian Carlo Cavalli, *Guido Reni,* Florence, 1955, p. 83 pls. 132-3.
5. Roli, *op. cit.,* 1973, p. 30 pl. 23b.
6. Ugo Ruggieri, "Nuovi disegni di Donato Creti," *Bollettino Annuale,* Musei Ferraresi, IV, 1974, p. 21

18.

GASPARE DIZIANI

(Belluno 1689 - Germany, Rome, North Italy - Venice 1767)

Christ in the Garden of Gethsemane

Pen and brown ink, grey wash, over red chalk; 195 x 162 mm.; extensive repairs on corners
Acquired 1974

Diziani was one of the most active draughtsmen in eighteenth century Venice, and during his lifetime his sketches were already being collected. First trained by Antonio Lazzarini in Belluno, he went to Venice in 1700 and entered Gregorio Lazzarini's studio where Giovanni Battista Tiepolo also was an apprentice. However, this contact with Tiepolo was brief, because Diziani soon moved on to the studio of Sebastiano Ricci. From 1717 he traveled extensively and was active in Munich, Dresden, Rome and Belluno, before settling in Venice around 1730. There he achieved considerable success as a leader among the painters of the second rank behind Giambattista Tiepolo (numbers 41 and 42).

This drawing is related most closely to Diziani's first years in Venice during the 1730's, while he was still learning from Ricci, whose influence is particularly evident in his paintings. Like Ricci, he drew with a quick, agitated touch to establish a skeleton of the form. His lines are minimal, irregular, abbreviated and angular. Their animation is intensified by the splashes of wash in different values, which are not only atmospheric in effect, but also suggestive of brilliant flickering light. The total effect is of impulsive draughtsmanship, indicating cosmic forces sweeping irresistibly through a tense world.

The profusion and variety of Diziani's drawn *oeuvre* makes it difficult to date or to associate individual sheets to specific paintings, particularly because the quality of the study often surpasses that of the finished work. Despite the range of his subjects, no painting corresponding to this sheet has been recognized. This draughtsmanship however is strikingly similar to that in the *Flight to Egypt* in the Museo Correr in Venice (inv. no. 5631)[1] which was preparatory for a painting of ca. 1733, while Diziani was still under Ricci's influence.

Diziani portrays the moment when Christ accepts the full burden of the sacrifice required of him. The relevant passage in the Bible is Luke xxii: 41-43: "He knelt down and prayed, saying, Father, if thou be willing, remove this cup from me: nevertheless not my will but thine be done. And there appeared an angel unto him from heaven, strengthening him." This representation is touching and tender, particularly in the suggestion of Christ's state of mind through his pose. But the vigor of the draughtsmanship also conveys the dramatic intensity of the event. N.M.

1. Pietro Zampetti, exhibition catalogue, *Dal Ricci al Tiepolo,* Venice, 1969, no. 107, p. 234, ill.

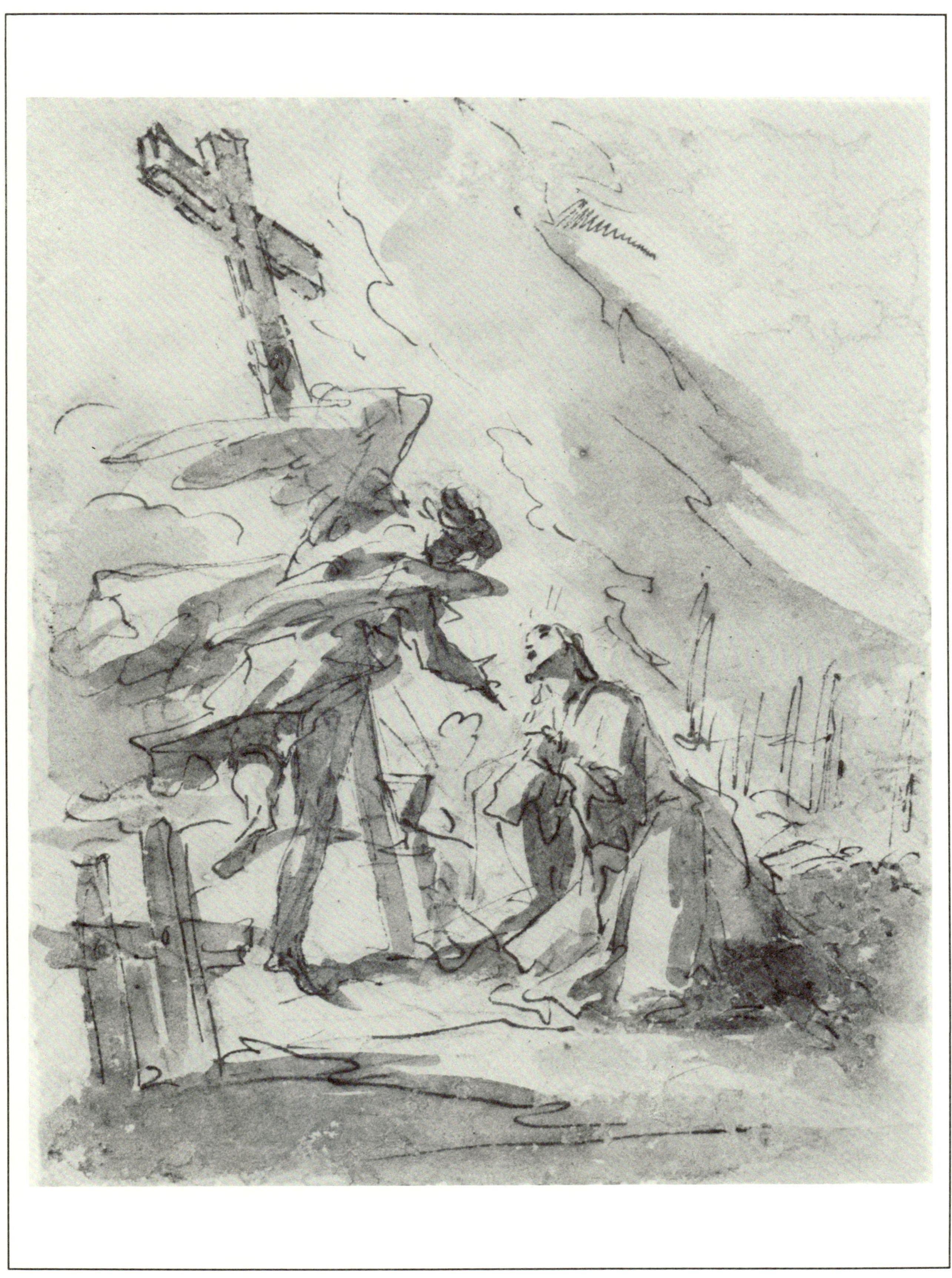

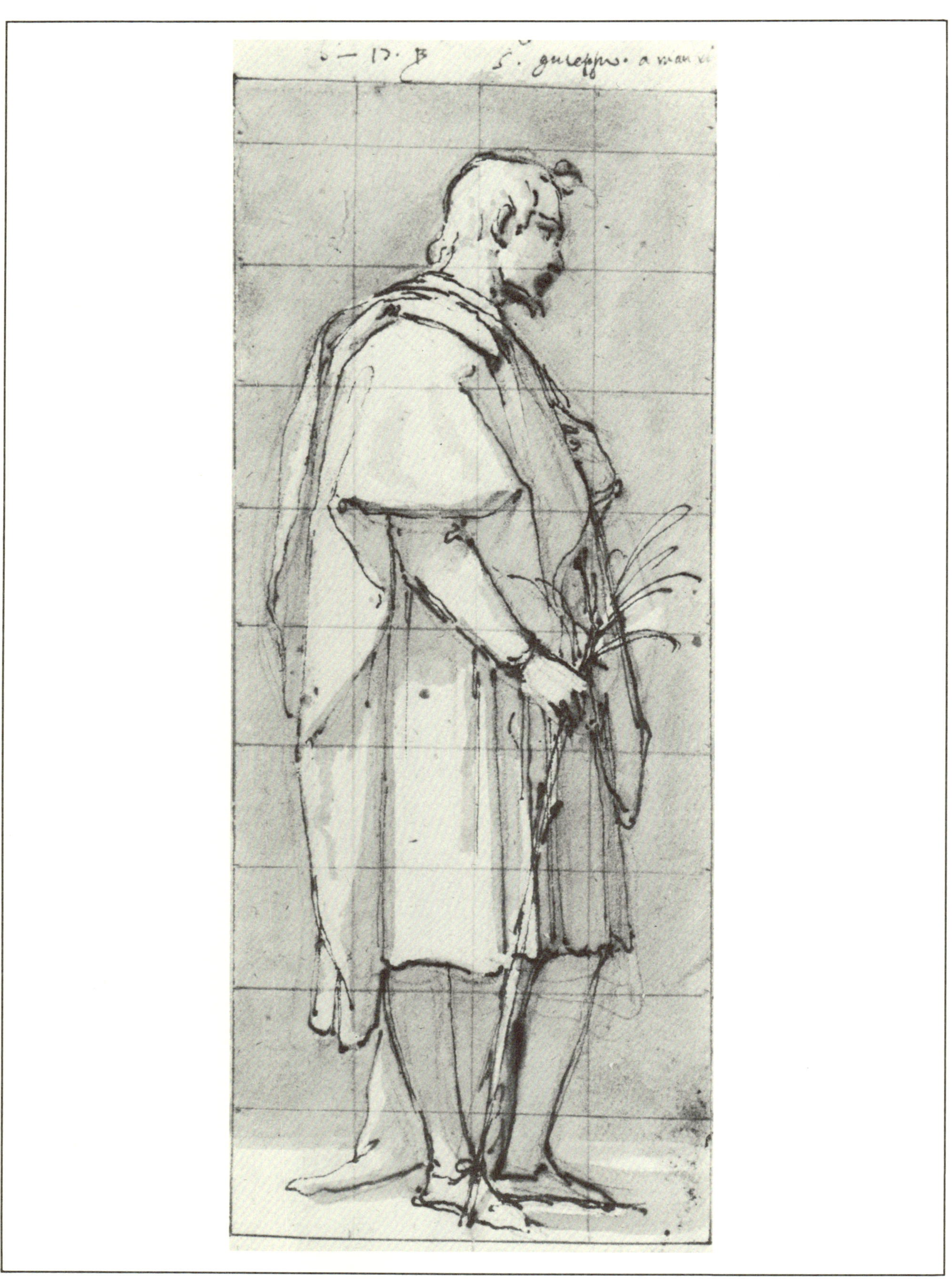

19.

JACOPO CHIMENTI called JACOPO DA EMPOLI
(Empoli 1551 - Florence 1640)

St. Joseph

Pen and brown ink, brown wash, over black chalk, squared with red chalk; 265 x 112 mm.
Inscribed recto, pen and ink: measurement numbers along left margin and top; *S. Guseppe. A Man. di. ta* [illegible: *dritta?*]
Provenance: Lucien Goldschmidt 1961; Ben Sonnenberg
Acquired 1979
Literature: Miles Chappell, ''Florentine Baroque Art: Recent Studies and Some New Proposals,'' *Southeastern College Art Conference Review X,* no. 5, 1985, pp. 253-4, fig. 16

A student of Maso da San Fiano, Jacopo da Empoli during his long life and active career not only spanned two centuries but also mastered two styles and facilitated the transition between them. Brought up in the tradition of the Florentine masters of the earlier 1500's, notably Andrea del Sarto, Fra Bartolomeo and Pontormo, he returned to their early Maniera style in preference to Vasari's High Mannerism of the 1560's and 1570's (number 48), and from that foundation evolved the early Baroque style of this drawing. He was an ardent draughtsman: over 400 of his drawings are preserved in the Uffizi.

This drawing has been identified by Chappell as a preparatory study for a panel painting in the Museo dell'Accademia Etrusca at Cortona. He compares the stance of the saint and the design of his drapery to those of the figure of Saint Thomas in Empoli's *Christ Appearing to the Doubting Thomas,* painted in 1602 for the Collegiata at Empoli. Presumably this drawing is contemporary.

St. Joseph carries his usual attribute, the blossoming staff, an allusion to the choice of Joseph as Mary's husband in preference to her other suitors when his staff flowered and theirs did not. The grid lines, drawn over the image to facilitate transfer to another surface on the larger scale of the painting, include numbers and figures along the top and left margins, probably notations for the scaling up of the drawing. The grid lines were drawn in a different medium, here red chalk, to contrast with the pen and ink of the image and be more easily read.

Empoli has noted the characteristics of his subject briefly but with sensitivity. The simplicity of line is common to his many studies of single figures. The wash, contrasting with the white of the paper, makes the folds of the garment palpable and voluminous. The figure stands out against the darker, washed background and the calligraphy is quick and descriptive. As is made obvious by the loose sketching in chalk around the knees, ankles and left hand, Empoli revised the figure as he drew it.

Although no pendant painting has been identified, there is a matching drawing of Saint Francis of Paola, which must have been made at just the same time[1]. It measures 265 x 110 mm. and is executed in pen and brown ink and wash. The figure is delineated in pen and ink, modeled in wash, and contrasted to the wash on the background; it too has been squared for transfer. There is also an inscription in what appears to be the same hand: *Fran.o. di Paola.* St. Francis, like St. Joseph, is presented very simply, but bearded and clothed in hooded sackcloth with a supporting staff, identifying him as a member of the order of Minims, which he founded. Because of all these similarities and the fact that St. Francis faces left while St. Joseph faces to the right, the two drawings seem surely to have been intended as pendants, perhaps flanking another work. T.L. and A.M.

1. Libiana Dal Pozzo, exhibition catalogue, *Disegni di Artisti Toscani dal Cinquecento al Novecento,* Stanza del Borgo, Milan, 1971, p. 35. She dates the St. Francis to the first decade of the 1600's.

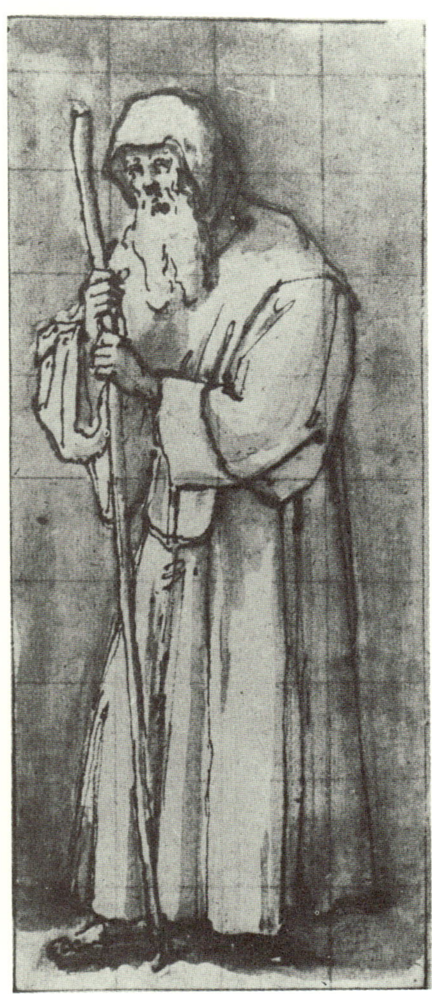

Jacopo da Empoli
Saint Francis of Paola
Stanza del Borgo, Milan

20.

CIRO FERRI
(Rome 1634 - Florence - 1689 Rome)

The Triumph of Flora (Allegory of Spring)

Black chalk, squared for transfer; 237 x 312 mm.
Inscribed lower right hand corner: *P. Cortona;* and upper right: *3.37* (?)
Acquired 1974
Loaned by Benjamin Fraker

At the age of sixteen, Ferri was apprenticed to the distinguished High Baroque painter, Pietro da Cortona (number 16), whom he trailed much the rest of his life. Ferri was recognized as a mature artist in 1657 when he became a member of the Academy of St. Luke, the painter's guild in Rome. Between the years of 1659-65 Cortona entrusted him, his favorite protegé, with the task of completing the fresco cycles in the Palazzo Pitti in Florence, for the Grand Duke Ferdinand II de' Medici. With his successes here, Ciro Ferri began to secure his own commissions and an independent reputation.

This drawing is a preparatory study for Ferri's late fresco, *The Triumph of Flora,* in his cycle of the seasons at the Villa Falconieri (formerly Rufina) in Frascati just outside of Rome[1]. The emphasis in the drawing on delineation without much regard for highlighting or shade, appears also in the only other extant study for the cycle, the *Bacchanal (Allegory of Autumn)* in the Gabinetto Nazionale delle Stampe, Rome (inv. no. 124338r). Jacob Bean[2] has pointed out that the wind god in Ferri's *Triumph* is close to Cortona's drawing of a wind deity in the Metropolitan Museum (inv. no. 61.129.1). Possibly the New York sketch was originally produced to guide Ferri while he was still assisting Cortona in the Sala di Apollo in the Palazzo Pitti, and he used the idea again at Frascati[3].

The Triumph of Flora has traditionally been dated 1688. Davis, however, has shown that the fresco cannot be that late, because Giovanni Francesco Grimaldi's garden scenes on the wall below Flora included putti by Ciro Ferri. The two artists' decoration must therefore be contemporary. Grimaldi stopped painting at the death of his wife in 1679, so the fresco cycle at Frascati must date earlier, according to Davis about 1675-77[4].

Flora was originally the Roman goddess of blossoming plantlife, honored with a sanctuary in 238 B.C. The temple's dedication was in the spring — April twenty-eighth — and after 173 B.C. this day also hosted licentious games held in the goddess' honor each year. Later Flora came to symbolize the season of spring. C.R.R.

1. Bruce Davis, *The Drawings of Ciro Ferri,* Ph.D. dissertation, University of California, Santa Barbara, 1982, p. 101, number 30 (pending publication by the Garland Press). The fresco is illustrated in Herman Voss, *Die Malerei des Barock in Rom,* Berlin, 1924, pl. 274, erroneously identified as *Winter.*
2. In a conversation with the Steiners in 1976.
3. Walter Vitzthum, "Pietro da Cortona" (Review of Briganti, 1962) *MD* II, 1963, p. 50.
4. Davis, *op. cit.,* p. 122.

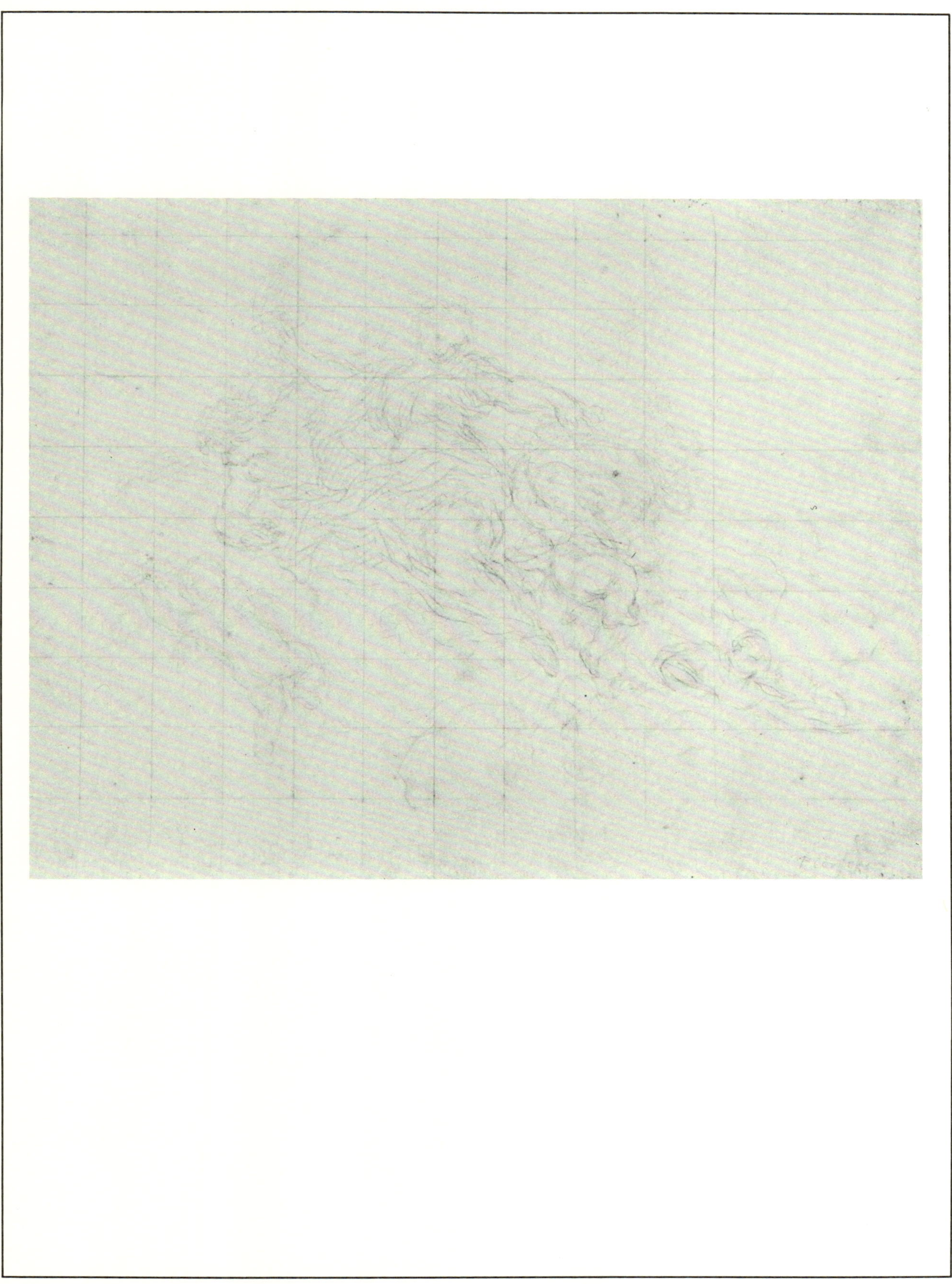

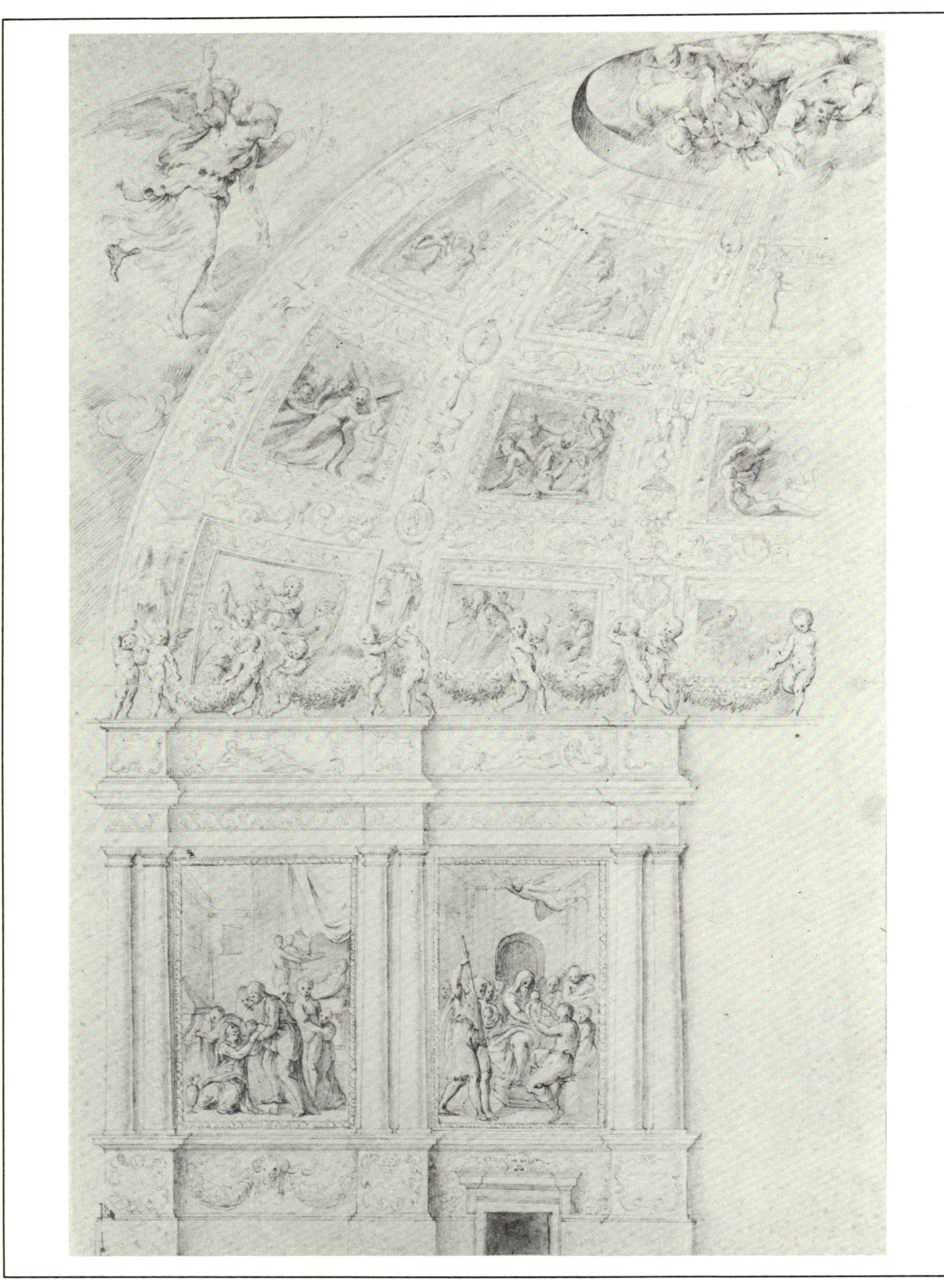

21.

BATTISTA FRANCO

(Venice 1510 - Rome, Florence, Urbino, Osimo, Fabriano - 1561 Venice)

Design for the Decoration of an Apse

Pen and brown ink, grey wash, over black chalk; 499 x 335 mm.; horizontal fold across the center, at the level of the knees of the putti. Watermark: crown b with cross, similar to Briquet 8090

Provenance: Sotheby's, London, 21 July 1966, lot 59

Acquired: 1974

Oberhuber, 1977, no. 13, pp. 49-51

Literature: Peter Ward Jackson, *Catalogue of Italian Drawings at the Victoria and Albert Museum,* London, 1979, pp. 68-69; Olszewski, 1981, no. 47, pp. 75-76

Franco and his *oeuvre* have been consistently belittled since Vasari, who knew him but wrote unsympathetically about his hard and dry labored style, his color without charm, and the monotony of his compositions. Olszewski repeats the libel: "This drawing is a good example of why the Duke of Urbino assigned Franco to design ceramic ware rather than large-scale projects. . . ." However, drawing designs for majolica was by no means a menial task, or to be despised (see Workshop of Taddeo Zuccaro, number 52). Furthermore, in the instance of this drawing specifically, a different analysis of Franco's style may redeem him.

Born and trained in Venice, when Franco was twenty he made his way to Rome, where he fell profoundly under the influence of Michelangelo. His first public activity was assisting Raffaello da Montelupo (who had been Michelangelo's assistant) in 1536-37 in Rome and in Florence, the beginning of a career which included important commissions in Rome, Florence, Urbino and Venice. In 1545, Franco left Rome for Urbino, where he frescoed the vault of the Cathedral tribune. Apparently this work was not too well received, and for the next four or five years, he made elaborate, highly successful designs for the majolica factory at Castel Durante. In 1550, he returned to Rome to fresco a chapel in Santa Maria sopra Minerva. The following year he was again in Urbino, to decorate the vault of a chapel in the Cathedral. In 1551 or 1552, he went home to Venice, where he remained for the rest of his life, carrying out a series of important commissions[1].

This drawing is for an apse, with scenes from the lives of the Virgin and of Christ. It is crowned by an oculus open to the heavens from which God is descending. Only half of the apse is visible, and not all of the scenes are legible, but the presence of the Archangel Gabriel in the upper left implies a corresponding virgin on the right, and therefore the *Annunciation.* A drawing of this left half of the apse dome alone is in the Victoria and Albert Museum. By an ingenious reconstruction of the dimensions, Ward Jackson has shown that "the width of the apse would be no less than 66 feet and the height not less than 60 feet . . . the only work on this scale that Franco is known to have carried out was in the tribune of the Urbino cathedral, destroyed in 1789 in an earthquake." Ward Jackson concludes "with an element of doubt [that] it is reasonable to assume that the two drawings are designs by Franco for the apse of the Urbino cathedral." However, neither drawing coincides with Vasari's description of the apse fresco: "The glory of the Saints, with all the choirs of angels about the Madonna . . . who . . . is received by Christ, who is in the act of crowning her...;" that is, he describes a single rather than this compartmentalized space, with the *Coronation of the Virgin* rather than these scenes. The identification of the two drawings with the apse fresco must therefore be suspect, either as an early rejected proposal or as a plan for some other monumental work.

Olszewski's criticism of the division of the surface of the apse into small units and his (and others') conclusion that it led the duke to assign "Franco to design ceramic rather than large-scale projects" does not seem justified either. This kind of division of large ceiling surfaces is traditional. Raphael (who incidentally came from Urbino) created a very similar effect in the Exedra of the Loggia of the greatly studied and admired Villa Madama in Rome — even the *grotteschi* surrounding the scenes in the drawings are similar to those at the Villa Madama. Furthermore this kind of compartmentalized decoration was standard in Venice, for instance in Franco's ceiling of the Grimani chapel of 1560 in the church of S. Francesco della Vigna.

Two other little drawings are related to the Steiner and London sheets, both of details: one, the *Birth of the Virgin,* was at Colnaghi's in 1965[2] and is now in a private collection in London; the other, in the J. B. Speed Art Museum in Louisville[3], for the *Adoration of the Shepherds,* is not identical to the scene in the drawings of the whole ensemble, but is similar enough to have been a suggestive first study. R.S.

1. This outline of Franco's career comes mainly from W. Roger Rearick, "Battista Franco and the Grimani Chapel," *Saggi e Memoria di Storia dell'Arte,* Venice, 1958-9, pp. 107-139.
2. no. 72 in the catalogue of June/July 1965.
3. *Bulletin,* J. B. Speed Art Museum, Louisville, XXVII, Oct. 1971.

22.

PIER LEONE GHEZZI (Rome 1674-1755)

Marco and Carlo

Pen and brown ink; 248 x 183 mm.
Inscribed bottom center, in the same brown ink: *Marco & Carlo*
Provenance: Edward Goddard; Dr. M. Goldstein (L.2824); Janos Scholz (L.2933b) (1943)
Acquired 1971

Grandson of a painter-sculptor-architect, Sebastiano, and son of a painter and man of affairs, Giuseppe, the artist was trained by his father. In 1708 Ghezzi succeeded his father as Painter of the Camera Apostolica, responsible for the papal art collections and director of the Vatican mosaic factory[1]. Like his father, Pier Leone Ghezzi was a man of many parts: in addition to his papal positions, he served as secretary of the Academy of St. Luke, painted genre, portraits, altarpieces and frescoes including in 1737 some charming *trompe l'oeil* at the Villa Falconieri in Frascati (see number 20), designed all kinds of decorations, and was a passionate antiquarian, musician and man-about-town.

Ghezzi was best known to his contemporaries, and today is remembered particularly, for his portrait caricatures, the first dated 1693. Their irreverence appealed to eighteenth century taste, and collections of them were already being formed while Ghezzi was still alive. Most of these collections were mounted in albums: three were in the court of Carlos IV in Naples, and the Duke of Wellington has two, gathered together, according to the title page in 1780, to save them from loss. Scores of the drawings hang in several *attico* rooms at the Villa Albani (now Torlonia) in Rome, presumably acquired by Cardinal Alessandro Albani during the 1760's. Other major collections are in the Vatican (over 1500 drawings), the Gabinetto Nazionale della Stampe in Rome, the Public Library in La Valletta (Malta), the British Museum, and formerly in the possession of Lord Braybrooke[2]. According to Janos Scholz[3], *Marco and Carlo* comes from an album assembled about 1800 by an English collector, Edward Goddard. Dr. Goldstein acquired it in London and his widow sold it intact to Mr. Scholz. It included a self-portrait of Ghezzi and his famous caricature of the celebrated *castrato* Farinelli (both now in the Morgan Library).

Ghezzi's English patronage was important for the developing popularity of caricature there; already in 1737-39, twelve of his caricatures were etched by Arthur Pond and published[4]. And during 1750-60 a German, Matthias Osterreich, published two volumes of etchings after Ghezzi and one of his followers, Giuseppe Internari.

Ghezzi worked in a caricatural tradition that went back to Leonardo da Vinci, whose caricatures were, however, more anatomical character studies than deliberately comic. It was a tradition that had attracted many leading seventeenth century artists (see number 30). Caricatural satire, social, moral and political, had been a popular art form, particularly as broadsheets, since the origin of print-making in the late fifteenth century. Ghezzi was the first to practice portrait caricature professionally. Over three thousand of his portrait drawings survive today, their models comprising a gallery of all levels of Roman society, all equally subject to burlesque. Ghezzi's willing victims included popes, nobles and cardinals, artists and librarians, a wigmaker, a German doorkeeper and a cardinal's gardener, foreign visitors, the famous — James Stuart the Old Pretender and Piranesi, for example — and the unknown, including an impenitent criminal waiting execution and Ghezzi's own housemaid, whom he labeled *"Marta Santa Serva."* Whether belonging to a high churchman or a humble blue-collar worker, large noses, protruding bellies, and similar physical idiosyncracies were subject to humorous exaggeration, as were quirks of personality, as is evident in fat, pompous Marco's scowl and lean Carlo's ironic grin. Typically Ghezzi characterized his subjects so perceptively that their modern counterparts are still recognizable in business suits and dresses on Roman streets. But his mockery is always cheerful and warm-hearted rather than mean.

Ghezzi did caricatures of individuals, couples (usually contrasting in physique and personality, like Marco and Carlo) and groups. Most of them stand still in rather stiff profile; occasionally he gives them an appropriate setting, but ordinarily no more than a few lines suggestive of a floor beneath them and a wall behind. His later caricatures tend to be carefully drawn with fine, regular contours and disciplined cross-hatching reminiscent of Jacques Callot's; his earliest tend to be spontaneous, with heavier lines, looser shading and even a little grotesque. *Marco and Carlo* falls somewhere in between; the date of the drawing, 1724, is established by the fact that all of the personages represented in the Goddard-Scholz album participated in the Lateran Congress of 1724. This date is confirmed by the comparable draughtsmanship in his portrait (in the Vatican Library, Fondo Ottoboniano) of Pope Benedict XIII Orsini, who reigned from 1724-30[5]. Marco and Carlo's costumes are not very different from those of Ghezzi's other male models, but each carries a tray or plate and a napkin or dishcloth, so they can be recognized as servants, a social status probably confirmed by Ghezzi's identification of them with given names only. Their employer at the Congress is not known. F.M. and A.M.

1. Mattia Loret, "Pier Leone Ghezzi," *Capitolium* XI, 1935, pp. 291-307.
2. Sold at Sotheby's, London, 10 December 1979.
3. In a letter to the editor of 3 January 1986.
4. Exhibition catalogue, *Caricature and its Role in Graphic Satire,* Museum of Art, Rhode Island School of Design, Providence, 1971, p. 8; William Feaver, in *Masters of Caricature,* (New York, 1981, p. 40), says Pond published 25 etchings after Ghezzi in 1744.
5. Illustrated in Loret, *op. cit.,* p. 295.

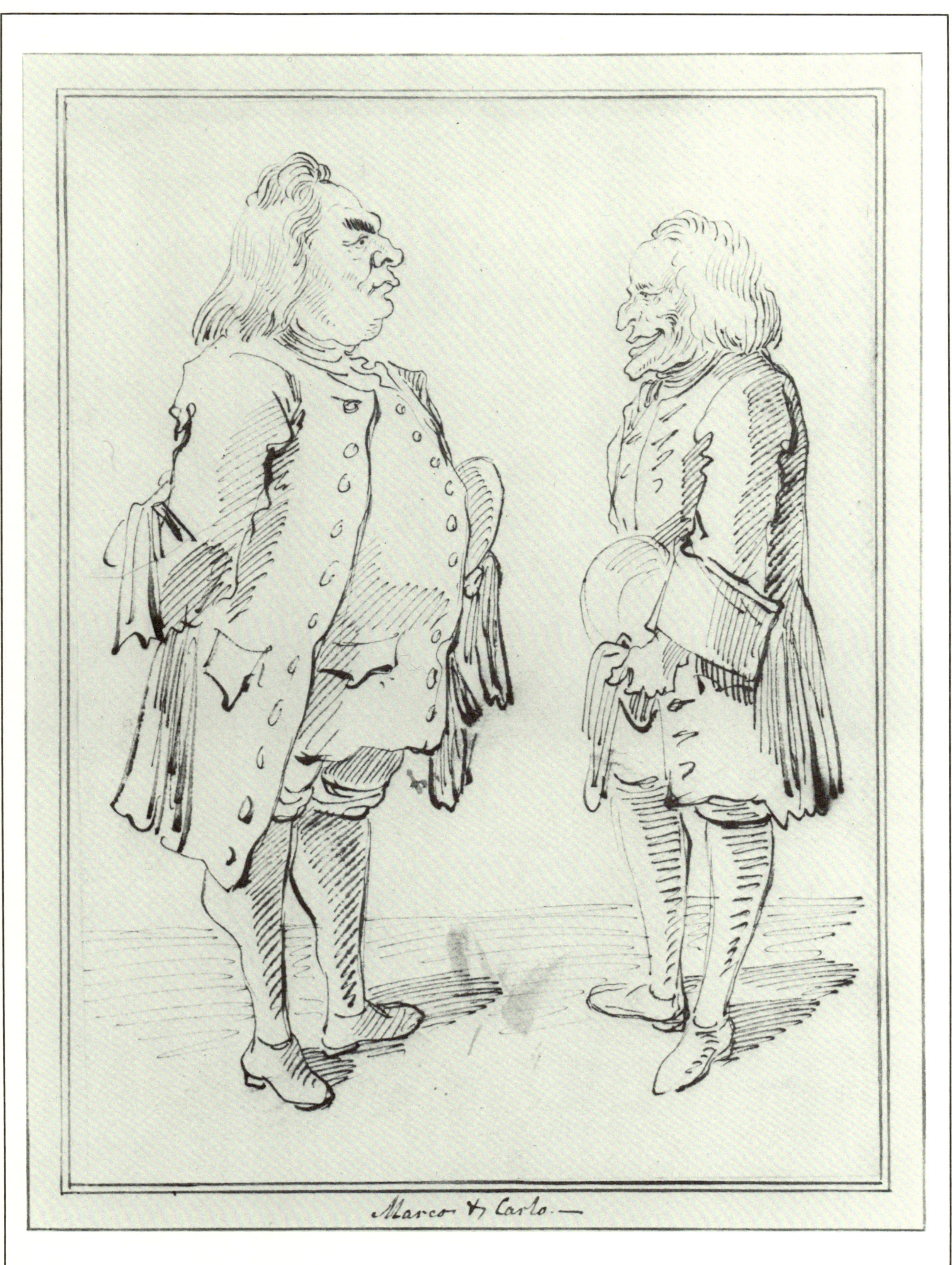
Marco & Carlo —

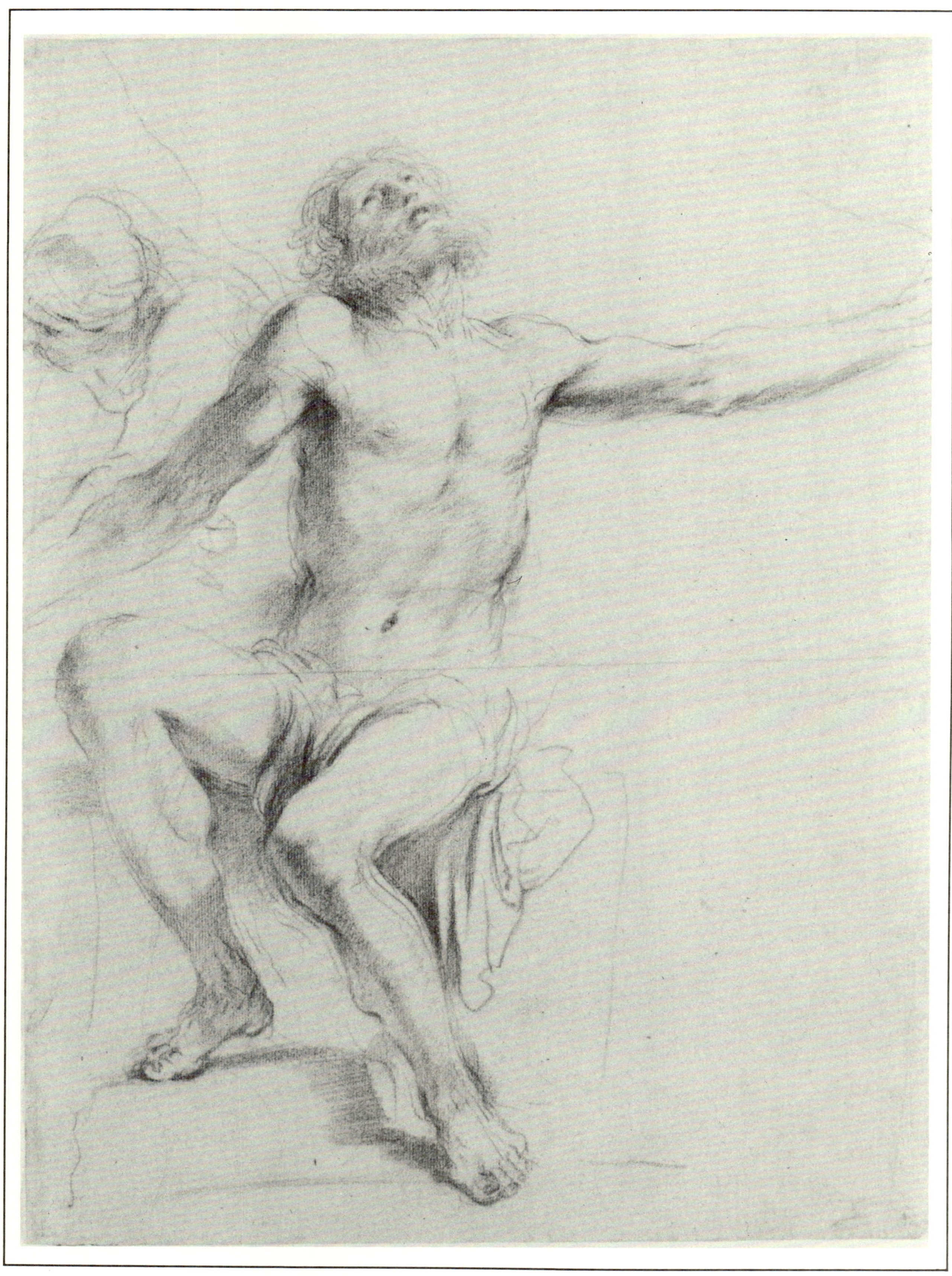

23.

GIOVANNI FRANCESCO BARBIERI called IL GUERCINO
(Cento 1591 - Bologna, Rome, Piacenza - Bologna 1666)

Seated Man

Red chalk, 372 x 284 mm.; horizontal line in red chalk across the center. Watermark: shield with crown and illegible device surmounted by a cardinal's hat similar to Heawood 793
Inscribed verso in graphite, lower right: *174576;* in brown ink, upper left, *34*
Acquired 1974
Susan J. Cooke in Oberhuber, 1977, no. 18, pp. 59-61

Guercino ("Squinty") developed the marvelously sensuous Baroque style of this drawing at home in Emilia, responding to what he could see there, particularly in the work of Lodovico Carracci (number 14). In 1621, when the Bolognese Cardinal Ludovisi was elected Pope as Gregory XV, Guercino went to Rome. There he produced his masterpieces, for St. Peter's and for the Villa Ludovisi. But he also came into contact with the more intellectual attitude toward art advocated by the theorist Monsignor G. B. Agucchi and practiced by the painter Domenichino, who had assisted and collaborated with Annibale Carracci at the Farnese Gallery (number 13). They persuaded Guercino to reorient his style, a process that continued in Emilia when he returned there after the pope's death in 1623. He remained in North Italy for the rest of his life, gradually replacing the charming pictorial ambiguity of his early work with an increasingly cold classicism. The climax of this late phase came in 1642 when Guido Reni died and Guercino moved from Cento to succeed him as Bologna's leading painter, a position he maintained until his death.

Although Guercino's draughtsmanship did not change as drastically as his painting, this drawing has been recognized as datable in 1618-19. Dennis Mahon, in giving it this date, associates it with a *Raising of Lazarus* painted in 1619, and Susan Cooke notes the similar poses of the seated male figures in the contemporary *Martyrdom of St. Peter* (in the Galleria Estense in Modena) and in the preparatory drawings for a lost *St. Sebastian.* However this model seems both too young for St. Peter and too old for St. Sebastian, who is usually clean-shaven. An alternative identification to be considered is Saint Bartholomew, and the other man as an executioner just beginning the grim task of flaying him. A pen and ink and wash drawing of the *Martyrdom of St. Bartholomew* at Princeton is not entirely dissimilar, although it is much later, preparatory for a painting for the church of San Martino in Siena recorded in Guercino's accounts for 1636[1].

The overlapping of the lines of the half-figure's left side with the right shoulder and arm of the presumed martyr suggests still another solution to the problem of the identification of the principal figure: that the two figures may not have been related thematically at all but are simply unrelated sketches, sharing the same sheet of paper. Lacking any attributes but assuming a pose that Guercino favored in various forms (even for a painted *Susanna in the Bath* of 1618, no. 234 at the Pitti), the drawing may be simply a study in which Guercino had the model take one of the somewhat empassioned poses that he liked and often used, particularly early in his career. The pose, the softly atmospheric modeling, and the pathos surely are characteristic of his appealing pre-Roman Baroque style, with imagery as fluent as its draughtsmanship. H.M. and A.M.

1. Gibbons, 1977, no. 272, pp. 102-3.

24.

GIOVANNI GUERRA (Modena 1544 - Rome 1618)

Unidentified Subject of Expulsion

Brown wash with pen and brown ink; 120 x 163 mm.
Provenance: Sotheby's, London, 10 December 1979, lot 262, as *A Biblical Scene: Men Chased from a Temple*
Acquired 1981
Literature: Antonella Pampatone and Marcello Aldega, *Disegni italiani dal XVI al XVII Secolo,* Rome, 1980, no. 13, pp. 11-12, ill.

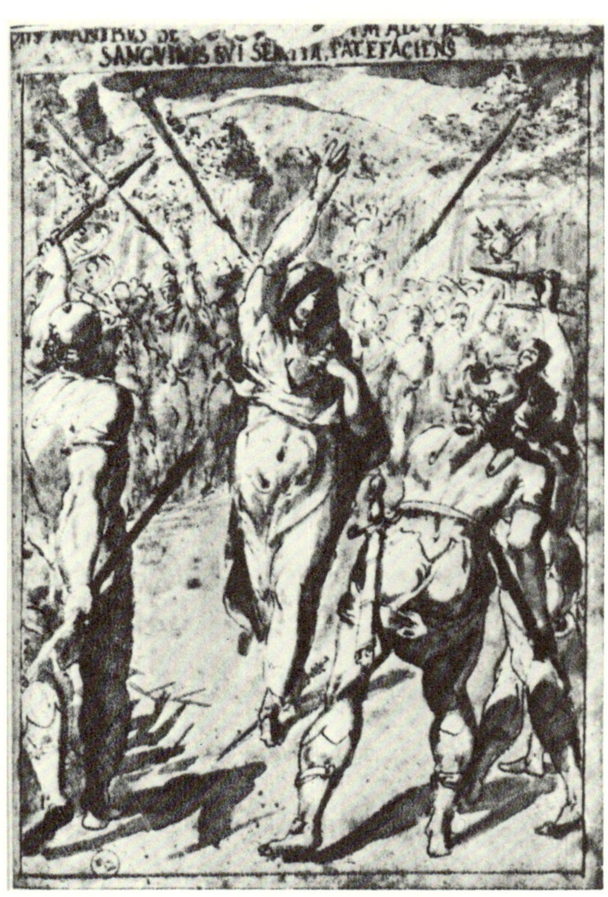

Anonymous Italian
Allegory
Biblioteca Reale, Turin

When he was 18, after training in Modena, Guerra entered the studio of Girolamo Muziano in Rome. He served there as a designer and supervisor of a large team of painters until the older master's death in 1592. Like many of his contemporaries in Rome, Guerra was under the shadow of Taddeo Zuccaro (numbers 51 and 52). His style at times is particularly close to that of Nicolo Trometta, one of Taddeo's closest followers. Guerra also collaborated extensively with Cesare Nebbia.

Guerra was quite versatile. In addition to the many walls he frescoed, often with Nebbia and a corps of assistants, he designed fountains, made drawings for engravings (including a series showing the transport of the Vatican obelisk), and illustrated books. This drawing is typical of his loose style of sketching. Executed primarily in wash with a few accents in pen and ink, it was probably made as a compositional study of the pattern of lights and darks and of the action. The wild gestures of the figures, their dislocated joints and rubbery limbs, and even some specific details are very similar to those in a drawing of ca. 1606, also of an unidentified subject from ancient history, in the Royal Library in Turin (inv. no. 16214)[1]. Both compositions are also emphatically central, although the Turin sheet with its vertical format is implosive rather than explosive.

Evidently the central figure is chasing the other active figures out of the building. Because the drawing is so loose and tentative, there are no attributes to specify the subject, whether Ulysses chasing Penelope's suitors out of the palace, or Christ expelling the merchants from the temple, or some similar event. Nor is the drawing's purpose clear, whether it is a preparatory study for a fresco or for one of a set of illustrations like those Guerra designed of the *Lives of the Legendary Kings of Rome* or the *Life of Esther.* R.S. and A.M.

1. Aldo Bertini, *Disegni italiani della Biblioteca Reale di Torino,* Rome, 1958, no. 530, as an *Allegory* by an anonymous Italian. Pouncey, in his review of Bertini's catalogue, (*Burl.* CI, 1959, p. 297) attributed the drawing to Guerra on the basis of its similarity to the Book of Judith album of 1606, in the Avery Library at Columbia University.

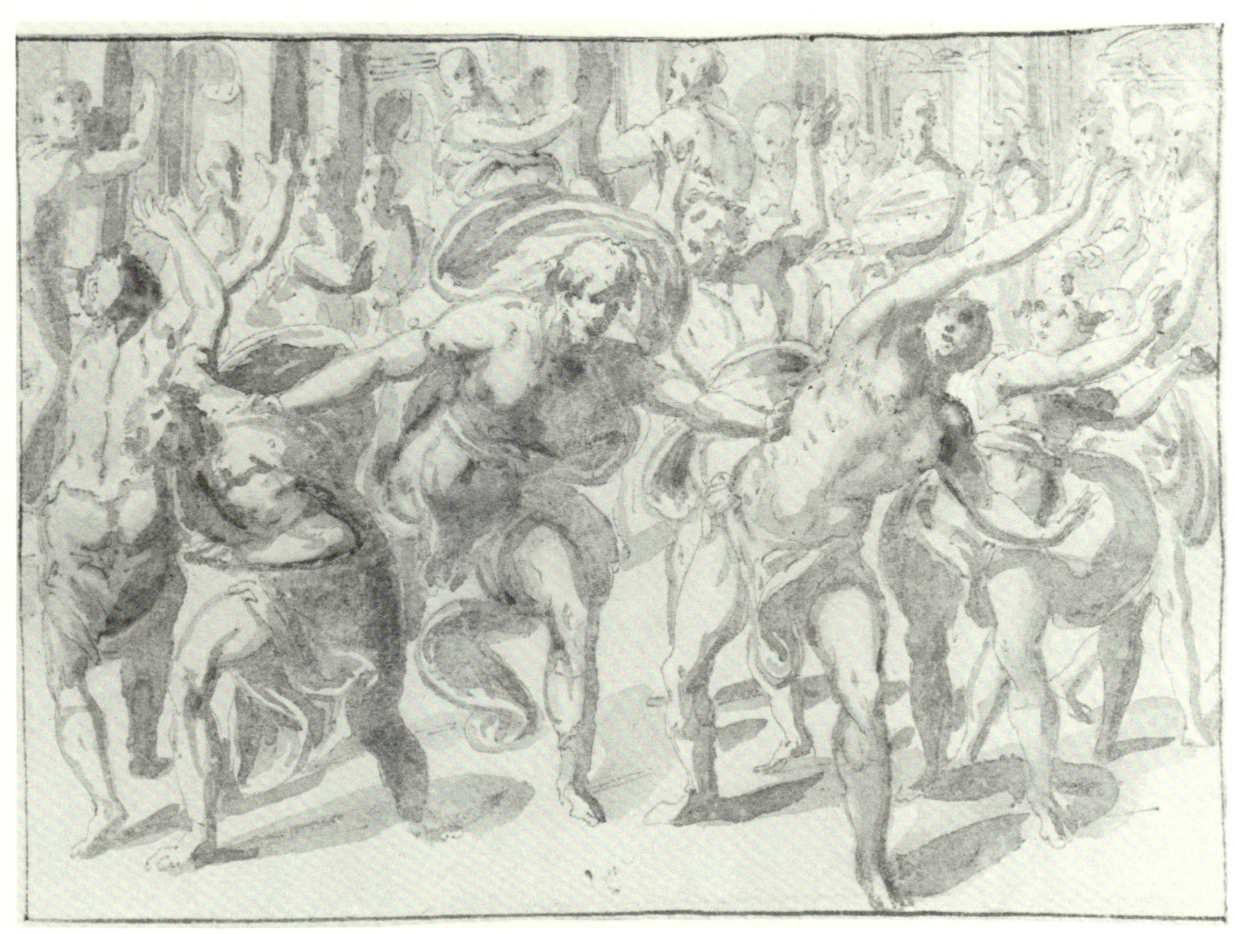

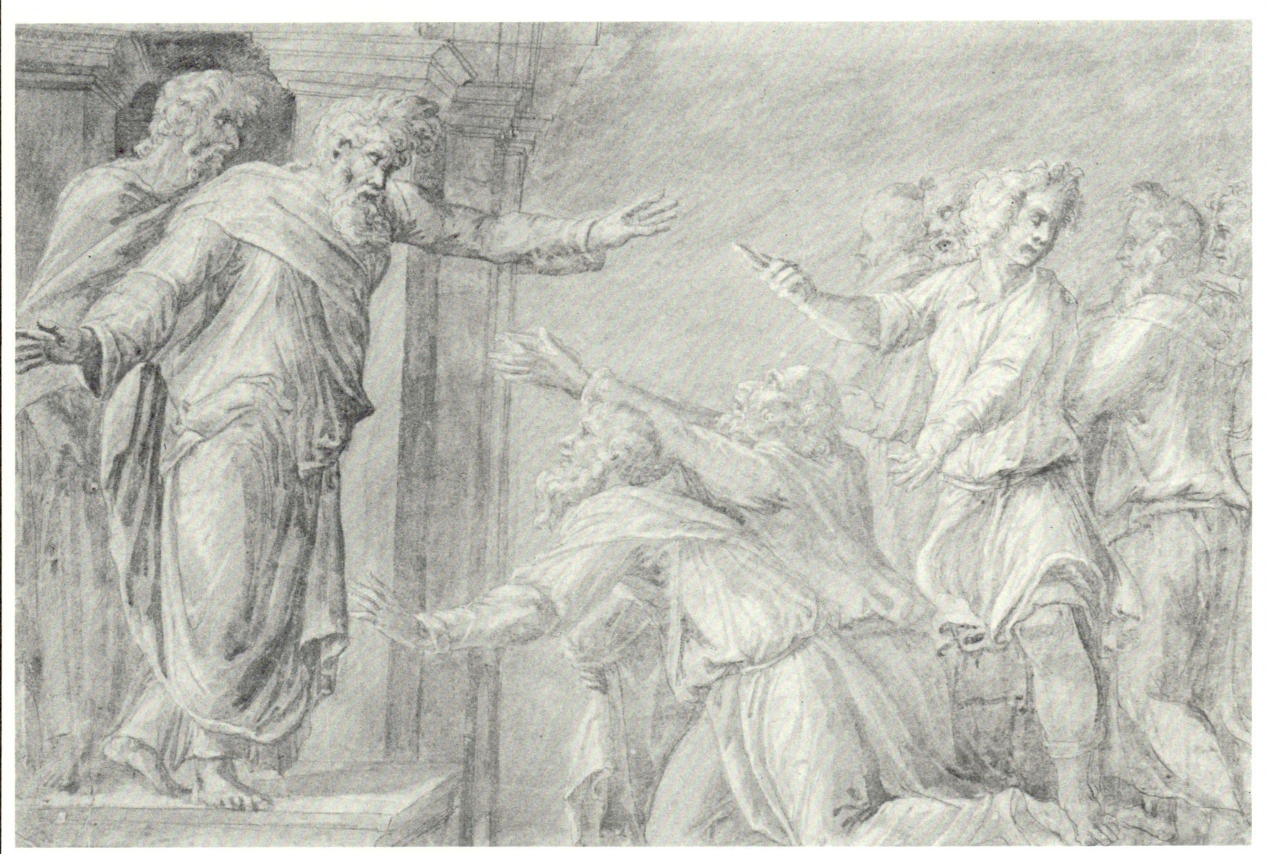

25.

PIRRO LIGORIO (Naples ca. 1513 – Rome – 1583 Ferrara)

St. Paul Preaching at Athens

Pen and black ink and brown wash heightened with white on paper washed green; 278 x 413 mm.; small tear on left lower edge
Acquired 1978
Loaned by Maud Fraker

Pirro Ligorio's birthdate is unknown[1], as is the precise date of his arrival in Rome, which must have been about 1534. He stayed there until 1568, when he was appointed antiquary to the Duke of Ferrara, Alfonso II d'Este. By 1569 he was in Ferrara, where he remained until his death[2].

Ligorio was a remarkable man — painter-architect, antiquarian-archaeologist and savant[3]. Unfortunately, all the facade frescoes that were his principal activity as a painter are lost, and only two other paintings, both frescoes of the mid 1540s in the Oratorio of San Giovanni Decollato in Rome, survive to show how great this loss was. A number of his drawings do survive, including not only sheets like this one but also studies of antique statues and ruins, and an extraordinary reconstruction map of the ancient city of Rome[4]. He is particularly remembered for his architectural accomplishments, less for his brief service in 1564-65 as Vatican architect in succession to Michelangelo, than for his two masterpieces: the exquisitely stuccoed Casino of Pope Pius IV in the Vatican, and the Villa d'Este, the many-fountained delight in the hills just outside of Rome at Tivoli.

This drawing is not specifically related to any of Pirro's documented works, although it seems typical. Pirro as a painter was most indebted to Polidoro da Caravaggio, but he was responsive to others of Raphael's successors as well. In this instance, the composition is related to a frescoed tondo by Perino del Vaga of the same subject in the Pauline Chapel (begun in 1545) at the Castel Sant'Angelo in Rome. Some details in the two frescoes are also nearly identical, particularly St. Paul's pose and physiognomy, and even his drapery. Ultimately the composition derives from Raphael's famous cartoon of *St. Paul Preaching* (in the Victoria and Albert Museum) he designed in 1515-16 for a set of tapestries for the Sistine Chapel. Raphael's figures are more solid and their gestures less sweeping and histrionic, and his composition is more spacious. Spatially, Pirro's frieze-like composition resembles not only his own facade decorations but also the borders of the tapestries, where Raphael created the effect of stone bas-relief, even including cast shadows.

This drawing is clearly similar in conception, style, and medium to others that are comparable and known to be by Pirro, notably to the unidentified ancient subject at Windsor (inv. no. 01234) and two at Chatsworth: the *Saint John Taking Leave of His Parents* (inv. no 46, case 73) and the *Holy Family* (inv. no. 128 case 33).

Pirro took particular care in drawing the figures of St. Paul and of the prominent standing man on the right. White is laid onto both more liberally and both are delineated with darker, heavier lines than the rest of the participants in the scene. He seems also to have exercised great care on the faces of all the foreground figures. This compositional study would not have been produced for its own sake, but would probably have preceded a full-scale cartoon for one of his many decorative schemes that have been lost. The strong influence of Raphael and his successors in this drawing may suggest a date earlier rather than later in his career.

The biblical source is Acts xvii: 22-34. St. Paul, preaching in Athens, was challenged by certain pagan philosophers, who invited him to explain his new doctrine at the high court, the Areopagus or Mars' Hill. He rebuked them for having many gods, and forecast the last judgment and the resurrection of the dead; and "some mocked . . . Howbeit certain men clave unto him and believed. . . ." R.S. and A.M.

1. But see Erma Mandowsky and Charles Mitchell, *Pirro Ligorio's Roman Antiquities,* London, 1963, p. 5.
2. Gere and Pouncey, 1983, vol. I, p. 113.
3. He even wrote a treatise on the hairstyles of ancient Roman women; See Luigi Damia, "An Unpublished Manuscript by Pirro Ligorio," *MD* XV, no. 1, 1977, pp. 22-25.
4. Mandowsky and Mitchell, *op. cit.*

26.

ATTRIBUTED TO LUZIO ROMANO
(active Genoa, Rome, mid-sixteenth century)

Design for a Narrative Frieze (recto and *verso)*

Pen and brown ink with brown wash (in figure scenes) and blue, yellow and orange washes (in the decorative borders); 222 x 398 mm.; vertical fold down the center

Inscribed recto: in pen and brown ink *Primo quadro* (upper right) *2do quadro* (center); in black ink, in a different hand, *Parmigianino* (lower right corner); verso in pen and brown ink *Ultimo quadro* (upper right center)

Acquired 1982

The attribution to Luzio is conjectural. Known also as Luzzi, de Lucij, or de Lutius da Todi, Luzio is recorded by Vasari as an assistant to Perino del Vaga (number 33) at the Palazzo Doria in Genoa in 1528-33. About 1537, he followed Perino to Rome, where he participated in frescoing the Palazzo Massimo and, during 1543-48, some of the Pope Paul Farnese rooms in the Castel Sant'Angelo[1]. After 1563 he collaborated with another student of Perino, Daniele da Volterra (1509-66), in designing and executing the ceiling of San Giovanni Laterano. He is last heard of in 1565, when he was paid for paintings and *stucchi* in the Vatican.

Because Luzio worked so closely with Perino, both his drawing style and decorative vocabulary follow that of his master. This sheet reflects the influence of Rosso Fiorentino's Fontainebleau style — surrounding a framed picture with figures and ornaments, a form of *quadri riportati,* as it was adapted by Perino in the Palazzo Massimo.

Each scene is framed by an elaborate border with figures and varied ornament. These scenes are pastoral and in sequence, as is made clear by the inscriptions — first, second, and last picture — and by the appearance in each of them of the same cast of characters: a bearded man, apparently a farmer; his donkey; and two other men, one bearded and the other clean-shaven. The interpretation of the sequence is undetermined. The donkey is central: he starts by plowing and ends by being drowned but no traditional myth or story seems to correspond exactly. It is not Apuleius' ass, as has been suggested. (Mrs. Steiner suspects the source may be an old German fairy tale, but none has as yet been identified.)

Although the attribution to Luzio is uncertain, the draughtsmanship does have much in common with other drawings that have been accepted as his. He used a choppy shorthand to define the general outlines of the principal elements but not their details. Comparison with the *Battle Scene* attributed to Luzio in the Uffizi shows similar heavy figures with small, almost unreadable hands, large calves and lumbering attitudes. The foliage of the trees in both drawings consists of clumps, characterized by little curl-like strokes of the pen that define general shapes without details; the trees have no secondary branches. The putti playing in the borders are like those in three *Studies for a Door Mantle* in the Dusseldorf Art Museum: they have tiny hands and feet, piles of curly hair, and plump bodies covered with rolls of fat. The general form of the decorative scheme is comparable to a *Study for a Frieze* at Windsor Castle.

In style and overall presentation the Steiner drawings are very similar to a couple of designs for friezes in the Kunstbibliothek, Berlin, attributed by Konrad Oberhuber to Perino del Vaga[2]. These drawings are studies for the decorative cycle executed in 1537-38 by Perino and members of his studio, including Luzio, in the Palazzo Massimo. All are drawn in a manner that makes the individual units of the decorative scheme clear without elaborating on particular details. This drawing and the Berlin designs also share such elements as the scrolled frame of the *"Ultimo quadro."* The length of the friezes in the Berlin drawings does not correspond to that in the final fresco where these scenes have been shortened to proportions closer to those in this sheet.

Whether or not this scheme was ever carried out is unknown. If it was, it may still exist, because so few of Luzio's works have been identified and published. R.S.

1. See Nicole Dacos, "Perino, Luzio, Zaga e Tibaldi: La Mostra dell'Appartemento di Paolo III a Castel Sant'Angelo," *Bollettino d'Arte* LXVII, ser. VI, 1982, pp. 142-148.
2. Konrad Oberhuber, "Observations of Perino del Vaga as a Draughtsman," *MD IV,* 1966, p. 172.

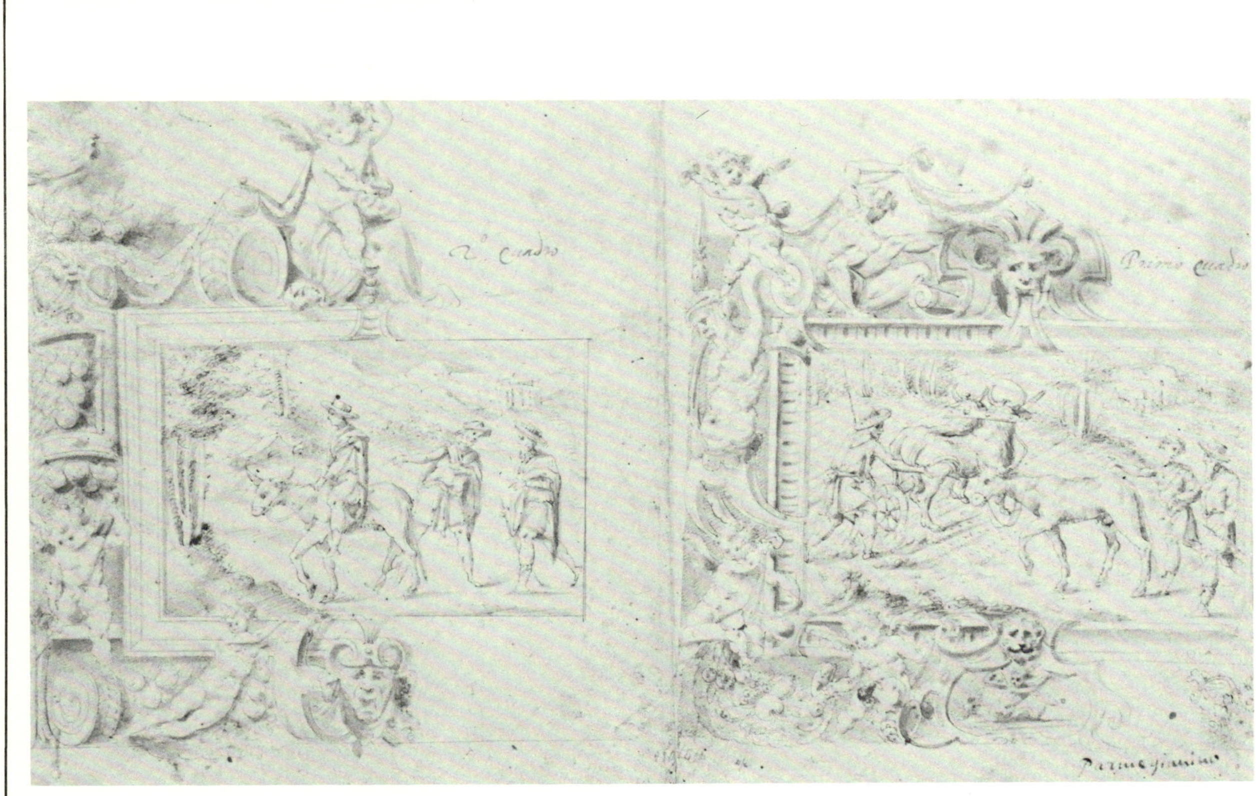

(recto)

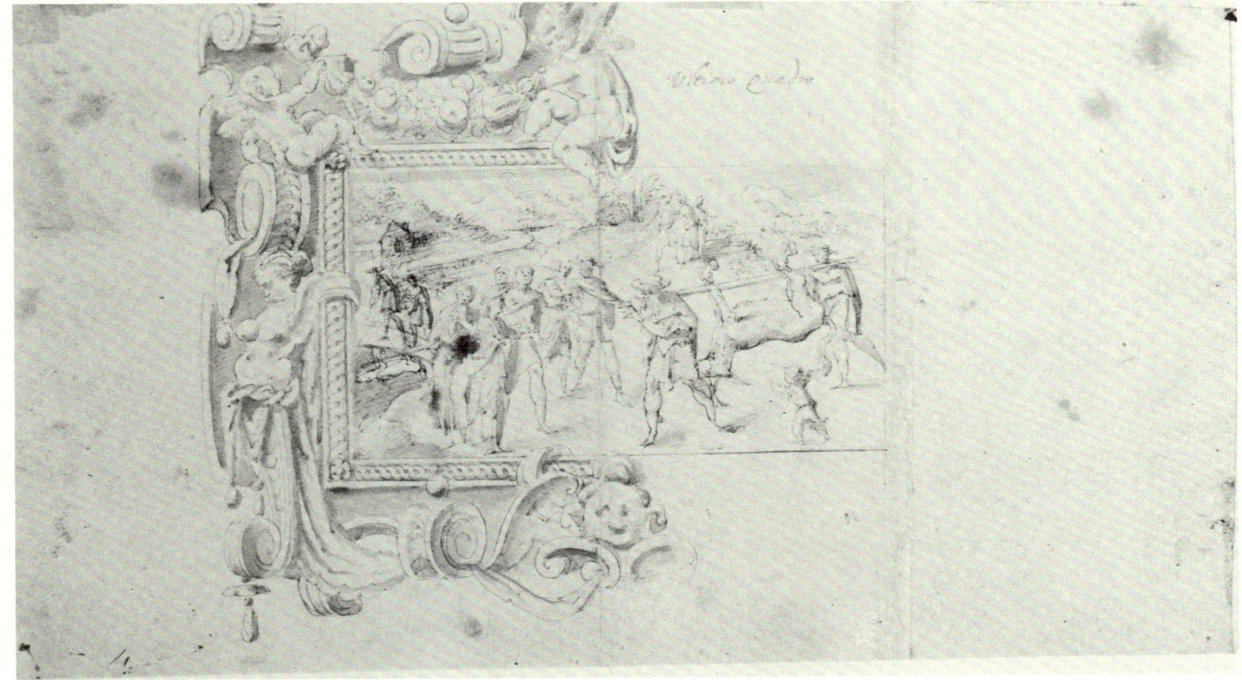

(verso)

27.

GIOVANNI BATTISTA TROTTI, called IL MALOSSO
(Cremona 1555 - Parma, Piacenza, Lodi, Milan - 1619 Parma)

The Three Magi

Pen and brown ink, brown wash, touches of black chalk, squared in black chalk; 366 x 377 mm. including 5 mm. strips added to top and bottom; repaired tears
Provenance: Paul Sandby (L.2112)
Acquired 1975
Andrea E. Kaliski in Oberhuber, 1977, no. 21, pp. 65-67

Malosso's nickname comes from his family name of De Malossis, contrary to the assertion of his old biographers, Malvasia and Lanzi. They reported it a reflection of the conflict he had with Agostino Carracci, his rival at the court of Parma. It was said that because of the trouble caused by the rivalry, the duke, Ranuccio Farnese, said he was a *"mal osso* [hard bone] to chew."

Giovanni married the daughter of Bernardino Campi, his first teacher, from whom he inherited his workshop. His first works, in Cremona, reflect Campi's style, mainly in the colors and in the typology of his dynamic and sentimental interpretation of religious subjects. He was also receptive to Correggio and Pordenone. Typical of Malosso's work in the 1580's are sculptural forms and theatrical compositions filled with histrionic gestures, clearly interpretive of the spirit of the Counter Reformation.

Malosso turned even more toward the style of Correggio when he moved to Parma in 1604 to become a court artist for Duke Ranuccio Farnese I. In succession to Agostino Carracci, he decorated the Palazzo del Giardino; but the Duke permitted him to leave the city from time to time to work in Piacenza, Cremona, Lodi, and in Milan, where many of his works remain.

Mario di Giampaolo[1] has clarified Malosso's draughtsmanship, seeing in it basically two pen and ink techniques. In the earlier drawings, those executed before the end of the century, line is more elaborate, and is very precise and clean. Many of these drawings are squared for transfer, making it clear that they were working drawings. Probably Malosso, as the head of the studio, executed the compositional drawings, and his assistants squared and transferred them either to full size cartoons, or directly to the surface to be painted. Malosso's later style was freer and appears to be more rapid and sketchy.

The Three Magi is related to his early period, where the treatment of line is more self-conscious, tidy and deliberate. There is a certain stiffness particularly evident in the angular folds of the Magi's drapery and in the firm contours of the legs and necks of the horses, which are Leonardesque in conformation. The heads of the Magi and their drapery are stylistically closest to the *Christ Disputing the Doctors* in the Uffizi (inv. no. 2030). In both drawings the drapery has been used as a dynamic compositional element that also increases the volume of the figures. The hatching with wash used to accentuate the dark areas is analogous in both these drawings.

The subject of the Steiner drawing is certainly exceptional, but it is probable that the figures do represent the three Magi. Following tradition, one is young, the one in the center is elderly, and the third is middle-aged. Malosso has depicted the moment when they first sight the star that guides them to the newborn Christ. Similar types were selected by Malosso for his *Adoration of the Magi* in the Cathedral of Casalmaggiore.

The drawing, like so many of Malosso's, has been squared for transfer. Because it is so large, it may be the cartoon for a small painting, but none has yet been recognized. R.S. and Y.R.

1. Mario di Giampaolo, "A Drawing by Malosso at Oxford and Some Additions to His Oeuvre," *MD* XV, 1977, pp. 28-31.

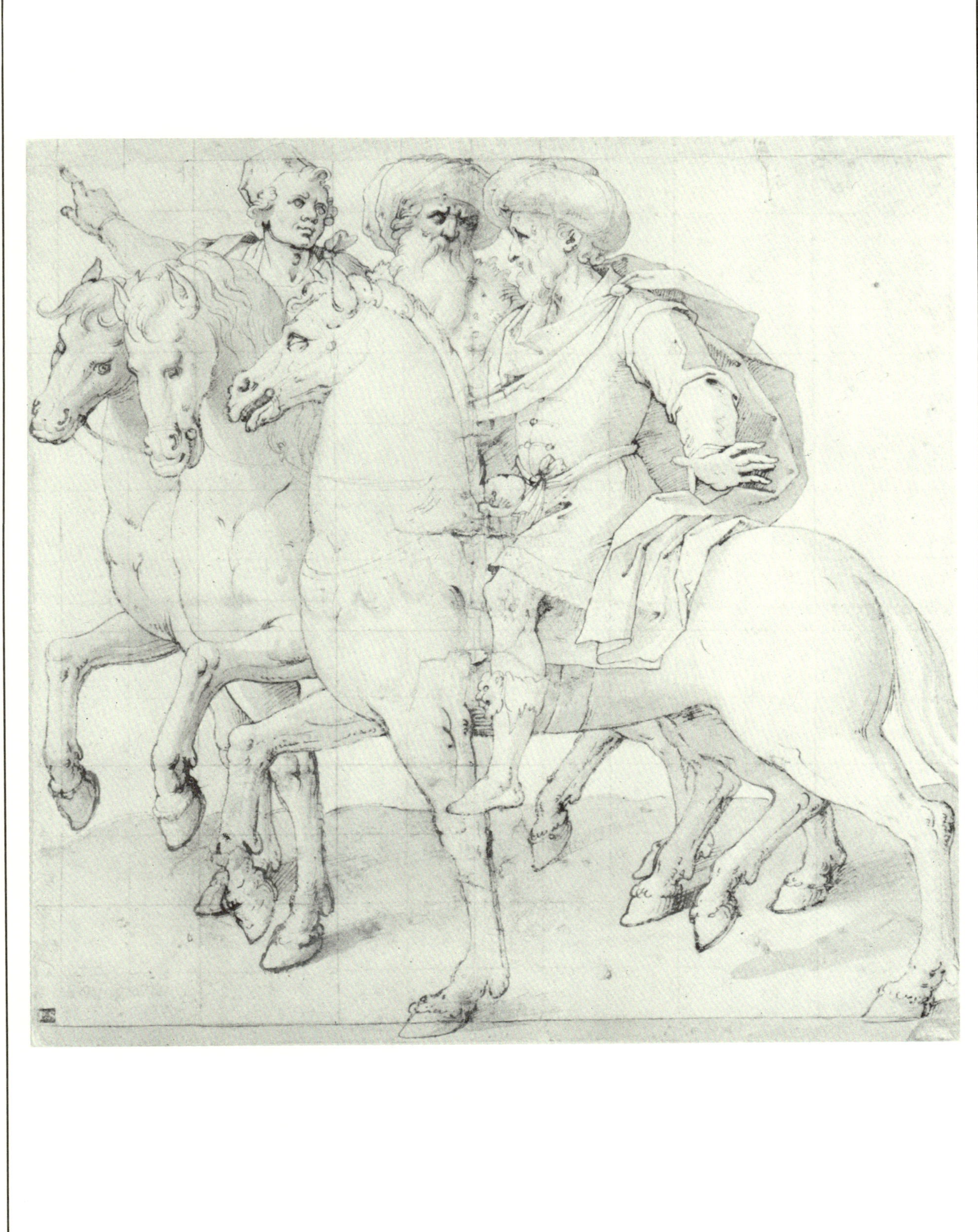

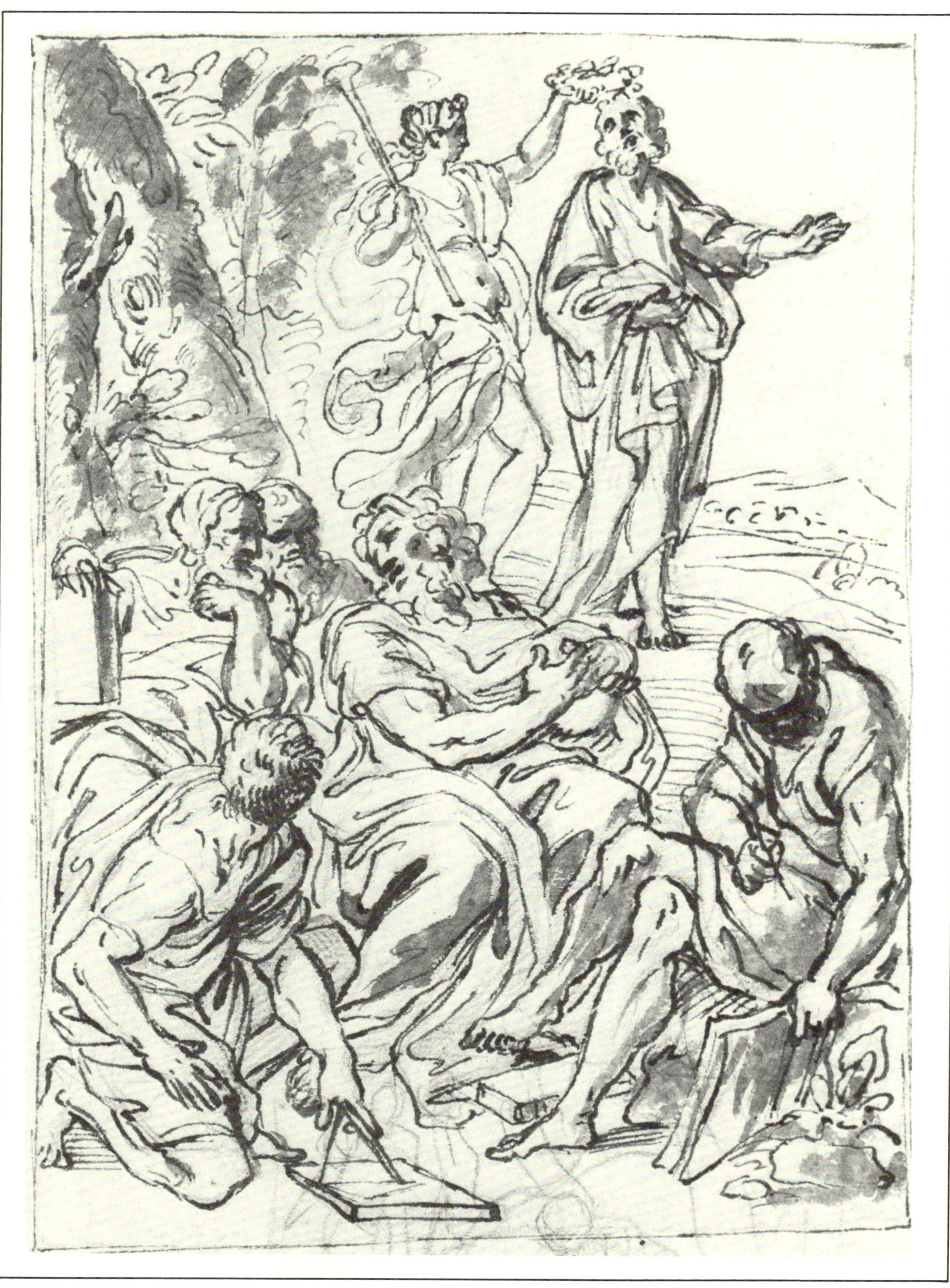

28.

CARLO MARATTA (Camerano 1625 - Rome 1710)

Fame Crowning Plato's Timaeus

Pen and brown ink, over black chalk; 237 x 176 mm.; previous studies in red chalk visible in bottom center
Acquired 1985
Loaned by Maud Fraker

Trained by Andrea Sacchi, Maratta was his heir both literally and figuratively. As the leading practitioner of the classicistic tradition continuing from Annibale Carracci and his successors, Maratta opposed Pietro da Cortona (number 16) in both theory and practice. In part because of aesthetic principle but also because of generally reduced patronage in Rome, Maratta's oeuvre consisted mainly of altarpieces. After Cortona's death in 1669, with only one real rival, Giovanni Battista Gaulli called il Baciccio (1639-1709), surviving, Maratta achieved so great an eminence as to be elected *principe* for life of the painter's academy in Rome and to be named painter to Louis XIV. During an active career of more than half a century, he served seven popes and trained a legion of young painters, so that his influence continued long after his death.

An eighteenth century print very similar to this drawing identifies its subject as *La Recompense des sciences*. Conceivably the three principal figures in the foreground of the drawing depict the fields of knowledge or "sciences," embodied in the *trivium* of the Liberal Arts: rhetoric in the center, geometry on the left and grammar in the lower right corner. But the drawing also includes a number of references to the idol of Baroque classicists, Raphael. Specifically, the bearded old man in the background resembles Homer in Raphael's *Parnassus* fresco in the Stanza della Segnatura; the most distant head in the foreground group is a portrait of Socrates, like that in the *School of Athens;* and the writer in the right foreground appears to be a portrait of Plato — not Raphael's Plato whose face is the aged Leonardo da Vinci's but rather derived from Hellenistic portraits of the ancient philosopher[1]. Raphael's Plato does carry a book, his *Timaeus,* which was particularly appealing to the Renaissance for its scientific yet spiritual explanation of the world.

The *Timaeus* dialogue is a discussion of the creation of the universe, in terms of biology, astronomy and physics. A key passage is Timaeus' statement that triangles form the basic elements of air, fire, water and earth[2]. This drawing appears to represent this dialogue, partly because of the triangle that the youth (Hermocrates) in the left center is measuring. Behind him is Plato's uncle Critias, who is bearded to show his age; he holds the book of the dialogue named for him. To his right is the unmistakable portrait of Socrates, in an appropriate position to fulfill his role as Timaeus' prompter. Timaeus is of course the central, expostulating man. Finally Plato, in the lower right corner, is rather awkwardly recording the dialogue in his book. The Homer-like man in the background who is being crowned by Fame, can be identified either as Timaeus or perhaps as a personification of the dialogue itself.

Although this drawing cannot be associated with any recorded work by Maratta, its complex and learned theme is certainly in keeping with his customary erudition, comparable to the arcane allegory of the frontispiece he designed for the *Fasti* . . . of the learned Sienese society of the Accademia degli Intronati. It is tempting to suspect that the references to Raphael's Stanza della Segnatura frescoes in the drawing were inspired by Maratta's having renewed his admiration for them when he was given responsibility for their restoration in 1702. The composition and many of the poses are comparable to his drawing of the *Allegory of the Old and New Dispensations* in the Metropolitan Museum (inv. no. 67.95.10), which was engraved in 1708[3]. However the flowing, relaxed but controlled delineation of the Steiner sheet is much closer to his earlier work, such as his drawing in the Morgan Library (inv. no. IV, 183) of the *Immaculate Virgin with Four Male Saints*[4]. The Morgan Library drawing was preparatory for the altarpiece of the Cybo Chapel in the church of Santa Maria del Popolo in Rome; the rebuilding of the chapel began in 1682, and the altarpiece is described as already in place by Titi in his 1686 guide, suggesting a date in the 1680's for the Steiner sheet. C.R.R.

1. See Margarete Bieber, *The Sculpture of the Hellenistic Age,* New York, 1961, particularly fig. 117.
2. Edith Hamilton and Huntington Cairns, eds. *Plato: the Collected Dialogues,* Princeton, 1980, p. 1180, sections 53 c-d, 54 b-d.
3. Bean, 1979, no. 280, p. 214.
4. Jean K. Westin and Robert H. Westin, exhibition catalogue, *Carlo Maratti and His Contemporaries,* Pennsylvania State University, 1975, no. 32, pp. 53-57.

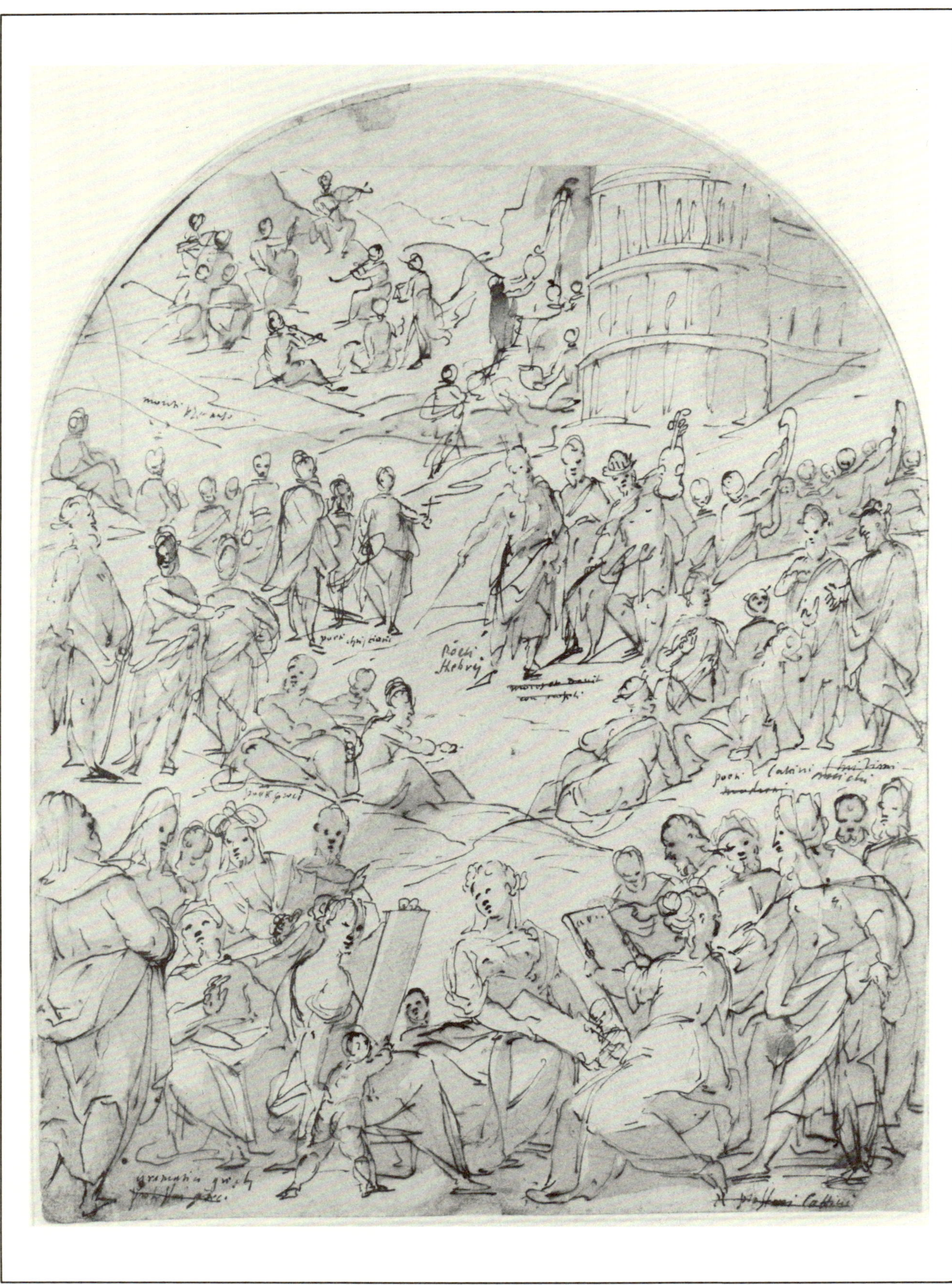

29.

PARRASIO MICHELI

(Venice before 1516 - Rome, Padua, Venice - 1578 Venice)

An Allegory of Learning

Pen and brown ink, brown wash, over traces of black chalk; 346 x 269 mm., including a strip approximately 27 mm. high added to the top; lower right corner missing. Watermark: hand surmounted by a flower; similar to Briquet 10681
Inscriptions: see text
Provenance: Mr. and Mrs. Stephen Kollmar, Cleveland
Exhibited: Cleveland Museum of Art, 1979, no. 177, ill. p. 101
Literature: Edward Olszewski, "Italian Drawings at Cleveland," *Connoisseur* CCVI, April, 1979, p. 287; Olszewski, 1981, p. 126, no. 101 (ill.)
Acquired 1981

Micheli[1] was mentioned by Aretino as a pupil of Titian's and a member of his circle. Although Micheli apparently had intellectual associations or pretensions, his few surviving identified works suggest his activity to have been as a portraitist and painter of *fêtes champêtres.*

The short, nervous lines in this drawing are characteristic of Micheli's draughtsmanship, as are the pointed noses and short slashes representing eyes. Olszewski dates the drawing 1565, and suggests that it was the preparatory sketch for a painting in the library of a humanist or academician. He associates it with a drawing in the Kupferstich Kabinett in Berlin (inv. no. 2369)[2], which is believed to be a study for a painting in the Doge's Palace that Micheli completed in 1563 but which was destroyed by fire in 1574. The figures in the Berlin drawing, which is about the same size, are also identified by autograph inscriptions.

Micheli's allegory follows the progress of learning from its basic foundations in grammar to the muses (which he, as an artist, slyly places at the pinnacle of learning) and the temple of knowledge itself. The three seated women holding tablets and surrounded by children in the foreground center are identified by the inscription *grammatica* in the lower left (followed by an illegible word, perhaps *grechi*), and represent the three liberal arts of the Medieval Trivium, grammar, rhetoric and logic. Because they are fundamental to all learning, their prominent position at the base of the drawing is appropriate. To their left and right are groups of old men. Although Micheli lined out the inscriptions, *profetti latini* and *profetti grechi,* presumably they do represent the Greek and Roman prophets, associating these wisest ancients with the foundations of learning.

The two groups of figures immediately above are labelled *poeti greci* and *poeti lattini.* Apparently Micheli changed his mind in the process of identifying these groups because he crossed out the original label of the group on the right transforming it from modern Christian [writers] *(christiani moderni)* to the latin poets. The [illegible] *-chi* (perhaps *antichi*) written with a different pen and in different ink, may refer to this change, for the same pen and ink describe the group immediately behind the latin poets as the Hebrew poets *(poeti hebrij).* The original inscription of this third group on the right, in the same pen and ink used elsewhere in the drawing, reads *Moses et David/con profetti.* This inscription is also cancelled, presumably to maintain the consistency of all the groups as generic rather than individual. The two chief figures of this group however are still recognizable as Moses — old, bearded, and with horns — and as David, who is younger, wears a crown, and carries a lyre. The corresponding group on the left represents the Christian poets *(poeti christiani),* the leading one of whom carries a cross. Thus Micheli has placed the learning of the Old and New Testaments, both literally and figuratively, above the Trivium and the ancient poets.

The summit, a hilly landscape labelled Mount Parnassus *(mont P . . . naso),* is peopled by ten figures, Apollo at the pinnacle and the nine muses who are performing for him. Beside them, four figures carry water in large amphorae from a spring. They are the Canephoroi, wise virgins who bore water from Mount Parnassus to the temple at Delphi where it was used for prophecy. (Another Canephoros appears in the Bedoli drawing, number 4 above). Perhaps the building on the right symbolizes the Delphic temple. It may also symbolize the temple of knowledge, attained by the pilgrim who has travelled the long upward path from the Trivium. It could also be read as the Tower of Babel, and as a Counter-Reformation warning to scholars who take too much pride in their learning by placing it above the Church and God.

In form, the tower may well have a contemporary reference — to the external staircase (the Scala del Bȍvolo, or, in the Venetian dialect, the Snail's Shell Staircase) of the Palazzo Contarini, built in 1499 and then as now a famous sight. The galleries drawn to the right of the tower are similar to those in the actual building. Micheli no doubt knew the staircase as a landmark. He was also connected with the family, having painted a portrait (now in the Doge's Palace) of the diplomat-politician Tommaso Contarini (1488-1578)[3]. Although Tommaso lived elsewhere, in the palace near the Madonna dell'Orto built by his brother, Cardinal Gaspare Contarini, conceivably this drawing was a *pensiero* presented by Micheli to the Contarini in hopes of another commission. R.T.P.

1. Detlev Hadeln, ("Parrasio Micheli," *JdPK* XXXIII, 1912, pp. 149-172). Hadeln, on the basis of descriptions ca. 1550 of Micheli as a young beginner suggested a later birthdate, of ca. 1525.
2. Detlev von Hadeln, "Eine Zeichnung des Parrasio Micheli," *JdPK* XXXIV, 1913, pp. 166-172.
3. von Hadeln, *op. cit.* 1912, p. 159, fig. 5.

30.

PIER FRANCESCO MOLA
(Coldrerio near Lugano 1612 - Rome, North Italy - 1666 Rome)

Caricature of a Duck Hunter

Pen and brown ink, 191 x 202 mm.; repaired losses due to corrosion of the paper by the ink; scatological detail erased lower right

Inscribed verso in pen and brown ink: *Mola, U. Price bought of Gialdoni at Rome, 1768* (in Uvedale Price's hand); in black ink: *1967;* in graphite: *5*

Provenance: Gialdoni; Uvedale Price (L.2048); Sir J. C. Robinson; John Malcolm; the Hon. A. E. Gathorne-Hardy; Geoffrey Gathorne-Hardy; the Hon. Robert Gathorne-Hardy

Acquired 1976

Ann J. Adams in Oberhuber, 1977, no. 23, pp. 69-71

Exhibited: P. & D. Colnaghi, 1971, no. 56; Ashmolean Museum, 1971; Metropolitan Museum 1976

Literature: J. C. Robinson, *Descriptive Catalogue of the Drawings by the Old Masters Forming the Collection of John Malcolm of Poltalloch, Esq.,* London, 1869, no. 265; *A Descriptive Catalogue of the Drawings in the Possession of the Hon. A. E. Gathorne-Hardy,* London, 1902, no. 22; *Loan Exhibition of Drawings by Old Masters from the Collection of Mr. Geoffrey Gathorne-Hardy,* London, P. & D. Colnaghi, 1971, no. 56; *Roman Artists of the Seventeenth Century, Drawings and Prints,* Metropolitan Museum, N.Y., 1976

Mola was one of the most important painters active in mid-seventeenth century Rome, ranking just behind Cortona, Rosa, Poussin, and Claude Lorrain. Born in North Italy, he was taken to Rome by his architect-father in 1616. He is reported to have studied with Cavaliere d'Arpino, the leading late Mannerist painter in Rome. But the primary influences on his style were North Italian. After visits there in 1633-40 and 1641-47, he returned to Rome and became the leading neo-Venetian painter of his generation there. His colorful manner of painting, at its best in narrative subjects, was quintessentially Baroque.

Mola was also a prolific draughtsman. Like all his contemporaries, he drew numerous spontaneous sketches and fluent preliminary studies for his paintings. He was also a caricaturist, in the tradition particularly practiced by the Carracci and their successors in Bologna and Rome, and among Mola's contemporaries in Rome most notably by Bernini. Unlike them, however, he drew not only individual caricatural sheets but also two series in which the same character appears in a sequence. This drawing is from one of those series. The protagonist is figuratively, and perhaps literally, an old acquaintance. He has a large, bulbous nose, a droopy moustache, frequently a heavy five o'clock shadow, and sometimes he wears a skull-cap. Ann Adams reports that Janos Scholz has identified seven other drawings of this man's adventures (mainly misadventures), ranging from his carving a fowl (Ashmolean Museum, Oxford, inv. no. 914) to his dictating his will from his bed (in Scholz' own collection, now in the Pierpont Morgan Library in New York). Although many of these drawings include scatological details, the man often is dressed as a cleric.

This drawing is the eighth in the series. Our hero, on his donkey which appears in two other scenes in the series, is hunting ducks with some success, judging by the two dead birds suspended from his saddle. But a cannon fired from the tower on the left is dispersing the rest of the flock and frustrating his hopes for bagging any more game. Perhaps we can read this image in a broader sense, as symbolizing the disappointment of man's hopes in life by superior external forces.

This broader interpretation seems appropriate to several of the drawings in the series. A ninth drawing (not included in Scholz's list) in the British Museum (inv. no. 1857-6-13-363) with an autograph inscription, *adio speranza* ("farewell hope"), shows the cleric leaning on an anchor, seated with another man, clearly disconsolate, and a jumble of objects, including a fallen cornucopia. This drawing has tentatively been titled *Two Philosophers,* perhaps because of its reminiscence of Durer's great *Melancholia* engraving; the message is much the same. In still another scene (in the Scholz Collection), the man reappears in bed (his deathbed again?); on the other side of the room is a skull and an hourglass that has almost run out, symbolizing the brevity and vanity of earthly affairs. But now there is hope, for the man holds in his hand a drawing of the Madonna and Child.

The inspiration of the series may be some literary source. But the theme hints at a remarkable presentiment of the sad last years of Mola's own life, when he suffered from the injustice of Prince Camillo Pamphili, who had been his patron during the 1650's. The prince's mistreatment of Mola culminated in a law suit that dragged on from 1659 until 1664, when the painter lost the case. During the 1660's Mola suffered from two illnesses, and the embittering experience with Prince Camillo may well have hastened his death in 1666.

These caricatures have been dated as from Mola's second visit to North Italy during the 1640's, specifically from his contacts in Bologna and with Guercino, who also made caricatures. However while Mola's paintings have been studied in a monograph[1], there has been no systematic analysis of his drawings, and their chronology is uncertain. This series may derive from his last years, and, if not made specifically in response to Prince Camillo's abuse of Mola, may at least be reflective of the artist's state of mind. C.R.R. and A.M.

1. Cocke, 1972, is the source of most of the information above.

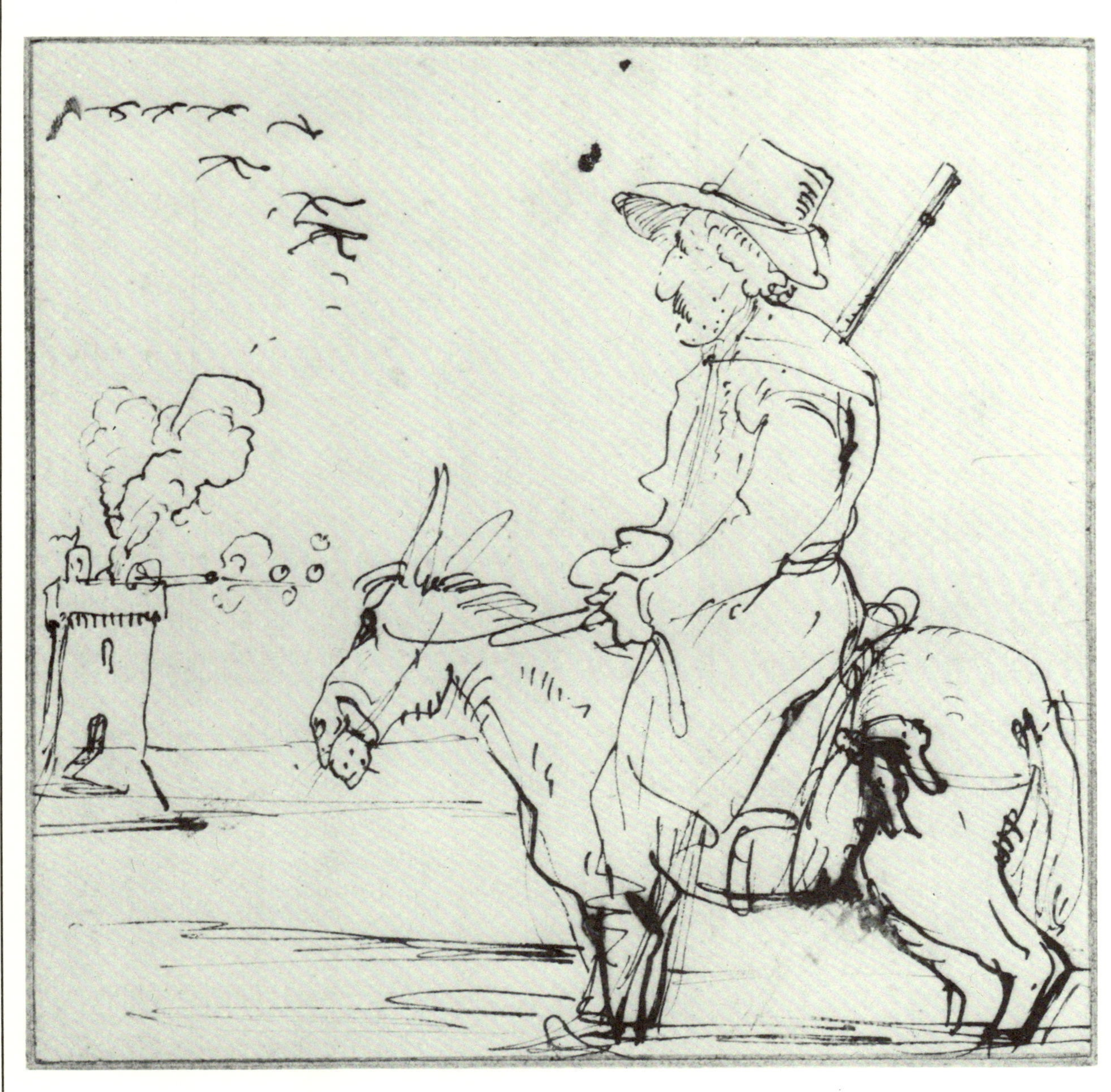

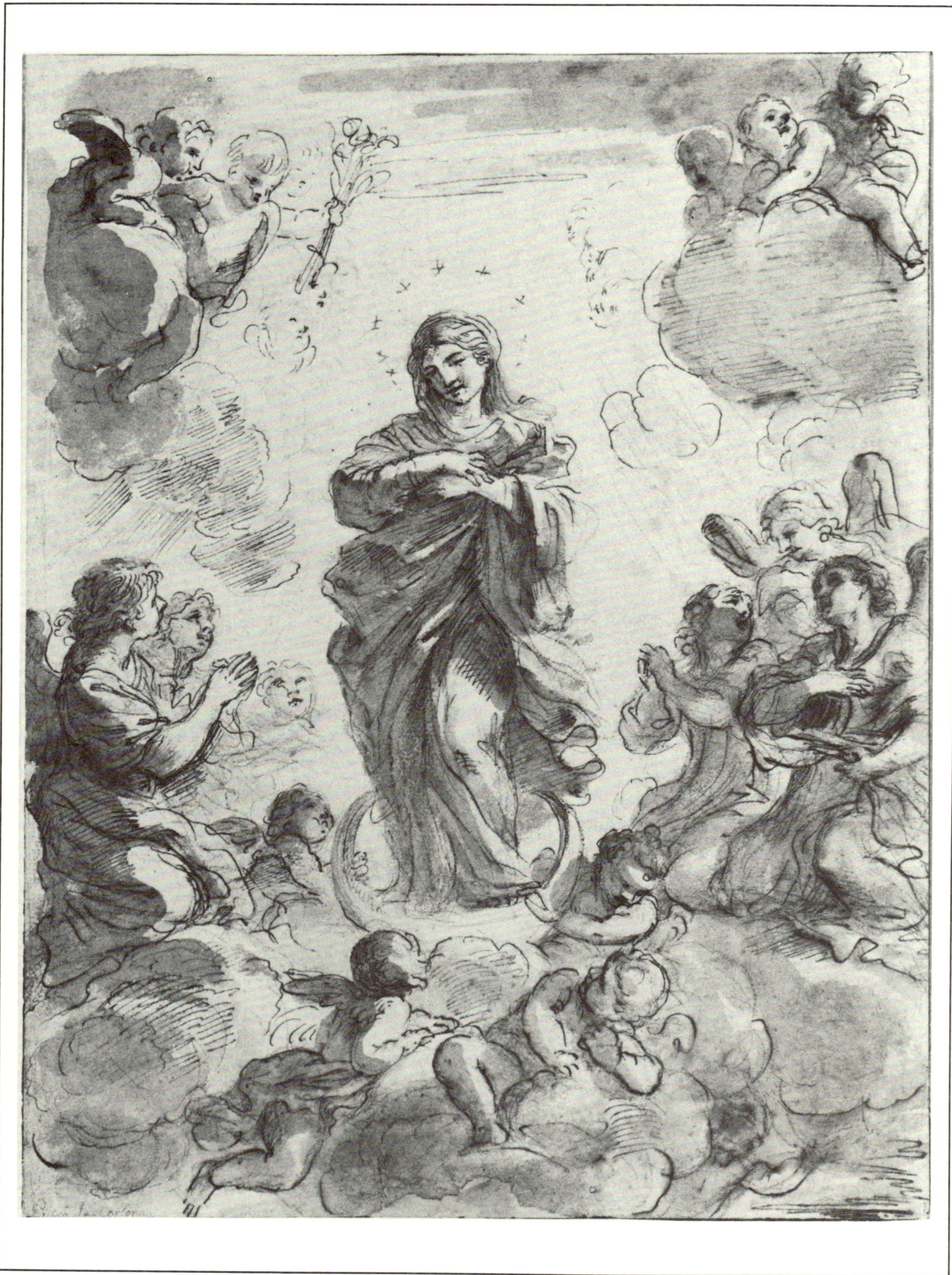

31.

PIER FRANCESCO MOLA

Immaculate Conception

Pen and brown ink and grey and brown wash over black chalk; 346 x 271 mm.

Inscribed recto lower left corner, in brown ink: *Pietro da Cortona*

Provenance: D. Huquier (L.1285); Christie's, 8 July 1975 lot 32

Ann J. Adams in Oberhuber, 1977, number 24, pp. 72-74

Acquired 1976

Adams proposes this drawing to be the first visual record of a church standard which has disappeared. It represented the *Immaculate Conception* or, according to Cocke[2] an *Assumption,* that Mola painted about 1656-57 for his difficult patron, Prince Camillo Pamphili. The confusion regarding the standard's subject matter is complicated by the London drawing where the Virgin is looking upward, as she traditionally does in the Assumption; the Virgin of the Immaculate Conception, with the attributes of "the moon under her feet, and upon her head a crown of twelve stars" (Revelations xii: 1) usually looks down. This Virgin's downward gaze, the hemicycle of stars around her head, and the cherub brandishing lilies (in the upper left) — all traditional attributes of the Immaculate Conception — establish the subject unmistakably.

Mystical subjects of this sort are relatively rare in Mola's *oeuvre,* and the model for the full-length angel kneeling to the left of the Virgin seems to have been borrowed from Pietro da Cortona. But nothing could be more typical of Mola's own hand and artistic vocabulary than the summary delineation, the pudgy body and the exuberant *contrapposto* of the *putto* in the upper right corner. This energy animates the whole drawing, even the generous forms of the Virgin's body, as if a great divine wind had swept the figures upward, relieving them of the weight of corporeal existence and transfixing them with joyful spirituality. Mola has succeeded remarkably in recreating the vision of the opening lines of Revelation xii:1: "And there appeared a great wonder in heaven; a woman clothed in the sun. . ."

Typical as the drawing is of the mid-century Roman Baroque, it betrays Mola's great debt to Venetian art of the preceding century, ultimately to Titian's epochal Frari *Assumption* of 1518. Its fervent virtuosity explains the esteem in which Mola's drawings are held.

A related drawing was on the London art market in 1981[1]. It differs from this sheet in details: the Virgin is more slender, joins her fingers in prayer and gazes upward; the draughtsmanship is sketchier; and the sheet includes three other figures and a profiled head that are unrelated to the Virgin. Presumably the London drawing is a preliminary sketch which was then developed, with changes in the figure of the Virgin, into this finished composition. C.R.R. and A.M.

1. Sotheby's, 9 July, lot 27, ill.
2. Cocke, 1972, pp. 4, 56, 72.

32.

JACOPO NEGRETTI THE YOUNGER called PALMA IL GIOVANE
(Venice 1554/8 - Urbino, Rome - 1628 Venice)

Saint Onophrius in the Wilderness(recto); two studies of the figure (verso)

Pen and brown ink, brown wash, over black chalk; 210 x 145 mm.; the ink has soaked through both sides of the sheet. Watermark: crossbow within a circle with illegible monogram, similar to Briquet nos. 753, 767, 769
Provenance: Vallardi (L.1223)
Acquired: 1972
Ann J. Adams in Oberhuber, 1977, no. 25 pp. 74-76

Palma Giovane, whose precise birthdate is uncertain[1], was the son and pupil of Antonio Palma and the great-nephew of Palma Vecchio, one of Giorgione's leading contemporaries. As a youth Palma Giovane studied in Urbino and Rome, where he was responsive to Michelangelo, Raphael, and particularly to Polidoro da Caravaggio. He returned to Venice to become the aged Titian's favorite assistant, but his style also reflects the influence of Jacopo Bassano, Tintoretto, and Veronese. He finished Titian's *Pietà* in the Accademia, Venice, after his master's death in 1576, and was among the painters who worked in the Doge's Palace after the terrible fire of 1577.

St. Onophrius (Humphrey in English) "the hairy Anchorite," is customarily depicted as an aged bearded hermit. Here, in a pose of great piety, he is seen in the rocky landscape with the date palms that supplied both his food and the fronds to cover his nakedness. He holds a rosary and his walking stick is leaning against the rocks on the right. Born in the fourth century, the son of a king of Persia, as a child he survived a trial by fire to prove that he was legitimate. An angel then ordered that he be baptised Onophrius, and when he grew up, he was led by a column of fire into the Egyptian desert, where he lived as a hermit for some sixty years[2].

The sketches on the verso are earlier versions of the figure: a strict frontal view in the upper right, and a smaller but better defined contrapposto pose at the bottom. Palma obviously gave considerable thought to the pose: an album of his sketches in the Fritz Lugt collection at the Institut Néerlandais in Paris, shows the saint in two other quite different positions[3]. Palma had a tendency to pull his pen, building up the trees with a series of simple rounded shapes, and defining the figures with quick and somewhat tentative contour lines, accented by touches of wash to develop their volume and effect of movement.

The Steiner drawing was preparatory, with a few changes, for one of three altarpieces Palma carried out

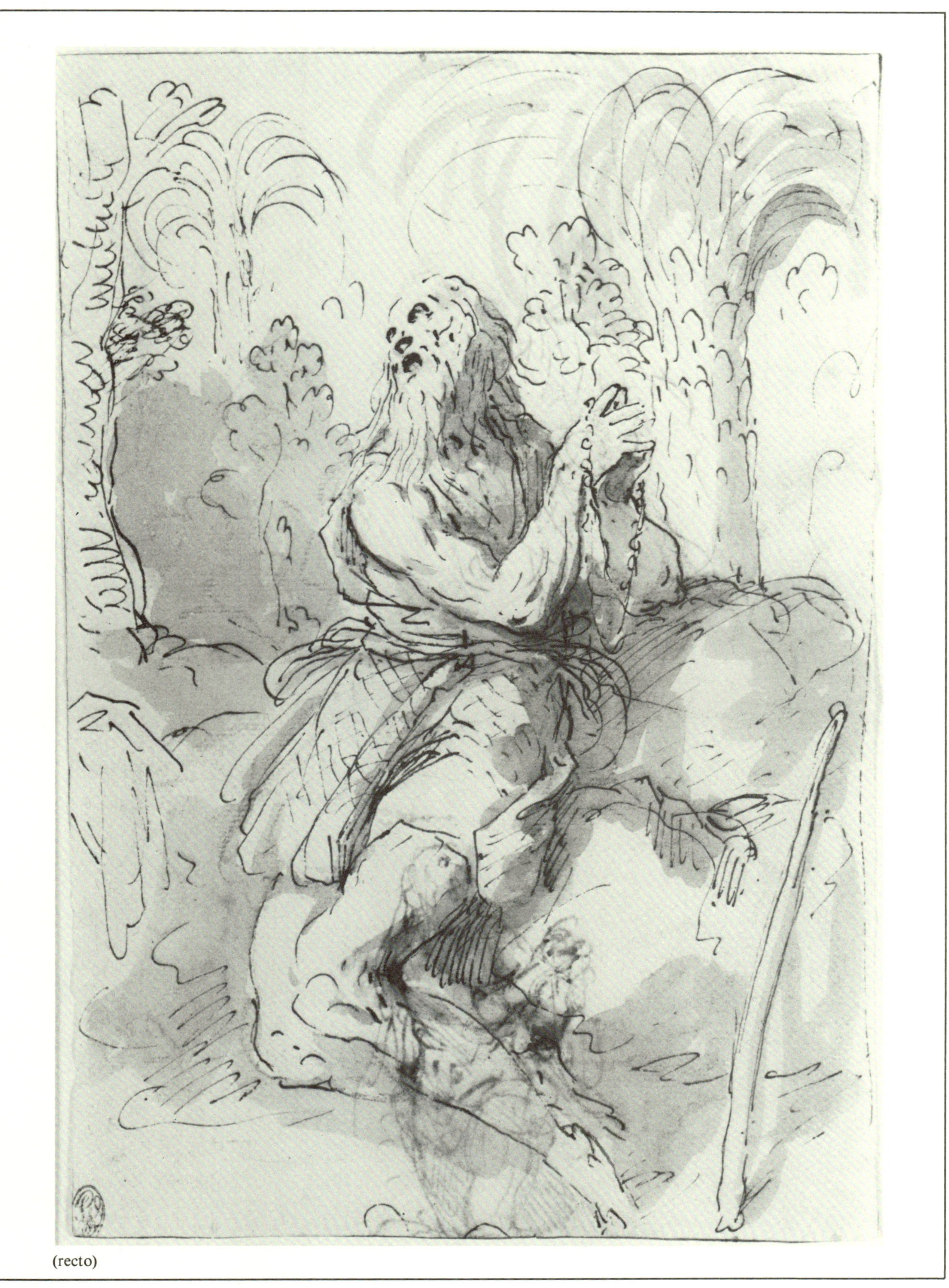
(recto)

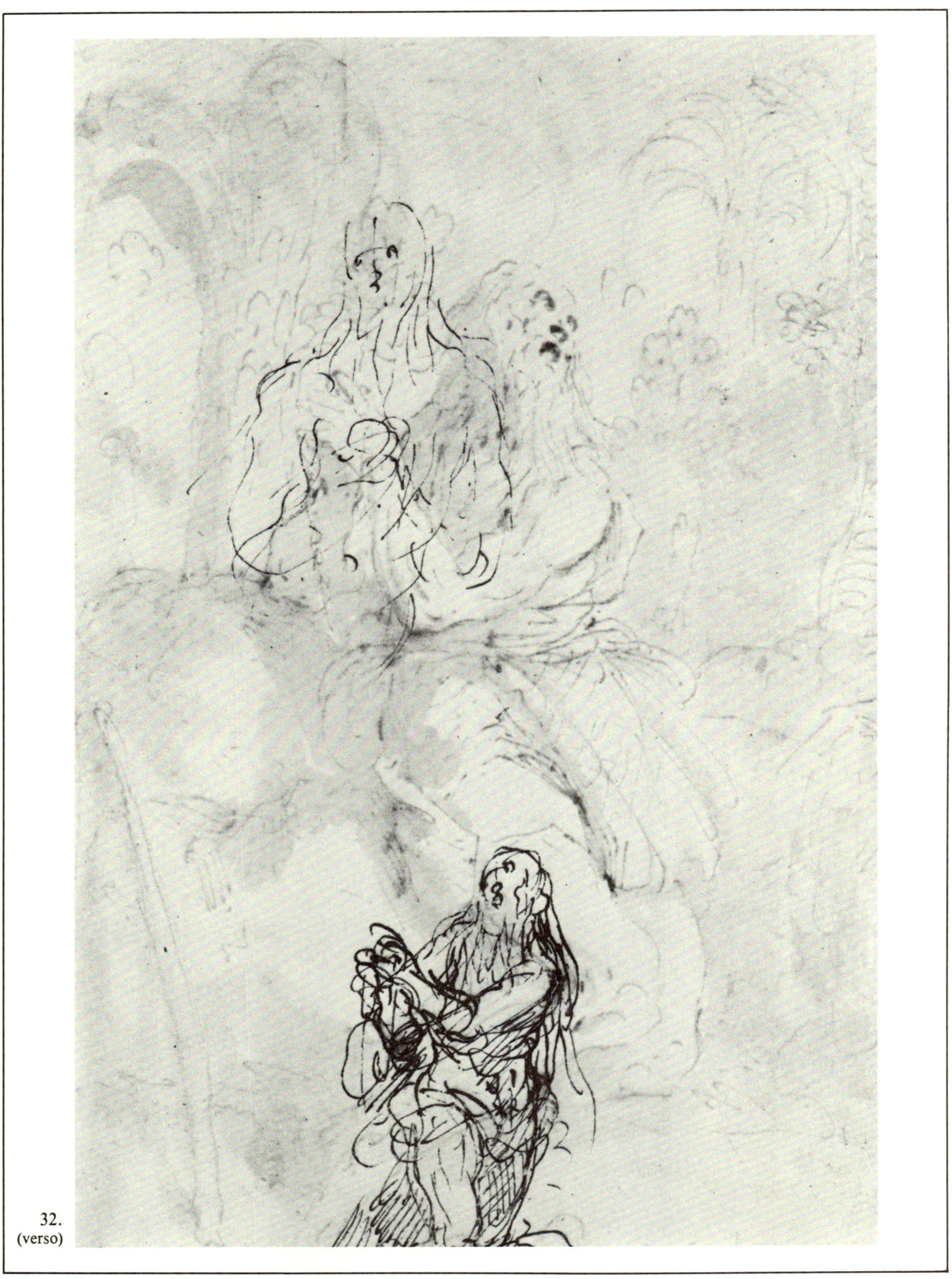

32.
(verso)

for three chapels in the Sanctuario della Madonna Inviolata at Riva del Garda, which was begun in 1603[4]. The chapels are dedicated to Saints Jerome, Charles Borromeo, and Onophrius as penitents, and a fourth is dedicated to the Cross. On the ceiling of St. Onophrius' chapel is a later fresco by Pietro Ricci showing the saint transported to heaven by angels[5]. The St. Charles Borromeo altarpiece is documented[6] as having been carried out by Palma on commission of Cardinal Carlo Madruzzo, but no date is given, nor are the other two altarpieces mentioned. Presumably the St. Charles altarpiece was painted after 1610, the year of his canonization, and the St. Onophrius and St. Jerome may have been part of the same commission or painted soon after. Mason Rinaldi suggests a date of ca. 1620[7].

The alterations made in the drawn composition of St. Onophrius as Palma developed the altarpiece seem typical of work from a drawing rather than a live model. The recto figure in the Steiner sheet was probably made up from the vast array of stock patterns Palma kept in memory and freely reassembled. It seems likely that the basic models for this and Palma's similar kneeling figures were such sculptures as the marble *St. Jerome* of ca. 1576 by his friend Alessandro Vittoria in the church of SS. Giovanni e Paolo in Venice.

Adams has pointed out the similarity of the figure to an engraving of the penitent St. Onophrius by Cornelis Cort after Girolamo Muziano. R.S.

1. For a summary of the arguments concerning the birthdate, see James Byam Shaw, *The Italian Drawings of the Fritz Lugt Collection,* Institut Néerlandais, Paris, 1983, vol. I, p. 258, n. 1.
2. Réau, 1958-59, vol. iii, pp. 720-721; Butler 1963, vol. 2, pp. 528-9.
3. Byam Shaw, *op. cit.,* cat. no. 249, fols. 20v and 21r.
4. Stefania Mason Rinaldi, *Palma il Giovane, l'opera completa,* Milan, 1984, p. 105, nos. 235-37.
5. Paolo Dal Poggetto, "La decorazione pittorica dell'Inviolata a Riva del Garda . . ." *Antichità Viva* XI, no. 5, 1972, p. 18 pl. 21.
6. In the *Miscelanea Madrizziana,* MS, 2915/134, in the Biblioteca Comunale, Trento; see G. B. Emert, *Fonti manoscritte inedite . . . nel Trentino,* Florence, 1939, p. 129 n. 6.
7. Mason Rinaldi, *op. cit.,* p. 105.

33.

PIETRO BUONACCORSI called PERINO DEL VAGA (Florence 1501 - Rome, Florence, Genoa, Pisa - 1547 Rome)

Saint Peter

Pen and brown ink, squared in black chalk; 214 x 312 mm.; iron-gall corrosion, some ink spots
Acquired 1975
Leslie Koenig in Oberhuber, 1977, no. 33, pp. 91-3
Exhibited: Cleveland, 1979, no. 68
Literature: Olszewski, 1981, p. 4, no. 68 (ill.)

About 1512, when he was eleven, Perino entered the workshop of Ridolfo Ghirlandaio, after preliminary training from another Florentine artist, Andrea de' Ceri. He served in Ridolfo's studio for several years and then became an assistant to a painter called Vaga, whose name he took. The two traveled to Toscanella (now Tuscania) near Viterbo and after a short stay moved on to Rome in 1515. Soon Perino joined the group of artists including Giulio Romano and Francesco Penni, who were decorating the Vatican Loggia under the direction of Raphael, and thus began his career as a designer of stucco decorations. During the 1520's he also came into contact with Parmigianino and Rosso Fiorentino.

Perino's activity centered in Rome, where he competed in the power struggle precipitated by Raphael's death in 1520 and Michelangelo's establishing himself in Florence. Twice Perino fled the city: in 1522 to avoid the plague, and in 1527 when he went to Genoa to escape the perils of the Sack of Rome. He stayed in Genoa until 1537 as court painter to the famous admiral, Andrea Doria, except for the years between 1534 and 1536 when he was in Pisa.

G. B. Armenini in 1556 saw hundreds of Perino's drawings at one time in Rome, and later gave this account of his method[1]:

> He would first of all sketch his intention roughly with charcoal or black chalk and then outline it with pen... Finally he would trace the composition on another sheet of paper and then finish it with so much grace that few or none ever equalled him and particularly in drawing in chiaroscuro.

Armenini points out that Perino's favorite medium was pen and ink and wash on tinted paper, heightened with white. Popham described Perino's pen lines as "spidery" because they describe contours so delicately.

Koenig connected this St. Peter with two other drawings, one in pen and ink (in an English private collection in 1969), which appears to be preparatory for the third, more finished with wash, in the Albertina[2]. All three drawings present the saint reclining within a triangular frame, which is doubled and more sharply

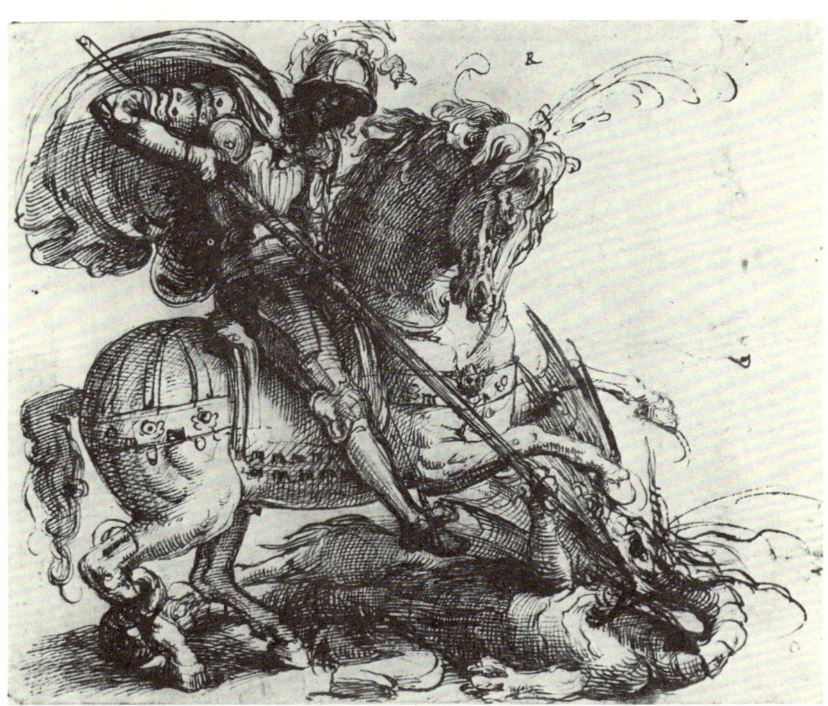

Perino del Vaga
Saint George and the Dragon
Museum of Fine Arts, Budapest

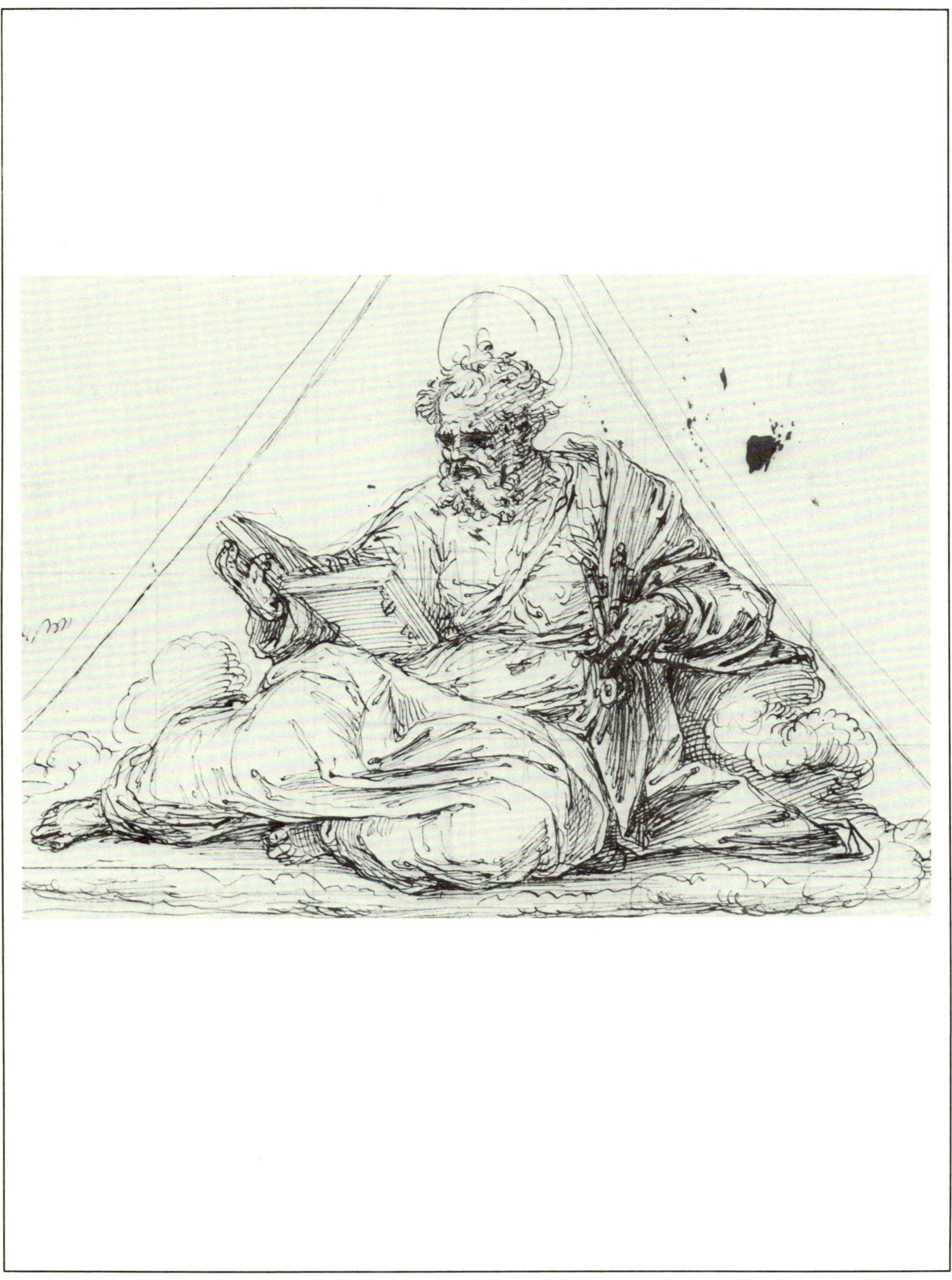

pointed in the Steiner drawing, and broader in the other two. The pose of the head and upper torso of the figure in the Steiner drawing, the heavy drapery describing the forms of the legs and clinging to the torso, betray Perino's dependence on Michelangelo's heavily muscular figures, particularly the figure of God in the Sistine Chapel *Creation of the Sun.* The poses in the other two drawings are more serpentine. The head and arms are now toward the right and the legs toward the left, with the keys in the saint's right hand and the book in the left, so that the poses extend to occupy all three corners of the triangular space. As a result, the Steiner sheet can be recognized as the first of three, a suggestive option in the artist's process of developing control of the forms and of the space they occupy, bringing them into harmonious balance.

Koenig would place this drawing at the beginning of Perino's stay in Genoa, while Davidson[3] sees it as after his return to Genoa from Pisa in 1636. These suggestions point to the interim period, that of Perino's activity in Pisa, as a likely date. Comparison with the pen and ink *St. George and the Dragon* in the Museum of Fine Arts in Budapest, which was preparatory for Perino's work at the Cathedral in Pisa, seems to confirm this supposition. There is a striking similarity to another pen and ink drawing in the National Museum in Budapest of *Saints Peter and Paul*[4]. Fenyo suggested a date for it of the early 1530's; Lorand Zentai proposes that it may have been preparatory for Perino's decorations in the Cappella Paolina in the Vatican of the mid 1540's. Again the possibility that it was drawn for a Pisan commission in the mid 1530's should not be overlooked. R.S.

1. Quoted and translated by A. E. Popham, "On Some Early Works by Perino del Vaga," "*Burl* LXXXVI," April, 1945, p. 59.
2. Bernice Davidson, exhibition catalogue, *Mostra di disegni di Perino del Vaga e la sua cerchia,* Uffizi, 1964, no. 25, p. 33, fig. 20.
3. *ibid.*
4. *In the exhibition catalogue, Leonardo to Van Gogh: Master Drawings from Budapest,* Chicago, 1985, no. 16, p. 48 (ill.).

34.

DOMENICO PIOLA (Genoa 1627-1703)

Adoration of the Shepherds

Pen and brown ink, brown wash, over black chalk: 276 x 417 mm.
Provenance: Giuseppe Vallardi (L.1223)
Acquired 1978

Part of a clan of artists, Domenico Piola was schooled by his brother Pellegro, and by Giovanni Domenico Capellino and Domenico Fiasella. He may have succeeded as head of Fiasella's workshop upon that master's death in 1669, but in any case, his studio dominated Genoese painting during most of the second half of the century. Leaving Genoa only once, in 1684-85, Domenico preferred to maintain his long leadership of the Genoese art world, together with his son-in-law Gregorio de Ferrari and Guidobono.

This drawing follows St. Luke's description of the scene in the New Testament (Luke ii: 15-17): "And they [the shepherds] came with haste, and found Mary, and Joseph, and the babe lying in a manger. And when they had seen it, they made known abroad the saying which was told them concerning this child." Their haste is captured by the shepherd rushing in from the left.

Both he and his kneeling companion bring gifts symbolic of Christ's mission[1]. Thrust into the belt of the entering peasant is a chalumeau, the forerunner of the clarinet, or possibly a shawm, which developed into the modern oboe[2]. This reed instrument refers to the disciples following Christ, like the enthralled crowds that accompanied the legendary pagan musician Orpheus (see number 66). The crouching shepherd has placed before Christ a staff and a lamb — allusions to Christ as the shepherd of souls and as a blood sacrifice for the purgation of mankind's sins. The woman on the left may also carry a present — a bundle perhaps containing the eggs, fowl, and milk that shepherdesses traditionally are thought to have brought to the Christ Child.

On the right a wreathed man tugs a donkey into view. This grouping is reminiscent of the processions of sacrificial animals and their attendants found on some ancient Roman reliefs[3]. The donkey in the Steiner drawing is probably the beast that Mary rode to Bethlehem, and the hindquarters of the animal directly behind the Madonna and Child are those of the ox brought along to sell for Roman taxes[4]. Its location so close to Christ may be a further reference to Christ's future sufferings, since oxen were frequent pagan sacrificial victims.

Another drawn *Adoration of the Shepherds* by Piola (in the London art market[5]) is close in composition and in style to the Steiner sheet. In both, the shepherds on the left take up similar poses, and the figure in the London drawing, wreathed with ivy and pulling a donkey, resembles the garlanded peasant on the right-hand side of the Steiner sheet. The human physiognomies are nearly interchangeable as are those of the two dogs.

Two etchings of the *Nativity* by Piola may be related to these drawings. One is signed and dated 1656. The other has been dated early in the same decade and can perhaps be linked with Piola's fresco of the *Nativity* on the nave vault of the church of S. Marta in Genoa[6]. But the etchings are vertical compositions, and much indebted to Valerio Castello and Bartolomeo Biscaino, who influenced the young Piola. Thus, despite some similarities in details and the siting of the Nativity in antique ruins, the two drawings do not seem to belong in

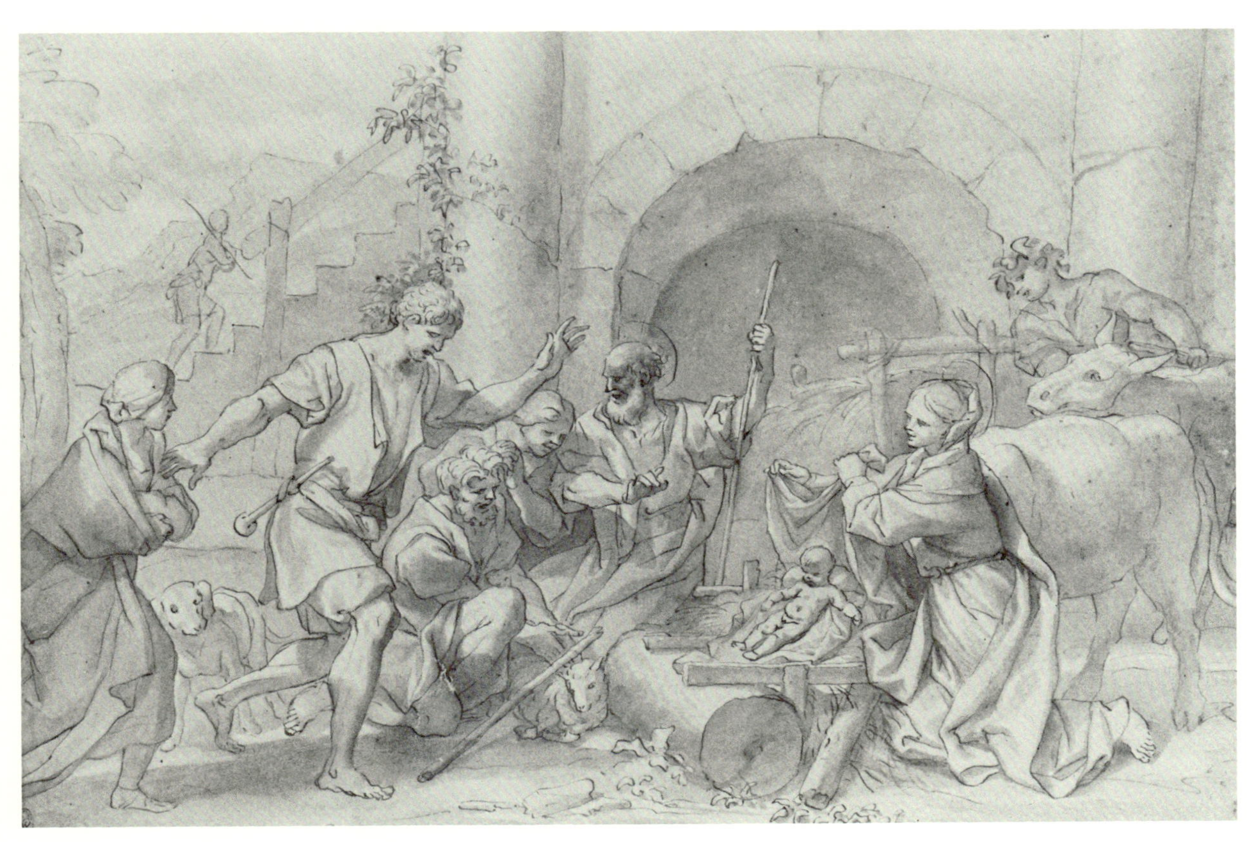

the 1650's with the etchings. They seem instead to share the drapery forms and wash effects of Piola's later drawings of the 1680's and 1690's. C.R.R.

1. Réau 1955-59, II, p. 234.
2. Sybil Marcuse, *Musical instruments, A comprehensive dictionary,* New York, 1975, pp. 87 (chalumeau) and 471 (shawm).
3. George M. A. Hanfmann, *Roman Art,* London, 1964, numbers 99, 106.
4. Réau, *op. cit.*, 1957, II, p. 228.
5. Christie's, London, 4 July 1984, Lot 51.
6. Mary Newcome, *Genoese Baroque Drawings,* Binghamton (NY) and Worcester (MA), 1972, p. 61, ill.

35.

FRANCESCO PRIMATICCIO

(Bologna 1504 - Mantua, Fontainebleau, Rome, Bologna - 1570 Paris)

Venus with Eros and Anteros (?)

Pen and brown ink, heightened with white, on tan paper, lightly squared off and lightly incised; 245 x 192 mm.
Inscribed recto, lower left: *229;* lower right: *CXL*
Provenance: Abbé Desneux de la Noue (L661, 774, 1855 and 3014)
Acquired 1981

Primaticcio studied at home in Bologna with Bagnacavallo and Innocenzo da Imola. He is first heard of as an artistic personality when he went to Mantua (in 1525 or 1526) to assist Giulio Romano in decorating the Palazzo del Tè. According to Vasari, Primaticcio was the executant of the classical friezes in the Sala degli Stucchi, and he is credited with other rooms there and in the Palazzo Ducale. It must have been from this experience that Primaticcio developed his system of decoration.

In 1531 or 1532, Francis I invited him to France where he joined the group of Italian and French artists working under Rosso Fiorentino (1494-1540) in decorating the palace at Fontainebleau. Except for trips to Rome in 1540-42 and 1546 and to Bologna in 1563, Primaticcio remained in France for the rest of his life. After Rosso's death in 1540 he became the leader of a large team of well-trained artists. They transformed the palace into a monument of his style, a combination of painting and high relief stucco not only reminiscent of the Palazzo del Tè but also comparable to work he had seen Perino del Vaga (number 33) carrying out contemporaneously in Rome. He also practiced architecture. From 1559 until his death, he worked in Paris for the Queen, Catherine de' Medici.

His main work before 1540, the Chambre du Roi, was destroyed, and only a few of his drawings from this period survive. Enough remain, however, to show that during the eight years of his first stay at Fontainebleau, he left behind Giulio Romano's solid classical style for Rosso's greater elegance. He developed both a *chiaroscuro* style with wash, and the almost purely linear manner of this drawing, in which smoothly controlled, even lines establish the contours of forms, and volumes are reinforced by touches of white. A date of about 1541-43, contemporary with the Cabinet du Roi (also destroyed) is likely for the Steiner drawing. The principal figure has shorter, more classical proportions, still a little reminiscent of Giulio, rather than the more elongated bodies and graceful movements of her sisters in the *Childhood of Mercury* of ca. 1545-47, formerly at Chatsworth[1].

Because of the moon in the upper left corner of this drawing, the woman has been identified as the goddess Diana. This would be appropriate inasmuch as the motif was used at Fontainebleau as a compliment to Diane de Poitiers (1499-1566), the mistress of Henry II from the early 1530's until his death in 1559. Furthermore, ancient gods and goddesses and heroes appear and reappear as the subject matter of the paintings at Fontainebleau, in celebration of the glory of the king and his court. Some familiar episodes were repeated so often that artists began looking for more unusual subjects, rich with possible, often ambiguous, allusions to the court. Hunting and bathing scenes were popular, "particularly in a romantic context . . . (and there was) a constant dialogue between Venus and Diana, between warm and frigid beauty[2]."

However, the woman has none of Diana's attributes at hand — neither the moon-crested crown, the bow and arrow, or the hunting dogs. The problem can be solved by identifying her as someone else, even the opposing principle of love, Venus. Venus had two children: Eros, the god of love, by her husband Vulcan; and Anteros, the god of unhappy love and the avenger of unrequited affections, by her lover Mars. The juxtaposition in the drawing of the female figure with the two boys is suggestive. Venus may be trying to convert Anteros to her way of thinking. But he resists and mocks her, grimacing and baring his teeth by pulling at the corners of his mouth and eyes, a traditional gesture of disdain *(das Gähnmaul).* In contrast, Eros, as Venus' follower, raises his hands in mock salute to the cold Diana, symbolized by the moon. His mother urges him on, adding with her right hand the ancient (and still potent) gesture of the *mano in fica* which is both a sexually explicit insult and a means of warding off the evil eye. R.S.

1. Sold at Christie's, London, 3 July 1983, lot 37.
2. Henri Zerner, *The School of Fontainebleu, Etchings and Engravings,* New York, 1969, p. 11.

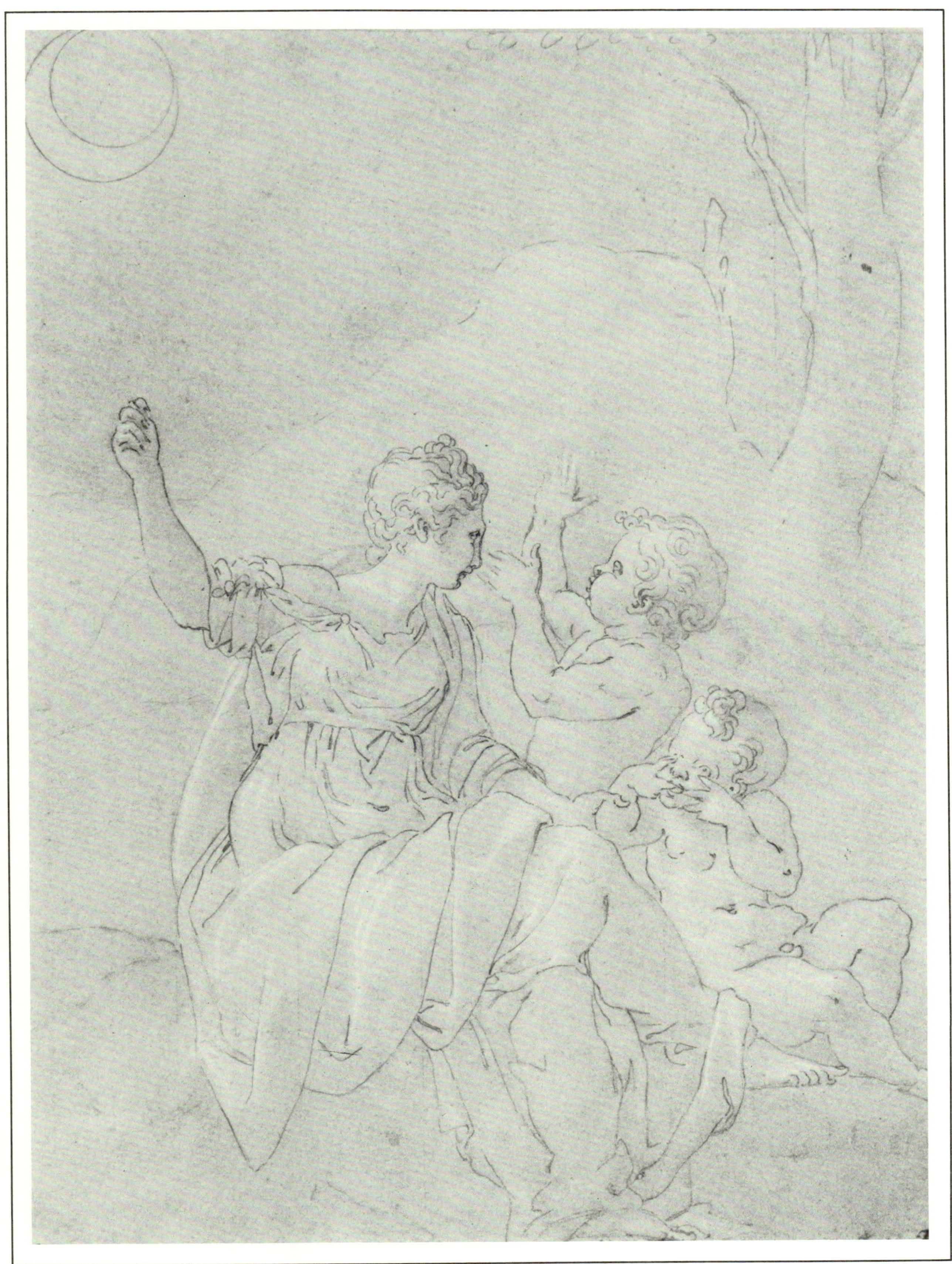

36.

CRISTOFANO RONCALLI called IL POMARANCIO (Pomerance 1552 - Volterra, Florence, Siena, Rome, Loreto - Rome 1626)

An Angel Playing a Viola da Gamba

Red chalk; 360 x 247 mm. Watermark: eagle above a star
Inscribed recto, lower left corner, in brown ink: *[C]orege*
Provenance: Hotel Drouot, Paris, 1877 (inscribed an old mount); Quentin Borthwick; Christie's, 5 April 1977, number 61 (ill.)
Acquired 1977
Oberhuber *Addenda,* 1977, pp. 2-4, number 63

Born into a middle-class Bergamask merchant's family, Roncalli was trained in Volterra and Florence. For a few years beginning about 1576, he established himself as an independent master in Siena, before going to Rome, where he was settled by 1582[1]. There he found great success, with numerous important commissions and highly placed and influential patrons and friends. He was closely associated with the Oratory of Saint Philip Neri, accompanied the Marchese Vincenzo Giustiniani on a famous four-month cultural tour of Europe during 1606, and was a favorite artist of Pope Clement VIII. The pope was instrumental in obtaining for him in 1605 the commission to fresco the New Sacristy of the Holy House in Loreto. He completed this commission in 1609, and then frescoed the giant octagonal dome of the church; sadly enough his dome frescoes deteriorated so badly that they were replaced in the late 19th century. The works at Loreto completed, he returned to Rome in 1615 and remained there until his death. Despite great success during his lifetime, he and his work were increasingly neglected, and until a decade or two ago they were all but forgotten. Fortunately, in recent years there has been a revival of interest in Roncalli and particularly in his drawings, which have come to be newly appreciated[2].

Like so many other artists included in this exhibit, he required many assistants to carry out his vast commissions. So he himself made many drawings, and his pupils and successors made many more in imitation of his. This drawing can be related to the sacred musicians nestled among the clouds at the base of the *Coronation of the Virgin* fresco in the cupola. The compositional scheme of the cupola decorations, distantly recollective of Correggio's in the Parma Cathedral, is preserved in a large presentation drawing in the Library of the Sanctuario at Loreto[3]. Although this exact figure does not appear, it is similar in pose and action to several that do. A number of Roncalli's other drawings for these musicians survive; the closest is also at the Sanctuario Library at Loreto[4].

The characteristically meticulous draughtsmanship of this sheet would seem almost obsessively neat, if Roncalli's touch were not so light and controlled. The effect of this fastidiousness is to reinforce the tenderness with which Roncalli has presented the concentration of the grave but passionate angel-cellist on his music. The reverberations are not only of sound but also of earlier Italian draughtsmanship, most obviously the mature Pontormo, as Kirwin has pointed out[5]. N.M. and A.M.

1. For documentation of his life, see Illeana Chiappini di Sorio, *Cristoforo Roncalli dello il Pomarancio,* in the series *I Pittori Bergamaschi, Il Seicento,* 1983, vol. I, pp. 23-32.
2. See W. Chandler Kirwin, "The Life and Drawing Style of Cristofano Roncalli," *Paragone* XXIX, no. 335, Jan. 1978, pp. 18-62; and exhibition catalogue, *Disegni dei Toscani a Roma (1580-1620),* Gabinetto Disegni e Stampe degli Uffizi LIII, Florence, 1979, pp. 17-54, nos. 1-31.
3. See Chiappini di Sorio, *op. cit.,* p. 192, no. 99/12.
4. Chiappini di Sorio, *op. cit.,* p. 194, fig. 5.
5. Kirwin, 1978, op. cit., p. 61, no. 140.

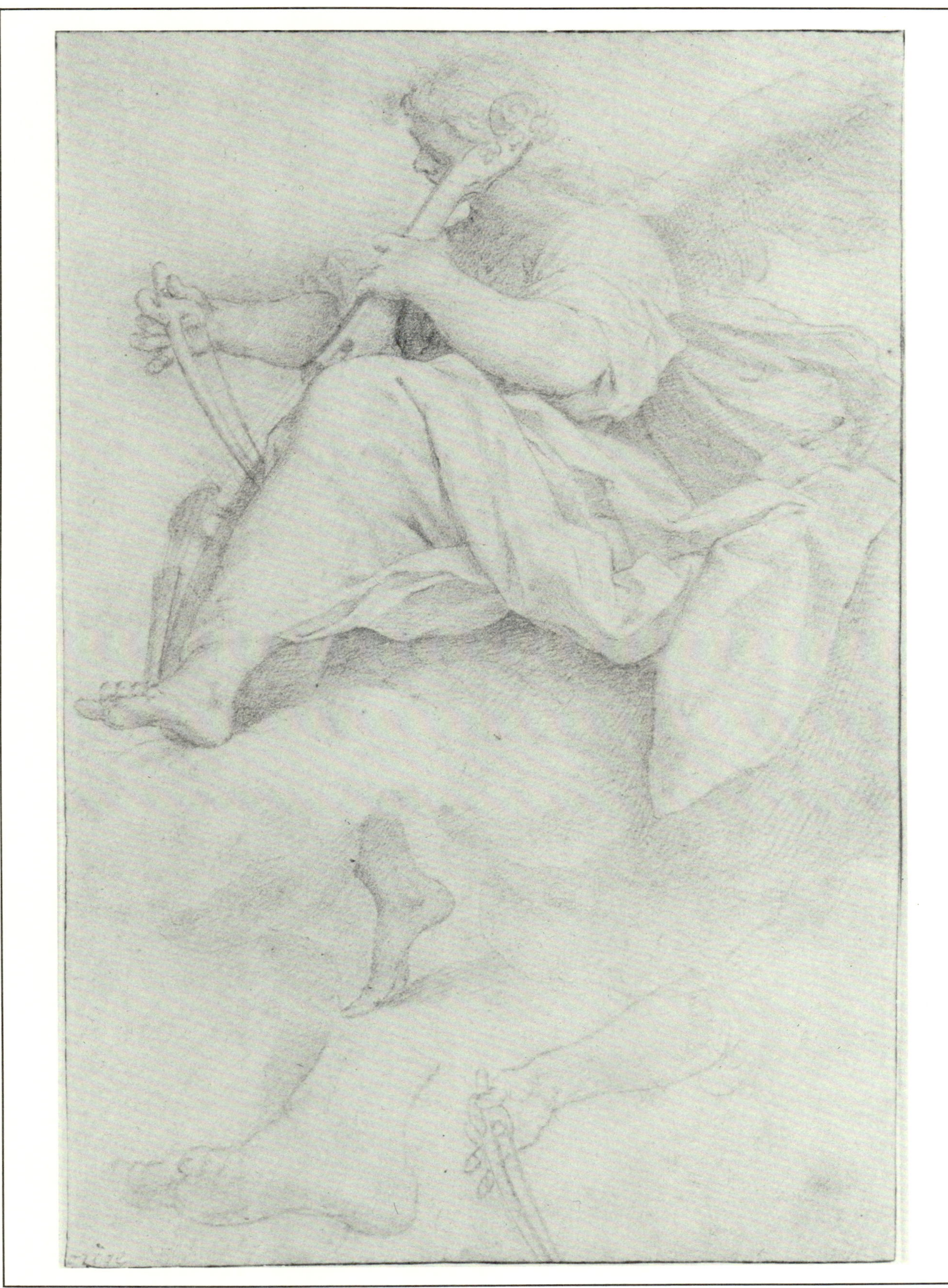

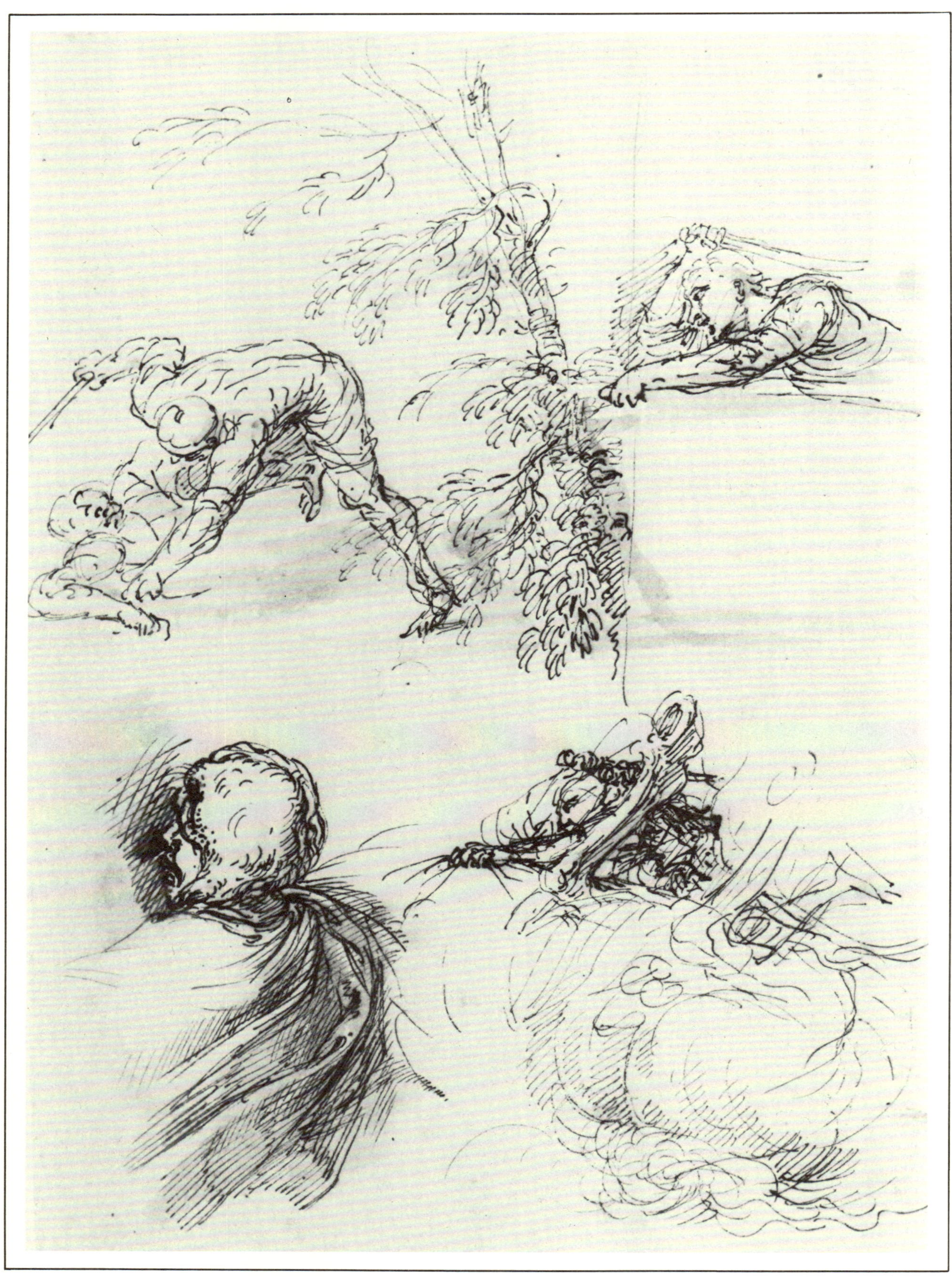

37.

SALVATOR ROSA

(Naples 1615 - Rome, Naples, Florence - 1673 Rome)

Studies

Pen and brown ink with grey wash; 273 x 196 mm.; upper edge cut and tinted red. Watermark: paschal lamb with pennant in a circle

Inscribed recto upper right: *29*

Provenance: Queen Christina of Sweden (?); Cardinal Decio Azzolini and Marchese Pompeo Azzolini; Prince Livio Odescalchi and heirs; Prince Ladislao Odescalchi

Acquired 1976

Rebecca Zurier in Oberhuber, 1977, pp. 81-82

Literature: Michael Mahoney, *The Drawings of Salvator Rosa,* New York, 1977, pp. 407-8, no. 40.12, ill.

Rosa was hardly more renowned in his time for his paintings and prints than for his poems, satires, and plays. He was something of a maverick, almost as disturbing in mid-century Rome as Caravaggio had been at the beginning of the century. After training in Naples in Ribera's circle, he moved to the papal city in 1639. But his wicked pen soon brought him Bernini's enmity, and he discreetly transferred to Florence. There he served the Grand Duke for nearly a decade before returning in 1649 to Rome where he spent the rest of his life.

As an artist he was very productive, and the range of his art was wide: he painted portraits, secular allegories, religious subjects, and the landscapes that were to be so admired by later generations; designed more than a hundred etchings; and made drawings almost beyond number. His brooding self-portraits provided the image for the Byronic hero almost two centuries later, and the picturesque energy of his landscapes, often savage and even menacing, inspired generations of Romantics. Rosa's dark palette, the violence implicit in many of his paintings, and the intensity of the passions depicted or evoked, were a marked contrast to the genial decorations and the serene meditations produced by his greatest contemporaries in Rome, Pietro da Cortona and Poussin (numbers 16 and 56).

This sheet of sketches proclaims Rosa's adherence to the Baroque cult of violence. Michael Mahoney has pointed out that it is related to a battle painting of 1652 now in the Louvre, a work originally intended as a present for Louis XIV (who did not like it particularly). Zurier has observed an even closer correspondence of the struggle in the upper left to a painting in Auckland, New Zealand, also of a great cavalry battle. Rosa must have acquired his taste for such battle paintings and skill in doing them from one of his teachers in Naples, Aniello Falcone (1607-56). Probably, as is characteristic of Rosa's unsigned drawings, he kept this sheet and those related to it in his studio for use as details in other battle paintings. But later in the 1650's, considering them unworthy of his hope for acceptance as a painter of serious "histories," he no longer painted them. Fortunately he did continue drawing with the exuberance of this sheet. The impetuosity of the delineation and of the action is still under the artist's absolute control, and the anthropomorphism of the foliage, reaching out like so many fingers to the struggling figures in the upper left, seems only a natural manifestation of the *élan vital* infecting Rosa and most of his work.

38.

GIOVANNI BATTISTA DELLA ROVERE
(Milan ca. 1551 - ca. 1630)

The Appointment of the Blessed Alessandro Sauli as Superior General of the Barnabites

Pen and brown ink, grey wash, white, over black chalk on grey paper; 231 x 338 mm.
Acquired 1974
Andrea E. Kaliski in Oberhuber, 1977, no. 29, pp. 82-84

There were three della Rovere brothers, all painters: Giovanni Battista, Giovanni Mauro (1575-1640), and Marco (fl. ca. 1625), the sons of Ricardo, a painter from Antwerp who settled in Milan. Marco is scarcely known, but Giovanni Battista and Mauro were active and very productive throughout Lombardy for fifty years. Both were shaped in late sixteenth century Milanese Mannerism by Ambrogio Figino and Giovanni Paolo Lomazzo, and evolved toward the more modern style of Pierfrancesco Morazzone, Giovanni Battista Crespi called il Cerano and Camillo Procaccini. With their skill in painting sacred narratives, they satisfied the demands made of artists by the Council of Trent and were officially encouraged in Milan by the Cardinal-Archbishop, Federico Borromeo. They often collaborated in series of paintings and fresco cycles, Giovanni Battista sometimes leaving a painting he had begun to Mauro for completion, making differentiation of their hands sometimes difficult.

However, comparison of this drawing with that of the *Last Rites of St. Dionysus* in the Ratjen Collection[1], shows the same hand unmistakably in both. On the mount in the Ratjen drawing, in an old hand, is an inscription in pen and ink: *Gio. Batta della Rovere . . . fece nel 1618.* This inscription would seem to establish the attribution of both drawings to Giovanni Battista; however the fresco in the little church of San Dionigi in Cassano d'Adda near Milan for which the drawing was preparatory, was a collaborative effort[2]. Nonetheless, the attribution to the older brother does seem to be confirmed by a number of other drawings that have been identified as his.

Kaliski has identified the subject matter of the Steiner drawing as a scene from the life of St. Charles Borromeo. However, neither of the principal figures has the very distinctive profile of the saint's physiognomy which was known through contemporary portraits (he had died only in 1584), and is unmistakable, with its small chin, bulging eye, and very prominent nose. Correct identification of the subject has been made possible by an illustrated manuscript in the archives of the Barnabite church in Milan[3]. This manuscript, prepared in the hope of the beatification of Alessandro Sauli, presents the program for a proposed cycle of paintings representing his life and miracles. The possibility of his beatification was first proposed in 1610 and was established by decree in 1620; the manuscript itself was written before 1622. The program of paintings followed the pattern established by the cycle of paintings in the Cathedral of Milan (to which, incidentally, the brothers della Rovere contributed five paintings in 1602-04) celebrating the life of St. Charles with paintings of twenty episodes and his miracles in twenty-five. Sauli's cycle was to consist of twenty-one scenes from his life and twenty-five miracles.

This drawing corresponds exactly with the illustration numbered "7" in the manuscript[4], and can therefore be identified as the preparatory study for one of the key events of his life. Alessandro Sauli was born in 1534 to a patrician Genoese family. At an early age, he joined the congregation of the Barnabites, and in 1565, he was appointed against his will its Superior General, the event depicted in this drawing. He served twenty years as a bishop in Corsica, and in 1591 was appointed Bishop of Pavia, where he died the following year. He was not beatified until 1742, and was canonized only in 1904.

Presumably the whole cycle of paintings was never carried out, as a result of a decree of Pope Urban VIII in 1625 which severely restricted the making of images of miracle-workers before their official canonization, and presumably brought the ambitious program to a halt. Two paintings in the Convent of San Barnaba in Milan were executed, but not until 1681. Apparently no painting was ever made from the Steiner drawing, which did however serve as the model for the corresponding illustration of the saint's life. Presumably, also, the drawing can be dated between 1610 and 1624.

Y.R. and A.M.

1. Exhibition catalogue, Stiftung Ratjen, *Italienische Zeichnungen des 16-18 Jahrhunderts,* Munich, 1977, no. 18, p. 48.
2. Nancy Ward Neilson, "Notes on the frescoes at S. Dionigi at Cassano d'Adda," *Arte Lombarda* XIII, no. 1, 1968, pp. 123-28.
3. Published by Maria Luisa Gatti Perer, "Un ciclo inedito di disegni per la beatificazione di Alessandro Sauli," *Arte Lombarda* XL, no. 1, 1974, pp. 9-86.
4. Gatti Perer, *op. cit.,* no. 7, pp. 24-26, ill.

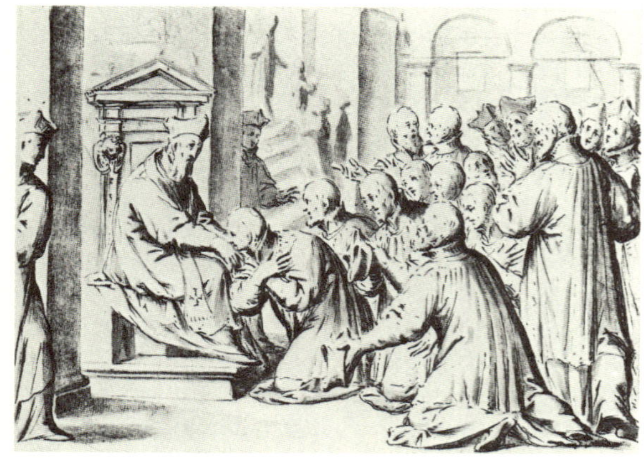

Giovanni Battista Della Rovere
The Appointment of the Blessed Alessandro Sauli as General of the Barnabites
Barnabite Church, Milan

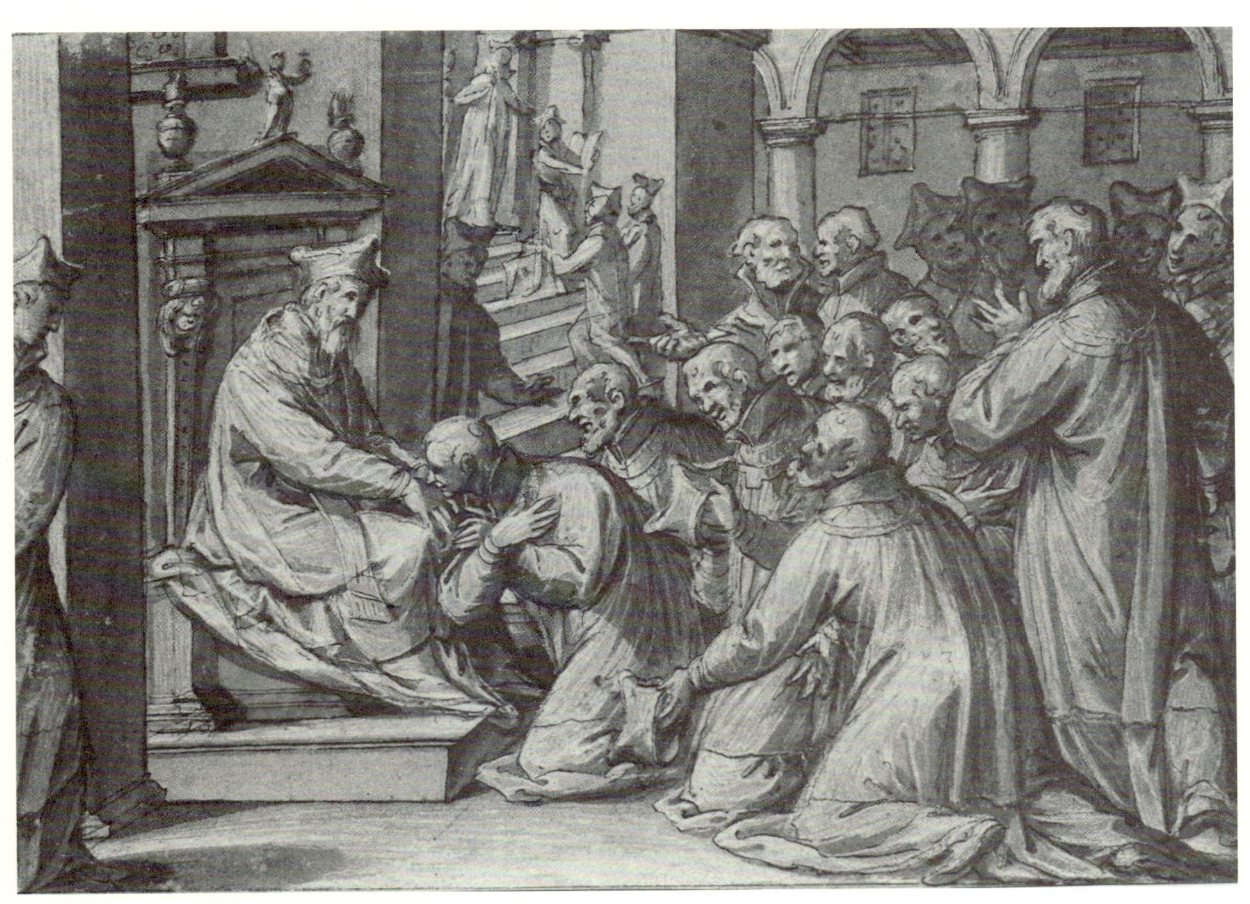

39.

ANDREA MELDOLLA called IL SCHIAVONE
(Zara ca. 1510/15 - Venice 1563)

Two Prophets

Brush and brown wash on tan paper prepared with pink wash, with white, over red chalk, with a few touches of brown ink; 248 x 168 mm.
Provenance: Benno Geiger; Kurt Meissner
Acquired 1982
Exhibited: Bremen-Zurich 1967; Stanford University Museum, 1969
Literature: Mina Gregori, exhibition catalogue, *Handzeich-nungen alter Meister aus Schweizer Privatbesitz,* Bremen-Zurich, 1967, no. 72; Françoise Forster-Hahn, exhibition catalogue, *Old Master Drawings from the Collection of Kurt Meissner,* Stanford, 1969, p. 34, no. 26 (ill.); Francis L. Richardson, *Andrea Schiavone,* Oxford, 1980, p. 135, no. 209

The date of Schiavone's birth in what is now Yugoslavia is uncertain. He is not mentioned in art literature until 1540, when Giorgio Vasari commissioned him to paint on a large canvas in oil the battle which had recently taken place between Charles V and Barbarossa[1]." In April 1548, the friend and publicist of artists, Pietro Aretino, wrote a letter to Schiavone, from which a short excerpt tells us about the artist's style and technique, as well as his position in the eyes of this influential writer[2]:

> . . . the marvelous Titian (no less dear to Charles V than Apelles was to the great Alexander) knows how I have always praised the virtuosity of your execution. Moreover the great painter himself is at times amazed by the technique you demonstrate in sketching your subjects, so well understood and composed that if you carried them out as carefully as you do speedily, you would confirm my recollection [of your work] as excellent. Your inventiveness in figure-composition is in itself praiseworthy, for paintings without it are hardly competent.

Schiavone's painterly style of drawing takes the concept of the Venetian *colorito,* in contrast to Florentine/Roman *disegno,* to its logical polar conclusion. Richardson[3] emphasizes this achievement by pointing out the frontispiece of Francesco Sansovino's *Delle Cose notabili della città di Venetia* of 1602, designed by Palma Giovane and engraved by Odoardo Fialetti. There Schiavone is pictured closest to the figure of *la pittura,* followed by Tintoretto, Jacopo Bassano and many artists representing the styles of Venice, Lombardy, Emilia, and finally Tuscany. At the end of this long procession is Vasari (number 48), who represents *disegno* and the anti-Venetian. The very colorful *Two Prophets* conforms to this conception of painterly creativity. Forms are built up loosely with washes of light and shade, roughly following the vague chalk underdrawing.

Richardson has noted that the figures are "apparently studies for pendentive or spandrel figures." He suggests the possibility of their connection with the Evangelists *negli angoli,* mentioned in 1648 by Carlo Ridolfi as in the choir loft in the church of the Carmine, and known today from a drawing in the Albertina (inv. no. 1580). The Albertina drawing shows four Evangelists in the corners. Although the shape of their allotted space is different, there is no problem in relating both drawings to the now-lost frescoes, considering how often an artist changes his conception of a project and tries out a number of variations before settling on a final solution (see number 32). The Albertina sheet could be the presentation drawing submitted for the commissioners' approval, and the Steiner sheet may present a later point, just before the execution of the fresco. Like the quasi-monochrome frescoes in the Grimani and Pellegrini chapels in San Sebastiano, Venice (dated c. 1548-53 and after 1557, respectively), the completed frescoes were probably not much more finished than the Steiner sheet shows.

Much of Schiavone's fame was based on his frescoes. Because very few of them have survived, and lacking a date for his lost work in the Carmine, it is not possible to date the Steiner drawing more specifically than somewhere in the last two decades of his life. Because of its close affinity to the loosely painted San Sebastiano frescoes, it broadens our knowledge of Schiavone's working method and indicates what another of his finished works probably looked like[4]. R.S.

1. Vasari, 1979, vol. III, pp. 1700-01.
2. *Lettere sull'arte di Pietro Aretino,* Milan, 1957, vol. II, p. 221; the very free translation is the editor's.
3. Richardson, *op. cit.,* pp. 13-14.
4. As this catalogue is about to go to press, Mrs. Steiner informs the editor that Giulio Bora following a suggestion of Julian Stock, believes this drawing to be by an unidentified Milanese early in the seventeenth century.

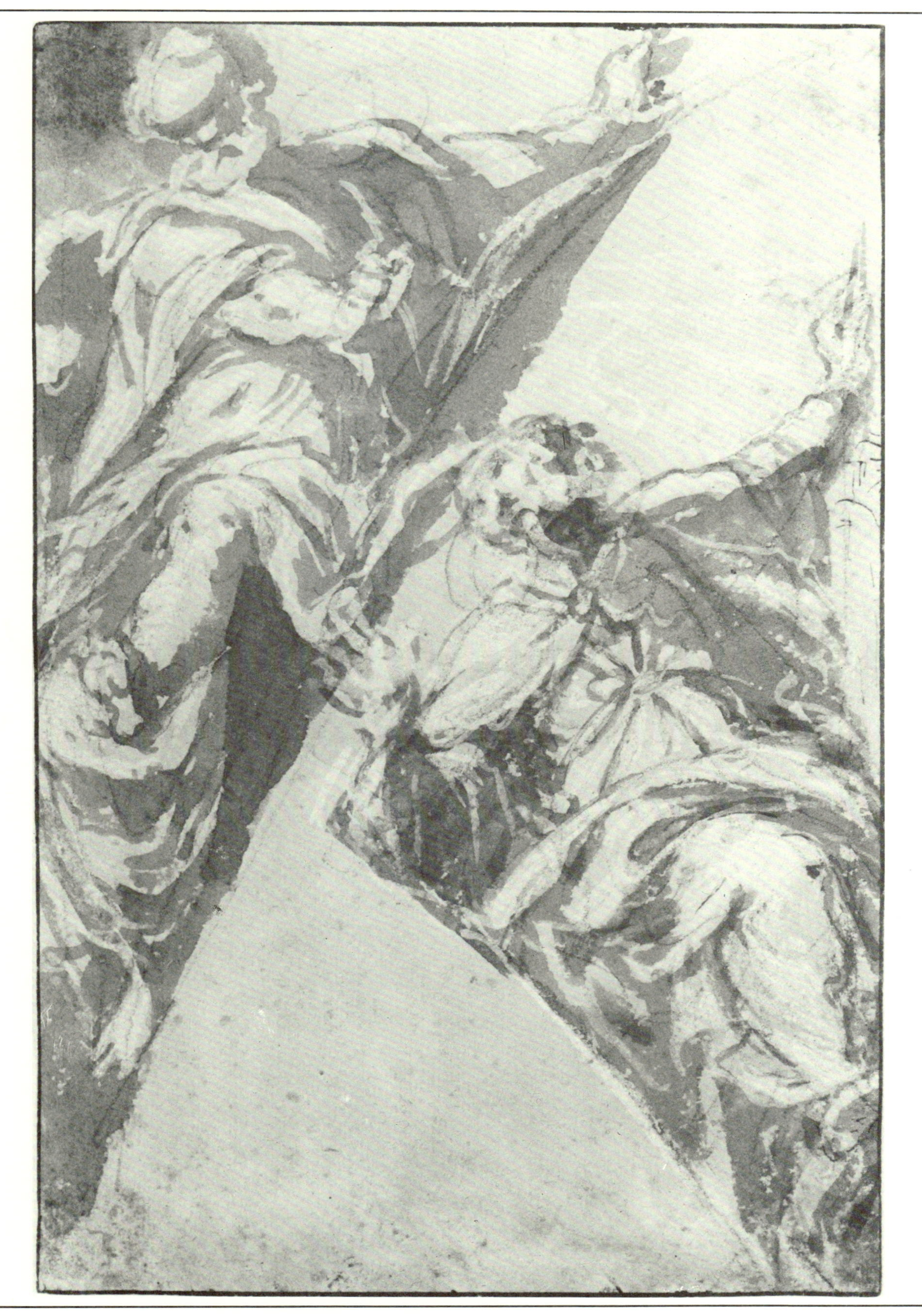

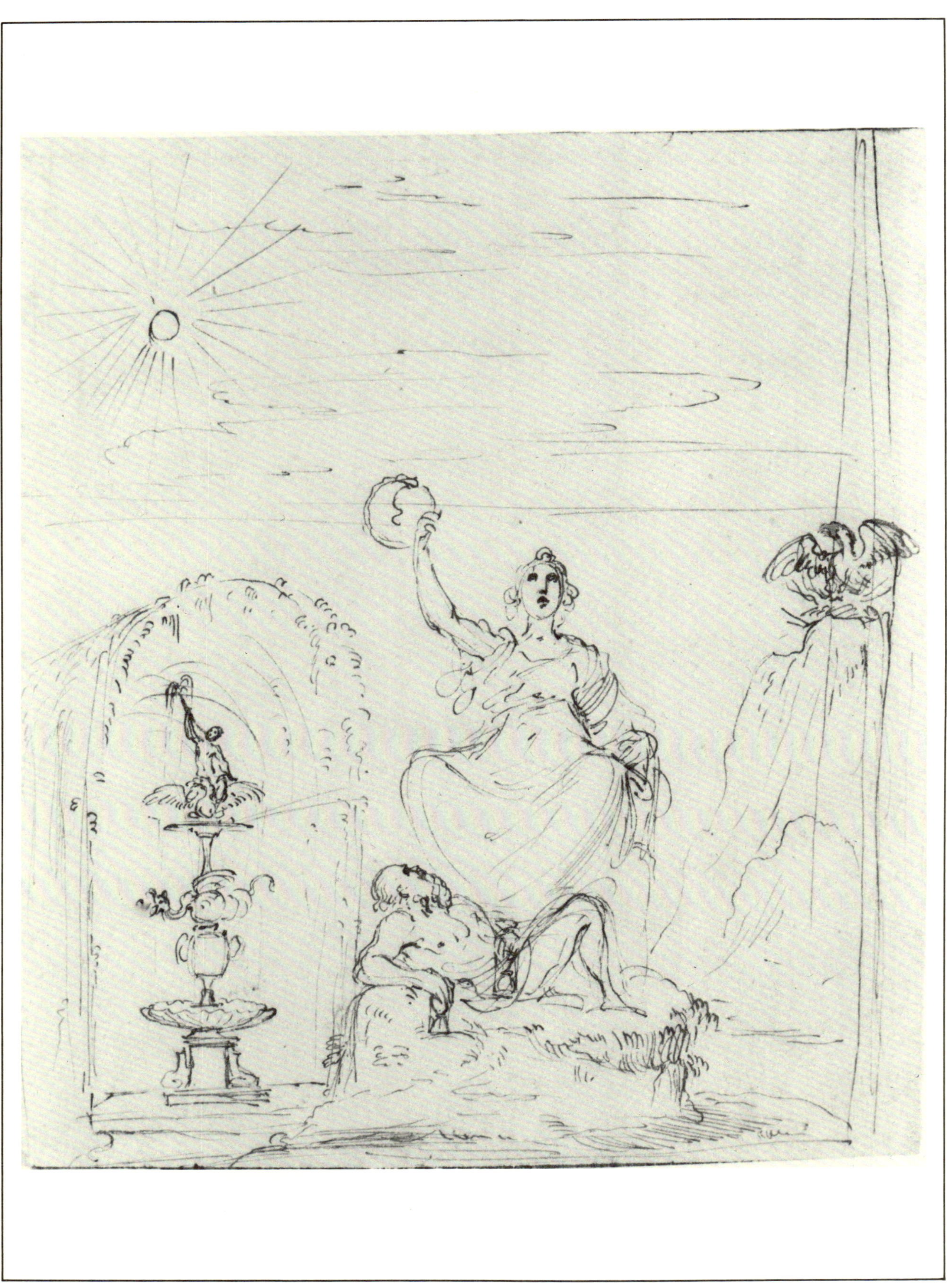

40.

AGOSTINO BUONAMICI called TASSI
(Rome 1581/2 - Livorno, Florence, Genoa - Rome 1644)

An Allegory of Time

Pen and brown ink; 221 x 197 mm.
Acquired 1980

Agostino Tassi is remembered primarily as a *quadraturista,* a painter of vast and elaborate architectural frescoes with complex perspective effects. Secondarily he is remembered for his landscapes and for the notorious profligacy of his life, which caused him to be expelled from Florence, to serve a term as a galley slave, and to be imprisoned at least twice in Rome. Perhaps it should also be noted that during 1613-15 Tassi was the first employer-master of the adolescent Claude Lorrain (1600-82), who assisted him in painting the frescoes at the Villa Lante (then Montalto) in Bagnaia near Viterbo. Tassi seems to have appeared in Florence about 1595, perhaps in the drawing school of Giulio Parigi (1571-1635), who was the chief designer of the almost ceaseless festivities in the Medici court. Leaving Florence in 1609, Tassi went briefly to Genoa before settling in Rome. There he developed a flourishing practice as a painter of illusionistic frescoes, often in collaboration with figure painters — with Orazio Gentileschi at the Casino delle Muse in the villa of the Cardinal-nephew Scipione Borghese in 1611-12, and with Carlo Saraceni and Giovanni Lanfranco at the Quirinal Palace in 1616-17 — and then independently in a series of frescoes at the Palazzo Lancelotti (1617-23) and in various other palaces and villas in Rome and its environs[1].

A figure drawing of this sort is rare in Tassi's *oeuvre,* although the allegorical subject matter would be suitable for a wall decoration. The attribution, originally made by Professor Ann Sutherland Harris, is confirmed by such Tassi drawings as the *Hermione and Shepherds* of the 1620's in the Uffizi (inv. no. 1057S)[2]. Usually Tassi drew with less fine a point, and with wash. But he used a similar pen in a drawing in the Ontario Art Gallery in Toronto, done during 1631 in connection with his paintings celebrating Pope Urban VIII's historically dubious appointment of his nephew Prince Taddeo Barberini as Prefect of Rome. So both the attribution and date of the Steiner drawing seem to be certain, although it may be a little earlier than 1631. The rather inelegant pose of the central figure is like some in the Quirinal Palace frescoes of 1616-17, and the charming gazebo and fountain are in accord with the ceiling in the Palazzo Lancelotti that Tassi frescoed just afterwards with birds and grapevines over a balustraded pergola.

At first glance the various elements in the drawing may appear too disparate to be related. However, they are brought together by the common themes of resurrection and eternal life[3]. The most obvious symbol of this eternal process is the sun on the upper left, renewing life every day by its cyclic action of rising and setting. The vegetation on the pergola just below may be grape vines, symbolic of Christ's Resurrection; the fountain within the pergola represents eternal life. The fountain's details elaborate the theme. The figure at the crest symbolizes apotheosis in general and probably stands specifically for the boy Ganymede; his trumpet showers water on his mount, the chief god Zeus disguised as an eagle, and thus signifies his triumph over death. Ganymede and the eagle rise victoriously over a dragon, a symbol of the underworld; the dragon, in turn, is perched on a funerary urn, reiterating the death *motif.* The whole fountain structure stands on a catch basin in the form of a shell, which in Graeco-Roman ritual also stood for resurrection.

On the far right, the mythological phoenix perched on its blazing aerie, takes up the theme of resurrection again. According to legend, when the bird began to age it built its own funeral pyre, ignited it with the rays of the sun, and then fanned the flames with its wings until the fire flared up and consumed it. Three days later, a new phoenix would rise from the ashes, completing the cycle.

The focus of the drawing is, of course, the woman enthroned on Time, the aged man with an hourglass in each hand. The ring she flourishes overhead is actually a serpent biting its own tail, another allusion to cyclic eternity. Her regal figure is obviously allegorical, following fairly closely Cesare Ripa's description of Eternity[4]: "A woman dressed like a matron, who in her right hand holds a serpent with its tail in its mouth, and who wears a veil on her head that covers both of her shoulders." C.R.R. and A.M.

1. The most recent information on Tassi's career is in Luigi Salerno, translated by Clovis Whitfield, *Landscape Painters of the Seventeenth Century,* Rome, 1979, vol. I, pp. 170-174.
2. Pl. 27 in Marco Chiarini, *I Disegni Italiani di Paesaggio dal 1600 al 1750,* Treviso, 1972, p. 18. The inscription is from *Gerusalemme Liberata,* VII, pp. 19 ff.
3. See J. C. Cooper, *An Illustrated Encyclopedia of Traditional Symbols,* London, 1978 and G. Sill, *A Handbook of Symbols in Christian Art,* New York, 1975.
4. Cesare Ripa, *Iconologia,* Padua, 1611; Garland Publishing Co. reprint, New York/London, 1976, p. 152.

41.

GIAMBATTISTA TIEPOLO
(Venice 1696 - North Italy, Wurzburg, Venice - 1770 Madrid)

A Bishop and Two Priests with an Acolyte

Pen and brown ink, brown wash over black chalk; 275 x 218 mm.; all four corners made up
Provenance: Prince Alexis Orloff sale, Galerie Petit, Paris, 30 April 1920, lot 122; Z. Birtschansky Collection, Paris
Acquired 1981
Exhibited: *Mostra del Tiepolo,* Venice, 1951, no. 83
Literature: Detlev von Hadeln, *The Drawings of Tiepolo,* 1925 (reprinted 1928 and 1970), vol. I, p. 27, pl. 101; George Knox, "The Orloff Album of Tiepolo Drawings," *Burl* CIII, 1961, p. 275, no. 74

According to von Hadeln, "Tiepolo was the greatest artist of his century, with superabundant fancy, incomparable in the certainty of his decorative taste, gifted with absolutely unbounded technical skill . . . [His] extremely fertile production appears like a long series of joyous festivals[1]." Tiepolo was no less incomparable as a colorist, with the subtility and refinement of the Rococo but more vigorous. Veronese's spiritual heir and the climax of the great Venetian tradition of decorative painting, Tiepolo, after responding to Sebastiano Ricci and Giovanni Battista Piazzetta, soon evolved his personal world, peopled by exultant superhumans, genially manifesting the beauties of this earth while often transcending it into a vast heavenly cosmos. He was a spectacular painter, the miracle of his inventiveness hardly less marvelous than the miracles that his paintings celebrated. Tiepolo's genius was recognized by commissions throughout North Italy, at the Prince-Bishop's Palace at Würzburg, and in Spain, particularly the ceilings of the throne and other principal rooms of the Royal Palace in Madrid. Working on so vast a scale required a corps of assistants, not only his sons Gian Domenico (numbers 43 to 45) and Lorenzo, but also two generations of lesser artists. Drawing was indispensable to all this activity. It was to Giambattista what melody was to Mozart, and flowed as easily. Furthermore the process of drawing allowed him to formulate his ideas; the drawings themselves instructed and guided his assistants. He created a huge corpus of drawn images, and used, reused, and transformed them in response to the demands made on him.

This drawing is typical. The head of the benign chief figure appears elsewhere in Tiepolo's *oeuvre* in various guises, like a single character actor made up for different, even contradictory, roles: he is a grandfatherly God the Father looking down benevolently on Pope St. Clement in the painting of 1737-39 in the Alte Pinacothek in Munich; he is again a bishop in the contemporary *Institution of the Rosary* at the church of the Gesuati in Venice and in the altarpiece of 1742-5 of *Saints Maximus and Oswald* in the church of San Massimo in Padua; or he is a leering Oriental in a drawing of a similar group for a *Scherzo di Fantasia* in the Civic Museum in Treviso (inv. no. 2033).

Not only the principal figure but also the whole group appears and reappears. Closest to the drawing is a little painting last heard of in the collection of Captain Langdon Douglas in London. The arrangement of the painted group is almost the same as this drawn group, although the shadowy figure behind the bishop has disappeared from the painting and the other cleric at his right elbow is now a young man. Aside from these changes and a few details, the major difference is in the placement of the group in an apse. This little painting can probably be associated with the altarpiece of *St. Augustine with SS. Louis King of France, St. John the Evangelist and a Bishop Saint* that was in the church of San Salvatore in Venice by 1733 or 1740, and was perhaps destroyed by fire in 1741; it had certainly disappeared by the end of the eighteenth century[2]. A much more ambitious composition, the San Salvatore altarpiece nonetheless included three of its saints in a similar cluster. Several other paintings, some probably autograph, a drawing and an engraving, are also related[3]. This bishop's lack of attributes prevents specific identification of him, if Tiepolo intended any.

During the past hundred years, the primary source for drawings by Giambattista and his son Domenico has been a series of albums in which their drawings were mounted, many of them at the time of the family's departure for Madrid in 1762. The dispersal of the drawings in the albums began in the late nineteenth century and has continued until as recently as 1965 (see number 43). This drawing comes from the Orloff album, which probably was put together in Tiepolo's studio before his departure to Spain, and was acquired by a late eighteenth or early nineteenth century ancestor of Prince Orloff who sold it in 1920[4]. Most of the drawings in the album were of religious subjects, and the majority were by Giambattista, although some by Gian Domenico were included. A few of the father's were of the 1720's; many were of the 1740's or 1750's. Knox identifies this drawing as a "half-sheet" of the 1740's, which coincides chronologically with the related paintings, although he believes none of the Orloff album drawings was a study for a specific painting.

1. von Hadeln, *op. cit.*, p. 2.
2. *Opera completa,* p. 103, no. 120.
3. Michael Levey, *The Eighteenth Century Italian Schools,* catalogue, National Gallery, London, 1956, pp. 96-97 no. 1193.
4. Knox, 1961, p. 272.

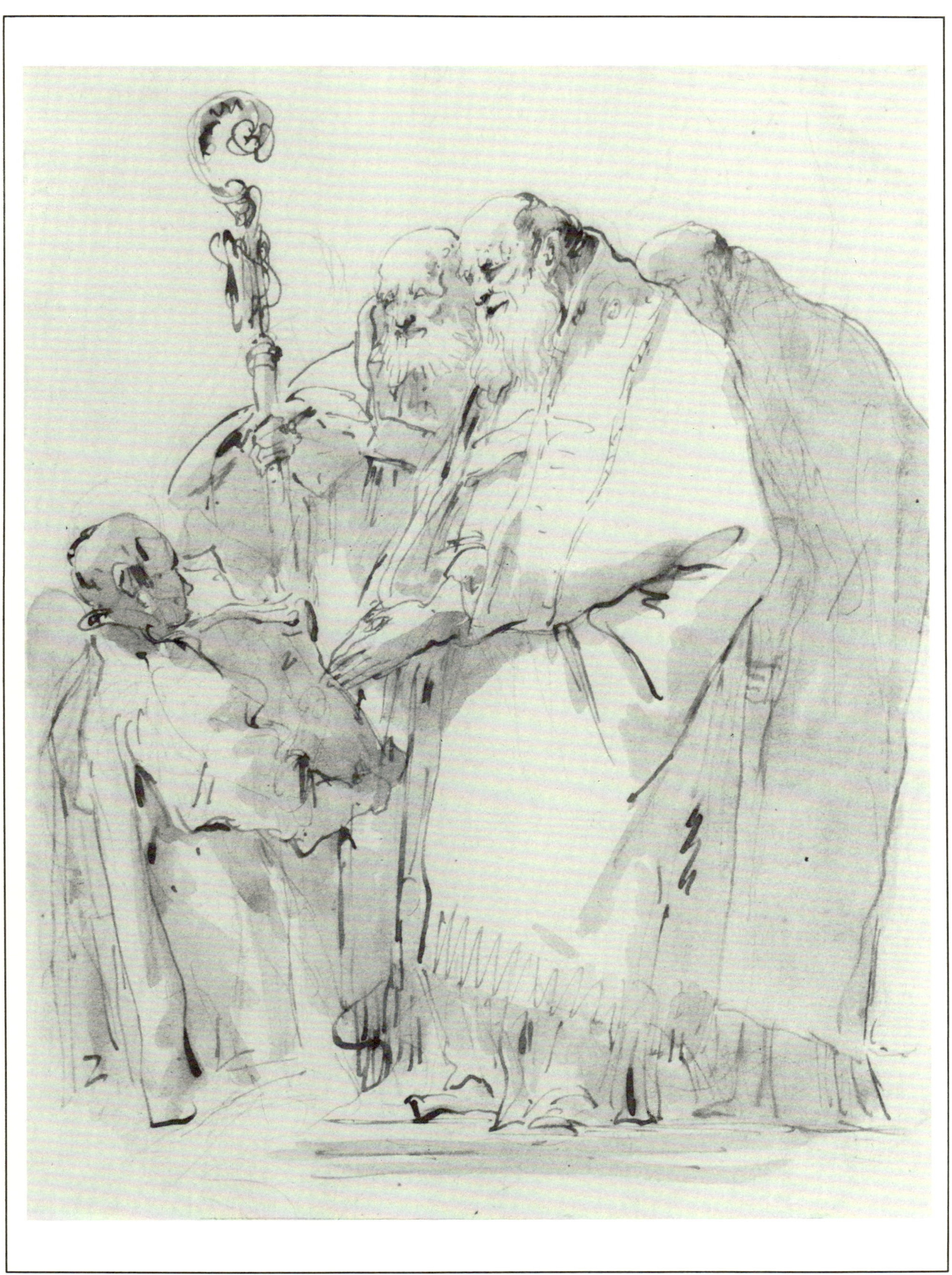

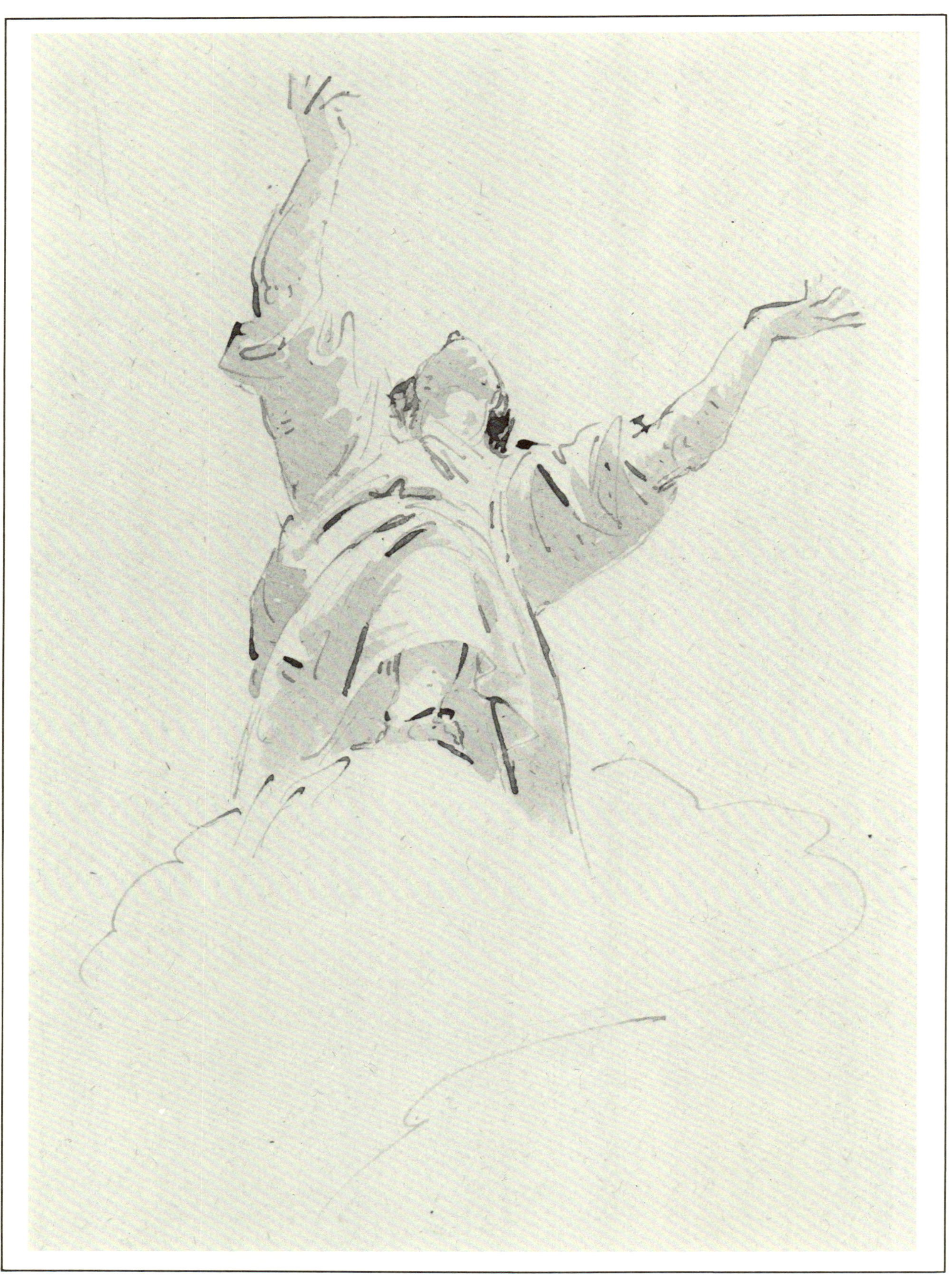

42.

GIAMBATTISTA TIEPOLO

Adorant

Pen and brown ink, brown wash; 247 x 185 mm.
Provenance: Conte Algarotti Corniani before 1852; Edward Cheney sale, Sotheby's, London, 29 April 1885; S.S. Bond sale, Christie's, London, 14 July 1914; Christie's, London, 9 June 1944, lot 85
Acquired 1982
Loaned by Lillian and Robert Fraker

This drawing appears to be a stock figure that Giambattista used a number of times with variations, as he did the preceding drawing. The gesture, the lack of any specific Christian iconographic detail (except perhaps for the rather indeterminate robe, which can be read either as secular or as a monk's tunic), and the *sotto-in-su* perspective view from below, have led to the vague identification of this figure as a magician. However, this pose appears to be almost identical to St. Dominick's in the ceiling representing his glorification in the vast fresco cycle of the church of Santa Maria dei Gesuati in Venice. The principal differences are that in the fresco the saint's arms are a little farther apart, he wears a black mantle, and he is supported by a cluster of angels. A *bozzetto* for the fresco is in the Johnson Collection in the Philadelphia Museum. The frescoes are documented as having been painted between May 1737 and October 1739.

This drawing was reported in the Bond catalogue to be from the Cheney Collection, presumably from the album entitled *Sole figure per soffitti,* from which Bond acquired ten drawings. The album originally contained about 115 drawings, which have been widely dispersed: some are in the Albertina, some at the Fitzwilliam Museum, twenty-four are at Princeton, and ten are at Yale. Like those in the Orloff album (see number 41), these were apparently gathered and mounted in the album about the time of the Tiepolos' departure for Madrid. George Knox has suggested a date of 1740 for the drawings in the album, which is in accord with the dates for the Gesuati ceiling.

Tiepolo undoubtedly conceived of the drawings of the *Sole figure per soffitti* without any particular ceiling in mind[1]. The association of the figure with St. Dominick's is not necessarily inconsistent with this statement, considering the number of variations on the same pose that appear in Giambattista's *oeuvre,* notably the bearded figure of Moses in the *Falling of Manna* canvas of 1738-40 in the parish church of Verolanuova near Brescia[2]. Moses is standing on the ground, as are some of the comparable painted figures, but he also is seen from below; St. Dominick is floating, as are others of the type, satisfying the Tiepolos' fascination with levitation. Both bring to mind the early Christian *orans* pose.

1. Haverkamp Begemann and Logan, 1970, no. 309, p. 169.
2. A similar drawing is in the Victoria and Albert Museum; von Hadeln, 1925, vol I, p. 18, fig. 4.

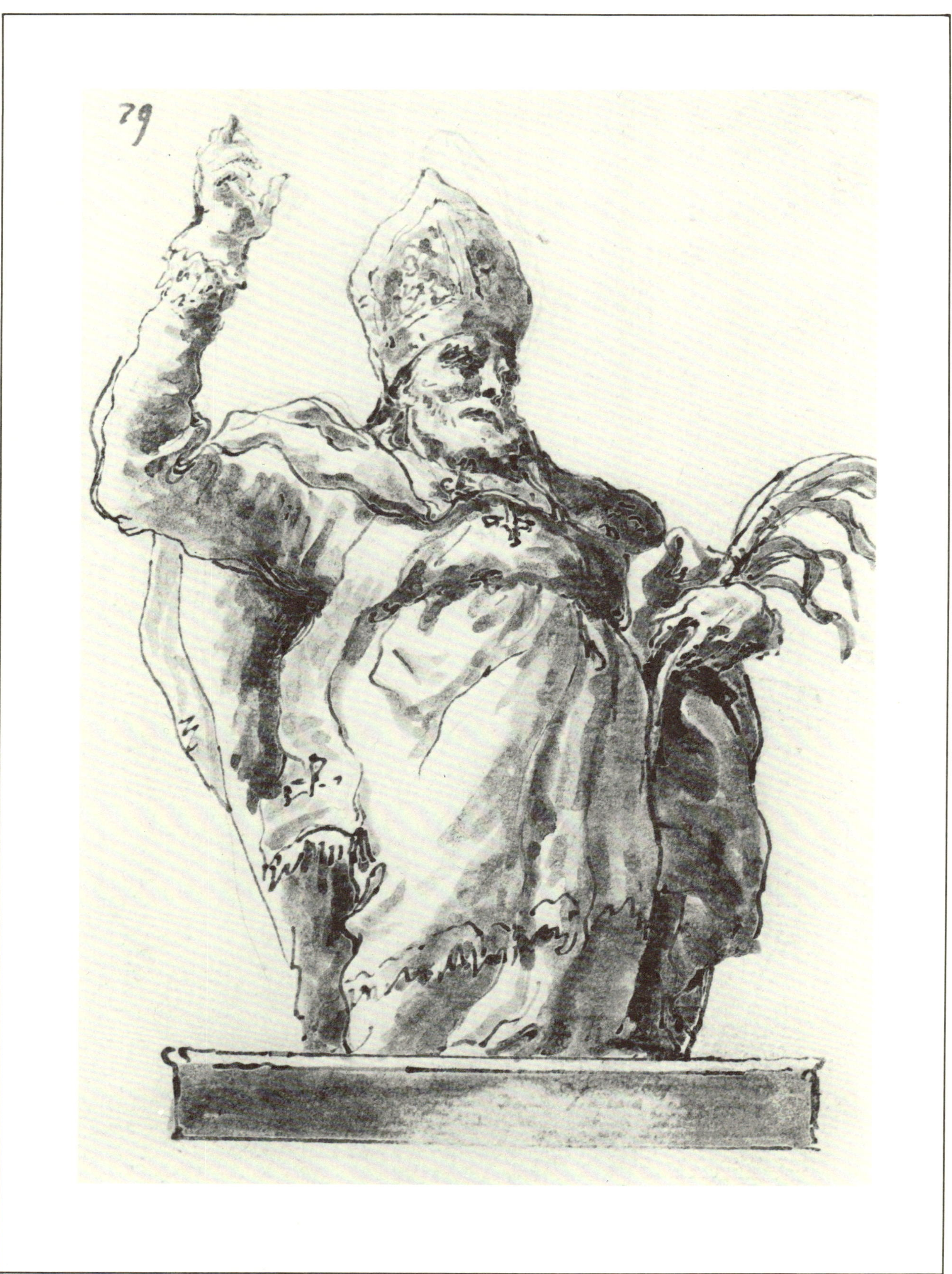

43.

GIAN DOMENICO TIEPOLO
(Venice 1727 - North Italy, Würzburg, Madrid - 1804 Venice)

Saint Ambrose

Pen and grey ink, grey wash, over black chalk; 191 x 140 mm.
Signed *DOM TIEPOLO* in brown ink on podium; rubbed out
Inscribed in pen and ink, upper left corner: 79
Provenance: Beauchamp sale, Christie's, London, 15 June 1965, no. 156, ill.
Acquired 1973
Exhibited: *Disegni Antichi dal Secolo XVI al XVIII,* Galleria del Giudice, Genoa
Literature: Byam Shaw, 1962, p. 42

Gian Domenico studied with his father and was so apt a pupil that Giambattista soon made him his chief assistant. This relation continued throughout the career and travels of the elder Tiepolo until his death in 1770. The close collaboration between father and son has created problems of attribution and dating of their drawings[1]. Both left us legacies of hundreds of drawings. They used the same media — chalk on bluish paper, and pen and wash on light paper — and they both made drawings preparatory to their oil paintings and frescoes. Gian Domenico also sometimes made record drawings of his and his father's paintings (or details from them) after they had been completed[2]. As a student, he copied his father's drawings; later he occasionally made drawings of his father's work — and signed Giambattista's name to them[3]. Both Giambattista and Gian Domenico did drawings independent of other works of art, presumably to work out their own ideas and (we may suspect) for their own enjoyment. To add to this confusion, many of the albums in which their drawings were preserved included works by both father and son (for example, the Orloff album; see number 41).

This drawing, however, not only comes from an album, formerly in the collection of the Earl Beauchamp (see number 44), devoted exclusively to Gian Domenico's drawings; but also it is characteristic of the son's own distinctive manner of drawing. For however close to his father, Gian Domenico also had his own identity and his own artistic career. As long as his father lived, he worked with him; but simultaneously he also worked on his own. In 1747, when he was only twenty and still very much in his father's shadow, he already had been given the major independent commission of painting fourteen *Stations of the Cross* for the Oratorio del Crocefisso in the church of San Polo in Venice. Correspondingly, although throughout his career he could (and did) imitate his father's manner of drawing convincingly, already during the 1750's Gian Domenico was evolving his own style of draughtsmanship.

Characteristically he worked in the medium of this drawing (as in numbers 44 and 45): pen and brown or almost black ink with grey or brown wash. This delineation is also typical: the drawing of contours is quite heavy and so relaxed as to seem meandering; and the wash appears to be laid on casually. But both pen and brush are in fact firmly controlled, so that together they map out the three-dimensional topography of the figure and its drapery very convincingly not to say powerfully. The easy flow of Gian Domenico's line and wash is less tense than his father's, but compensates for this relaxation with suavity.

Gian Domenico's distinctive personal style began to emerge in the early 1750's, at the time of the decoration of the Archepiscopal Palace at Würzburg (1750-53). The patron, the Prince-Bishop Carl Phillipp von Grieffenklau, was so impressed with young Gian Domenico's talent that he allowed him to paint three overdoors in the Kaisersaal, the climax of the great fresco cycle. One of these three overdoors represents *Saint Ambrose and the Emperor Theodosius,* in which the saint, the Bishop of Milan, forbids the excommunicated emperor from entering the church until he has done penance for the massacres he caused in Thessalonia in 390.

St. Ambrose, one of the four Latin Doctors of the Church, had become Bishop of Milan in the year 374. He is usually depicted in a bishop's robe, with a miter and a crozier. The beehive is his usual attribute, but he is sometimes shown, as apparently he is here, holding a scourge with three knots, symbols of the Trinity.

Several drawings related to the Würzburg *St. Ambrose* commission survive: one of the saint's hands, from the Gatteri album in the Museo Correr, Venice; the second, a record drawing of the whole figure, in the Fogg Museum; and a third, of the whole composition, in the Mainfrankisches Museum in Würzburg. Comparison with these three makes it clear that the Steiner sheet is related to them only in subject matter. The Kaisersaal overdoor is the only known painting of St. Ambrose by Gian Domenico. This drawing evidently belongs to a much later phase in his career, even after his father's death.

The drastic foreshortening and the inclusion of the podium have led Byam Shaw[4] to suggest that this drawing might have been preparatory for a fresco decoration in the Tiepolo family villa at Zianigo. In the fresco the figure would have been placed on the dado that runs around the rooms and would have been high on the wall and therefore foreshortened. The *St. Ambrose* is very similar stylistically to another drawing from the Beauchamp album, a *Hercules* (no. 146), which is also foreshortened on a podium and would have been appropriate for the Camerino dei Centauri at the Villa. Possibly the date of the Camerino, 1791, is therefore appropriate for this *Saint Ambrose.* J.I.

1. As, for example, a drawing recently sold in an auction house in London. The auctioneer attributed it to Giambattista; a

leading authority on the Tiepolos to Lorenzo; and the other expert thought it was possibly by Gian Domenico.

2. See George Knox, exhibition catalogue, Tiepolo: A Bicentenary Exhibition 1770-1970, Cambridge (MA), 1970, pp. xx and no. 55.
3. For example, the *Head of Cleopatra* in the Warsaw Museum. Byam Shaw, 1962, no. 2, pl. 2.
4. Byam Shaw, 1962, p. 42.

44.

GIAN DOMENICO TIEPOLO

The Baptism of Christ

Pen and brown ink and wash; 282 x 203 mm.
Signed recto, lower right center, in brown ink: *Dom Tiepolo f*
Inscribed recto, upper left corner, pen and brown ink: *45*
Provenance: Horace Walpole; Beauchamp sale, Christie's 15 June 1965, lot 7, ill.; Lucien Goldschmidt, New York; Mr. and Mrs. Lester Francis Avnet
Acquired 1980
Exhibited: University of Pennsylvania, 1969; Minneapolis Institute of Art
Literature: exhibition catalogue, *Old Master Drawings from the Collection of Mr. and Mrs. Francis Avnet,* Philadelphia, 1969, no. 91 ill.

This drawing, like the one preceding, also comes from the Beauchamp album[1]. The album included 166 drawings, with an inscription on the front cover reading: DISEGNI PENA DA CUARDRETTI GIO: DOMENICO FIGLIO DI GIO: BATA': TIEPOLO CON ALCUNI DISEGNI DEL SUDETTO. The back cover was also inscribed, on the inside: *Questi Disegni Sono no. 160. tutti Originali Costa Cechini 15 da Lire 22 L'uno;* and *Queste Libro de disegni originalli tutti al natural è di Gio. Batta è Figlio Tiepolo Pitori del anno 1770. Cosa Sechini no. 8.*

The calligraphy of the cover inscriptions is the same as that of an inscription on the last page of the Gatteri album of drawings by the Tiepolo father and son, which is in the Museo Correr, Venice. The writer has been identified as Gian Domenico's maternal uncle, the great Venetian *veduta* painter Francesco Guardi (1712-93), who apparently possessed several of these albums. The others were probably put together in 1762 at the time of the Tiepolo's departure for Spain and may have come into Guardi's possession then or in 1770 when Giambattista died. The drawings in the Beauchamp album were gathered together later, perhaps because they are all by the son, who survived his father by a quarter of a century and continued active. The compilation of the album can be placed during the decade beginning in 1783, because it includes a drawing for *The Apotheosis of San Jacopo Giustiniani* which Gian Domenico painted in that year; and the album must have been complete by 1793 when Guardi died.

Presumably Walpole, whose bookplate was on the title page, acquired the album at that time. What happened to the album after his death in 1797 may be indicated by an inscription on the title-page: *162 Dessins de Dominique Tiepolo fils de Jean-Baptiste Tiepolo Venetien;* probably the album passed into the possession of some French collector.

Throughout his life, Gian Domenico did series of drawings, no one exactly like any other, all of them variations as it were on a single theme. Perhaps these later series were prompted by the success of the twenty-two compositions of the *Flight to Egypt* and the fourteen Stations of the Cross he drew in his youth. Among the sacred themes he depicted were *St. Anthony with the Infant Christ, God the Father, Clouds of Angels,* and the *Baptism of Christ.* Of the *Baptism,* he did at least 98 drawings. many of these "series" drawings, like this one, have a number inscribed in the upper left corner. These numbers are sometimes repeated in an album but never in their series. This suggests that at some point, perhaps late in his career, Gian Domenico placed his drawings into some sort of order and numbered them accordingly. The Beauchamp album contained thirteen *Baptism* drawings, similar in size, (approximately 290 x 200 mm.). They are numbered 2, 14, 25, 35, 40, 42, 45, 50, 61, 77, 86, 89, and 98. Thirteen more *Baptism* drawings are in the Graphische Sammlung in Stuttgart, but they are about 20 mm. less in height, and only two have numbers, suggesting that the other numbers were cut off.

This drawing is rendered in the unhesitating, undulating lines characteristic of the entire series, but its composition is simpler than most. Like all but two of the *Baptism* drawings, there is relatively little development of deep space. The figures of Christ and John the Baptist, and to a lesser extent of the angels, are emphasized by a heavier and darker line. The whole drawing seems a quick and fluent virtuoso performance, of the sort that Byam Shaw terms a "doodle"[2]. The figure squeezed in between Christ and John the Baptist even seems like an afterthought.

Both father and son painted the same subject, the father in 1732-33 for the Colleoni Chapel in Bergamo and later in a lost work known through an etching by the son[3]. Gian Domenico's only known painting of the subject, in the Museo Stibbert in Florence[4], can perhaps be described as a greatly expanded version of the etching. But all three of these works, the two paintings and the etching after the lost painting, are horizontal in format. So none seems directly related to the series of drawings of the *Baptism,* which can probably therefore be recognized as the artist's turning the subject over in his mind without any specific project in view. J.I.

1. Most of the information about the album comes from the introduction to Christie's sales catalogue.
2. Byam Shaw, 1962, p. 63.
3. Aldo Rizzi, exhibition catalogue, *Tiepolo disegni e acqueforti,* Udine, 1971, no. 73.
4. Adriano Mariuz, *Giandomenico Tiepolo,* Venice, 1971, pl. 305, who dates it 1775-85.

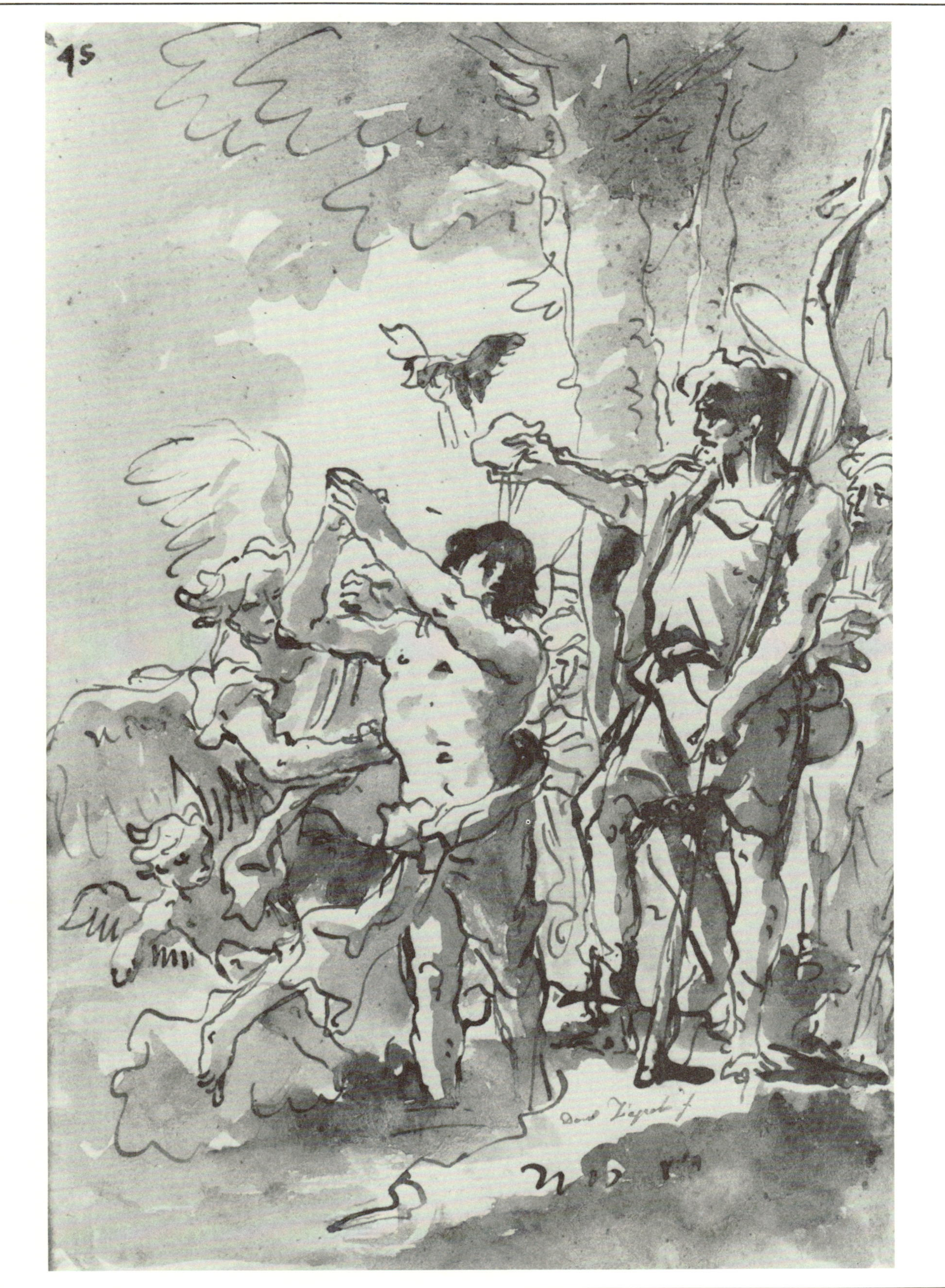
45

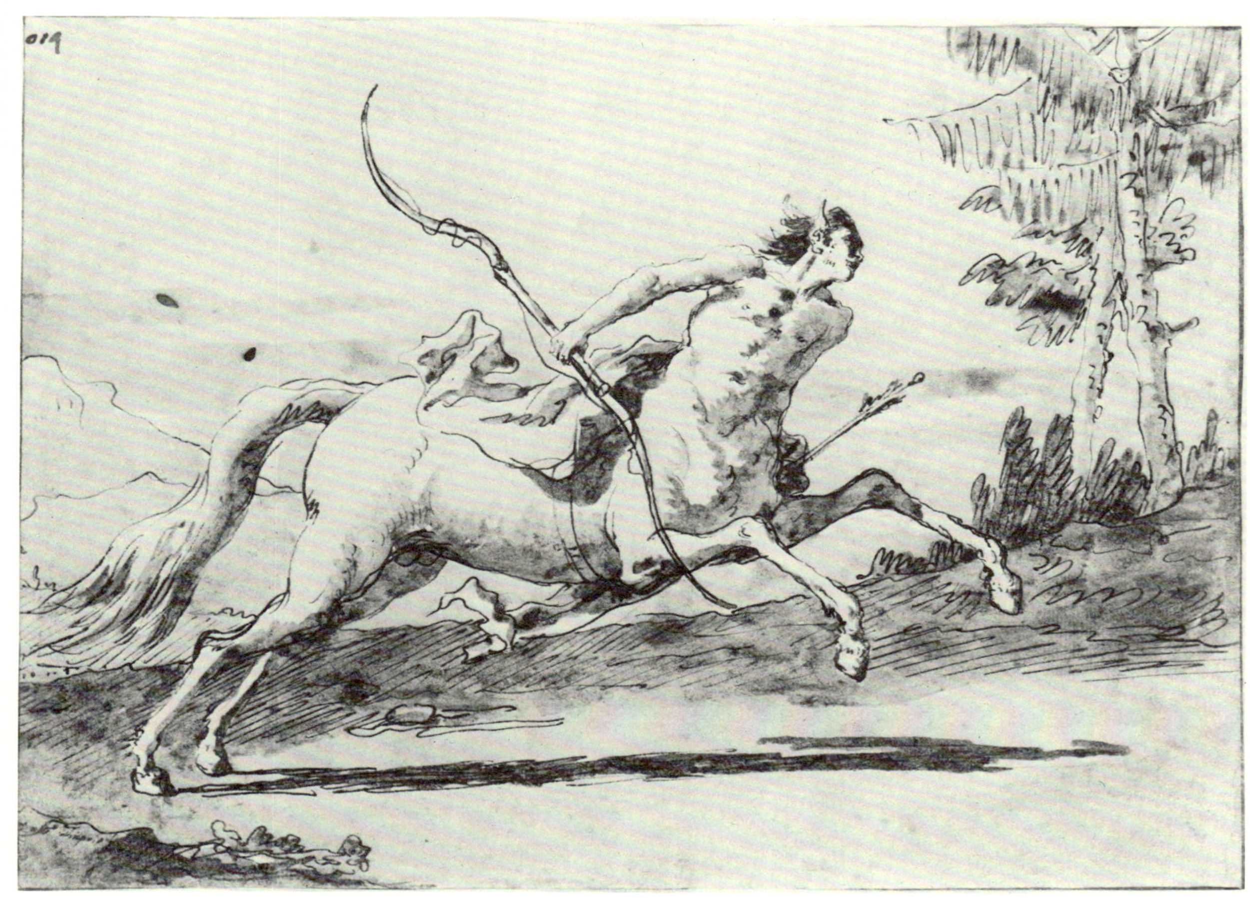

45.

GIAN DOMENICO TIEPOLO

A Galloping Centaur

Pen and brown ink and wash over black chalk; 192 x 275 mm.
Signed *Tiepolo F.* in pen and ink lower left corner
Inscribed, recto upper left corner in pen and ink: *019;* verso, in pen and ink: *345*
Acquired 1978

Centaurs and satyrs, derived from classical mythology, tend to be associated, not only because both types of creatures combine human with animal anatomy but also because of their symbolic meaning, of untamed nature, of the uncivilized natural man. Perhaps inspired by publications of mid-century discoveries at Pompeii and Herculaneum, both Giambattista and Gian Domenico treated centaurs and satyrs in frescoes, oil paintings, and drawings, the father from 1735 at the Palazzo Clerici in Milan, and the son as early as 1754 in the Camera dei Satiri in the Palazzo Panigai at Nervesa in the Veneto. In 1757, collaborating with his father, Gian Domenico painted a medallion with a centaur at the Villa Valmarana near Vicenza, and two years later he decorated the cornices of the Palazzo Correr at San Fosco in Venice with satyrs. Obviously, the Tiepolos enjoyed these motifs for they decorated two rooms in their own villa at Zianigo with frescoed medallions of centaurs and satyrs, which have been transferred to the Ca' Rezzonico in Venice.

Gian Domenico also did a series of drawings of centaurs, which can be divided into five sub series: centaurs alone (like this drawing), centaurs fighting, centaurs enamoured of female fauns, centaurs and satyrs as friends or fighting, and the centaur Nessus with the nymph Dejanira[1]. All these drawings are horizontal in format and in pen and ink with wash. The delineation is crisp but flowing, perhaps with somewhat more variation in the weight and breadth of the sinuous contour lines than in numbers 43 and 44, and with wash applied more in his father's manner, as is particularly noticeable in this centaur's chest and abdomen. The presence of hatching in some of the shadowed areas in the landscape is unusual.

Cailleux[2] lists 100 drawings of centaurs as known to him; this drawing, which he did not list, is the 101st. Apparently there were even more: twenty-two are numbered; the highest number is 144. There was apparently no chronological sequence or systemization according to subject in the numbering; for example, four of the five lone centaurs are numbered 19, 32, 100, and 138. Of the 101 known drawings, only nine can be associated with the frescoes in the Tiepolo villa, and only four of those specifically to the Camerino dei Centauri. This drawing does not relate to any known painting. The time span between the Camerino dei Satiri (1759) and the Camerino dei Centauri at Zianigo (1791) is more than thirty years[3]. Because of the subtle yet unmistakable affinity of this drawing to Giambattista's draughtsmanship, it probably belongs to an earlier rather than a later date in Gian Domenico's *oeuvre.* Cailleux suggests a date as early as 1755 for some of the series.

Neither Gian Domenico nor his father was a *peintre-philosphe,* but can we not suspect that Gian Domenico used the centaur to convey some personal meaning? Perhaps the centaur is his device to comment on the natural man, comparable to his use of Punchinello to depict man's condition in society. Certainly the centaur lives elementally — fighting, coupling, or like this creature, simply exercising his energy and power, unrestrained and unthinking but joyful. J.I. and A.M.

1. Jean Cailleux, "Centaurs, Fauns, Female Fauns and Satyrs among the drawings of Domenico Tiepoli," *Burl,* 1974, advertisement supplement, pp. iii-iv.
2. Cailleux, *op. cit.*, p. iii.
3. Byam Shaw, 1962, p. 42.

46.

TIZIANO VERCELLIO called TITIAN
(Pieve di Cadore ca. 1480/90 - Venice, Padua, Emilia, Rome, Augsburg - 1576 Venice)

A Grove of Trees beside a Pool

Pen and brown ink over charcoal; 238 x 207 mm.
Acquired 1976
Oberhuber, 1977, No. 31, pp. 86-88
Literature: Konrad Oberhuber assisted by Hilliard Goldfarb, exhibition catalogue, *Disegni di Tiziano e della sua cerchia,* Venice, 1976, no. 36 bis., pp. 90-91; Terisio Pignatti, "Disegni di Tiziano: tre mostre a Firenze e a Venezia," *Arte Veneta* XXX, 1976, p. 268; Michelangelo Muraro, "Grafica tizianesca," *Tiziano e il manierismo europeo,* Florence, 1978, p. 137; Konrad Oberhuber, "Tiziano disegnatore di paesaggi," *Tiziano e il manierismo europeo,* Florence, 1978, p. 118; Terisio Pignatti, *Tiziano Disegni,* Florence, 1979, Pl. XXX

Titian went from his birthplace[1] in the Dolomites to Venice about 1500, and soon entered the studio of Giovanni Bellini, whose work had a lasting effect on him. More influential, however, was the poetically conceived painterly manner of Giorgione. Throughout his career Titian remained faithful to Venetian *colorito,* but as he matured this loyalty did not prevent him from absorbing Michelangelo's heroic figural style as well. His fame was hardly less universal than Michelangelo's. Patronized by many European heads of state and leaders, he excelled in both sacred and secular compositions, and also produced a great number of imposing and perceptive portraits. His travels took him from Rome to Augsburg; in Venice he produced many important works for his numerous local clientele and many others for shipment to Spain.

This landscape was first associated[2] with Titian because of its similarity to the *Edge of a Wood* drawing at the Metropolitan Museum (inv. no. 08.227.38), although the two drawings were recognized as differing in many respects. Most obviously, the Metropolitan drawing focuses on the gnarled and almost withering tree trunks and branches, arranged with the foliage as an almost opaque screen. The Steiner drawing, on the other hand, represents a whole grove of trees beside a tranquil pool; the foliage is rich, but its dense mass is penetrated by dark, mysterious, atmospheric depths, particularly toward the center. A few very faint figures in charcoal on the lower right do not upset the tranquility of the landscape or its concentration on the organic nature of the plants.

Since the celebration of the Titian anniversary year of 1976, the authenticity of the Metropolitan Museum sheet, and in turn of every other landscape drawing attributed to Titian, has been under scrutiny and subject to question. In that year and in subsequent publications, Dr. Peter Dreyer suggested that the *Edge of a Wood* was not a true drawing at all but rather a forgery, a print cleverly redrawn by one of Titian's contemporaries[3]; Byam Shaw has proposed Domenico Campagnola as the culprit[4]. A decade earlier Felice Stampfle and Jacob Bean had already observed that the lines were blurred, and had suggested that two counterproofs had been made from the sheet[5]. Dreyer showed that the drawing itself was composed of two offsets, pulled from a four-block woodcut *Abraham and Isaac* designed by Titian about 1514-15, and then carefully fused together at the joints with drawn lines in pen and ink. Recent microscopic observation seems to confirm Dreyer's analysis; faint traces of printer's ink appear under (or mixed with) practically all the lines drawn in brown water-soluble ink[6].

Dreyer's analysis applies not only to the Metropolitan *Edge of a Wood;* three other landscape drawings attributed to Titian appear to be forgeries made by the same method[7]. However, Dreyer's thesis has not been universally accepted. For example, David Rosand has cautioned against overturning the attribution of the Metropolitan drawing too readily, it having "stood as a central monument in the accepted canon of Titian's drawings . . . [since the Tietzes' book in 1944][8]."

Throughout this discussion, the Steiner drawing has continued to stand up undoubted. It is free of *pentimenti* or other evidence that might relate it to a print. The use of the pen is spontaneous, continuous and very clear throughout. And the conception and draughtmanship are consistent with two drawings at Chatsworth, which also seem unquestionably Titian's. Particularly notable is the identical treatment of the water surface and reflections by means of vertical and horizontal lines in both the Steiner drawing and the Chatsworth *Landscape with a Horse.* Dreyer has not questioned the Steiner drawing, and its attribution to Titian has been confirmed by Oberhuber and others[9]. The importance of the sheet therefore can hardly be understated, both because it is so beautiful a drawing and because it gives such insight into the mind of the greatest Venetian master. R.S.

1. The most recent, and reasonable, study of the vexing question of Titian's birthdate is Charles Hope's in his *Titian,* London, 1980, pp. 11-12.
2. Oberhuber, 1976, no. 36 *bis.*
3. Peter Dreyer, "Tizianfalschungen des sechzehnten Jahrhunderts, Korrecturen zur Definition des Delineatio bei Tizian und Anmerkungen zur Datierung seiner Holzschnitte," *Pantheon,* XXXVIII, Oct.-Dec. 1979, pp. 365-75; Peter Dreyer, "Sulle silografie di Tiziano," *Tiziano e Venezia, Convegno Internazionale di Studi Venezia 1976,* Vicenza, 1980, pp. 503-11.
4. James Byam Shaw, "Titian's Drawings: a Summing Up," *Apollo* CXII, Dec. 1980, pp. 387-89.
5. Felice Stampfle and Jacob Bean, exhibition catalogue, *The Sixteenth Century in Italy. Drawings from New York Collections,* New York, 1965, p. 45, no. 58.
6. From a conversation in July 1985 with Merritt Safford, Conservator of Paper at the Metropolitan Museum, 1970-83.
7. Dreyer, *op. cit.,* 1979.
8. David Rosand, "Titian Drawings: a Crisis in Connoisseurship?" *MD* XIX, no. 3, 1981, pp. 300-08.
9. In conversation and correspondence with the Steiners.

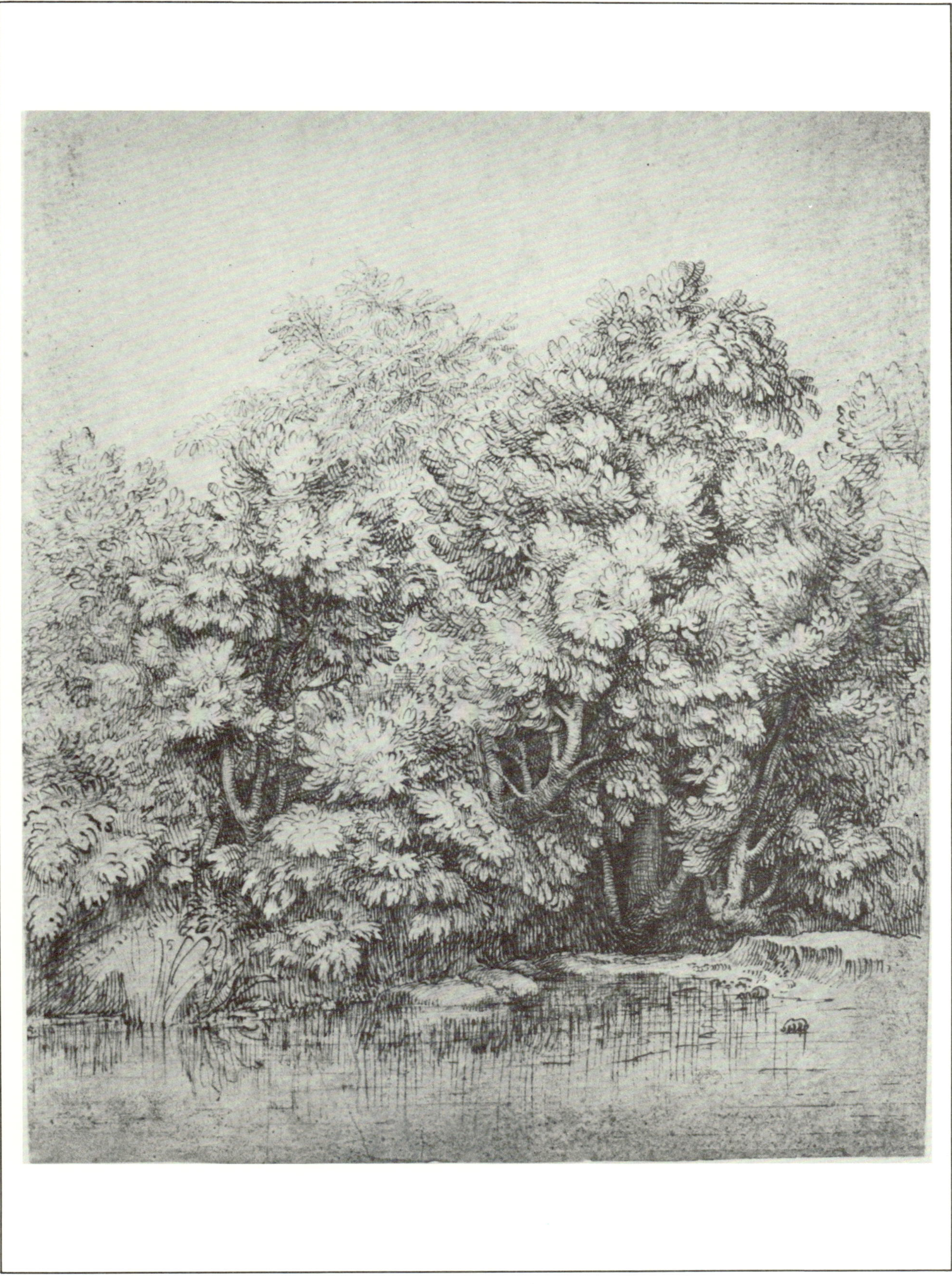

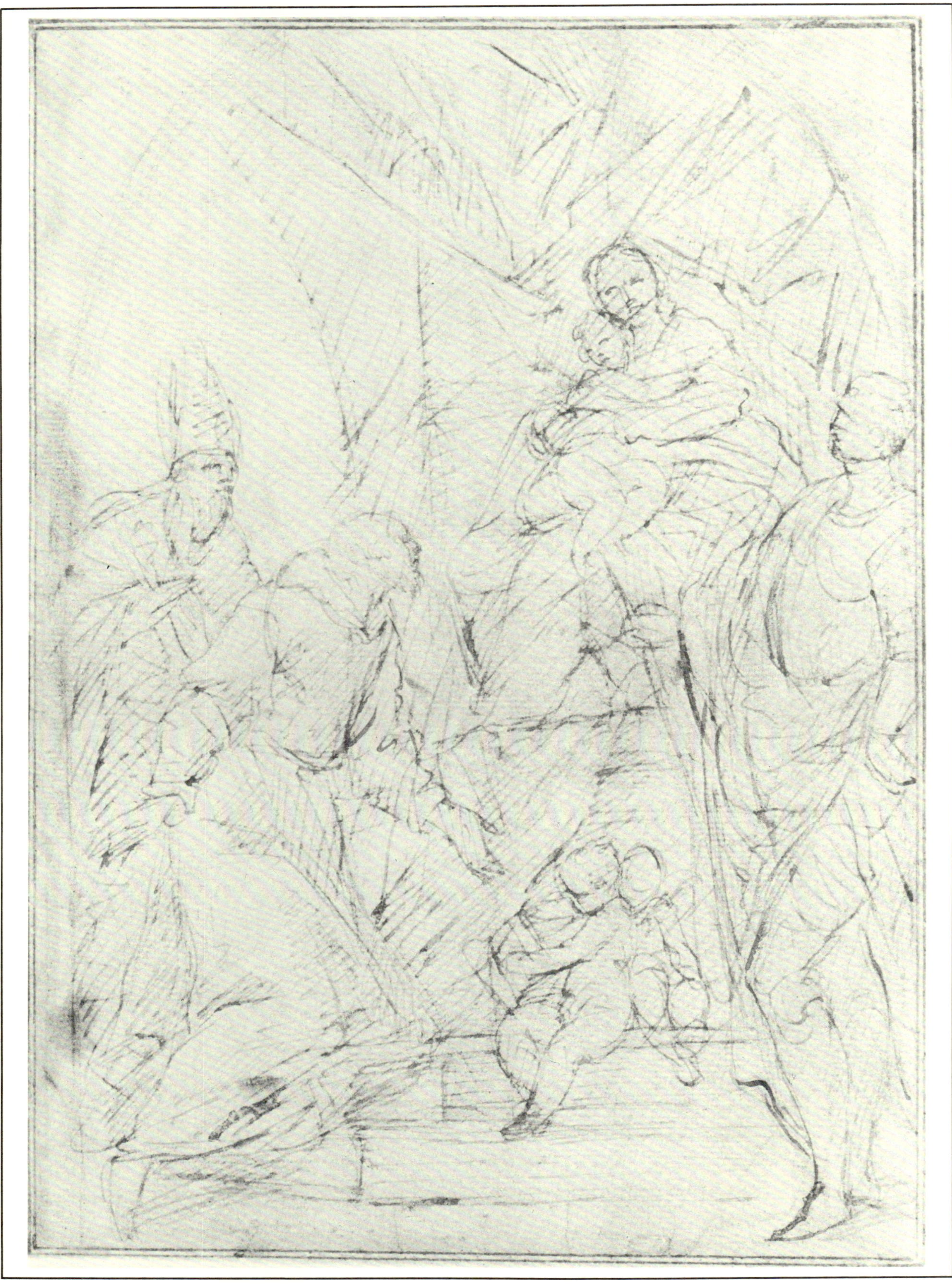

47.

ALLESSANDRO VAROTARI called IL PADOVANINO
(Padua 14 April 1588 - Rome, Bergamo - 1648 Venice)

The Virgin and Child Adored by a Bishop and Two Saints

Brown ink and black chalk; 279 x 201 mm.; discolored along left edge; small creases (tears?) along lower edge; bordered with two parallel lines
Acquired 1974

Padovanino was born into a family of artists — his father a Paduan painter, his mother the daughter of a painter — and his artistic career after 1614 was centered in Venice. He apparently left the city only twice after that; once for Rome between the years of 1616 and 1618, and once for Bergamo in 1631. Padovanino's style was greatly influenced by Titian's early works, and his copies of Titian's *Bacchanal* still exist[1]. His rejection of contemporary Venetian painting for the Titianesque tradition gave Padovanino a certain measure of renown, and he became the teacher of Girolamo Forabosco, Pietro Liberi, Giulio Carpione, and Pietro della Vecchia.

Terence Mullaly has assigned the Steiner drawing to Padovanino's *oeuvre,* and linked it to an altarpiece now in the Chiesa dell' Assunta in the southern Adriatic town of Polignano a Mare[2]. Both Alessandro Ballarin[3] and Harold Wethey[4] have accepted this attribution; Wethey confirmed the sketch as a preliminary study for the painting in Polignano a Mare. The altarpiece depicts Mary and the Christ Child enthroned between two saints, identified by Semenzato as Anthony and John the Baptist[5], they have also been described as Saints Vitus and Blaise[6]. The figure on the left must be St. Blaise because of his attributes of a miter and a carding comb. He might also be the saint represented by the left background figure in the Steiner drawing. However, because this figure lacks the instruments of Blaise's martyrdom, he can be identified with certainty only as a bishop. The figure on the right of the altarpiece could be one of the healing saints, Vitus, although he is generally associated with a white cock and a pot of boiling pitch[7] and only occasionally with a dog[8]. Another saint who is evoked for medical assistance is St. Roch, who also has a dog as his attribute along with the cross, a cape, and the signs of a pilgrim. However, although similar to the young man in the altarpiece in stance and overgarment, the youth in the drawing does not seem to be either St. Roch or St. Vitus. Both of them were civilians, and he is clearly a soldier, with armor and a hatchet. The third figure in the drawing, dressed in a Franciscan habit, does not appear in the altarpiece.

The drawing's combination of a bishop, a Franciscan friar, and a soldier-saint appears, perhaps significantly, in Guido Reni's Plague altarpiece of 1631-32, and in his *Pietà with the Patron-Saints of Bologna,* both in the Pinacoteca Nazionale, Bologna. The saints in Guido's paintings are Petronius who was an early bishop and the patron saint of Bologna; Francis or Anthony of Padua; and Proculus or Florian.

The Steiner drawing appears not to be preparatory specifically for the Polignano altarpiece. Instead, it embodies a compositional formula which Varotari employed in several altarpieces. The similar *Sacra Conversazione* in the Parish Church at Pontevigodarzere near Padua[9] is composed according to this formula; its date of 1630 is probably appropriate for this drawing as well. C.R.R.

1. Rodolfo Pallucchini, *La Pittura Veneziana del Seicento,* Milan, 1981, vol. I, p. 101.
2. According to the Steiners' documentation.
3. In a conversation with the Steiners.
4. In a letter 4 April 1977.
5. Camillo Semenzato, "Un Padovanino ed un Celesti in Puglia," *Arte Veneta,* XI, 1957, pp. 213-215, fig. 224.
6. Exhibition catalogue, *Mostra dell'arte in Puglia dal tardo Antico al Rococo,* Rome, 1964, p. 99, fig. 106.
7. Réau, 1955-59, vol. III, pp. 622-23.
8. Donald Attwater, *The Penguin Dictionary of Saints,* London, 1982, p. 338.
9. Pallucchini, *op. cit.,* I, p. 103

48.

GIORGIO VASARI
(Arezzo 1511 - Rome, Naples, Venice, Florence - 1574 Florence)

Incredulity of St. Thomas

Pen and brown ink over black chalk, brown wash, squared in black chalk; 215 x 176 mm.
Inscribed in pen and ink in the cartouches above and below the image: *Beati qui no viderut/et crediderunt*
Acquired 1976
Charles R. Saumarez-Smith in Oberhuber, 1977, no. 35, p. 95
Literature: Anna Maria Petrioli Tofani, exhibition catalogue, *Giorgio Vasari,* Arezzo, 1981, p. 300, no. 59, fig. 125

Vasari's greatest gift to posterity was his *Lives of the Excellent Italian Architects, Painters and Sculptors,* published in two editions, in 1550 and 1568. The second edition, including not only biographies of earlier artists but also first-hand reports on his contemporaries, became the basic source for the history of Italian art. Its colorful style, rich with anecdotes (many of which have turned out to be true), has also informed and delighted generations of amateurs. Vasari was also an architect, most memorably of the Uffizi in Florence, and a very prolific and influential painter. Although his greatest activity as a painter was in Arezzo, Rome, and Florence, he traveled throughout Italy from Naples to Venice, doing research for the *Lives* and carrying out his commissions. These commissions were so numerous and their scale often so large as to require the assistance of many students and collaborators. His style was based on Florentine drawing rather than Venetian color. Derived from his Florentine predecessors, most notably Rosso and Pontormo, and from his idol Michelangelo, Vasari's style was indispensable to the evolution of Mannerist painting.

Although this drawing is a complete composition and squared off for transfer, it is not related to any known painting. Saumarez-Smith links the subject to the altarpiece of the *Incredulity of St. Thomas* in the Guidacci Chapel, the fourth on the left in the church of Santa Croce in Florence. Stylistically, she associates it with a painting in the Staatliche Museum in Berlin which represents *Saints Peter and John the Apostle Blessing* and is similar in composition. The Berlin painting was in fact a processional banner that Vasari painted in 1557 for the Compagnia dello Spirito Santo in Arezzo. The Steiner drawing may well have been intended to serve a similar purpose, particularly because its dainty border is too thin and too light for a tapestry and inappropriate for a painting[1]. Although the Santa Croce altarpiece has also been dated 1557, it was apparently not painted until 1569[2]. The correspondence between the Steiner drawing and the *St. Roch Healing Victims of the Plague* altarpiece in the Museo Civico of Arezzo, with similarities in the poses and physiognomies of St. Thomas and St. Roch, suggests that the two works are contemporary. The Arezzo picture was also a banner, painted by Vasari for the Compagnia di San Rocco in Arezzo in 1568. Therefore the later date, at the end of the 1560's rather than the 1550's, seems likely for the Steiner drawing.

It is somewhat less icy and sculptural than most of Vasari's finished drawings; the figures are a little less three-dimensional and lighter, and the delineation of contours is less firm. The composition is relatively flat, a graceful tangle of sinuous lines, and the only effect of depth is created less by modeling and atmospheric wash than by displacement of space by the crowd of disciples behind Christ and St. Thomas. The figures are very gentle and solicitous of each other, as if their manners were as exquisite as Vasari's draughtsmanship.

The inscription, from St. John's Gospel xx: 29: "Blessed are they that have not seen, and yet have believed," is Christ's response to St. Thomas, who was so sceptical of His Resurrection that he said "Except I shall thrust my hand into His side, I will not believe." This exhortation to faith was often repeated in paintings at the time of religious controversies of the sixteenth century.

There is a copy of this drawing in the Uffizi (inv. No. 233S) in red chalk with touches of black. It has been attributed by Petrioli Tofani[3] to Giovanbattista Naldini, who was working with Vasari during 1567[4].

1. Petrioli Tofani, *op. cit.*
2. Walter and Elisabeth Paatz, *Die Kirchen von Florenz,* Frankfurt am Main, 1955, vol. I, p. 580; Petrioli Tofani, *op. cit.*
3. Petrioli Tofani, *op. cit.*, who however dates the Steiner drawing much earlier.
4. Paola Barocchi, *Vasari pittore,* Milan, 1964, p. 57.

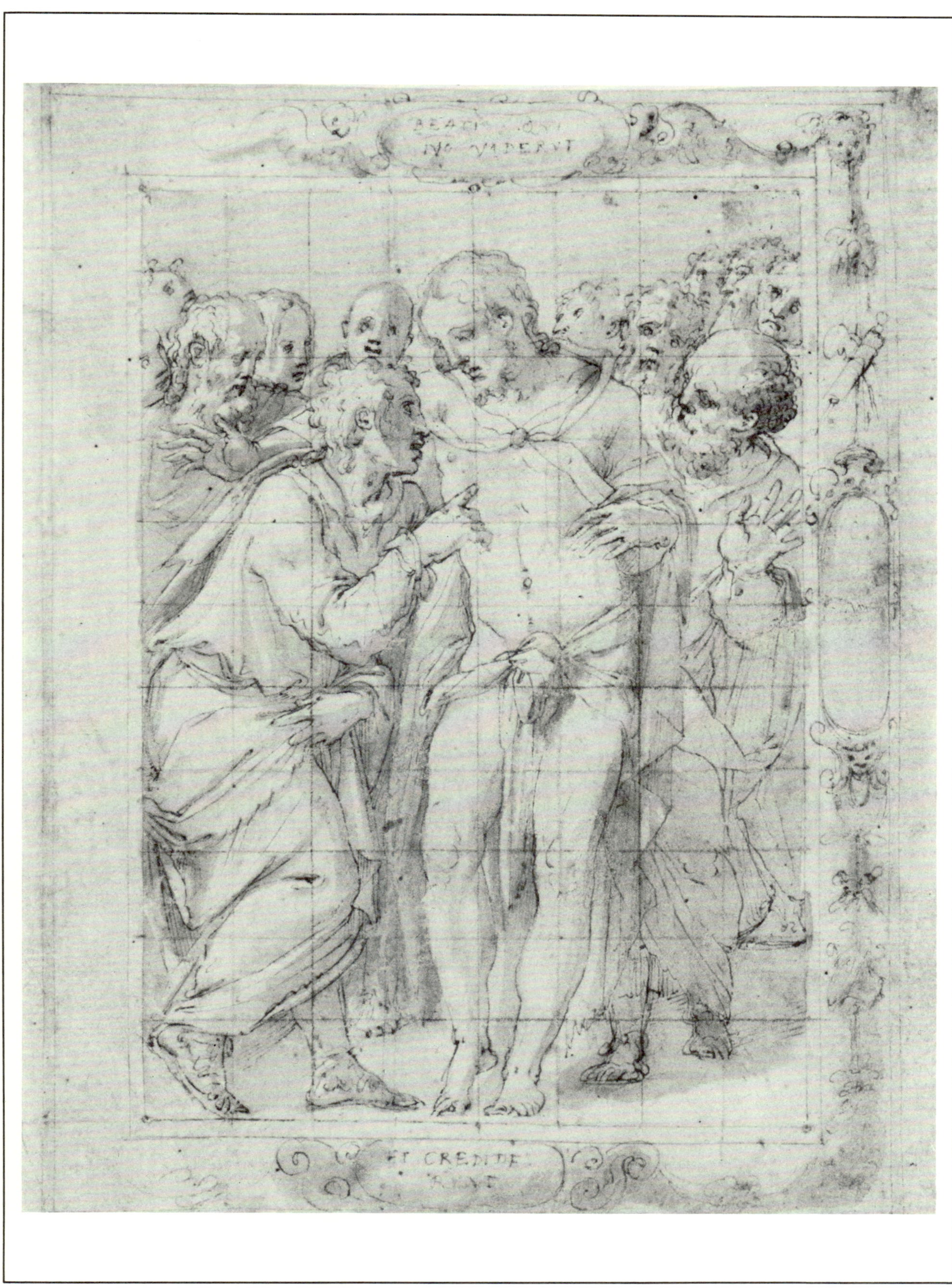

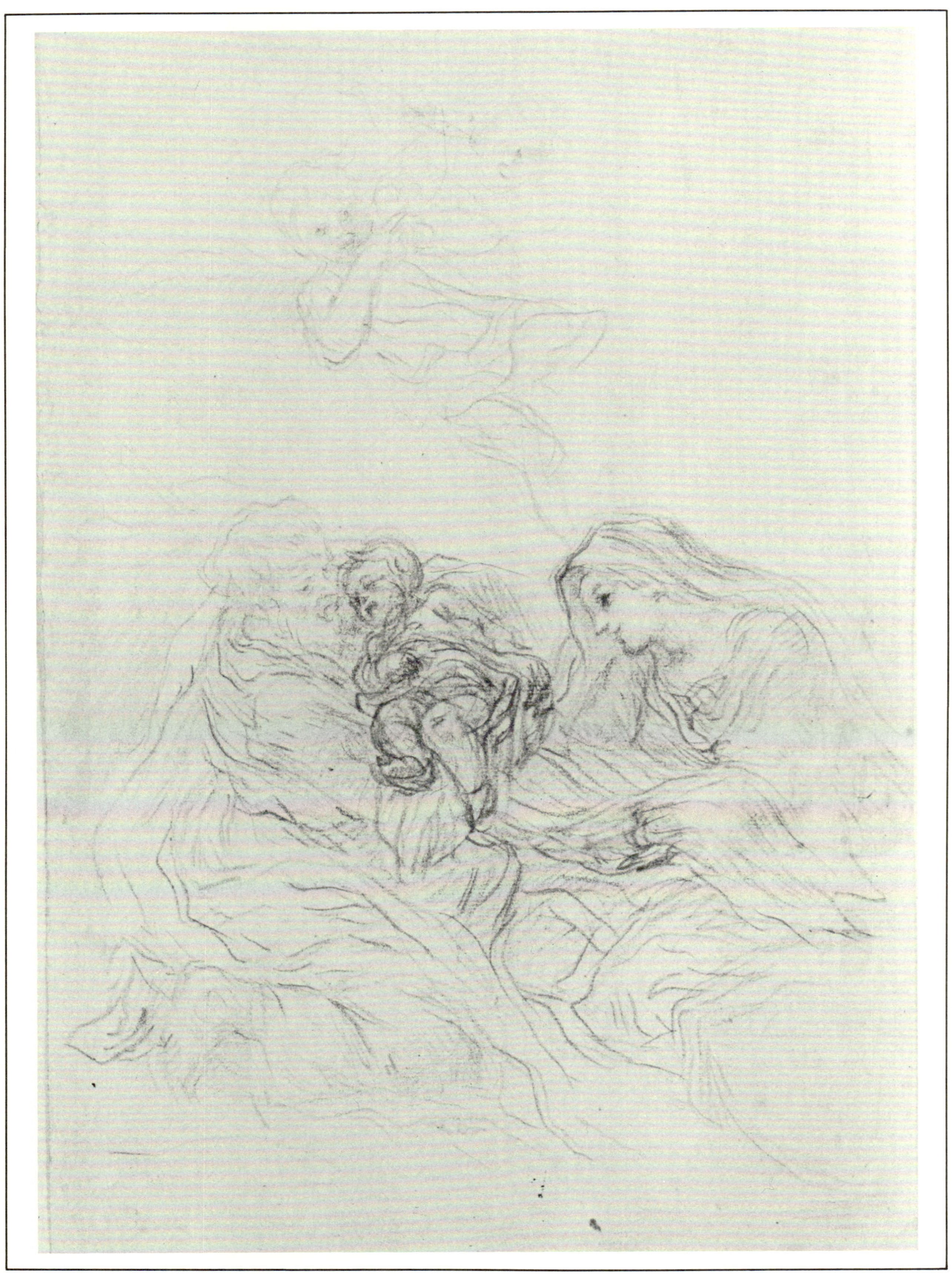

49.

BALDESSARE FRANCESCHINI called IL VOLTERRANO (Volterra 1611 - Florence 1689)

Holy Family

Black chalk; 298 x 205 mm.
Acquired 1980

Son of a sculptor, Gaspare, his first teacher, Volterrano in 1628 began training in Florence, first with Matteo Rosselli and soon afterwards with Giovanni da San Giovanni. By 1635, he had become Giovanni's assistant for decorations in the Palazzo Pitti, and in the following year, he was working independently, painting frescoes in the Medici Villa Petraia. In 1640 and 1652, Don Lorenzo de' Medici and another important patron, Filippo Niccolini, sent Volterrano on educational journeys to Bologna, Parma, Ferrara and Venice, and to Rome; he responded particularly to the work of Correggio and of Pietro da Cortona (number 15). Volterrano's main activity, decorating palaces and churches, established him as one of the most distinguished fresco painters in Italy during the second half of the seventeenth century.

He was an indefatigable draughtsman. His early work in red chalk, during the 1630's, was careful, each detail studied with exact attention, but with a liveliness owing to Giovanni da San Giovanni. As time passed, Volterrano began to envision complete compositions in studies marked by a whirlwind energy of line. By the early 1640's he had developed his characteristic process of drawing and redrawing forms until they became a mass of superimposed lines, as much fields of energy as palpable figures.

Volterrano assimilated aspects of the styles of other artists but his own style remained personal. Thus he did not fall completely under the spell of Pietro da Cortona during the 1640's, although similarities can be found between the two in the vivacity of their delineation, their gentle modeling, pretty body and physiognomic types, and the consistently cheerful mood of their art. One specific effect Cortona had was to induce Volterrano to switch from red to black chalk, often heightened with white, as his primary drawing medium. Cortona's influence must have reinforced the appeal that Correggio's soft atmospheric effects and tender sentiment evidently had for Volterrano.

Volterrano made many paintings and drawings of the Holy Family and of the Virgin Mary, but none corresponds to this drawing, nor do any of the lost works described by the Florentine historian of art, Filippo Baldinucci. The arrangement of the figures is strikingly similar, however, to the figure group in a pen and ink *Mystical Marriage of St. Catherine,* in the National Gallery, Scotland (inv. no. 1613). Because of the medium, the drapery in the *St. Catherine* is quite different; and the composition is more finished, with a towered city in the background. Otherwise, the two drawings are variations in subject on the same compositional theme.

Volterrano was prone to work his ideas out by drawing the same theme, figure, or group again and again, each time with subtle changes. Perhaps this drawing was preparatory for some painting that was small and intimate and never recorded. But it is likely to be a product of Volterrano's practice of thinking with chalk. N.M.

50.

BALDESSARE FRANCESCHINI called IL VOLTERRANO

Study for the Coronation of the Virgin with the Heavenly Hosts

Black chalk, gone over (in the two lower ranges) in pen and black ink; 390 x 261 mm.; horizontal fold at springing of arch with traces of red chalk along the fold
Acquired 1980

Volterrano had a thirty-year association with the Santissima Annunziata, the richest and most fashionable church in Florence of his time. It was a 13th century construction but rebuilt during the 15th century. During the 17th century, the entire interior was remodeled and redecorated as a result of the enthusiasm for sumptuous Baroque beautification that had swept over Italy. Volterrano designed the lavish nave ceiling, executed in 1664-69, centered on his giant painting of the *Assumption of the Virgin,* and in 1666 he was commissioned the frescoes of the tribune cupola. According to Baldinucci, he did not begin preparations for the tribune frescoes until a decade later, and the actual frescoing of the cupola took place between 1681 and 1683. The subject is the *Coronation of the Virgin,* and this drawing is probably a preliminary study. Its sketchiness suggests that it is only a tentative formulation of the image, presumably one of many first thoughts preliminary in the very prolonged process of conceiving and carrying out the frescoes.

There is a hint of a hilly landscape at the bottom of the sheet beneath the clouds, as if Volterrano wanted to establish the vision in relation to earth. The vision is of the heavenly host, arranged in three levels, each one of which is further divided into three choirs, each labeled. Whether these labels were written by Volterrano himself or not is debatable. Not all of them correspond correctly with the figures and their symbols: for example, that for principalities has been exchanged with that of archangels. The bottom level consists of the intercessors between God and man, and the executors of His will: principalities, the dispensers of the fate of nations, with crowns on the left; in the center, archangels, the warriors of heaven, with the scales of justice; and on the right the guardians of the innocent and the righteous, angels, holding little figures representing souls. This angelic host is illuminated by the choirs on the level above, of governors of the stars and elements: of Virtues on the left, with lilies symbolic of Christ's Passion; Dominions in the center representing the power of God and carrying orbs as emblems of authority; and on the right, armoured Powers, God's warriors victorious over evil. Their power is bestowed on them by the uppermost choirs: seraphim holding burning candles; cherubim with books; and thrones who should wear robes and carry staffs of authority. They are the representatives, respectively, of Divine Love, Wisdom, and Justice; they receive their glory directly from God.

The crowning of glory, faintly drawn above the fold, represents the Coronation of the Virgin, with the Madonna on the left (the heraldic right) of Christ who is seated in the center, following I Kings ii: 19: "And the King rose to meet her, and bowed himself unto her, and sat down on his throne, and caused a seat to be set for the King's mother; and she sat at his right hand." The biblical reference is from the Old Testament, and the king is Solomon; but traditionally the episode was conceived as describing also the Coronation of the Virgin. The Madonna is crowned as the Queen of Heaven; Christ, as the Saviour of the World, holds the globe and scepter and wears the crown of thorns and a nimbus. The figure to the right of Christ is probably God the Father in which case the Dove of the Holy Ghost would have appeared in front of them, to complete the Trinity. But this figure and the others may stand in for the patron saints of Florence.

Perhaps Volterrano's conception of this vision was inspired more by Venetian sources where heavenly hosts seem to have been a popular subject for paintings like Tintoretto's great canvas in the Doge's Palace, than by Correggio's frescoes in the domes of the church of San Giovanni Evangelista and the Cathedral in Parma. The cathedral dome, representing the *Assumption of the Virgin,* was surely relevant to the SS. Annunziata commission, and may well have inspired Volterrano as it did so many other seventeenth century painters. N.M.

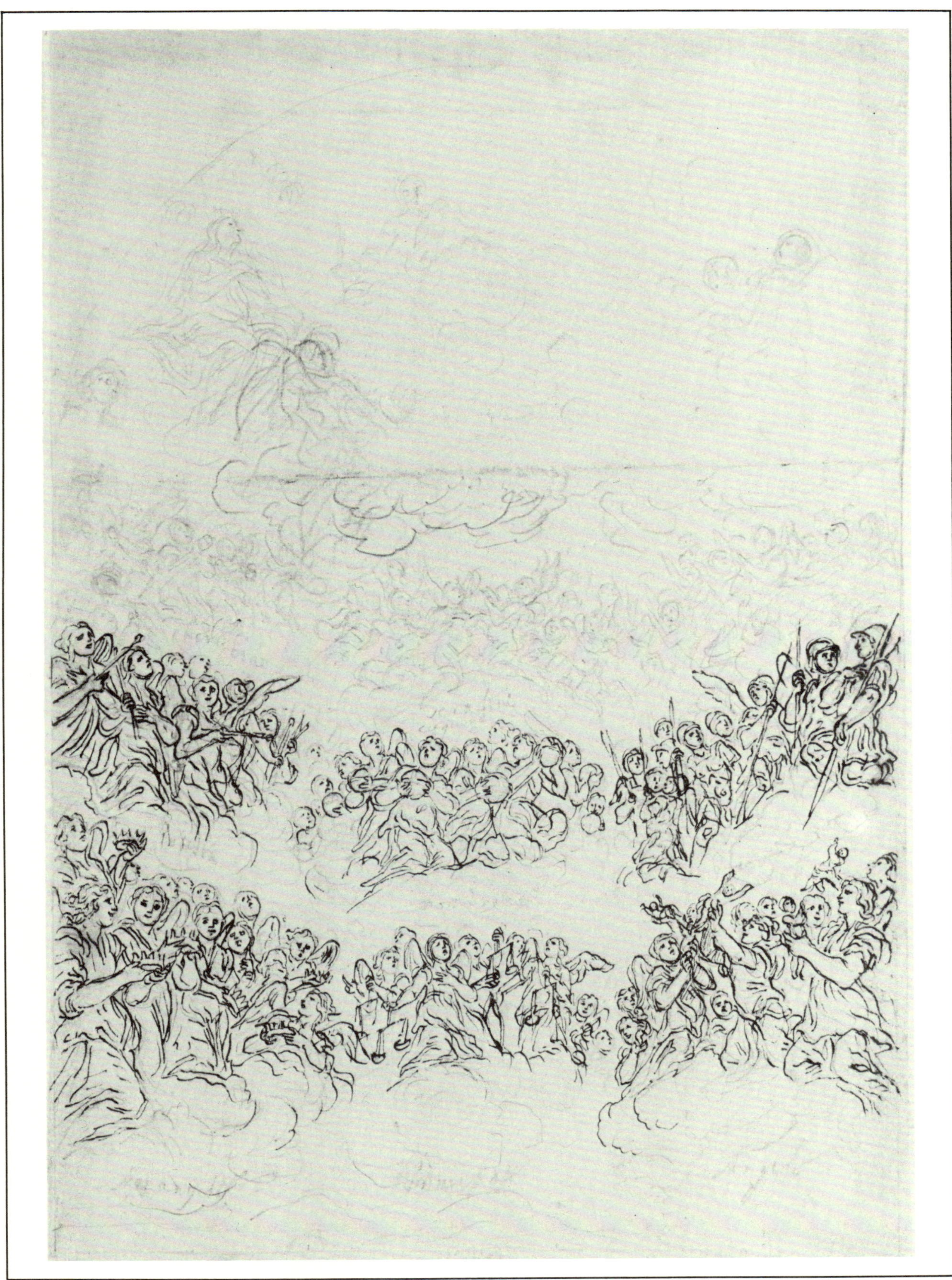

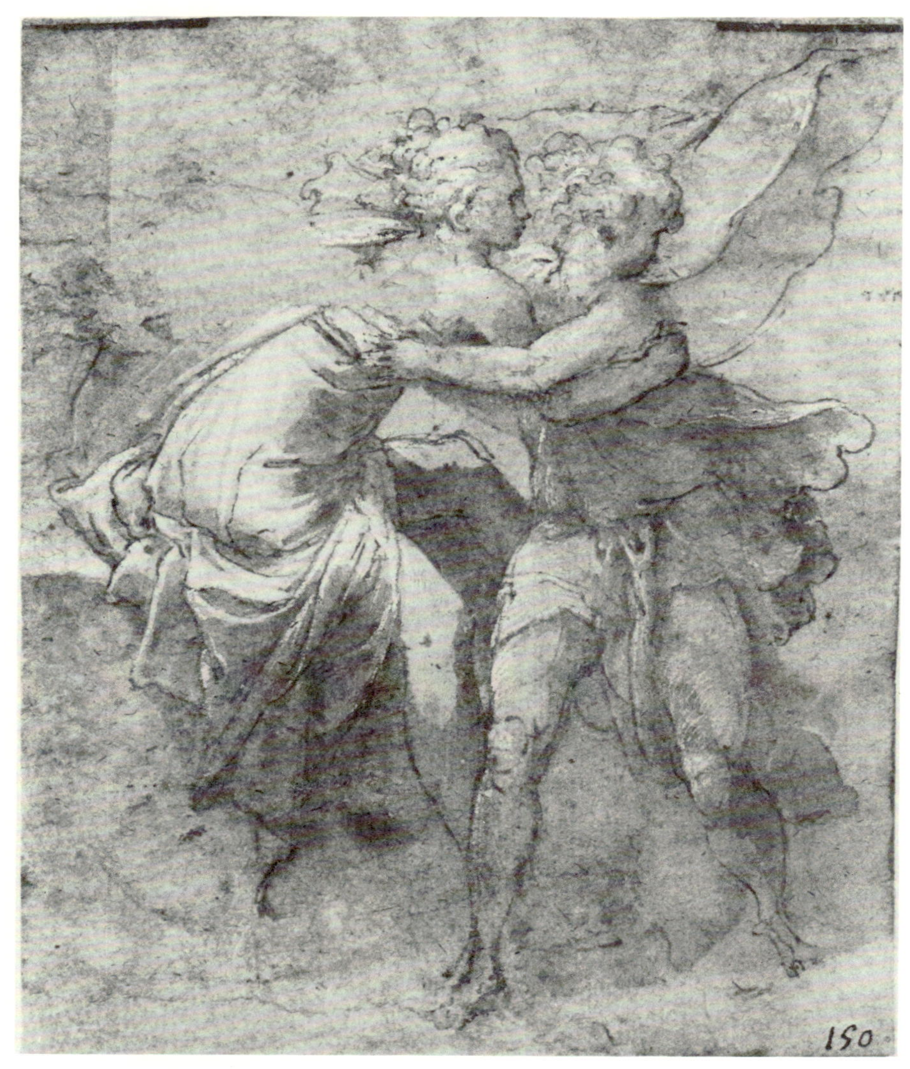

51.

TADDEO ZUCCARO
(Sant'Angelo in Vado 1529 - Rome, Urbino, Caprarola - 1566 Rome)

Joseph and Potiphar's Wife

Pen and brown ink and wash, heightened with white on prepared blue paper; 132 x 111mm.; extensive repairs Originally mounted, in a cartouche in pen and brown ink (now in the Fogg Museum, Cambridge, Mass.) attributed to Francesco Morandi called il Poppi, with the arms of Pope Pius V Ghislieri (reigned 1566-72)
Inscribed recto, lower right corner in pen and ink: *150* On the original mount, in pen and ink, just below the lower left corner of the drawing: *Parmesan;* in a cartouche below the drawing: a bear with stars on his back (i.e. the Great Bear of the Zodiac) under the motto *Sine occasu felix;* lower left corner: *Vasari;* bottom center: *Federico Zucchero*
Provenance: Jan Pietersz, Zoomer (L.1511); Sir Thomas Lawrence (L. 2445); John Viscount Hampden sale, 1827; Mr. and Mrs. Hugh Squire, London
Acquired 1979
Exhibited: London, Messrs. Woodburns' Gallery, 1836, no. 10 (as Parmigianino); Royal Academy, London, 1960, no. 477 (as Parmigianino), p. 190
Literature: Gere, 1969, no. 120, pp. 50-51, pl. 34

Taddeo arrived in Rome in 1543 at the age of fourteen and was apprenticed to Daniele de'Porri da Parma, who introduced him to the work of Correggio and Parmigianino. Taddeo was also profoundly influenced by the works of Raphael and his followers, and studied the facade frescoes that were then so popular and still visible in Rome, particularly those by Polidoro da Caravaggio. No work by Taddeo has been documented before 1553, but he was very active and prolific throughout his life — as brief as Raphael's — and his work was so much in demand that he used many assistants, including his younger brother, Federico, who carried on his style.

The attribution to Taddeo is owing to Gere who owns another, previous, study of the composition. The two drawings were made, perhaps about 1550, for an etching (B.XVIII, 11.1) by Bartolomeo Passarotti, who was living with Taddeo at the time. Gere suggests that the relation betwen the two artists may have been like that of Michelangelo and Sebastiano del Piombo, with the greater master providing drawings for his friend. Passarotti's print is reversed, and differs from this drawing in the setting and a few details, so it may in fact have been from an even more detailed preparatory drawing. A second print, in the same direction as this drawing, may therefore have been made derived from Passarotti's etching. Gere notes that this second print is of the type "made in about 1636 by Lucas Vorsterman and Hendrick van der Borcht after drawings in the Arundel Collection." Included in that collection were many drawings by Parmigianino, which were copied in reproductive prints by Vorsterman and van der Borcht, and which may therefore explain the earlier unfounded attribution of this drawing to Parmigianino.

The confusion of authorship is understandable, considering the elegant brio of this drawing and the psychological effectiveness of the action. The bodies in a drawing of *The Shepherds in Adoration* at the Christ Church, Oxford (cat. no. 1420) of ca. 1553-56 are bulkier, but similar in the subtle modeling of lights and shadows and rhythmic delineation of contours.

The subject, a favorite in the seventeenth century, presumably for its erotic suggestiveness, is from Genesis xxxix: 6-20, where Joseph resists seduction by the wife of his master the Pharaoh; she then accuses him of having made advances to her, with the result that he is thrown into jail. R.S.

52.

WORKSHOP OF TADDEO ZUCCARO

Battle on the Gulf of Morbihan

Brown wash and white, over black chalk, on tan paper; 308 x 436 mm. Vertical double fold down the center; pin-prick holes in the upper right and left edges
Watermark: Briquet no. 3395
Provenance: Baron von Kuhlen (?)
Acquired 1973
Oberhuber and Leslie Koenig, 1977, no. 38, pp. 100-103

Guidobaldo II della Rovere, Duke of Urbino (1538-74) employed not only Battista Franco (see number 20) to make designs for his majolica factories, but many other artists. When the Duke invited Taddeo Zuccaro to Urbino in 1560 to paint a portrait of his daughter, Virginia, on the occasion of her marriage, he also commissioned of Taddeo the design of a service set to be executed in the celebrated majolica factory of the Fontana family. The set, illustrating the life of Julius Caesar, was completed in December 1562 and sent as a gift to Philip II of Spain. Most of the pieces of this "Spanish service" have been lost, but Gere has identified a number of them and reconstructed others with the help of majolica copies and drawings by the brothers Zuccaro and their assistants[1].

The scene in this drawing was correctly identified by Oberhuber as from Caesar's *Conquest of Gaul.* It represents the Roman defeat of the powerful fleet of the Veneti (the tribes of Brittany) in the Gulf of Morbihan in 56 B.C. The specific passage reads:

> Forthwith, gliding out from the Auray, appeared the hostile squadron, numbering two hundred and twenty sail. They stood out of the water like floating castles. The Roman [ships] were over-topped by the lofty poops, and could not throw their javelins with effect. But the Roman engineers had prepared an ingenious contrivance. Two or more galleys rowed up close to one of the enemies' ships. Then, with sharp hooks fixed to the ends of long poles, the Romans caught hold of the halyards, and pulled them taut: the rowers plied their oars with might and main; and the sudden strain snapped the ropes. Down fell the yards: the troops clambered on to the helpless hulk; and the struggle was soon ended by the short sword. When several ships had been thus captured, the rest prepared to escape. The swift little galleys ran in and out among them, and captured them one after another[2].

This drawing is carefully composed to show a variety of these specific battle actions precisely, almost as a paraphrase of Caesar's text. In the center foreground, small but elaborately designed rounded boats containing five or six men each, are assaulting the "hulk" in the center of the composition that towers above the small boats with their new hooked inventions. To the right, the troops are clambering onto the enemy ship, and the short sword used to end the struggle is seen in the hand of the figure at the front (right) of the foreground boat. To the left a large boat tries to escape and has two small boats assailing it. The battle continues to the horizon, with the upsetting of a small boat in the middle ground.

The original majolica for which this design was created is not known, but there is an elaborate wine cooler in the Wallace Collection in London with a faithful copy of the design on its inner surface.[3] It might have been the centerpiece of the set, befitting its depiction of the "battle that decided the war." The signature F.F.F. is interpreted by Rackham as "Flaminio Fontana faciebat," and is dated 1574, eight years after Taddeo's death.

Gere and Pouncey discuss the composition in an almost identical drawing at the British Museum, a pendant of a drawing at Windsor[4]. They do not believe that this composition (and therefore by implication the Steiner drawing) was made for the Spanish service, but describe it as a pastiche made in Taddeo's shop, possibly after his death in 1566. Nonetheless, they acknowledge Taddeo's "ultimate responsibility for the composition" because of its correspondence in a number of details to Taddeo's fresco of the *Battle of Tunis* on the end wall of the Sala Regia in the Vatican.

Gere also observes that the technique "seems to have been peculiar to Taddeo"[5] and Oberhuber points out that this wash technique corresponds to Taddeo's "only known finished drawing" for the Spanish service. Oberhuber also observes the nicety with which the round forms of the ships fit into the round format, and considers the Steiner sheet as "a working drawing produced by one of the major assistants in Taddeo's shop...without quite the crispness expected from Taddeo's own hand." R.S.

1. John A. Gere, "Taddeo Zuccaro as a Designer for Maiolica," *Burl* CV, no. 724, 1963, pp. 306-15.
2. T. Rice Holmes, *Caesar's Conquest of Gaul,* London, 1903, pp. 65-66.
3. William King, "Two Pottery Specimens from the Museum Leverianum," *Apollo* XLII, 1945, pp. 298-300 citing Rackham.
4. Gere and Pouncey, 1982, no. 341, p. 213, pl. 334.
5. Gere, 1969, pp. 192-3.

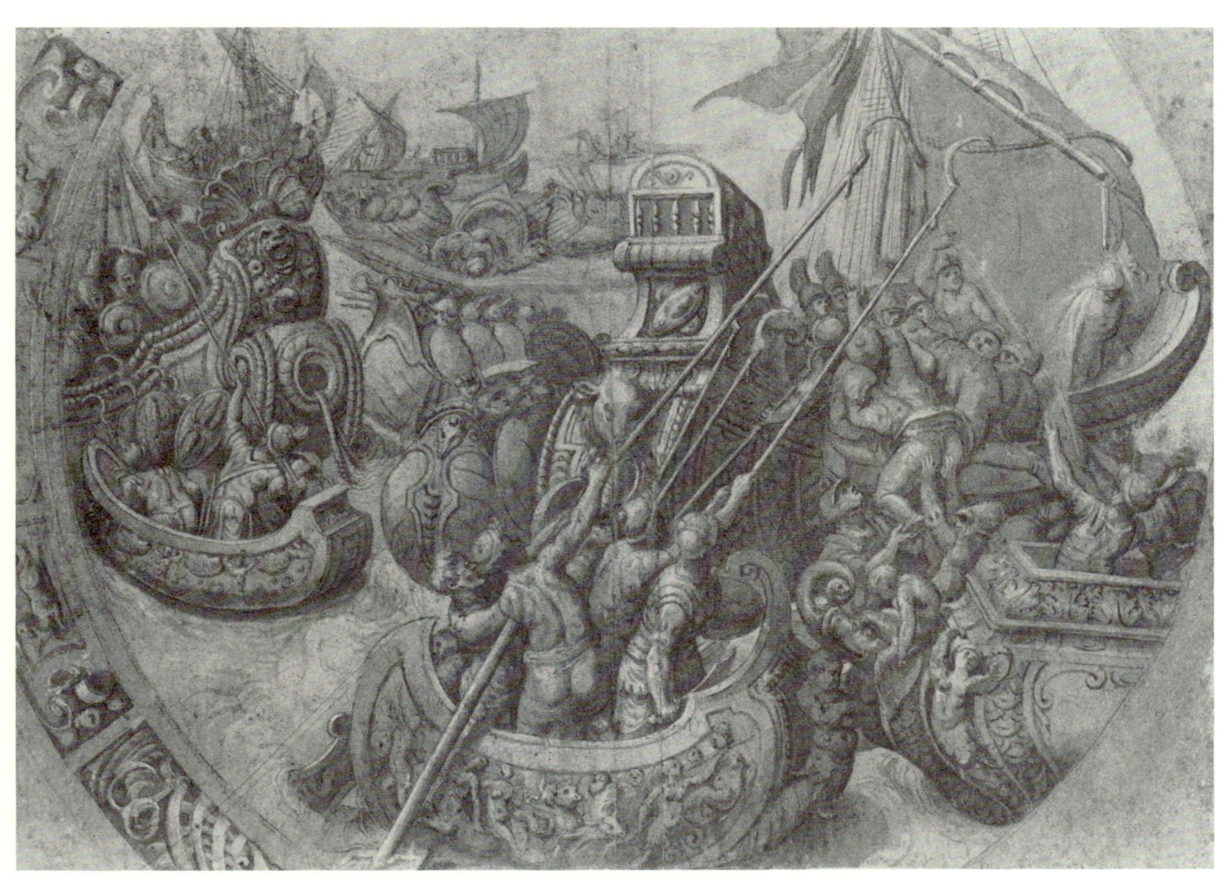

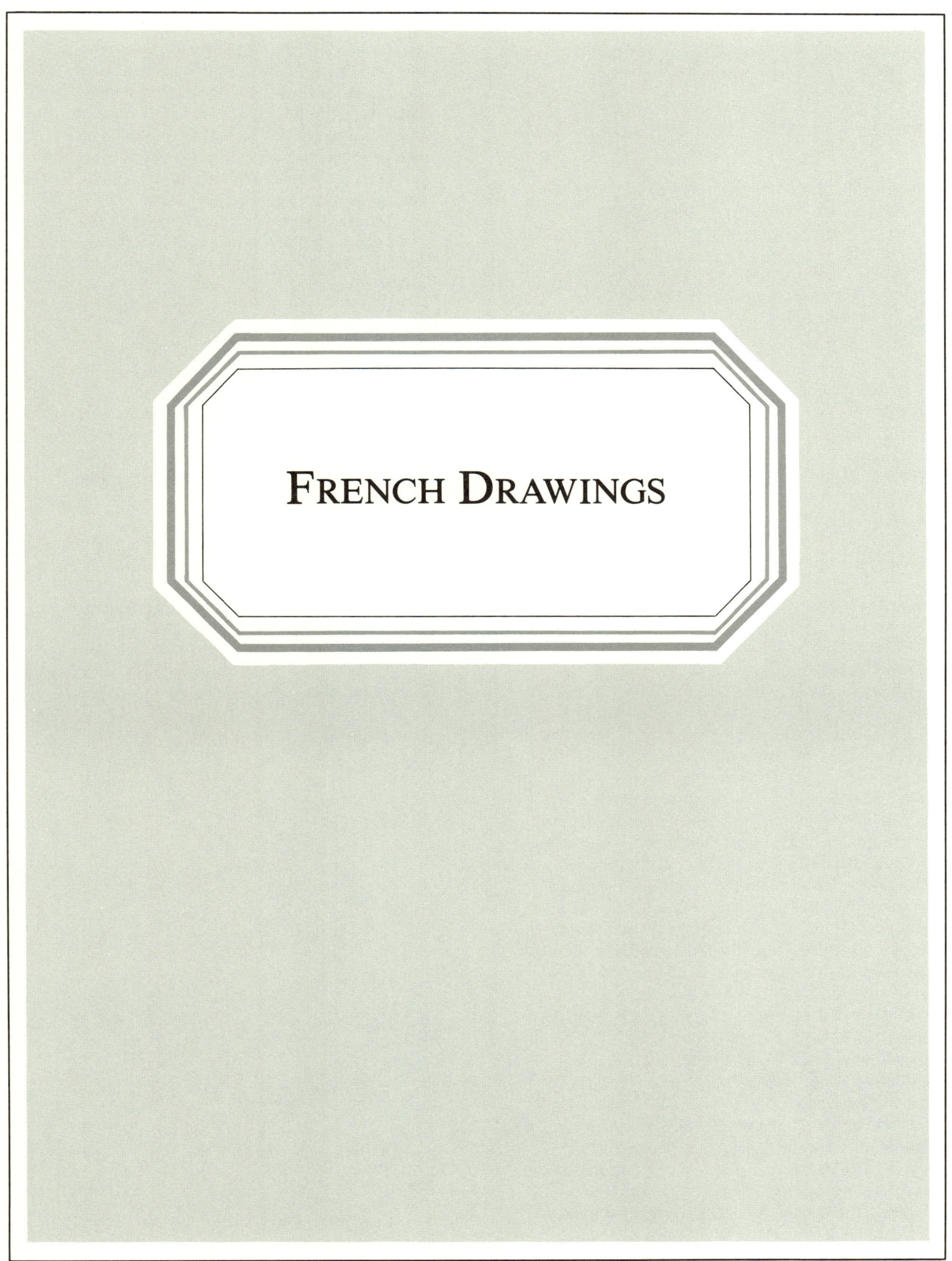

French Drawings

53.

ANONYMOUS FRENCH ARTIST, OF LORRAINE (?)
ca. 1620's

Pilgrims with Guardian Angel (recto): *An Angel, Sheep, Hands* (verso)

Black chalk, black charcoal, with grey wash and white (recto); black chalk (verso); 283 x 425 mm.
Provenance: Hubert de Marignane (L.1343a)
Acquired 1981
Loaned by the Harvard University Art Museums, (Fogg Art Museum), Cambridge, Mass.

This drawing, like the Anonymous Tuscan *Baptism* (number 2), presents an unsolved problem of attribution. The dealer from whom it was purchased believed it to be by one of the Le Nain brothers, an attribution that does not seem tenable, especially since no drawing by any one of them has ever been identified. The hand does seem to be French and of the first half of the seventeenth century, but without the Mannerism that lingered on in much of France after it had been outdated in most Italian art centers.

Perhaps because the draughtsman presented the old peasant man and the boy without any condescension, Oberhuber has suggested some possible relation to the great master of Lorraine, Georges de La Tour (1593-1652)[1]. But no drawing by La Tour has ever been identified either. Yet, quite apart from the artist's straightforward and sympathetic acceptance of the humble subjects, the man does resemble some of La Tour's models, specifically the old man (Job?) in the little painting in the Palace of the Legion of Honor in San Francisco, and the *Penitent St. Jerome* in the Museum of Grenoble. However it requires too great a feat of the imagination to transform these figures into those in La Tour's paintings; their anatomy and action flow too articulately to be La Tour's, while the calligraphy seems too suave. Nonetheless, the possibility of locating the artist in or around Lorraine is worth considering, if for no better reason than these hints of some affinity to La Tour. The artist in question clearly was sophisticated. If his origin and perhaps his main activity may have been in the French provinces, his training must have been more urbane, even specifically Roman; his aesthetics certainly were.

Oberhuber has also suggested Claude Deruet (1588-1660) as a possible author. Deruet's biography certainly would seem to qualify him: born in Nancy, after training with the wonderful late Mannerist painter-printmaker of Lorraine, Jacques Bellange (fl. 1602-17), he went to Rome where he stayed during the second decade of the century, having enough success to be commissioned an altarpiece in a chapel of the Palazzo Borghese about 1616 and to be awarded a knighthood in 1619 by the Borghese pope, Paul V. Deruet's paintings in Rome were enough admired to cause Jacques Callot and his teacher Philippe Thomassin to make some reproductive prints of them. But when Deruet went home to Lorraine in 1619/20, he seems almost immediately to have put his promising Roman style behind him, and replaced it with a stiff and artificial *retardataire* Mannerism. This maladroit mature style earned him great success in court, church and civic circles, and he became very rich and was ennobled.

However, Deruet's manner of painting in Lorraine is contradictory of this drawing, which has a suave style that would also have been out of place among French artists in Rome during the 1610's when Deruet was there. It would have been more at home during the next decade, with such paintings as Claude Mellan's *Transport of Saint Peter Nolasco,* which was also engraved by Thomassin in 1627. We might even suspect that the artist was familiar with Vouet's Roman work.

The figure on the right, lacking wash, is not so finished as the other two. But it has sprouted wings and is therefore unquestionably an angel. Otherwise the drawing might reasonably be classified simply as subjectless genre, particularly because of the sheep on the verso. The presence of the angel, however, apparently in the same space as the other two figures, requires explanation. Possibly the subject is the *Return from Egypt,* which was not all that rare in the seventeenth century even though it often is not recognized as such in the twentieth; but where then is the Virgin? More likely it represents a guardian angel, either Tobias' (see number 71) or simply the companion of pilgrims, which the old man and the boy, with their staffs, appear to be.

1. According to the Steiners' records.

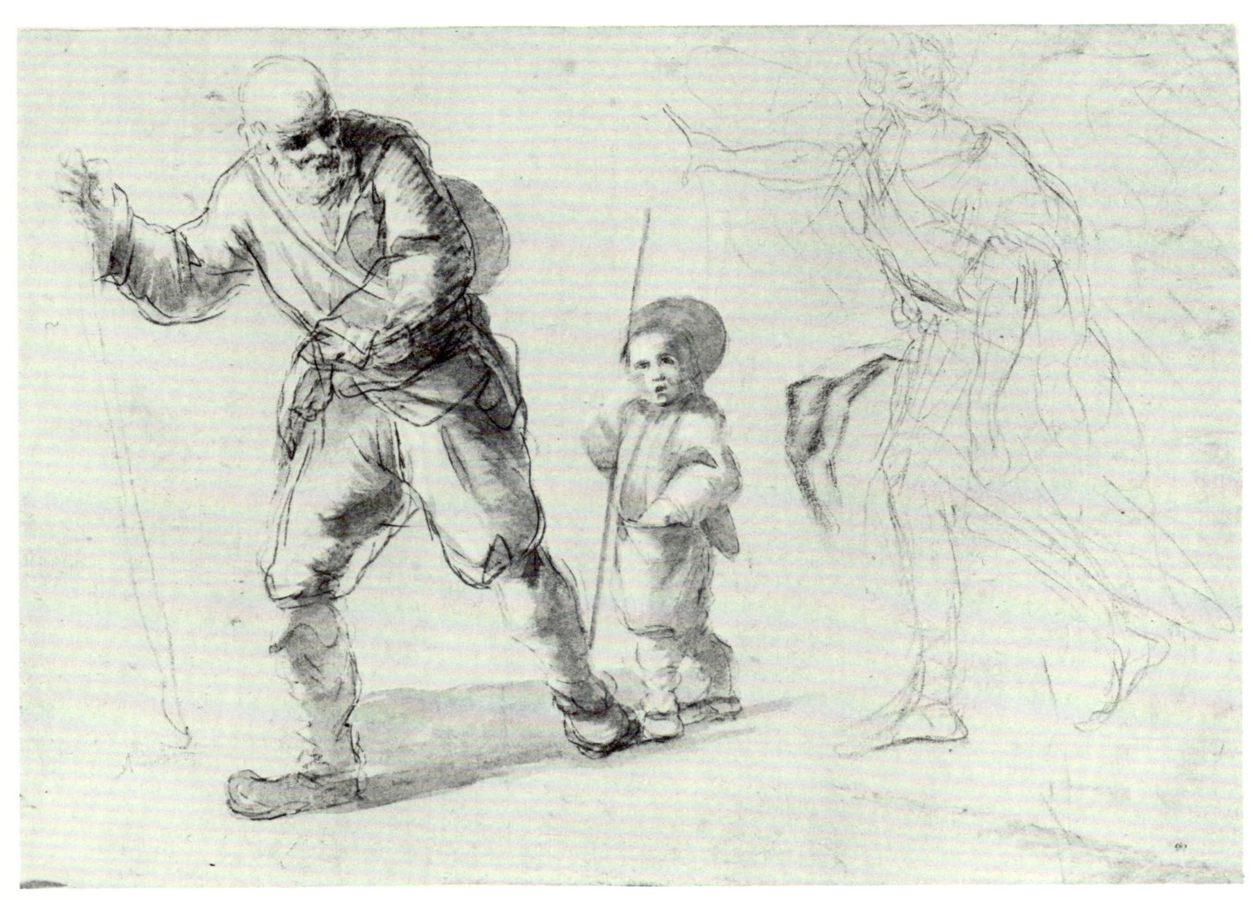

(recto)

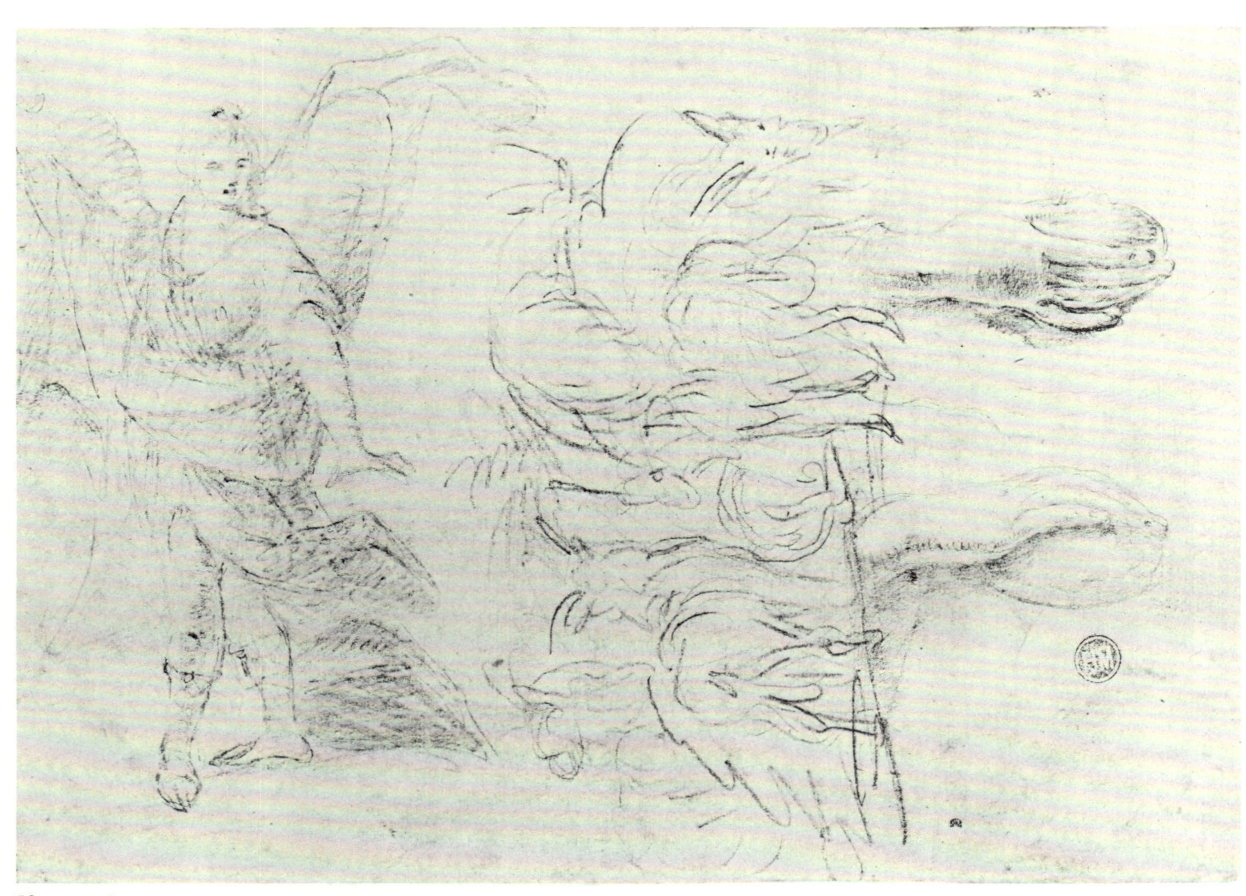

53. (verso)

54.

FRANCOIS BOITARD
(Paris [?] ca. 1670 - England, Holland - The Hague after 1717)

Birth of Venus (recto): *Bacchanale* (verso)

Pen and red and grey ink with grey wash; 152 x 195 mm.
Provenance: Roderer Collection
Acquired 1974

Little is known about Boitard's life, except that he described himself as a student of the eccentric and short-lived Raymond Lafage (1656-84), and that the French art historian Mariette complained that he was debauched and made pornographic engravings, including a famous suite wrongly attributed to Marcantonio Raimondi[1]. Like Lafage's, Boitard's *oeuvre*, so far as it is known, consists entirely of drawings and prints. He provided the designs for some if not all the illustrations of the 1709 edition of Shakespeare[2], and two years later he published a book, *Oeuvres de divers parties, figures et groupes Conservant L'Art Du Dessein* in Amsterdam, illustrated by rather clumsy drawings. In the same year his drawings, probably engraved by Elisha Kirkall, illustrated an edition of the works of the Elizabethan playwrights Francis Beaumont and John Fletcher[3]. A few drawings by him are in public collections (at Yale, Princeton, the Louvre, and the Kunstbibliothek in Berlin) and in recent years they have appeared from time to time in London auctions.

Pierre Rosenberg has described[4] Boitard's "nervous uneven line... as utilized with an almost total lack of concern for construction or unified composition, and by an impressive though gratuitous virtuosity." These words might be appropriate to this drawing, which is characteristic of Boitard's oeuvre, but they seem too harsh. The recto of the sheet, which is a kind of loose version of Agostino Carracci's *Galatea* fresco in his brother Annibale's Galleria Farnese, invites comparison to Boitard's *Flood* at Princeton (inv. no. 48.818)[5]. The effect of spontaneous improvisation is like that for which Lafage was famous, and together with the verve of the calligraphy and the spirit, conception, and actual composition, it remarkably anticipates Matisse's *Joie de Vivre.*

1. Pierre Jean Mariette, *Abecedario,* Paris, 1851-53 (1966 reprint), vol. I, p. 145.
2. H.A. Hammelmann, "Shakespear's First Illustrators," *Apollo* LXXXVIII, August, 1968, pp. 2-3.
3. *ibid.*
4. Pierre Rosenberg, exhibition catalogue, *French Master Drawings of the 17th and 18th Centuries in North American Collections,* translated by Catherine Johnston, London, 1972, p. 135.
5. *ibid.*

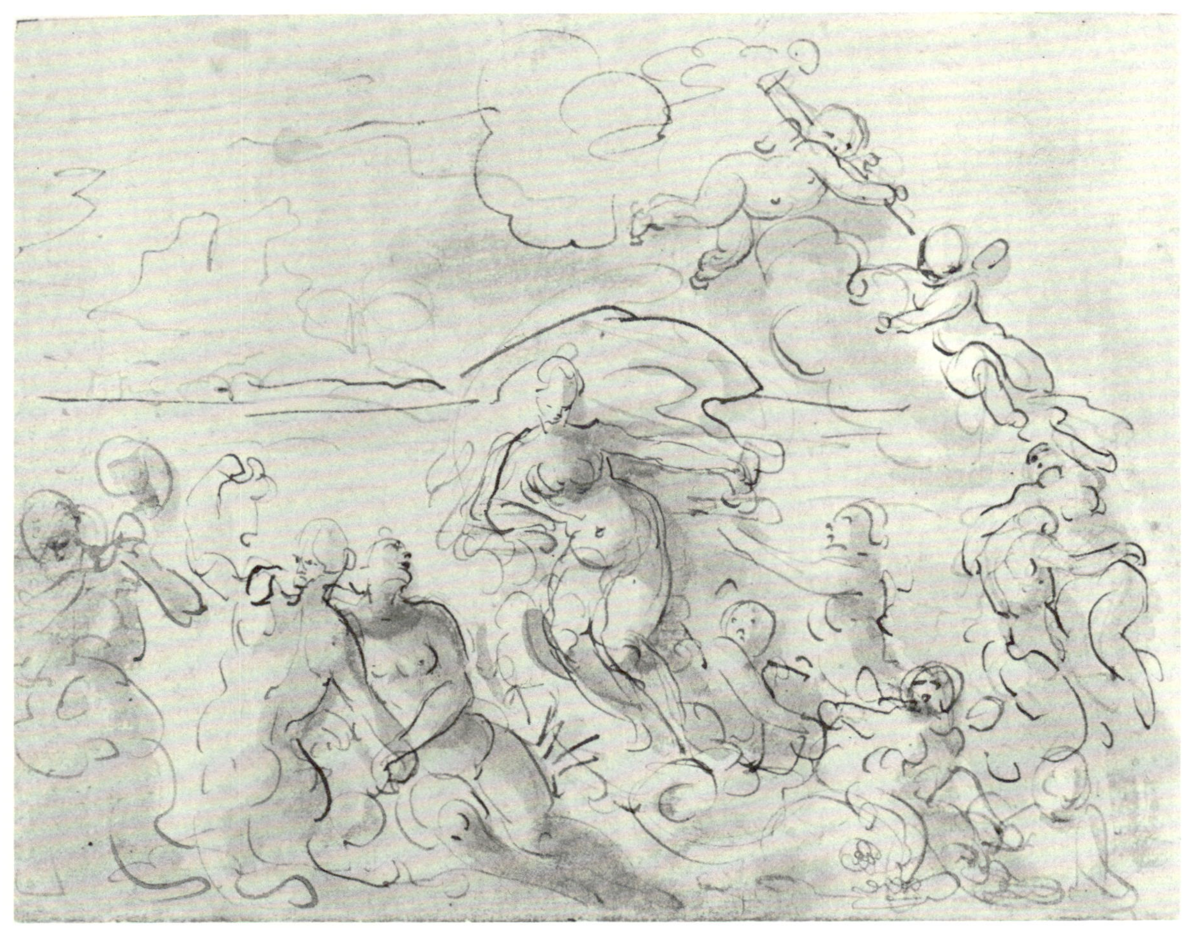

54. (recto)

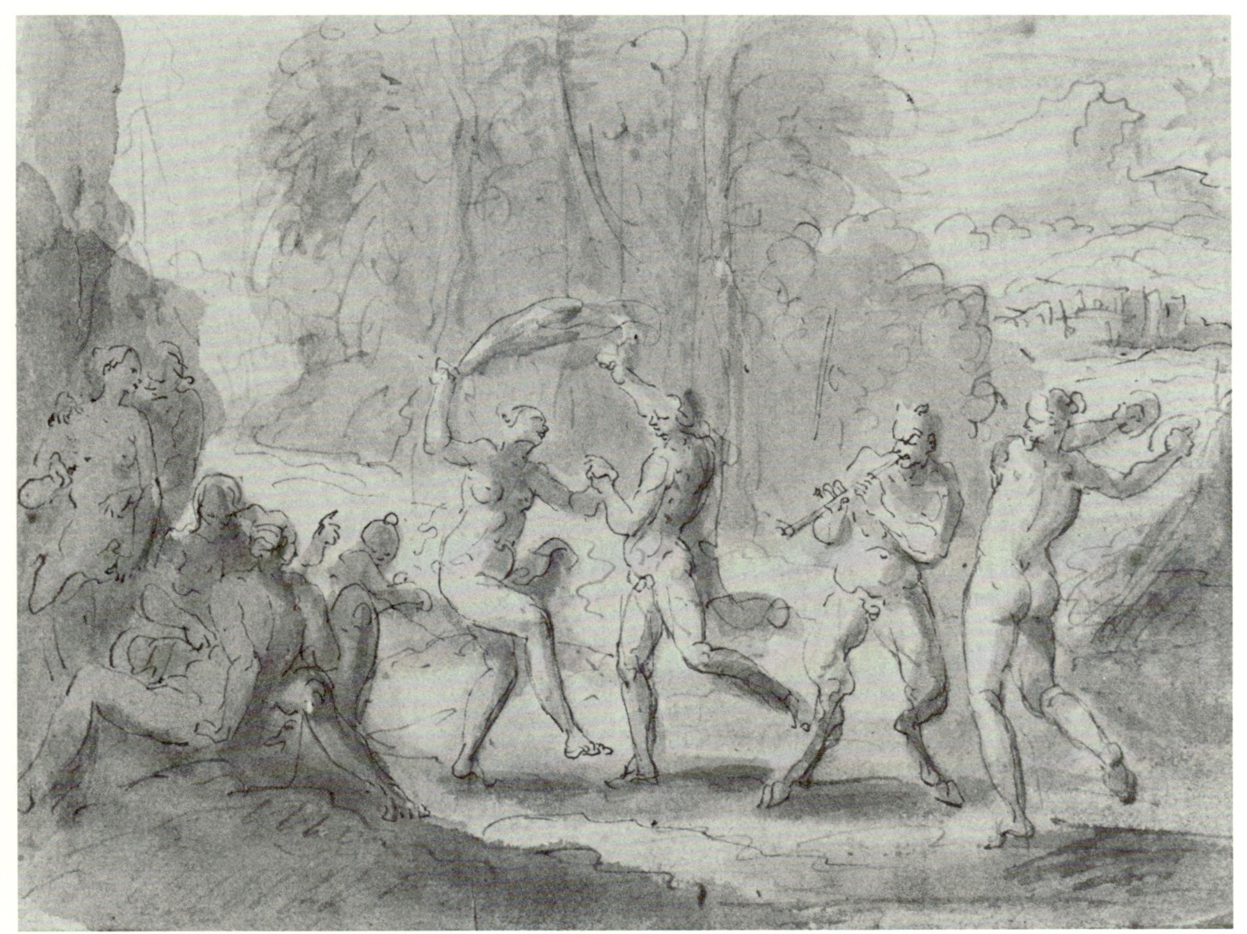

54. (verso)

55.

JEAN HONORÉ FRAGONARD (Grasse 1832 - Paris, Rome, Naples - Paris 1806)

Ruins of the Colosseum

Red chalk on buff paper; 368 x 267 mm.

Signed recto lower left corner, in pen and brown ink: *fragonard Rome 1758*

Inscribed recto bottom center to right corner, in black chalk: *Vue de la cour de l'Hermite au Colisée*

Provenance: Charles Natoire, Rome ?; Janos Scholz, New York; Schaeffer Galleries, New York; Private Collection, New York

Acquired 1975

Exhibited: Metropolitan Museum, New York, February-April 1978; National Gallery, Washington, November 1978 - January 1979; Fogg Art Museum, Cambridge (Mass.), February-April 1979; Frick Collection, New York, April-June 1979

Literature: Anatole Ananoff, *L'Oeuvre dessiné de J.-H. Fragonard,* Paris, 1964, vol. I, no. 385, fig. 136; Eunice Williams, exhibition catalogue, *Drawings by Fragonard in North American Collections,* 1978, p. 30, no. 2 (ill.)

This drawing comes from what must have been a very happy time in Fragonard's life, during his first stay in Rome, from 1756 to 1761, when he was a much appreciated and indulged *pensionnaire* at the French Academy[1]. Earlier in Paris he had been a student of Chardin briefly, then of Boucher, and finally of Charles van Loo. When he returned from Rome to Paris in 1761, he embarked on his career as a painter of charming Rococo reveries, and was highly successful — until neo-classicism and the French Revolution put his work out of style and destroyed his patronage. His long Roman interlude must have been a period of bliss, of few responsibilities and constant discovery, no less of himself than of the marvels of the Roman past. He returned to Rome in 1773-74, but now as an established master, with a wife and a reputation to maintain.

Fragonard apparently drew constantly on both Italian trips. Most of the drawings of the later visit are in wash; most of the earlier ones are, like this, in red chalk. This sheet can also be recognized as a working drawing rather than one intended as a finished work of art. It is actually an archeological study, forthrightly and rather literally recording an unpretentious subject. He made many drawings of this sort, particularly during his travels in 1760-61 with his friend, Hubert Robert (number 57), and their patron, the Abbé de Saint-Non (1727-91)[2]. However, the date and location of this drawing make clear that it was made earlier, as a part of Fragonard's studies at the French Academy.

The day that Fragonard drew this sheet, he and Robert must have gone out sketching together, because the same site appears in a red chalk drawing by Robert in the Museum at Besançon[3]. According to the collector-architect Pierre-Adrien Pâris (1745-1819), Robert's drawing of the scene was the first that he made in Rome[4]. But this is hardly likely, Robert having been there since 1754. Whatever the case, it must have been done at the same time as Fragonard's. There is more foliage and the hatching is different, but under the arch appear the same ladder, boards, cloth, basket and jugs, as a kind of workman's still life — perhaps set up by the young draughtsmen themselves — of objects they brought with them or found on the site.

The motif itself is characteristic of the eighteenth and nineteenth century Romantic fascination with ancient ruins rather than with monuments' grandeur. It is the kind of image that would reappear in the background of both artists' later paintings, transformed by imagination into architectural fantasy. The sublime decrepitude of the ruin exposes the folly of man's pretentions, of his vain hope to construct monuments that would survive relentless nature.

Williams suggests that the drawing may have belonged to Natoire, the director of the Academy, or that he may have sent it back to Paris as an *envoi de Rome,* "as evidence of progress made by the *pensionnaires.*"

1. Although the officers of the Academy were wary of Fragonard's painting — his colors were "dangerous" — they liked his drawings: "dessinés avec finesse et verité" *(Correspondence,* 1901, vol. XI, p. 217). And his term at the Academy was extended twice (*ibid.* pp. 283, 305, 363, 369).
2. Louis Guimbard, *Saint-Non et Fragonard,* Paris, 1928.
3. Inv. no. D2987, 392 x 275 mm.
4. M. L. Cornillot, *Collection Pierre-Adrien Pâris, Besançon,* Inventaire Général des Dessins des Musées de Province, vol. I, Paris, 1957, no. 131. The drawing is inscribed in Pâris' hand *"Premier dessin de Robert d'après nature."* It has an additional inscription in a hand neither Robert's nor Pâris': *"Cortile del heremità de Collosseo".*

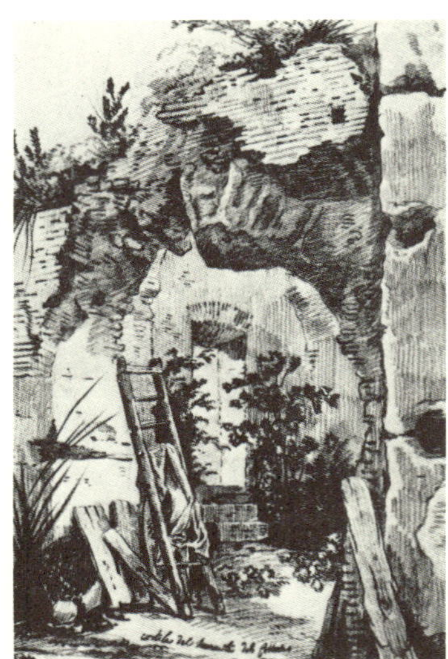

Hubert Robert
Ruins of the Colosseum
Musée des Beaux-Arts, Besançon

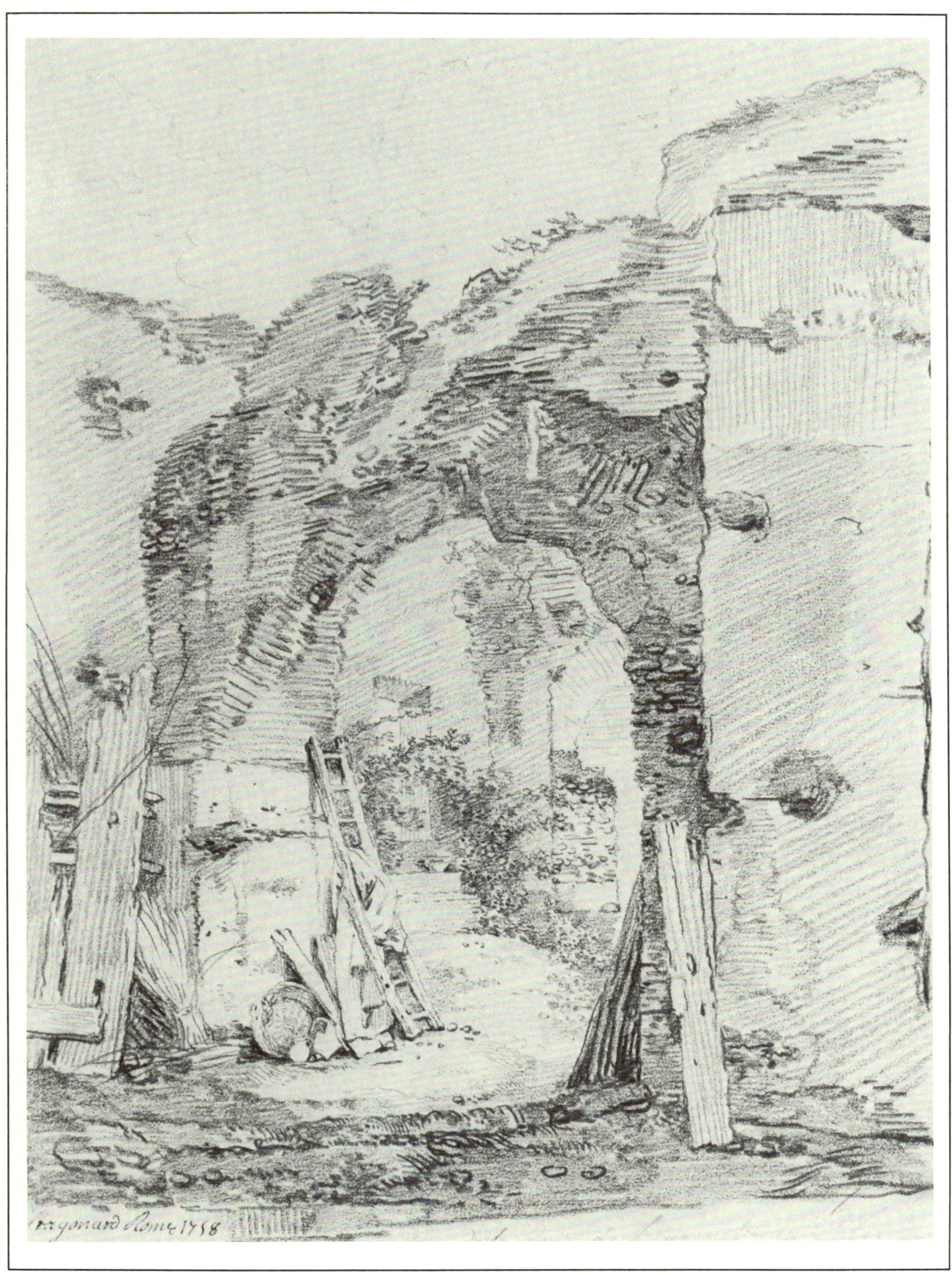
ragonard Rome 1758

56.

NICOLAS POUSSIN
(1594 Les Andelys [Normandy] - Paris, Rome - 1665 Rome)

Studies of Trajan's Column, Rome

Pen and brown ink, brown wash, over traces of black chalk; 304 x 225 mm.; lightly foxed; laid down
Inscribed on the backing (verso), in graphite: *Nicolas Poussin, No. 2550 N. Poussin, 173a*
Provenance: Lord Overstone (before 1878); C. Lloyd, Lockinge, Berkshire; Thomas Agnew and Sons, London, 1967
Acquired 1975
Nichole Harris in Oberhuber, 1977, no. 51, pp. 130-33
Exhibited: Fogg Art Museum, Cambridge, Mass., 1975; Metropolitan Museum, New York, 1976
Literature: *Catalogue of Works of Art at Overstone Park, Lockinge House and Carleton Gardens,* London, 1875-77, p. 33 no. 140; Walter Friedlaender and Anthony Blunt, *The Drawings of Nicolas Poussin,* London, vol. V, 1974, no. 331, pl. 248; exhibition catalogue, *Roman Artists of the Seventeenth Century, Drawings and Prints,* Metropolitan Museum, New York, 1976; Christopher Lloyd, exhibition catalogue, *Dürer to Cezanne; Northern European Drawings from the Ashmolean Museum,* Rutgers University, New Brunswick, N.J., 1982, p. 105; Anthony Blunt, *Nicolas Poussin,* 1958, National Gallery of Art, Washington D.C., p. 228; Anthony Blunt, "Newly Identified Drawings by Poussin and His Followers, *MD* XII, no. 3, 1974, pp. 239-248

Poussin was born in Normandy and trained there and in Paris. By 1621 he had begun his mature activity, working in Paris with Philippe de Champaigne on the decorations of the gallery in the Luxembourg Palace that was to house Rubens' Marie de'Medicis series. In 1624 he left for Rome, where he remained for the rest of his life, except for a brief, unhappy return visit to Paris in 1640-42.

In Rome Poussin became the ideal learned painter, and the focal point of the group of artists, theorists, and connoisseurs devoted to a revival of classical art. Although he had few public commissions (and those few were not particularly well received), he became something of a cult figure, encouraged and supported by a select, admiring clientele, particularly by a remarkable amateur, the Cavaliere Cassiano dal Pozzo. Under his auspices, Poussin developed his interest in Roman archaeology, participating in a project to draw all the classical remains surviving in Rome, which finally produced over 1500 drawings by Poussin, Pietro da Cortona (number 16), Pietro Testa, and less memorable hands[1]. These drawings were all mounted in twenty-three albums.

Although Poussin probably developed the practice of drawing antique remains from his participation in the project, this drawing is one among many others that he made entirely on his own account[2]. Harris dates it after Poussin's return from his Parisian trip in 1642, on the basis of "the very abstract and geometric outlines, frequently breaking up into small strokes, and the planar conception of the figures stressed by the washes..." which features she relates to the drawings Poussin did ca. 1645 to prepare for his second series of paintings of the *Seven Sacraments*[3]. Particularly notable, also, is Poussin's success in using wash to recreate the effect of relief sculpture and in maintaining both the clarity and the intricacy of the details of the prows of the galleys in the upper left quadrant of the drawing.

Trajan's column, over 135 feet high, including its base but excluding its pedestal, stands in the remains of the Forum of Trajan in the center of ancient and modern Rome. Covered with carved marble reliefs, it commemorates the Emperor Trajan's military campaigns against the Dacians; these reliefs twist up the column in a continuous spiral about a yard high and, all told, more than 650 feet long. Even in the optimum conditions of weather and light, the reliefs are difficult to see; as they ascend the column they become increasingly so, and, without the use of binoculars, are all but illegible toward the top. So there has been some debate about the source for this and Poussin's other drawings of the column reliefs. Plaster casts of the reliefs did exist, which might have solved the problem and saved the draughtsman's eyes and neck from the strain of attempting to draw on the spot, from the column itself. But apparently Poussin drew from some engravings by Francesco Villamena that were published in 1576. All the more remarkable, therefore, is the fresh spontaneity of this drawing, which gives every appearance of being made from the sculptures themselves in natural light rather than from a second-hand source.

The scenes were identified by Anthony Blunt from another set of engravings made in 1673 by Pietro Santi Bartoli. In the lower range, the Emperor (on the left) is being presented with a captive Dacian spy, an episode from the earlier campaign. The upper range is confusing, because it is a composite of two episodes: the bows of the boats on the left are from a river scene in the first campaign, while the two mounted cavalrymen on the right form part of the Emperor's retinue in the episode of the surrender of the Dacian children during the second campaign. Another drawing of the bows of the ships, from the Dal Pozzo Collection, is in the British Museum.

1. Francis Haskell, *Patrons and Painters,* 2nd ed., New Haven and London, 1980, pp. 101-2
2. See Walter Friedlaender and Anthony Blunt, *op. cit.,* nos. 292-327 and 335a-368.
3. Friedlaender and Blunt, *op. cit.,* p. 36, date the drawings after Trajan's column as "from the late 1630's or early 1640's."

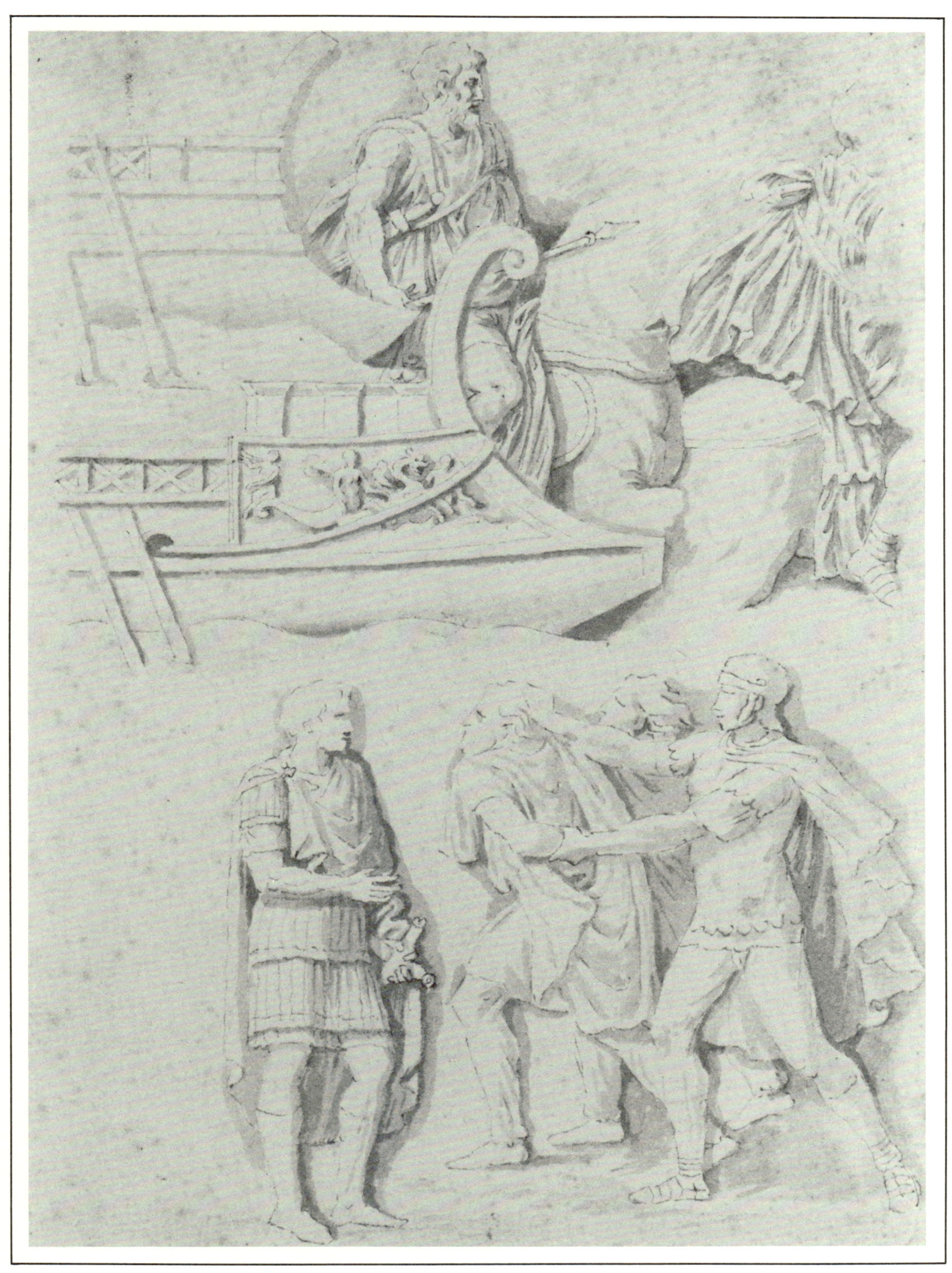

57.

HUBERT ROBERT
(Paris 1733 - Rome, Naples, Florence - Paris 1808)

A Roman Capriccio

Pen and black ink with water color; 364 x 271 mm.
Watermark: a Strasburg lily
Provenance: J.F. Gigoux (L.1164)
Acquired 1982

Robert had gone to Rome in 1754, in the entourage of the French Ambassador to the Pope, Comte de Stainville (later Duc de Choiseul), whose father Robert's father had served as *valet de chambre.* Although not holding a *Prix de Rome,* Robert was eventually favored with accommodation at the French Academy and with a stipend. The director, the painter Natoire, described him[1] as working very diligently *("avec une ardeur infinie...")* in the manner of the great Italian architectural painter, Giovanni Paolo Pannini (ca. 1692-1765/68), who taught perspective there. Robert must also have had contact at this time with Piranesi, whose shop was just across the street from the Palazzo Mancini (now the Bank of Sicily) in the Corso, the seat of the Academy, with which he was much involved. In the Spring of 1760 Robert went to Naples, Pompeii, and Herculaneum with his patron, the Abbé de Saint-Non, and he spent that summer in Tivoli with the Abbé and Fragonard. Returning to Paris in 1765, he became a successful painter of architectural scenes and fantasies, keeper of the king's pictures, and after the Revolution a curator at the Louvre.

This drawing is characteristic Robert's architectural *capricci,* of the type made popular in contemporary Italy by Pannini in Rome and Francesco Guardi (1712-93) in Venice. For these *capricci* artists often started with actual architectural and sculptural monuments and remodeled and rearranged them to suit their fancy. This building is quite similar to the so-called Temple of Vesta on the bank of the Tiber in Rome, which was a popular subject and certainly known to Robert in intimate detail. Later in his career, he painted the Temple *in situ* with the Arch of Janus visible in the background; the painting, in the museum at Cherbourg, reverses this composition and is deliberately archaeological, with a frieze of garlands and ox skulls.

The drawn temple has an order of fluted Corinthian columns, like the Temple of Vesta, but lacks its frieze. The broken friezes at the base of the drawing are unidentified, but they seem too large in scale to belong to the temple. The water in the foreground may be the Tiber, which had low earth embankments in the eighteenth century, although only at floodtime did its level rise so high. The presence of the shepherds with their staffs, an echo of the seventeenth century *bamboccianti* perhaps suggested by Piranesi's comparable prints, may seem anomalous today, when the temple has become an isolated island in a swirling sea of automobiles. But in the eighteenth century the area was nearly deserted and used for grazing. Basically, however, the scene is a fantasy: if the building was inspired by the Temple of Vesta (or alternatively by the equally popular so-called Temple of the Sibyl at Tivoli) it has been transformed into a pastoral dream.

Victor Carlson[2], noting the striking similarity of the figures to Pannini's, dates the drawing as ca. 1757-59 very early in Hubert Robert's career, contemporary to the Steiners' Fragonard.

1. *Correspondence...,* 1901, vol. XI, p. 262.
2. In a telephone conversation with the Steiners in 1983.

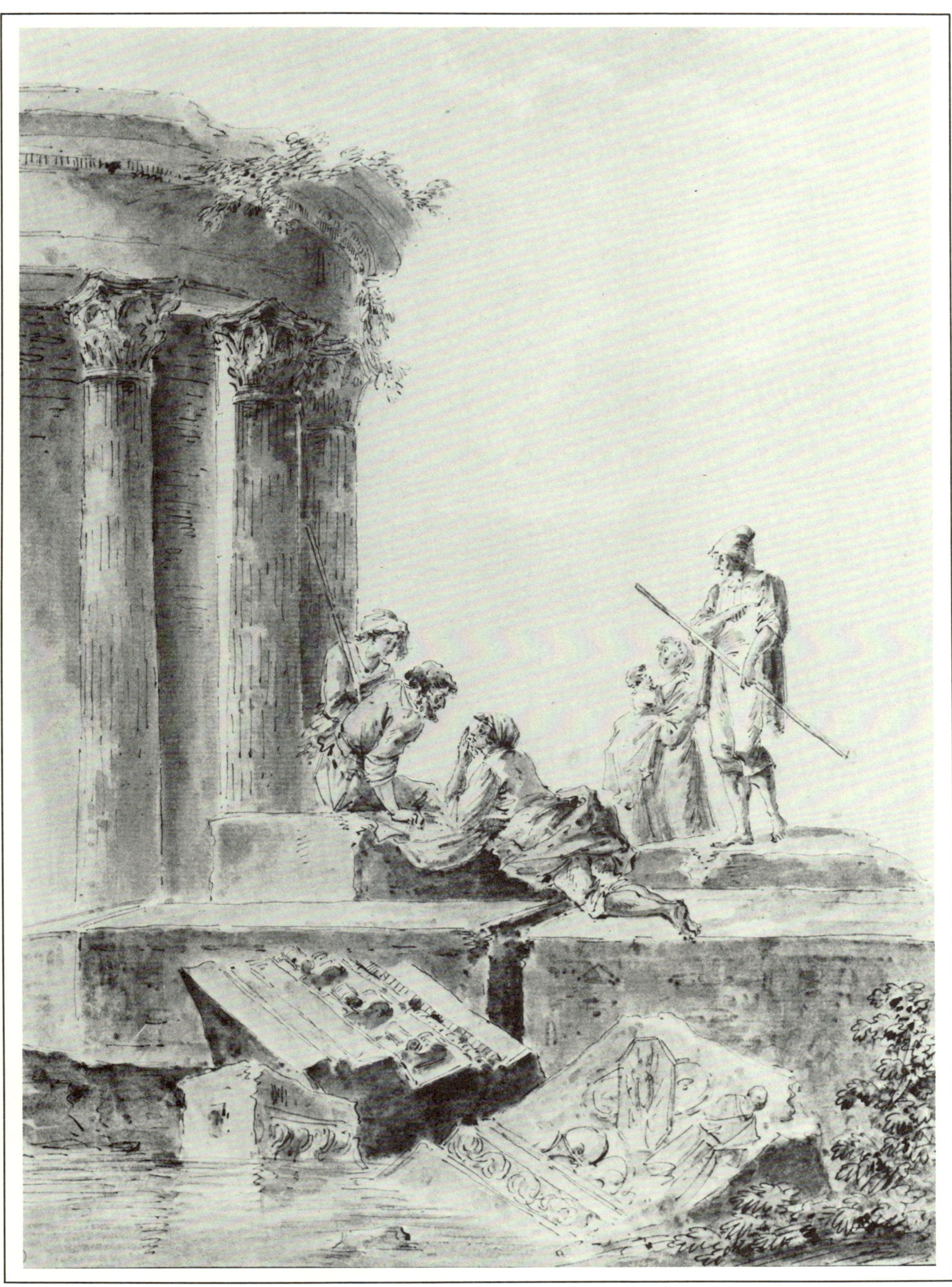

58.

JACQUES STELLA

(Lyons 1596 - Florence, Rome - Paris 1657)

Three Peasant Women

Pen and brown ink, grey wash, over black chalk; 167 x 241 mm. Watermark: IHS with letters AB
Inscribed on the backing: *Stella x 10/No 2816*
Provenance: Anonymous eighteenth (?) century collection
Acquired 1983
Loaned by Lori Steiner

Stella went to Italy while young, first to Florence and then in 1622-3 to Rome. Returning to France in 1634, he became painter to the king and prospered. Usually pigeonholed as one of Poussin's many sycophants, Stella in fact led a double artistic life. He did develop a cool and Poussinesque manner of painting, particularly in his maturity. But he also did scenes of the daily life of his contemporaries in prints and in drawings like this one. His "realist" activity was most prominent during his Roman sojourn in the 1620's[1], but it continued at least as an undercurrent throughout his career. There are even hints of it in some of his most pretentious representations of inspiring subjects, as for example in his pretty painting of the *Holy Family* in the Musée des Augustins in Toulouse. The setting there includes a classical columned portico, and the figure-types and costumes are nobly Roman; but relations among the holy family are very *gemütlich,* with St. Joseph warming the sacred infant's diapers near the fire and an angel-chef cooking supper on a campfire. Correspondingly, the series of *Children's Games,* engraved by Stella's niece Claudine after her uncle's images, represents cheerful, ordinary innocent pastimes. At the same time, the playful figures are in a frieze-like arrangement, so if they were costumed *all'antica,* the composition would appear to be as classicistic as Stella's paintings.

Two of the women in this drawing are squabbling. But the woman holding the baby establishes the mood of amusement at the low wrangling of her friends or relatives. Stella uses her to convey his own attitude, of indulgent condescension at the picturesque vulgarity of her companions. However shrill, they are not miserable. The message is not social protest, for these protagonists belong to the same properous peasantry depicted by the brothers Le Nain[2]. Nor is the dispute so acrimonious as in George de La Tour's painting of the *Beggar's Brawl* at the J. Paul Getty Museum in Malibu. Rather, the drawing conveys Stella's usual cheerful mood; he sees these people as droll and worthy of passing notice not only to reassure the viewer of his own superiority but also to confirm the basically benign nature of the world.

This drawing clearly belongs with the corpus of Stella's comparable humble subjects, in the same medium, like the *Old Soldier Smoking with a Companion* in the Wolf Collection in New York[3]. Davidson at first placed the Wolf drawing in 1633-40 but later accepted Oberhuber's redating of it to ca. 1650[4], which seems appropriate for the Steiner sheet as well.

1. For example, in the nine drawings he made representing the *Miracles of St. Philip Neri* in the Yale University Art Museum; six are dated 1629 and 1630, and all must postdate 1622, the date of St. Philip's canonization.
2. For the reality of the social situation of the brothers Le Nain, see Neil MacGregor, "The Le Nain brothers and the changes in French rural life," *Art History* II, no. 4, 1979, pp. 401-412.
3. Published by Gail S. Davidson "Some Genre Drawings by Jacques Stella," *MD* XIII, 1975, pp. 147-157; the Wolf Collection drawing is pl. 14.
4. Exhibition catalogue, *French Drawings from a Private Collection: Louis XIII to Louis XVI,* Fogg Art Museum, Cambridge (Mass.), 1980, no. 5b.

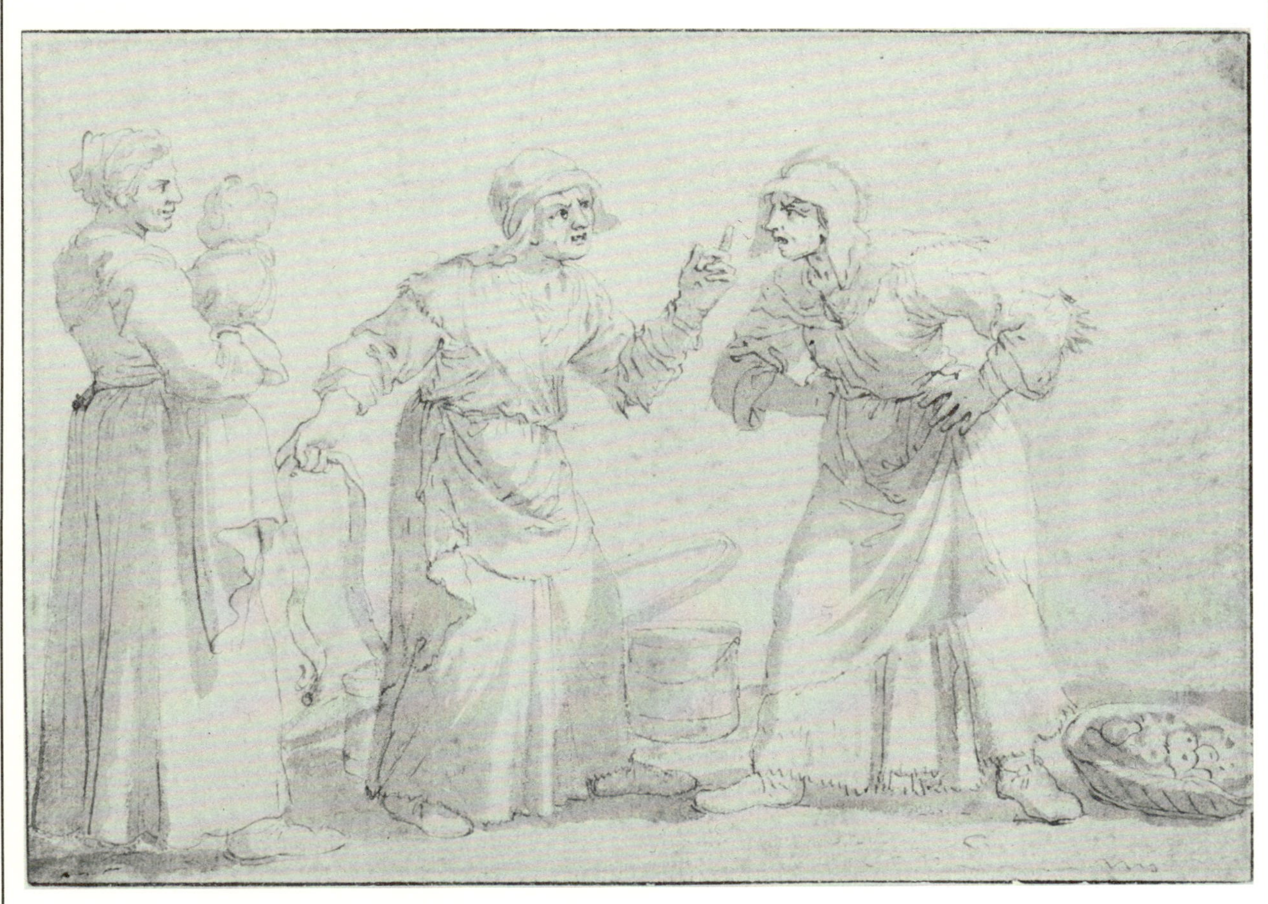

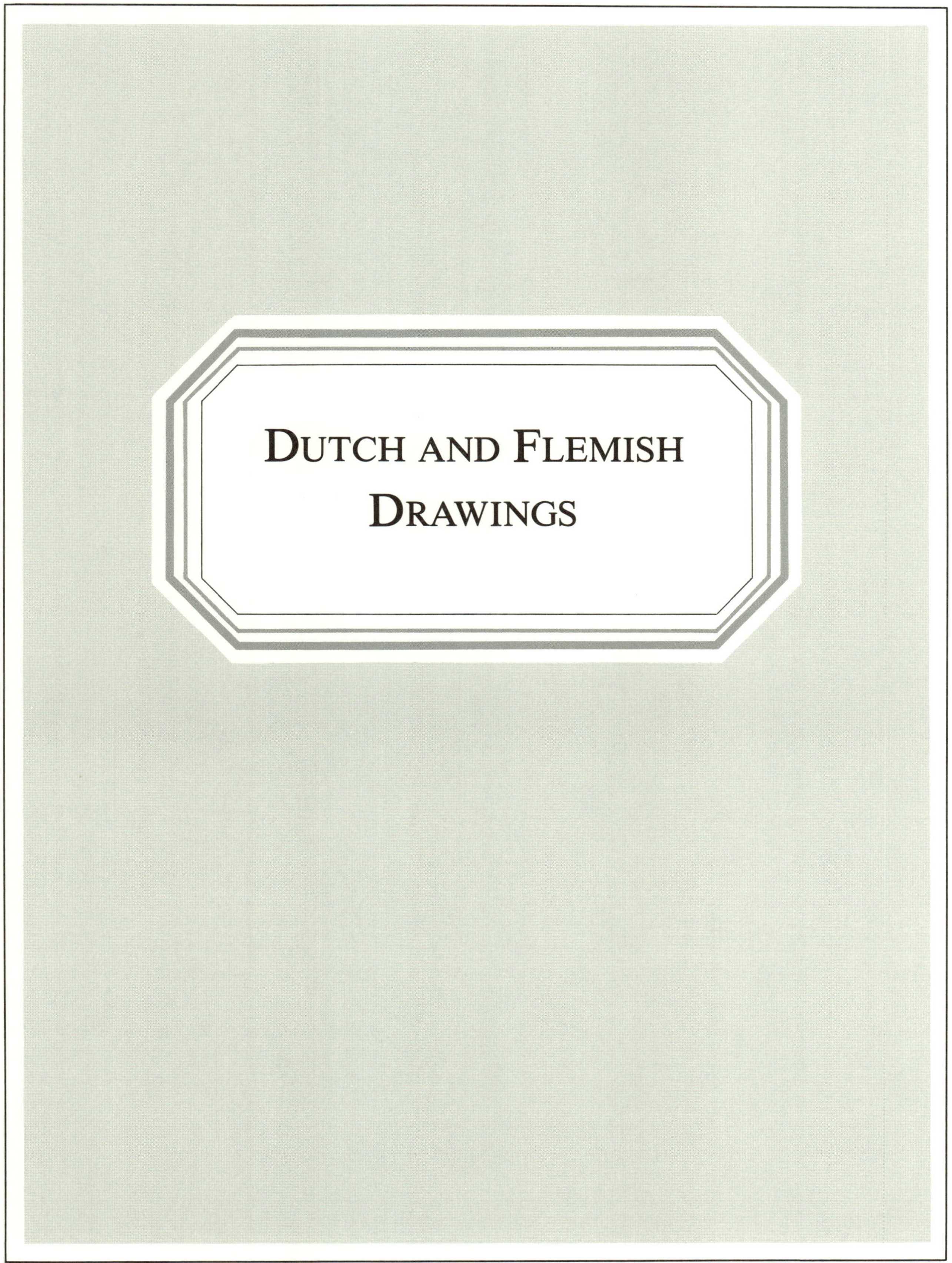

Dutch and Flemish Drawings

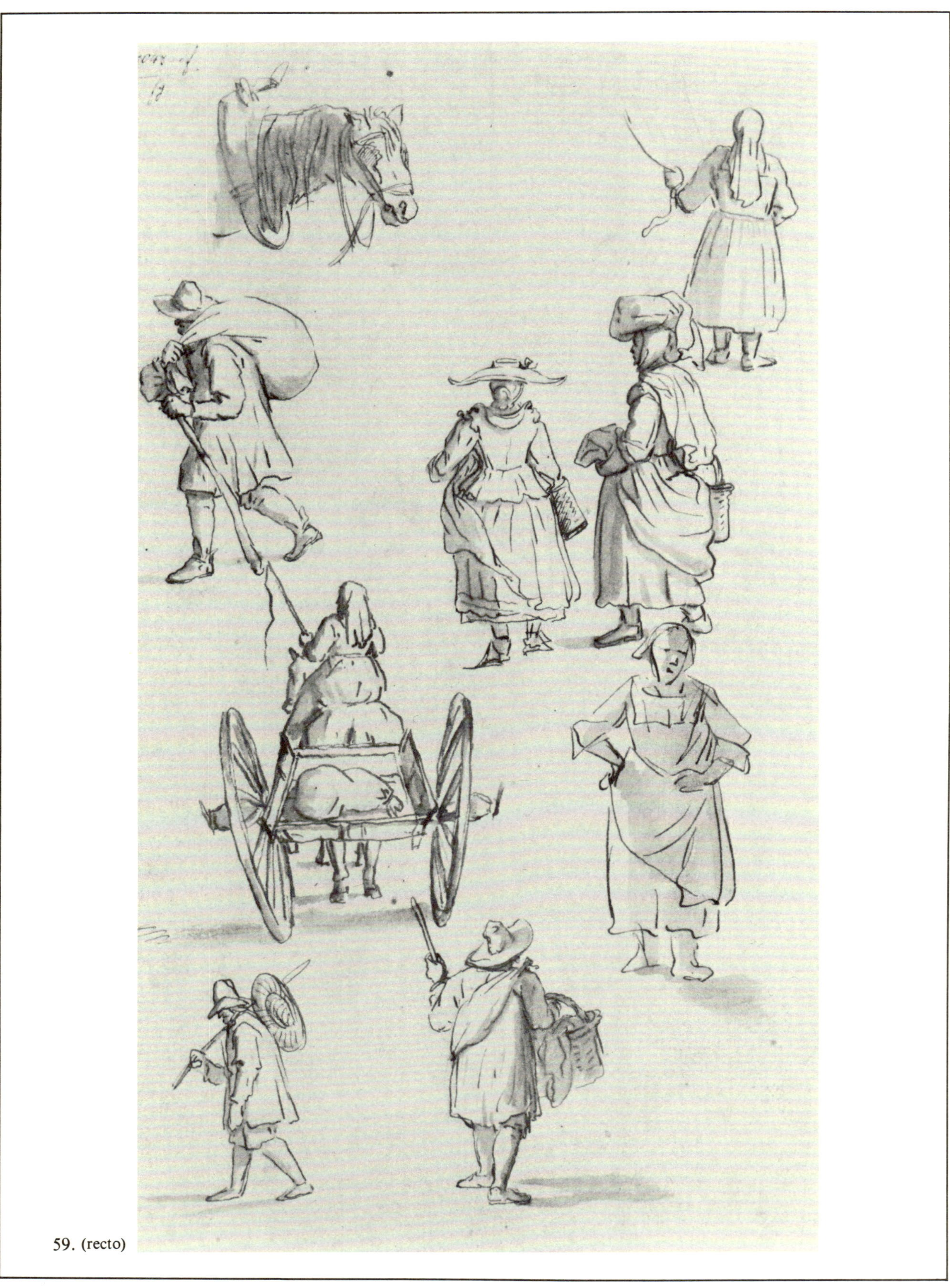

59. (recto)

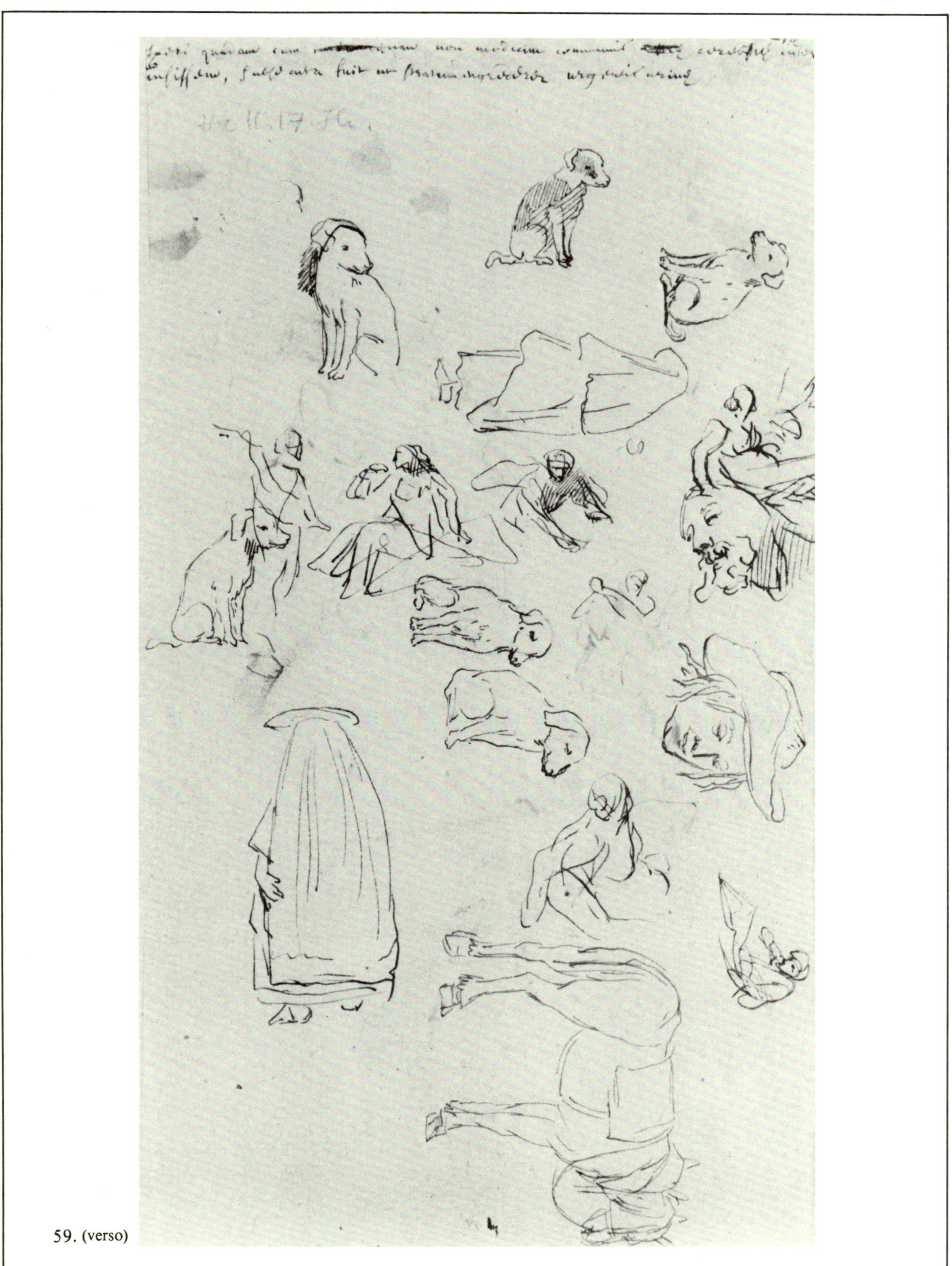

59. (verso)

59.

ANONYMOUS SEVENTEENTH CENTURY DUTCH DRAUGHTSMAN

Studies of Working Peasants

Pen and brown ink, grey wash (recto); pen and brown ink (verso); 352 x 191 mm. Watermark: shield with lily
Inscribed recto upper left corner, in pen and brown ink: *1043 cf./fy;* verso, pen and brown ink: *Lydri quandam cum i d...* (cancelled) *non non modicum comunnio apud* (cancelled) *lorum/* (illegible) *anta fuit ut psalum* (illegible); graphite; Holl. *17 Jh*
Provenance: Paul Sachs (L.2091); La Porte (L.1170)
Acquired 1971

Despite a tentative attribution to the minor and all but forgotten Dutch engraver Jacob Lutma[1], this drawing remains without identification with a known hand — or hands. Quite apart from the use of wash on the recto and of pen and ink only on the verso, there are enough differences in the calligraphy on the two sides to suggest the possibility of two hands. The one of the recto seems more assured: the draughtsman had a very sharp eye for the characteristic gestures and mannerisms of his models, whether the man ambling disconsolately out of the lower left corner, the creaking wheels of the cart above him, or the slightly defiant stance of the woman just to its right. The short, angular, brisk lines are similarly effective in animating the little figures. The total effect of the delineation of the recto is so pungent as to be nearly caricatural.

The verso in contrast is drawn more carefully, even hesitantly. As the six sketches of the little dog suggest, this draftsman was interested in anatomical structure and characteristic pose. But his hand was less spontaneous and his mind's eye less summary; he was less clever but more studious and perhaps more sympathetic. The recto brings to mind comparable quick sketches of peasants by Adrian Brouwer (1605-38); and the verso, perhaps some sketches by Jan Brueghel the Elder (1558-1625). The verso is closest to a drawing of peasants in the Hofstede de Groot collection, tentatively attributed to Nicolaes van Haeften or Haften (ca. 1663-1715) and described in the catalogue as probably the work "of a late genre painter copying an example of ca. 1660"[2].

These drawings are included in the exhibition to demonstrate that Dutch artists did not make only finished compositions. They also made quick sketches direct from nature, of landscapes or figures. Furthermore these studies are casual, and their models are anonymous, without literary identity or historical position but simply common people engaged in the process of daily living. The contrast with the Italian drawings is evident: only Stefano della Bella's (number 6) seems comparable, and it has an aura of wit and stylishness as contradictory of the plainness of these figures as poetry is of prose. The Stella and Ribera drawings (numbers 58 and 99 respectively) are closer in spirit, but they present finished thoughts in contrast to these fragments. Stella's hints of condescension toward his models are even more contradictory; Ribera's objective but sympathetic observation is closer.

1. Jacob Lutma is barely mentioned by the Dutch art historian Arnold van Houbraken (1660-1719), as an engraver who died in 1654 in Amsterdam.
2. J. Bolten, *Dutch Drawings from the Collection of Dr. C. Hofstede de Groot,* Groninger Museum voor Stad en Lande, Utrecht, 1967, no. 36, p. 73.

60.

ANONYMOUS SEVENTEENTH CENTURY DUTCH ILLUSTRATOR

Camillus and the Schoolteacher of Falerii

Pen and brown ink, brown wash; 168 x 281 mm.
Provenance: W. Beck (L.2603)
Acquired 1973

The attribution of this drawing to Jan Luyken (1649-1712), a leading Dutch illustrator, has been denied by Haverkamp Begemann. Despite the distinctive mannerisms — all the pen and ink and wash dots in the middle and background, and the slender, long-legged body-types with rather inarticulate anatomy — no alternate attribution has been proposed. However, these same mannerisms do appear in a drawing of an unidentified subject from Jewish history in the Louvre, from the Mariette collection where it was identified as by Jan Goeree, whose *Death of Herod* is also in this exhibit (number 75). If an attribution to Goeree could be confirmed, it would establish not only the authorship of this drawing but also its role in the process of making an illustration. The contrast between its loose spontaneous calligraphy and the exactitude of the *Herod* makes clear that it was a preliminary study rather than a finished design ready for engraving on the printer's copper plate. In any case, the composition was almost certainly intended eventually to be engraved as an illustration for an edition of the ancient Roman historian Livy.

If the attribution is uncertain, the subject matter is not. It is from Livy's *History of Rome* V/XXVII and recounts an event during the campaign in 394-395 B.C. of the Roman military tribune. Marcus Furius Camillus, against the Faliscans in Etruria. The Romans having overrun their camp, the Faliscans retired to their city of Falerii Veteres (the modern Civitā Castellana near Viterbo), most famous in ancient times for its excellent Falernian wine. The Romans then put the city under siege. The Faliscan schoolteacher, thinking to lift the siege, took his pupils into the Roman camp and offered them to the Roman tribune as hostages to force their fathers to surrender the city. Camillus responded contemptuously that such an act of perfidy was inconceivable to Romans, who won their victories by fighting rather than treason. So he had the schoolteacher bound and stripped, gave the boys scourges with which to whip him, and sent them back home. According to Livy, the Faliscan fathers were so grateful to him and so impressed by his uprightness that they surrendered the city forthwith.

61.

NICOLAES BERCHEM
(Haarlem 1620 - Italy - 1683 Amsterdam)

Cattle and Figures in a Landscape

Black chalk; 182 x 290 mm.
Signed ? in lower left corner: very faint and illegible possible signature
Provenance: Sir Robert Witt, London (L.2228b)
Acquired 1972

Berchem studied first with his father, Pieter Claesz (1597-1660) the great still life painter. He studied figure painting as well but he must have turned to landscape painting very early, for he is reported by Houbraken to have been a student of Jan van Goyen, Jan Wils and Jan Baptist Weenix, although as Haak points out[1], this last association is not very likely, considering the birth dates of Berchem and Weenix. In any case, Berchem must have had contact with the first generation of Dutch Italianate landscape painters early in his career, and surely must have visited Italy, perhaps in 1642-43 with Weenix or perhaps in 1653-56. He is recorded in 1677 as living in Amsterdam where he stayed until his death, and was much appreciated in his own lifetime, hardly more for his paintings than for his drawings. More than 500 drawings survive, many of them signed[2]. They establish him as the best draughtsman among the Dutch Italianate landscapists.

Even this monochromatic drawing clearly shows Berchem's delight in sun drenched atmospheric scenes and his skill in conveying their visual effects. The composition and draughtsmanship here are strikingly similar to a drawing of *Pack Mules Descending a Mountain Road* in the Morgan Library[3]. The Morgan Library drawing is larger, its foreground topography more rugged, and the distant landscape is Alpine. Stampfle suggests that it may represent a scene that Berchem saw on his travels and drew on the spot. In contrast, this drawing is of an ordinary nondescript hilly landscape, of the sort that he might have seen north of Rome (or in eastern Holland) which he, and the other Italianate landscapists, repeated again and again. Stampfle places the Morgan Library drawing in the mid-1650's, and lists a number of other comparable drawings Berchem made about the same time. The drawing of figures in the Steiner sheet is identical to that of a *Landscape with a Fort* at the Hermitage in Leningrad (inv. no. 179), which is also of the mid-1650's. The tranquility of the landscape is characteristic of Berchem's youthful works and confirms this relatively early date.

1. Haak, 1984, p. 383.
2. See Ilse von Sick, *Nicolas Bercham Ein Vorlaufer des Rokoko,* vol. V, *Kunstwissenschaftliche Studien,* Deutscher Kunstverlag, Berlin, 1930, pp. 66-67, for a compilation of the changes in Berchem's signatures, arranged chronologically.
3. Stampfle, 1979, pp. 126-27, no. 100.

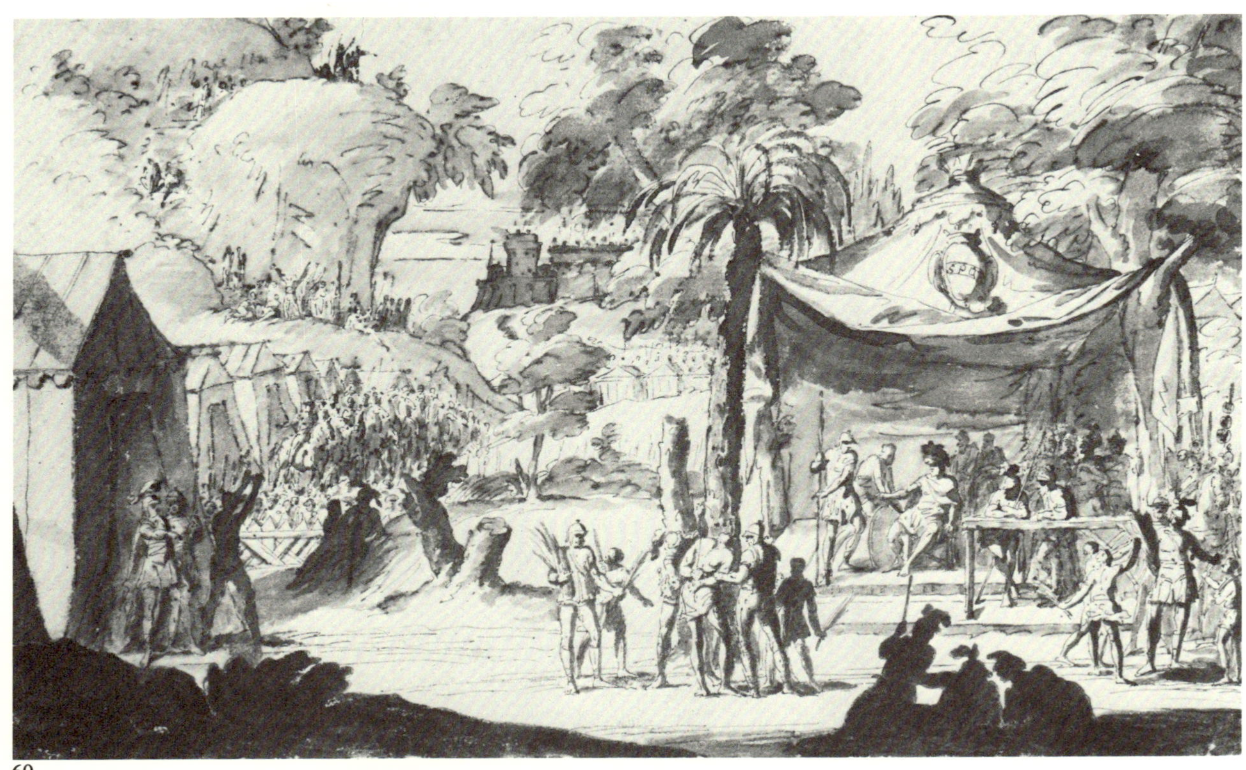

60.

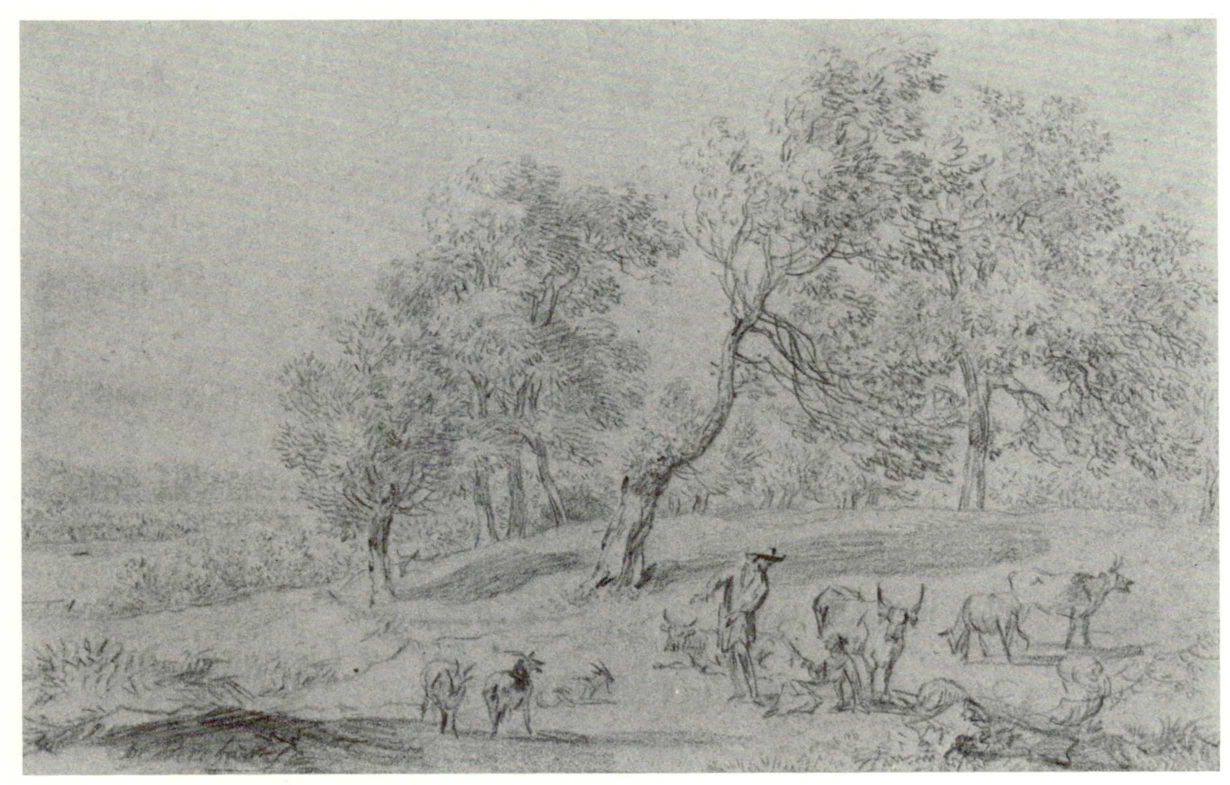

61.

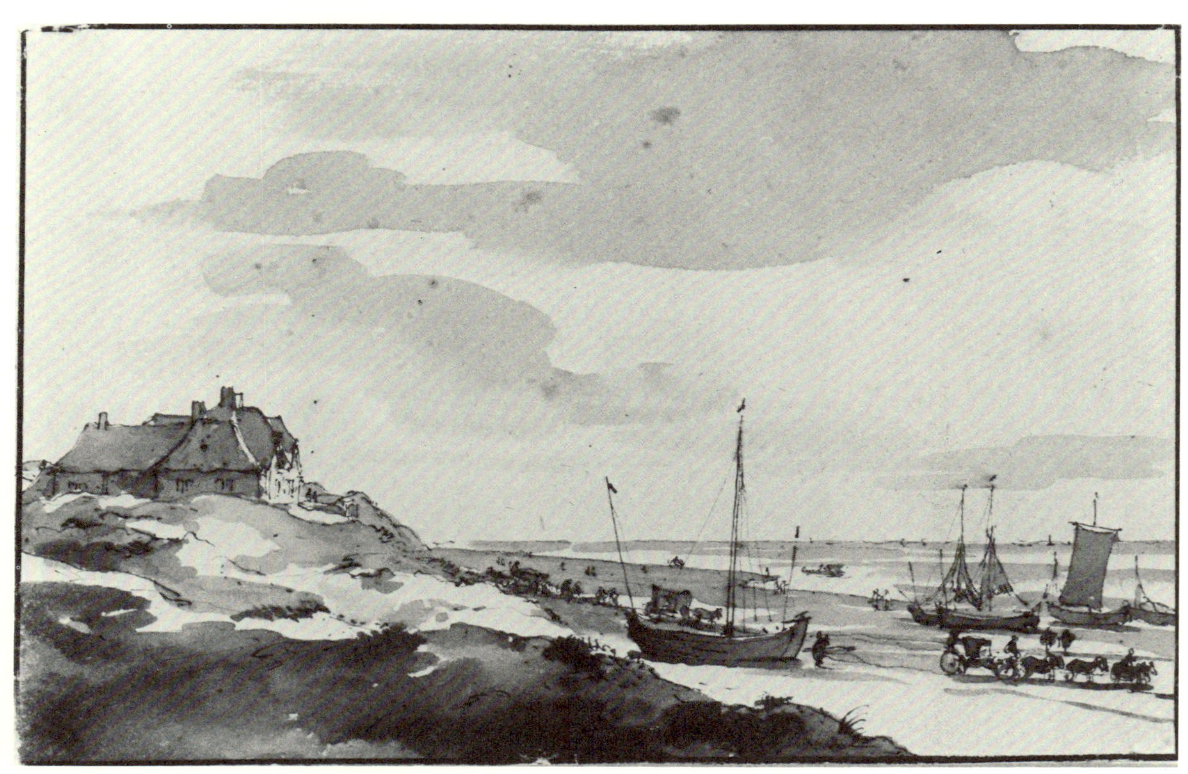

62.

JAN DE BISSCHOP
(Amsterdam 1628 - Leiden, Italy - the Hague 1671)

Coastal Scene, Scheveningen

Pen and brown ink, brown wash; 97 x 154 mm.
Inscribed verso: *Schevelings*
Acquired 1982

Arnold Houbraken specifically states that Jan de Bisschop never painted but remained an amateur draughtsman and printmaker throughout his life. Born in Amsterdam, he was educated at Leiden, then settled in The Hague and practiced law for the rest of his life. A friend of the sons of Constantijn Huygens, he was apparently influenced by Huygens' attitude, (inspired by Castiglione's *Il Cortigiano [The Courtier]),* that the study of drawing was part of a good education. In 1661 together with several friends, Jan de Bisschop opened a private drawing academy, where he emphasized principles based on those of classical antiquity[1].

Jan de Bisschop's work consists of two major groups: drawn or engraved copies of other works of art, most of them made during a tour of Italy in the mid-1650's; and works of his own invention, done both at home and abroad, from the beginning of his activity as an artist in about 1648 until his death in 1671. The drawings in this second group belong to the tradition of the *"playsants"* of Esaias and Jan van de Velde; their style suggests that de Bisschop may have been a pupil of Bartholomeus Breenbergh.

In landscape drawings, de Bisschop's style went through three major phases. In early drawings dated 1648, edges of forms are carefully outlined in pen, and volume is suggested by a uniform area of wash. By the mid-1650's (as in this drawing), edges of forms are sometimes outlined in wash as well as in pen; and wash is occasionally brushed over wash, creating darker effects. After 1660, often only wash is used. In depicting buildings, wash is used with precision, one stroke suggesting both the volume of a form and its clearly defined edge. After 1660, in depicting trees de Bisschop used wash in a loose, sketchy way, to suggest light and shade.

The attribution of this drawing is confirmed by its similarity to a drawing in the National Gallery of Canada, Ottawa[2]. In both drawings, outlines of forms are precisely rendered by pen or wash, or by a combination of pen and wash; wash is brushed over wash in areas representing shadows. The Ottawa drawing is inscribed *'t strandt tot Schevelingen* (the beach at Scheveningen) on the verso in the artist's hand; it comes from a series of drawings of which the first is dated 1652 and initialed J.E. in monogram, meaning Johannes Episcopius, the Latin form of the artist's name.

The style of the Steiner drawing is also similar to that of a drawing by de Bisschop in a private collection in Augsburg[3]. The Augsburg drawing, along with many others, documents the embarcation of Charles II at Scheveningen for England in 1660, when he was called back from exile for restoration to the British throne. Jan de Bisschop apparently spent the day at different viewing-points making quick sketches of the event. Valerius Rover, an eighteenth century Dutch collector, owned twenty-one Jan de Bisschop drawings of the event. After Rover's death, the collection of drawings was dispersed[4]. The similarity in subject matter and style between the Steiner and Augsburg drawings suggests that the Steiner drawing was part of this collection. A.L.

1. The authoritative study of the artist is J.G. van Gelder, "Jan de Bisschop," *Oud Holland,* 1971, pp. 201-259.
2. Arthur E. Popham and Kathleen Fenwick, *European Drawings in the...National Gallery of Canada, Toronto,* 1965, p. 120, no. 175. The dimensions of the drawing are 99 x 153 mm.
3. *ibid.,* pp. 208-9, pl. 21
4. According to van Gelder *(op. cit.,* p. 208, n. 32) some of these drawings are now in the Rijksprentenkabinet in Amsterdam, the Municipal Archives in The Hague, the British Museum, and the Fondation Custodia (F. Lugt Collection) in Paris, f. 32.

63.

ABRAHAM BLOEMAERT
(1564 Dordrecht - Paris, Amsterdam - 1651 Utrecht)

Pomona and Vertumnus (recto); *Reclining Figure; hand* (verso)

Pen and brown ink over black chalk, brown wash heightened with white, squared in black chalk (recto); black and red chalk (verso); 136 x 105 mm.; incised
Provenance: Christie's, London, 10 July 1973, lot 141
Acquired 1980

Bloemaert's life spanned two centuries, and he was so adaptable that his art evolved from late Mannerism into the full Baroque. Born in Dordrecht, he was taken as a child to Utrecht where he studied with Joos de Beer. Apart from visiting Amsterdam and a trip to Paris in 1580-83 where he was exposed to the School of Fontainbleau (see number 35); he stayed the rest of his life in Utrecht. He had great influence through his numerous students including not only his sons, Frederick, Cornelis and two others, but also most of the city's most distinguished painters, Hendrick Ter Brugghen, Gerard van Honthorst, Cornelis van Poelenbergh, Jan van Bijlert, Jan Both, Jăcob Gerritsz. Cuyp, Jan Weenix, and Nicolas Knupfer. Many of Bloemaert's works were engraved, particularly by his sons. Frederick engraved an instruction book, the *Tekenboek,* after his father's drawings of figures in different poses seen from different angles, and a textbook by his father, *Artis Apellae Liber.* These books extended Bloemaert's influence into the eighteenth century; François Boucher owned a copy of the *Tekenboek* as well as a small collection of Bloemaert's drawings[1].

Although his subject matter covered a wide range of themes, Bloemaert was often repetitive, and the story of Vertumnus and Pomona appears a number of times in his *oeuvre.* He presented the story in two forms: either the two female figures are shown full-length within a luxuriant landscape and usually in a horizontal format; or as in this drawing they are three-quarter or half-length in a vertical close-up bordered with a few botanical details. Characteristically, the images also include a billhook, the curved instrument in the foreground of this drawing, a medieval gardening tool used for pruning trees. There are several variations on this composition, drawn, painted, and in prints. The closest seems to be a pen and ink drawing with wash in the Centraal Museum in Utrecht (inv. no. 11832), which is somewhat larger (166 x 132 mm.) and is squared for transfer[2]. A painting in the New York art market during 1968 is possibly related[3]. Although the drawing is incised, none of the prints seems to have been made from it.

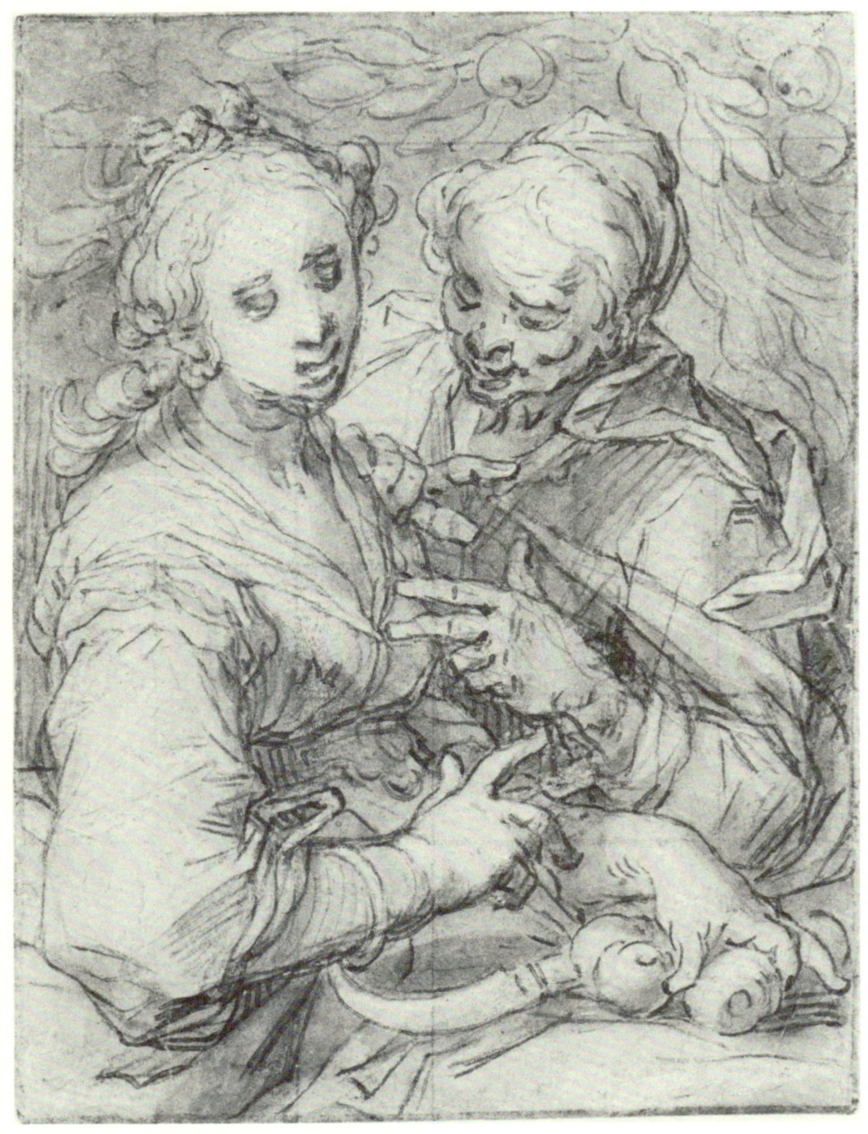

(recto)

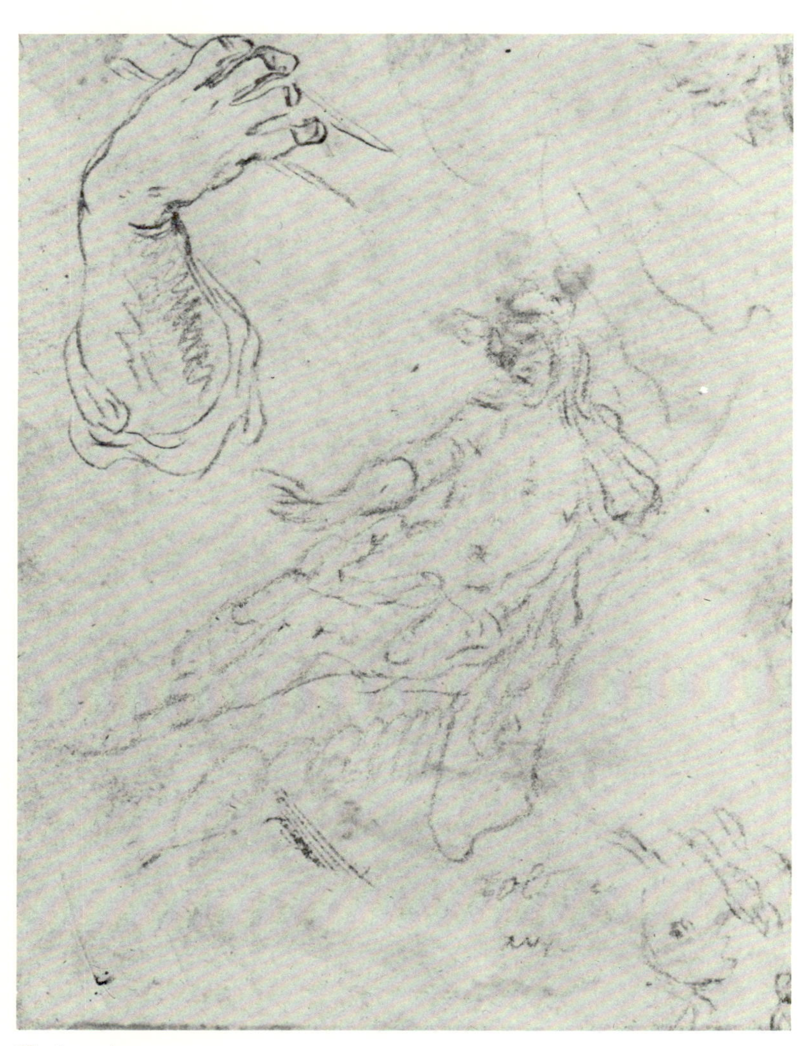

63. (verso)

The subject of the drawing is from Ovid's *Metamorphoses* XIV. Vertumnus, the god of changing seasons, adored Pomona, goddess of fruit trees. Because she had rejected so many suitors, Vertumnus transformed himself into an old woman in order to speak on his own behalf. Evidently he pleaded as ardently as a young man; Pomona listened, and he won his suit.

The Steiner drawing is marked by compactness to the point of crowding, by linear rendering of the inner contours of the rather substantial figures, and by handling that is somewhat angular in the drapery folds and flat and decorative in the background details. All these features are indicative of Bloemaert's responsiveness to the art of Bartolomeus Spranger (1546-1611)[4]. A native of Antwerp. Spranger visited Paris briefly and then went to italy, remaining in Rome for almost a decade before becoming court painter to the Emperor Rudolf II in Prague. Bloemaert's *Mystical Marriage of St. Catherine* in the National Gallery of Canada, a pen and ink drawing with wash, is similarly influenced by Spranger. It is signed and dated 1597 and the similar draughtsmanship in the Steiner drawing suggests that they are contemporary. A.L.

1. Regina Schoolman Slatkin, "Abraham Bloemaert and François Boucher: Affinity and Relationship," *MD* XIV, no. 3, 1976, p. 252.
2. Others are: Colnaghi's, London, 1955, pen and grey-green wash with white on brown paper, from the H.S. Reitlinger Collection (very similar); Sotheby's, London, 10 Dec. 1975, lot 285; 165 x 130 mm. (much sketchier).
3. Known through a photograph in the Getty Museum archives, otherwise unidentified.
4. Wolfgang Stechow, exhibition catalogue, *Dutch Mannerism,* Vassar College, 1970, p. 18.

64.

ABRAHAM BLOEMAERT

A Standing Man (an Apostle?)

Red chalk with white; border in brown ink; 310 x 193 mm.
Inscribed lower left corner in black chalk: *van Dyke*
Provenance: Sotheby Mak van Waay B.V., Amsterdam, 3 May 1976, lot 104
Acquired 1977
Oberhuber, 1977 (supplement), no. 64, p. 4

Although Bloemaert apparently never went to Italy, most of his students did. As they returned to Utrecht, they affected Bloemaert's own art, which became increasingly Italianate and Baroque. He was particularly vulnerable to the Caravaggesque manner of Gerard van Honthorst (1590-1656) who returned to Utrecht in 1620 after a decade in Rome. The affinity of Bloemaert and his pupils for Italy is not surprising because, as Oberhuber reminds us, Utrecht "was an island of Catholic faith in the Protestant Northern Netherlands."

Although he has never been identified, according to Oberhuber this figure is "surely the study for a religious painting, presumably for an Apostle in either the *Assumption of the Virgin* or the *Ascension of Christ.*" Oberhuber cites a half-length drawing in the Albertina for an *Ascension*[1] as appropriate evidence. This pose, with the arms apparently spread in astonishment and the head looking upward, does suggest either subject, but it might appear as well in an apotheosis or any event requiring a spectator to look upward. Specifically, the figure of St. John at the right of Bloemaert's signed and dated *Crucifixion* altarpiece of 1623 in the Roman Catholic Church at Scheveningen might be cited[2]. St. John is, of course, younger than this model, his cloak is less voluminous and his hands are clasped; but otherwise the attitude is the same. Furthermore, St. John's heavy drapery falls in similar natural folds without the linear mannerisms of Vertumnus and Pomona's clothing (number 63).

This fully draped figure appears early in Bloemaert's career, for example, on the left in the *Christ and the Adulteress* drawing in the Metropolitan Museum. So does the physiognomy with the distinctively bristling beard: in the elder in the center of Bloemaert's *Judith Displaying Holofernes' Head* of 1593 in the Kunsthistorisches Museum, Vienna. But the naturalistic treatment of the drapery in the Steiner drawing, with the development of its effect of full volume in an atmospheric space, clearly places it later in Bloemaert's career, no earlier than his most Caravaggesque painting, the *Supper at Emmaus* of 1622 in the Musées Royaux des Beaux-Arts in Brussels of 1622, and probably later, like the St. John in the Scheveningen altarpiece or the figure of St. Paul before Agrippa in a painting signed and dated 1635 in the Centraal Museum, Utrecht.

Both the figure in the Steiners' drawing and the Vertumnus figure manifest Bloemaert's interest in old age. He repeatedly portrayed elderly men and women, and very sympathetically, not only when required by the narrative but also, presumably by preference, as incidental figure details. While certainly personal, this interest may also be reflective of the Baroque preoccupation with time. Just as scientific developments in the seventeenth century created a new concept of time as a measurable property of nature, so Baroque art indicates an awareness of the passage of time, of the mutability and brevity of life. A.L. and A.M.

1. Benesch, 1928, no. 458.
2. See Gustave Delbanco, *Der Maler Abraham Bloemaert,* Strassburg, 1928, no. 24, p. 75, pl. 12, fig. XXVII.

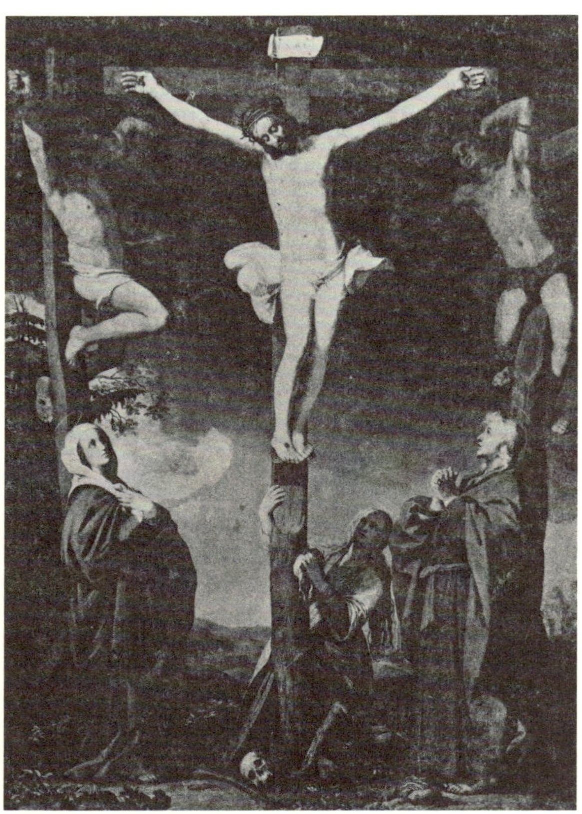

Abraham van Bloemaert
Crucifixion
Roman Catholic Church, Scheveningen

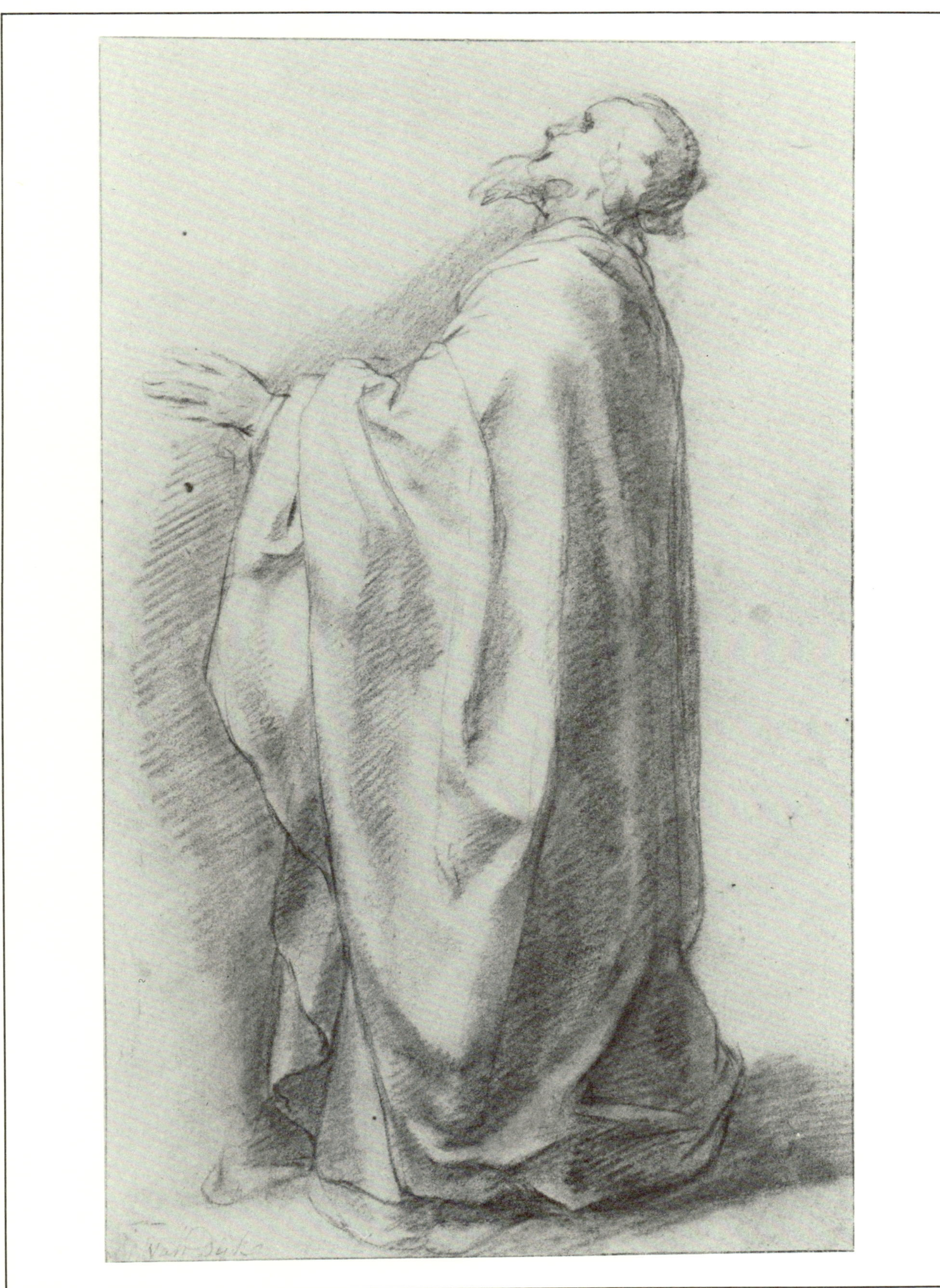

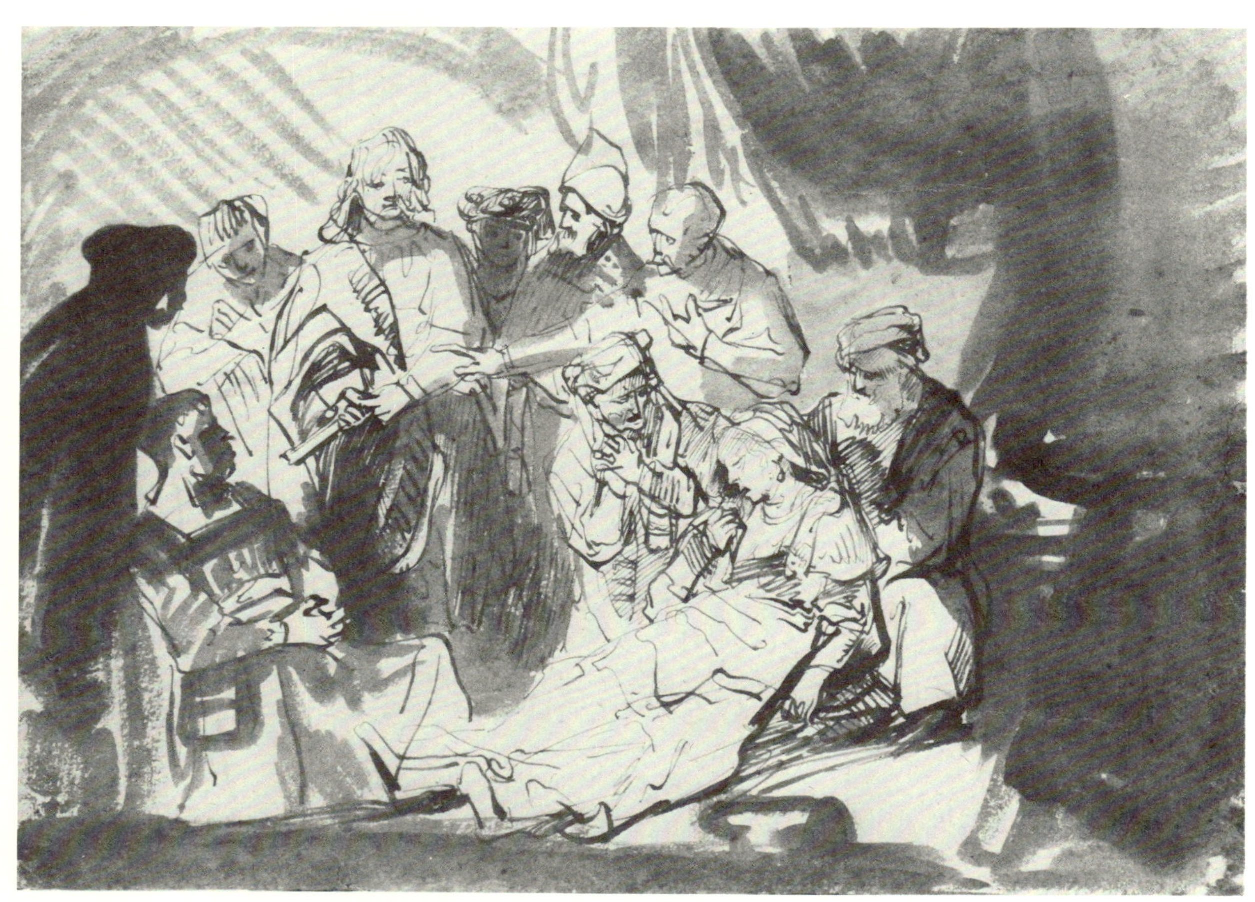

65.

FERDINAND BOL
(Dordrecht 1616 - Amsterdam 1680)

The Raising of the Daughter of Jairus (?)

Pen and brown ink and brown wash over graphite on buff paper; 201 x 286 mm.; cracks throughout, mended on verso; tips of four corners replaced
Provenance: Christie's London, 2 July 1954, lot 291 (as School of Rembrandt, *Raising of the Daughter of Jairus);* Fischer, Lucerne, 1 December 1956, ill. (as School of Rembrandt, *Christ Healing the Sick);* Galerie am Neumarkt, Zurich, 25 May 1972, no. 17b, pl. 1 (as School of Rembrandt, probably Aert de Gelder)
Acquired 1973
Cynthia Schneider in Oberhuber, 1977, no. 40, pp. 107-8
Exhibited: Palazzo Strozzi, Florence, 1971
Literature: Sumowski, 1979, vol. I, no. 194x, p. 412, ill. p. 413 as *The Death of Lucretia*
Copies: A. Laurentz, etching in the same sense, 1756, as after Rembrandt, *Christ Taking Leave of Mary;* in R. Weigel catalogue of 1865, p. 635, no. 7513

Bol is one of the leaders among the many artists in Rembrandt's circle. He studied with the master from 1636 to 1640, and imitated him until the 1650's — often so successfully that his works have been mistaken for Rembrandt's own. From the 1650's onward, however, he adopted the more stylish manner of Bartholomew van der Helst. After 1669 when he married a rich widow, he apparently stopped painting; at least no known works are dated later.

There seems to be no question as to the authorship of this drawing. Sumowski sees another Bol drawing of the *Death of Lucretia* in the Rijksprentenkabinet, Amsterdam (no. 193x, p. 410) as a partial study for it, and dates both to the early 1640's. He suggests that Rembrandt's *Death of Jacob* of 1640-42 in Montreal[1] may have inspired its style.

The identification of subject matter, however, is not so certain. Sumowski thinks it represents the death of Lucretia because the woman appears to be dead and the most prominent man is holding what, he suggests, is the knife she used to kill herself. Furthermore, her position is similar to that of the woman in a painted *Death of Lucretia* in the Detroit Art Institute attributed to another Rembrandt pupil, Jan Victors.

There are problems with this proposal. Lucretia was a Roman heroine, and the figures in the Steiner drawing do not appear in any respect to be Roman. The fact that the victim is fully dressed suggests that she is not Lucretia. Benesch[2] gives Lucretia as a possible subject of two Rembrandt drawings, and she is bare-breasted in both, as she is in most Baroque paintings. In fact, the figure on which the composition is focused appears to be Christ. His robe is the same as that of Christ in other drawings by Bol as well as in those by Rembrandt. While he lacks the radiance with which Christ is often depicted, this is not unusual, especially in compositions of the healing of the sick. Nor does the object that he is holding in his hand appear to be a knife.

There is less problem in reading the subject as *The Raising of the Daughter of Jairus.* The two figures closest to the young woman may be her mother and father. Mark v: 40 states that they were present when Christ raised their daughter from the dead. The earrings worn by the girl suggest that she is from a prosperous family, and would be appropriate for the daughter of a ruler of the synogague. However, this young woman seems too mature to be Jairus' twelve year-old-daughter (Mark v: 24). Furthermore, she is lying on the floor or on the ground, while in Rembrandt's drawings of Jairus' daughter, she is lying on a bed. According to the biblical account, Christ is brought into her room, while this setting is indeterminate and could be anywhere, indoors or outdoors.

Sumowski mentions *Christ Taking Leave of Mary* as another possible subject. But this woman's earrings and fashionable dress are inappropriate for Mary and are inconsistent with Bol's other representations of her; and she is usually represented as sitting up. Finally, and perhaps most reasonably, the subject could be simply *Christ Healing the Sick,* a theme Rembrandt favored. A.L.

1. Benesch, 1973, vol. III, no. 493, fig. 651, pp. 136-37.
2. Benesch, 1973, vol. I, No. 117 and vol. II, no. C22.

66.

PIETER VAN DER BORCHT THE ELDER
(Mechelen 1545 - 1608 Antwerp)

Landscape with Duckhunters

Pen, brown and grey ink, on vellum; 77 x 86 mm.
Acquired 1977

Van der Borcht received his initial training in the productive workshop of his father Jacob, a prominent painter in Mechelen. After the sack of the city in 1572, Pieter fled to Antwerp where he prospered, primarily as an engraver and draughtsman.

In Antwerp, he was offered refuge by Christoffel Plantin (1520-89), a successful and flamboyant man, a generous protector, and a famous publisher/printer of humanistic literature and illustrated books. Plantin revolutionized the printing and publishing trade in the second half of the sixteenth century, by being the first systematically to use copper engravings instead of woodcuts for the illustration of the vast quantity of books turned out by his internationally renowned press *De Gulden Passer* (The Golden Compass), also known as *Officina Platiniana.* Series of copper engravings were utilized for the first time in Andreas Vesalius' illustrated anatomical study, *Vivae Imagines Partium,* published by Plantin in 1566. Soon engraving became an Antwerp specialty, which attracted industrious draughtsmen like van der Borcht from all over the Netherlands and beyond. Along with very successful printers like Plantin and Hieronymous Cock, a great number of smaller publishers very quickly adopted copper engraving, not only to illustrate books but also for albums, in small series, and even in separate prints. As a result, Antwerp established an international reputation as one of the most important centers for illustrated books and engravings.

Van der Borcht apparently recognized Antwerp's rapid rise in the print trade from the beginning and took advantage of it. He began to furnish Plantin with drawn and engraved projects as early as 1565, and worked for other publishers as well. His range of subjects was wide; most active as an illustrator of the Bible, he also produced single leaf prints and small printed series of hunting scenes and landscapes.

Hunting scenes appear in Late Gothic manuscript illuminations, symbolizing the month of December in Book of Hours calendars. The subject enjoyed increasing popularity throughout the 16th century, especially after Cock's publication in 1566 at Antwerp of Pieter Bruegel the Elder's *Landscape with the Hare Shooting,*[1] and became a well defined genre on its own.

This panoramic landscape is staged in three steps, with a triangular *repoussoir* in the right foreground, a diagonal stream in the middle ground and rugged, sharply pointed mountains in the background. This composition, with these almost standardized features, is typical of Flemish panoramic landscapes in the tradition of Joachim Patinier, which continued to be much favored in Antwerp, even in van der Borcht's days.

This sheet is one of four by the artist in the Steiner Collection, all of about the same size. Because it shows a distinctive affinity in style, technique and composition to *Orpheus Enchanting the Animals* (number 67) and the other two, it is probably contemporary. Small printed sets of hunting scenes were popular from the mid-16th well into the first half of the 17th century, as exemplified by Lucas van Uden's *Landscape with Hunter and Three Dogs,* part of *Six Landscapes* (B. VI, p. 29. 28) (see also Verhaecht, number 92). Whether this drawing served as a design for an engraved book illustration or not, is unknown. Probably it was a *modello* of ca. 1585-90, and part of a small series of engravings, depicting both landscape and hunting scenes. H.V.M.

1. Hollstein, 1949 ff., vol. IV, p. 186, no. 150.

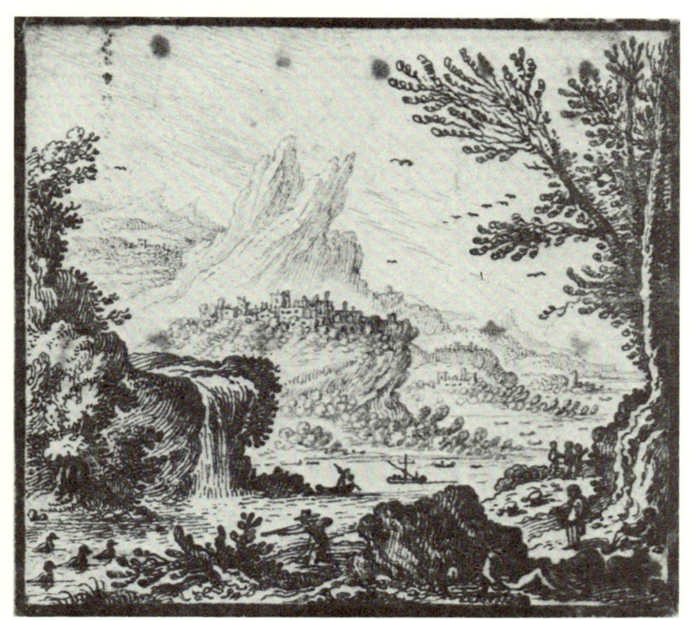

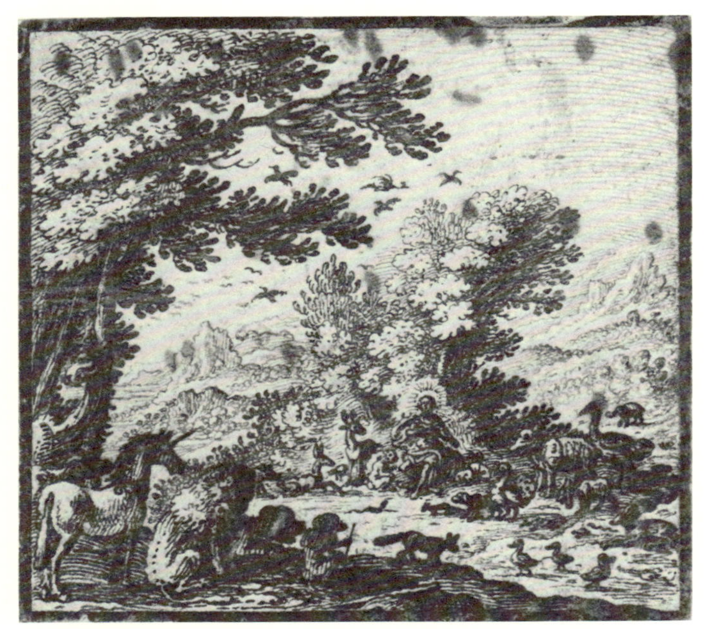

67.

PIETER VAN DER BORCHT

Orpheus Enchanting the Animals

Pen, brown and grey ink, on vellum; 77 x 88 mm.
Acquired 1977

> Here, while the Thracian Bard's enchanting strain
> Sooths beasts and woods and all the listening plain...
>
> Ovid, *Metamorphoses,* Book XI, Chapter I

This drawing bears witness to an Antwerp tradition of combining the two themes of the legend of Orpheus and the Paradise landscape. Popularized in the first half of the 16th century, the combined themes were still popular in Rubens' time. Roelandt Savery (1576-1639) set the standard for representations of fantastic landscapes with animals, and of combinations of paradise-like landscapes with Ovid's tragic hero. Furthermore, van der Borcht's contemporary, Jan Bruegel the Elder (1568-1625), painted at least 106 exotic landscapes, and he or his workshop also combined the two themes.

Orpheus belongs to a very ancient tradition. Found sporadically from the 5th century BC onward, the scene of *Orpheus Enchanting the Animals* was frequently depicted in the Roman Empire, when Orphism was a popular religion. The theme remained popular in Early Christian times when Orpheus, with his power to end discord with music and eloquence, became the principal model for representations of Christ. Between the sixth and fourteenth centuries the scene was relatively rare. It owed its revival in pictorial arts to the writings of Christian commentators, who interpreted pagan myths in Christian terms. The anonymous author of the *Ovide Moralisē,* probably a Franciscan writing in about 1300, went to great lengths to Christianize every detail of Ovid's *Metamorphoses.* Orpheus is interpreted as Christ, and his song represents the preaching of the divine word by which the souls of men are drawn away from damnation. Because this Orpheus wears a halo, van der Borcht probably intended to endow him with a similar Christian significance, a common practice during the Counter Reformation.

In this version Orpheus enchants not only a lion and a unicorn, but also a great variety of other animals, many of them exotic. These animals are not described in detail in Ovid's text and belong essentially to a visual tradition begun in the fourteenth century. The mythical unicorn which is firmly placed within the enchanted circle, has no obvious link with the Orpheus legend. It was known during the Middle Ages from the *Physiologus* manuscripts and bestiaries, which explained that the unicorn was caught because he rested his head in the Virgin's lap, but which contain no mention of a lion. Throughout the Middle Ages and the Renaissance, however, the lion and unicorn were widely recognized as traditional enemies. The appearance here of the two animals seated peacefully side by side demonstrates Orpheus' ability to enchant the wildest of animals and to reconcile the deepest of foes. Closely parallel are those many scenes of Paradise from the 14th century onward in which, for the same reason, the lion and unicorn appear together. The two beasts appear during the late 15th century also, in early illustrated printed editions of the *Metamorphoses.*

Orpheus' popularity was not limited to the visual arts. In the fifteenth century his music was discussed by Marsilio Ficino, among others, and two epic poems were devoted to his story: Angelo Poliziano's *La Festa di Orfeo* (ca. 1470) and Pierre de Ronsard's *Orphēe en Forme d'Elēgie* (1563-4). However, painting and the graphic arts provided by far the most popular means of presenting the combined Orpheus and Paradise themes. Orpheus and the Animals also appear sometimes in allegorical series of *The Five Senses,* as in the elder Jan Bruegel's painted *Music* in the Prado in Madrid. Van der Borcht illustrated Plantin's 1591 edition of Ovid's *Metamorphoses,* but this drawing does not correspond in composition to the appropriate engraving. So this drawing may have been the design, executed around 1590, for an illustration in another moralised version of the *Metamorphoses,* or it may simply have been a single leaf. It could also have symbolized the faculty of hearing in a *Five Senses* suite, but none of the other four drawings by van der Borcht in the Steiner Collection refers to any of the senses. So, if they were drawn as a group, which their similarities suggest, it was not as an allegory of the *Five Senses.* H.V.M.

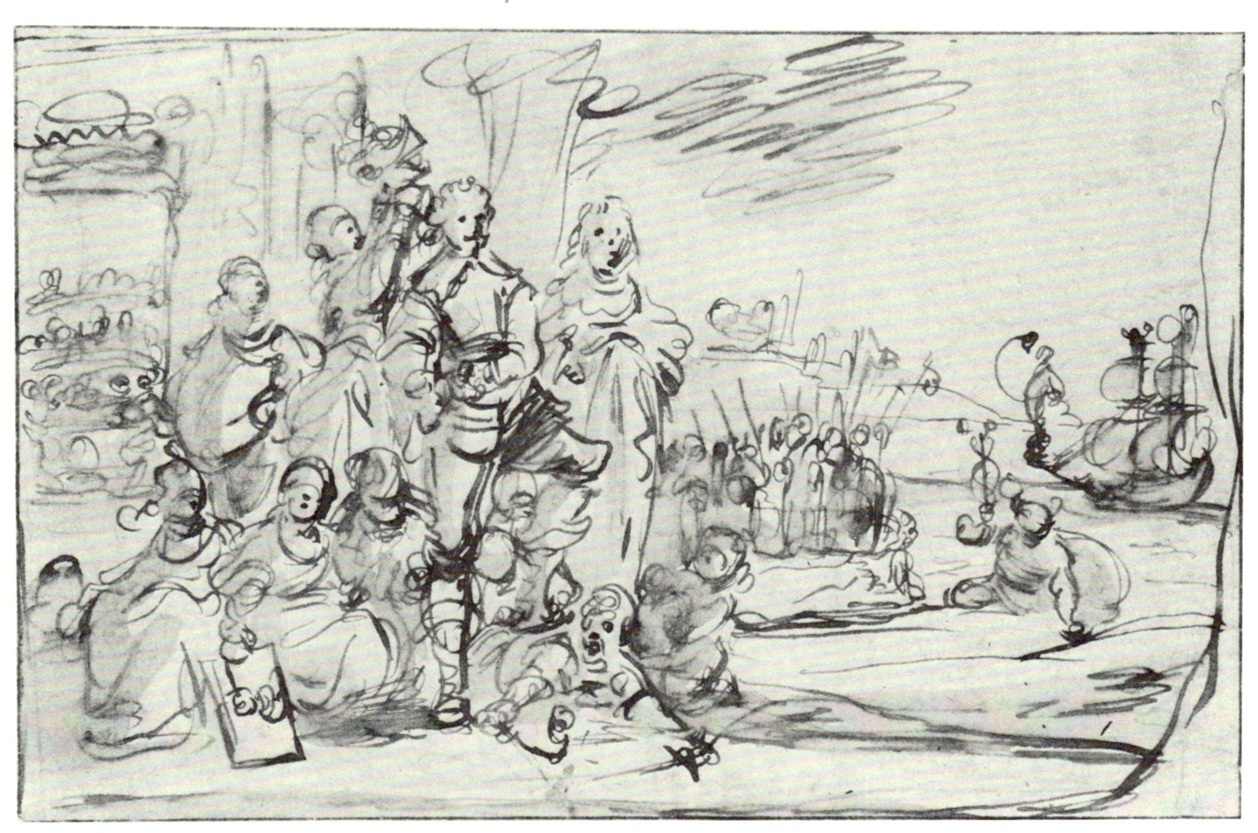

68.

JAN PHILIPSZ. VAN BOUCKHORST[1]

(Haarlem ca. 1588 - The Hague - Haarlem 1631)

An Allegorical Portrait of a Naval Commander

Pen and brown ink, grey and brown wash; 127 x 198 mm.
Provenance: William Esdaile (from inscription on the mount); Hatvany Collection
Acquired 1980

Bouckhorst's *oeuvre* includes a variety of media. He was trained as a glass-painter and is included in Houbraken under this profession only. It was a respected art form, its practitioners being acknowledged by membership in the painter's guild. But in addition Bouckhorst designed coats of arms, made prints and drawings, and painted Biblical, historical and allegorical themes. He was also a portrait-painter, practicing his trade in Haarlem contemporaneously with Frans Hals (1581/5-1666) who was second only to Rembrandt among Dutch portraitists.

No drawing by Hals has ever been identified, and his *oeuvre* lacks the kind of allegory Bouckhorst introduced here. Nonetheless this chauvinistic image shares something of the character of the group-portraits of military companies that Hals was painting at just the same time and displays much of their spirit of nationalistic confidence. The calligraphy is florid, as is typical of Bouckhorst and of his and Hals' sitters. It is in notable contrast to the careful refinement of Jan Goeree's *Death of Herod* illustration of nearly a century later (number 75). The difference is not only that between the personal styles of two artists, but also the product of changes in the attitudes and expectations of Dutch society: from the robust and aggressive optimism of Hals and Bouckhorst's time, to the more reserved and consciously cultivated prudence of Goeree's.

Bouckhorst drawings are rare; it may be more exact to say that not many have been recognized. However enough are known — including sheets in the Prentenkabinett in Leiden, the Graphic Collection in Munich, the Ashmolean Museum, and Yale — to confirm this attribution. The Yale drawing[2], of St. Nicholas of Bari, is particularly pertinent. Similar in medium and style, particularly in the *putti* at the saint's feet — the siblings of this swarm of children — the Yale drawing is signed and dated 1622, which may also place this drawing in time. A pen and ink self-portrait[3] in the Rijksprentenkabinett in Amsterdam, signed and dated 1628, offers confirmation of a date in the 1620's.

Professor van Gelder suggested that this drawing might represent Prince Frederick Henry of Nassau (1584-1647). Son of the great Dutch leader, William the Silent, and a military genius, he was elected *stadtholder* and served with notable success as commander of the forces of the United Provinces in the Dutch war against Spain. If so, the drawing represents him with his wife Amalia van Solms. He is being crowned with a helmet while a second figure behind him carries what might be a breastplate, but is more likely a coat of arms. The number of children at the feet of Frederick Henry and Amalia is not clear; there may be seven, which could be an allegorical reference to the seven provinces forming the Dutch republic. The prince's role as naval commander may be symbolized by the ship in the background, and the presence in the middle-ground of Mercury rather than Neptune may be a reference to the success of Dutch maritime trade.

1. Houbraken gives the name as Bockhorst or Boechhorst.
2. Haverkamp Begemann and Logan, 1970, no. 356 pl. 208.
3. Peter Schatborn, exhibition catalogue, *Dutch Figure Drawings,* the Hague, 1981, pp. 42, 132, no. 25.

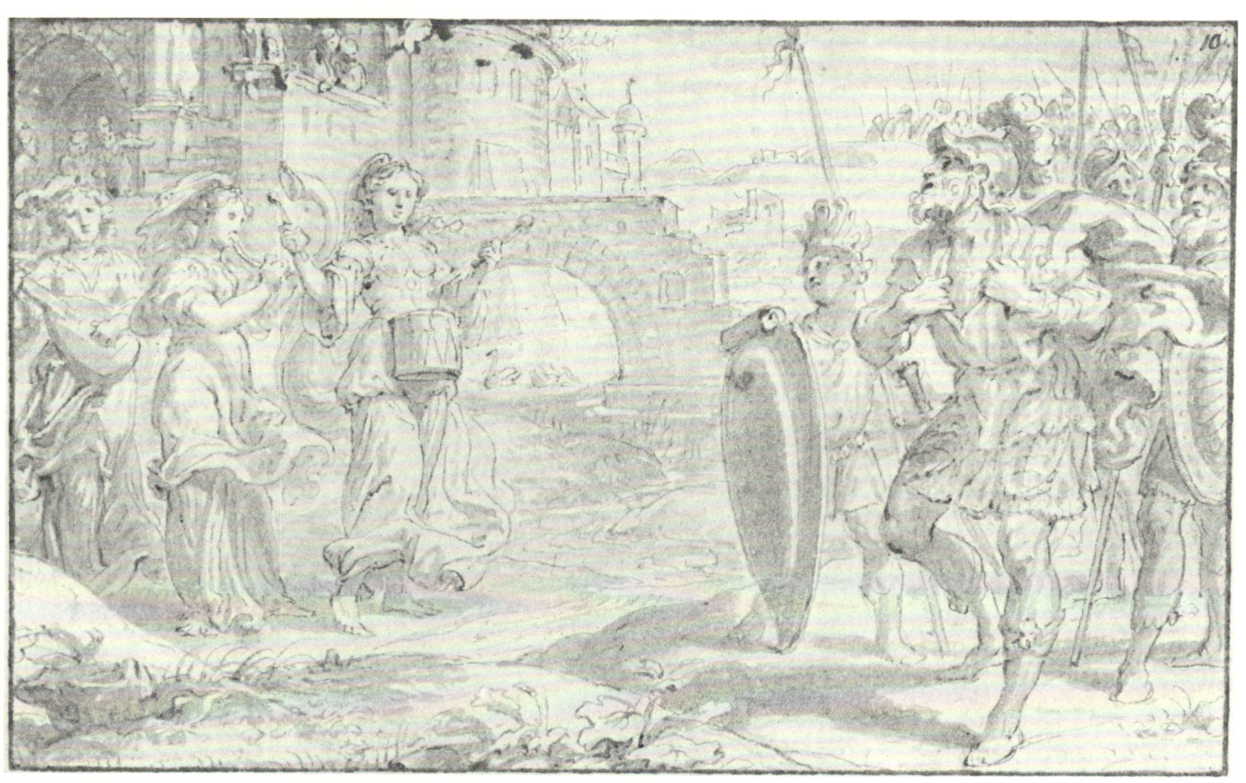

69.

ABRAHAM VAN DIEPENBEECK
(Hertogenbosch [Bois-le-Duc] 1596 - Antwerp, France - Antwerp 1675)

The Return of Jephtha

Pen and brown ink, brown wash, with white over graphite; 97 x 157 mm.
Inscribed recto upper right, in pen and brown: *10;* verso in graphite: *Sacrifice De Jephte/Diepenbeck*
Acquired 1973
Margaret P. Morgan in Oberhuber, 1977, no. 43, pp. 113-15

Diepenbeeck, an imitator of Rubens, was something of a jack of all artistic trades, a glass-painter, designer of church windows and an engraver. The first years of his career he devoted to glass-painting, and only in his mid-thirties did he turn to making paintings, of which about fifty survive. Most of his work is in the form of drawings for engravings: Steadman[1] estimates that over 750 of these drawings survive. Diepenbeeck went to Antwerp about 1621, became a citizen of the city a decade later, and was sufficiently recognized there to be elected dean of the painters' guild in 1641. He soon quarreled with the other members however, and was expelled, not to be re-admitted until 1672 after almost a decade of litigation. He was also involved in a suit involving some copies of van Dyck paintings[2]. Steadman doubts that he made the trips to Italy and England that have been proposed, but accepts as autograph his drawings of the Duke of Newcastle and English equestrians; he did visit Paris in 1650, and perhaps earlier.

Surprisingly, among his numerous drawings and commissions for engravings, scarcely any treat Old Testament subjects, making this sheet something of a rarity. A few others are listed by Morgan, who conjectures a new edition of the Bible as having been proposed and begun but never completed. This subject is not often repeated, and when it is, Jephtha usually is mounted. Diepenbeeck, who customarily utilized compositions from Rubens, in this instance used one of his own, a pen and ink drawing in the Louvre[3] representing the triumphant return of David, which easily transforms into Jephtha's horrifying return.

The biblical source is Judges xi, which tells the story of Jephtha, who was born out of wedlock, so the legitimate sons of his father drove him into exile. However, when the Israelites, who had sinned against the Lord, were menaced by the hostile Ammonites, they recalled him, now a general, to take command of their army. He indiscreetly promised the Lord that if given victory, when he went home he would sacrifice "whatsoever cometh forth...to meet me...[as] a burnt offering." The Lord duly delivered the Ammonites into his hands and he slaughtered them. But when he went home, as the drawing shows, "his daughter came out to meet him with timbels and with dances: and she was his only child...When he saw her...he rent his clothes, and said, Alas my daughter! thou hast brought me very low...for I have opened my mouth unto the Lord and I cannot back down." Nor did she ask him to, but retired into the mountains for two months, and when she returned "her father...did with her according to his vow..."

1. David Steadman, *Abraham van Diepenbeeck,* Ann Arbor, 1982, p. 33.
2. Steadman, *op. cit.,* p. 3.
3. Lugt, 1949, no. 554.

70.

LAMBERT DOOMER
(Amsterdam ca. 1628 – France, Germany, Alkmaar – 1700 Amsterdam)

Rebecca and Eliezer at the Well

Pen and brown ink and colored washes; 259 x 406 mm.
Signed recto lower right (on well) in brown ink: *1696 Doomer*
Provenance: J. der Bosch sale, Amsterdam, 5 October 1767, G-411; Yver; J.W.B. Wayters sale, Utrecht, 15 Sept. C-47; Chevalier Ignace-Joseph de Claussin sale, Batignolles, 2 Dec. 1844, lot 27; Defer-Dumesnil Collection sale, Hôtel Drouot, Paris, 10 May 1900, lot 66; Henry Oppenheimer; Colnaghi's; Sir Karl T. Parker
Acquired 1976
Nancy D. Nizer in Oberhuber, 1977, no. 44, pp. 15-16
Exhibited: Colnaghi's, London, 1959, no. 48; National Gallery, Edinburgh, 1965, no. 55
Literature: Karl T. Parker, "Lambert Doomer," *OMD* IV, 1929, p. 9 (ill.); H. Dattenberg, "Lambert Doomer als Zeichner," *Pantheon* XXV, 1940, p. 16; Andor Pigler, *Barockthemen,* Budapest, 1956, vol. 1, p. 47; *Loan Exhibition of Drawings by Old Masters from the Collection of Dr. and Mrs. Francis Springell,* P. & D. Colnaghi, London, 1959, no. 48; *Illustrated London News,* 24 Oct. 1959; *Old Master Drawings from the collection of Dr. and Mrs. Francis Springell,* National Gallery, Edinburgh, 1965, no. 55; Wolfgang Schulz, *Lambert Doomer Sämtliche Zeichnungen,* Berlin, 1974, no. 42, fig. 19; Robinson, 1977, p. 68, pl. 66; Sumowksi, 1979 ff., vol. II, no. 375, pp. 798-9 (ill.); p. 948

Doomer, surely one of Rembrandt's most appealing students, was the son of a framemaker, best known to history through the portrait Rembrandt made of him and his wife in 1640. The son seems to have drawn more than he painted; at least more of his drawings survive. Many were made on his travels through provincial France in 1645-6 along the Loire, down the length of the Rhine in the 1660's (although not into Switzerland as has been supposed), and even (in 1646) to Cowes on the Isle of Wight[1]. Later drawings show that he never forgot these foreign landscapes, for they appear and reappear throughout his work.

This drawing is a good example, as Sumowski has pointed out. The rock and the road in the middle ground are copied from Doomer's drawing in Berlin of the Loire landscape near Nantes[2]. And the mountains in the background could be based on the preparatory drawing for the *View of the Falls of the Rhine* in the de Boer Collection in Amsterdam[3]. In fact, the city on the right has been tentatively identified as Bacharach seen from the North[4] and the castle on the left as "recalling Stahleck, but...possibly Sonnek Falckenberg or Ehrenfels."[5] Characteristically, Doomer has not described the actual topography literally. Rather he has adapted it imaginatively as a setting. Furthermore, Sumowski has suggested that the poses of the two central figures are self-plagiarism, taken from a drawing in the Louvre (R.F.4.770).

This drawing is significant for combining in a single scene the draughtsman's principal interests: landscape, animals, genre, and religious themes. Comparison with Doomer's earlier version[6] of the subject in the Munich Print Room, casts him in role of a stage designer working out a new presentation, Doomer used a different landscape background and different details in the setting, and changed the poses and actions of some of the human particpants and the animals. Apparently, however, he liked some details like the camel on the far left of the earlier drawing too well to change them, and he continued to arrange the composition like a frieze.

Use of the pen and wash medium in the Steiner drawing is, however, different — the wash is so much softer and atmospheric that Parker described it as "foggy." The effect is of tranquility, while the modest little figures are going about their daily chores quietly. Schulz sees Saftleven's influence in Doomer's Romantic landscapes. The humility of the figures and their gentle solicitude for each other are surely owing to Rembrandt who drew this subject at least three times,[7] although never with this composition.

The subject, from Genesis xxiv: 11-20, reports how Abraham's servant, Eliezer, found Rebecca as a wife for Abraham's son, Isaac, in the city of Nahor in Mesopotamia. Abraham, who was living with the Canaanites, had sent Eliezer back home on this mission. By inspiring Rebecca to offer water to Eliezer and his camels, the Lord made known to him that she was the chosen bride. Having met her family and discovered that she was the granddaughter of Abraham's brother Nahor,[8] Eliezer took her home to the eagerly awaiting Isaac. Their arrival was depicted by Eeckhout (number 71). A.L. and A.M.

1. Sumowski, 1979 ff., vol. II, no. 393, p. 844
2. Sumowski, *op. cit.*, no. 385
3. Schulz, *op. cit.*, 1974, fig. 124
4. Sumowski, *op. cit.*, vol. II, no. 406, p. 876, a view by Doomer of Bacharach from the South, with similar towered buildings.
5. Parker, *op. cit.*, 1929, following Hofstede de Groot and Wilhelm Spies "Rheinlandschaften van Lambert Doomer", *Wallraf-Richartz Jahrbuch* III/IV, 1926/7, p. 183 ff.
6. Schulz, *op. cit.*, 1974, cat. no. 16, fig. 11; Sumowski as "substantiated," *op. cit.*, vol. II, p. 962x.
7. Benesch, 1973, nos. 491, 503 and 566, plus A13 (attributed) and C30 and C64 (copies). According to Sumowski (*op. cit.*, vol. III, No. 442x, p. 948), C64 is not a copy of Rembrandt at all, but rather an original by Doomer of ca. 1644.
8. Depicted by Doomer in a drawing in the Prentenkabinett at Leiden (inv. no. AW 309); Schulz, *op. cit.*, 1974, no. 11, fig. 7; Sumowski as "substantiated," *op. cit.*, vol. II, p. 974, no. 455x.

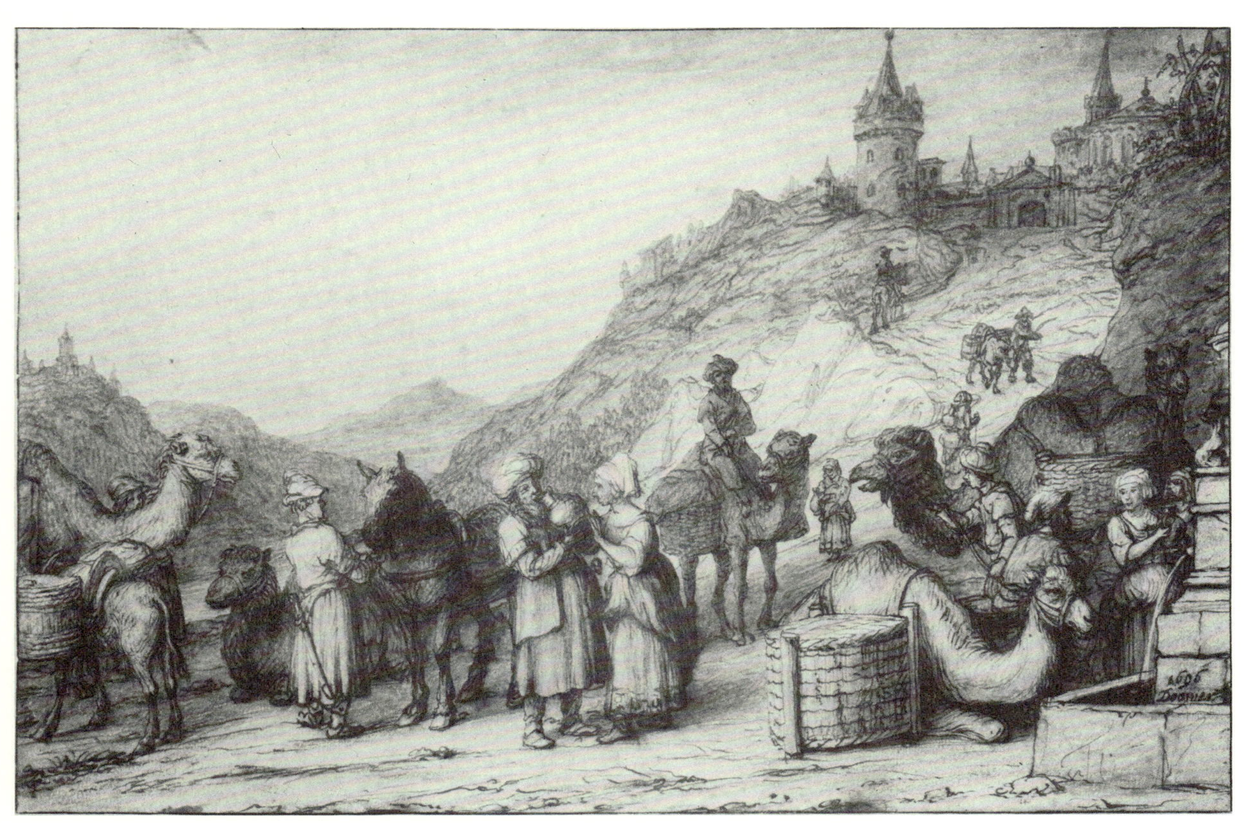

71.

ABRAHAM VAN DYCK

(Alkmaar 1635 - 1672 Amsterdam)

Tobias, Tobit and Anna

Pen and brown ink, brown and grey wash, over black chalk; 190 x 251 mm.

Acquired 1982

Provenance: D. Neyman, Amsterdam; Lansdowne-Heseltine Sale, Sotheby's London, 25 February 1920, lot no. 57; F. Leverhulme and other collections Sale, Anderson Gallery, New York, 2 March 1926, no. 253 as Rembrandt

Literature: Sumowski, 1979, vol. III, p. 1262, no. 578 xx as attributed to van Dyck, whereabouts unknown

Loaned by Lori Steiner

The refined and very detailed manner of drawing, the delicate *chiaroscuro* and the coloristic washes are characteristic of Van Dyck's drawing style. The sensitivity and atmospheric quality are akin to the Rembrandt's idiom of the 1650's, while the staging of the scene, especially the placement of the furniture, is remarkably close to Rembrandt's *Tobit, Anna and the Goat* of 1647 in the Morgan Library in New York[1]. Like the mature Rembrandt, Van Dyck stresses mood rather than action. All these similarities support the assumption that Van Dyck was a student of Rembrandt in the late 1640's. They may also explain some of the confusion existing between the drawings attributed to Van Dyck and to Nicolas Maes, Barent Fabritius, Ferdinand Bol, or even Samuel van Hoogstraten, each to some degree echoing Rembrandt's manner of that period.

At the time of Van Dyck's presumed apprenticeship to Rembrandt, the master was preoccupied with the story of Tobit, which he illustrated several times in highly personal drawings and prints. Humble interiors of this sort were popular with many of Rembrandt's immediate predecessors. Elsheimer in particular often depicted common folk sitting before an open fire to illustrate biblical or mythological events, as in his conversion of *Jupiter and Mercury visiting Philemon and Baucis,* from Ovid's *Metamorphoses* into a genre scene of farmers resting before an open fire (see number 97).

An etching by the English engraver, William Baillie known as Captain Baillie, of 1767 after this drawing, then in the Neyman Collection attributed to Paul [sic] Rembrandt, is entitled *L'Histoire Touchante (The Moving Story).* In fact, the similarities to Rembrandt's drawings from the Book of Tobit point to the correct interpretation of this drawing, previously identified only as *An Interior with a Reader.* One of the so-called apocryphal books of the Old Testament, Tobit formed part of Luther's Bible and of the Dutch Bible established at the Synod of Dordrecht in 1618, but it was not included in the King James version. The Book of Tobit is one of the greatest scriptural examples of piety and confidence in God's unfailing wisdom. This scene, from the Book of Tobit ii, iv, and v in the Jerusalem Bible (1966), shows the aged, blind Tobit at the right, listening to his son Tobias who is reading. Tobit's wife, Anna, is standing behind her husband. Her spinning wheel is at the left, following the text "Anna then undertook woman's work; she would spin wool..." (Tobit ii: 11-12) to support the family after old Tobit's had been blinded. Probably Tobias is checking the debtor's note given to his unfortunate father according to Tobit v: 3-4. Immediately after this scene, Tobias goes out and finds the Archangel Raphael, whom he does not recognize, but who miraculously rescues the family from its predicament.

Menno Simons, the founder of the Mennonite sect, referred several times to the Book of Tobit as a model for Christian education, singling out Tobit's patience, his piety, his charity, and his concepts of sexual morality. Rembrandt was acquainted with several Mennonites, notably the preacher Cornelis Claesz. Anslo, whom he portrayed in 1640, and Van Dyck probably was also. Inspired by Rembrandt and by their mutual contacts with the Mennonites, Van Dyck is likely to have made this drawing in the late 1640's[2]. Like his master, he was interested not only in the moral connotations of the story, but also in the depth of the relations within the family, particularly between the father and son. He succeeded remarkably in fusing his theme and his artistic means to produce an image as humbly appealing and sympathetic as Rembrandt's own. H.V.M.

1. Benesch, 1973, vol. III, no. 584, p. 158, fig. 755.
2. Sumowski, *op. cit.,* says the drawing must pre-date 1654. Because of the contemporary costumes, he denies the possibility that the subject could be biblical.

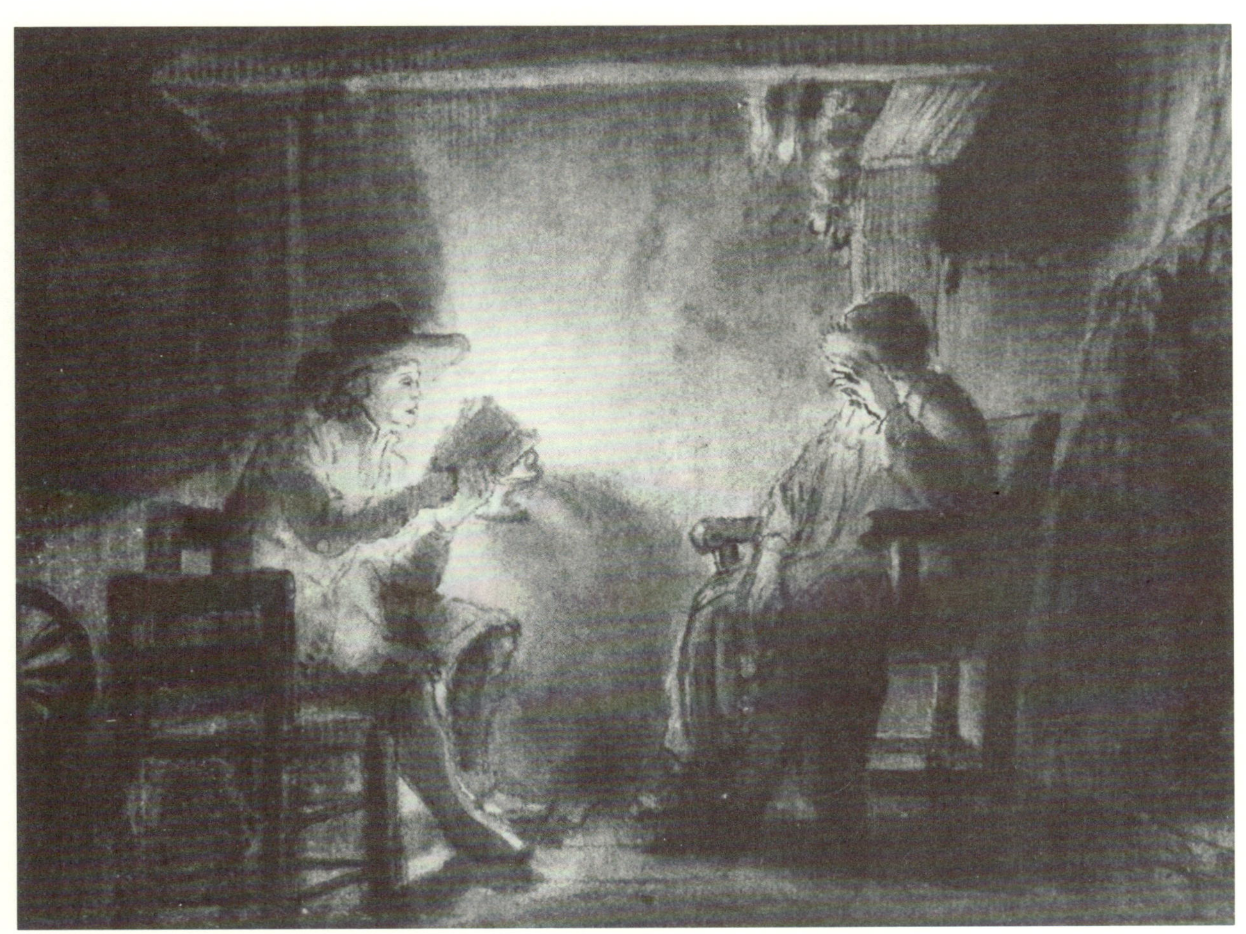

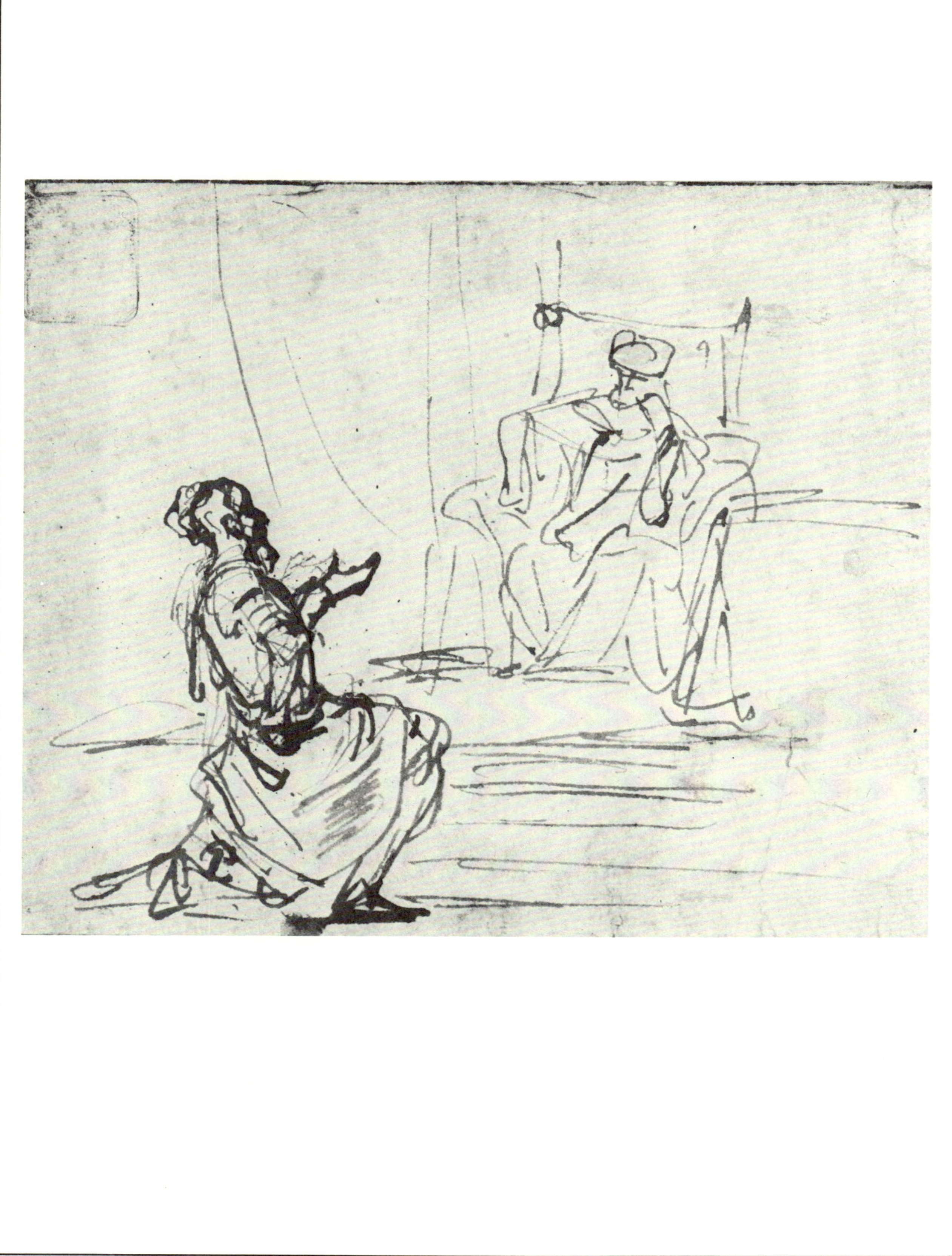

72.

GERBRAND VAN DEN EECKHOUT
(Amsterdam 1621–1674)

King David and Uriah

Pen and brown ink; 133 x 177 mm. (sight); tears lower right corner, repair upper right
Inscribed: unidentified collector's mark upper right corner
Provenance: Count C. de Robiano sale, Amsterdam, 15-16 June 1926, lot 425 as Rembrandt; F. Muller, Amsterdam, 1932 as Ferdinand Bol; Sale, F. Muller, Amsterdam, 27 April 1937, lot 559 as Rembrandt; H.C. Overbosch, Amersfoort; Sotheby's, London, 13 December 1973, lot 97 as attributed to Samuel Hoogstraten; Hatvany Collection
Acquired 1980
Literature: Per Bjurström, exhibition catalogue, *Drawings from Stockholm,* New York, 1969, p. 37; Werner Sumowski, "Gerbrand van den Eeckhout als Zeichner," *Oud Holland,* 1962, pp. 19, 23 fig. 25 as Haman before Ahasuerus; Sumowski, 1979 ff., vol. III, no. 644, p. 1398 as Uriah Before David

Described by Houbraken as a friend of Rembrandt, Eeckhout also studied with him from 1635 to 1640, and his earliest independent work can be dated 1640 or 1641. Although the range of Eeckhout's subject matter was as wide as Rembrandt's own, he apparently preferred scenes like this one from the Old Testament, the source according to Haak[1] for more than half of Eeckhout's history paintings. His allegiance to Rembrandt was intense during the mid-1640's, and continued into the 1660's and beyond, with some gradual modification. At its best, his draughtsmanship was worthy of Rembrandt. As this spontaneous sketch shows, he shared much of the master's ability to evoke with very few lines an expressive encounter between convincing personalities.

However, just what this encounter is, has been questioned. It has been identified as either from the second Book of Samuel xi: 7-12, showing the cuckholded Uriah before King David (see number 82), or from the Book of Esther, with its account of the attempt of Ahasuerus' prime minister Haman to persuade the king to persecute the Jews. The composition and its details are not unique in Eeckhout's *oeuvre;* similar motifs appear in several of his paintings. Most relevant are a similar painted composition preserved in a photo in the Witt Library in London, and a couple of drawings. The little painting, which was sold at Dorotheum in Vienna at some unspecified date, unmistakably represents Haman, but he is standing beside the aged Mordecai who is kneeling before Ahasuerus. One of the drawings, of the enthroned figure (with minor changes), is in the Louvre identified as King David[2]. The second drawing, in the National Museum in Stockholm,[3] is believed to be preparatory for a painting sold in 1708, and is a slightly more elaborate version of this composition. It is identified as Uriah before David, presumably because the kneeling figure is in armour, as the soldier Uriah should be. Close inspection of the same figure in the present drawing indicates that he too is armoured: the four short curved lines on his upper arm must represent arm guards, and there is a hint of a shoulder plate in the hook-shaped line on his upper back. It seems likely therefore that he represents Uriah the soldier, rather than Haman the unscrupulous politician. The meaning of the encounter between the two figures thus becomes clear: Uriah, out of loyalty to his battle-weary comrades who are confined to their camp, refuses the home-leave offered him by David after the king's secret seduction of the soldier's wife, Bathsheba; thus he not only frustrates the king's attempt to cover up Bathsheba's illegitimate pregnancy, but also seals his own doom. The psychological content is conveyed by the poses. Uriah is unsure and somewhat apologetic; King David is restless, his irritation betraying the arrogance that will bring him to send the hapless soldier ruthlessly to his death in battle.

Sumowski dates the drawing ca. 1664.

1. Haak, 1984, p. 366
2. Wolfgang Schulz, "Anne et Samuel à propos d'une peinture...de Lambert Doomer," *Revue du Louvre* XX, 1970, pp. 29-36, figs. 2 and 3.
3. Per Bjurström, *op. cit.,* p. 37; Sumowski, 1979, III, no. 645, p. 1400.

73.

GERBRAND VAN DEN EECKHOUT

Isaac's Reception of Rebecca

Pen and brown ink on light brown paper; light foxing; 162 x 243 mm.
Provenance: Andreossy; A. Sans, Beziers (L.178a); E. Giscaro, Toulouse, 1941; Crewer
Acquired 1980
Literature: Sumowski, 1979, vol. III, no 774x

Another one of Eeckhout's scenes from the Old Testament, from Genesis xxiv: 62-67, this event continues the history of the courtship and marriage of Abraham's son Isaac and Rebecca, the sequence that begins with Doomer's *Meeting of Rebecca and Eliezer* (number 88). Eeckhout also drew the *Meeting,* (in the Musée des Beaux-Arts, Brussels),[1] and the scene of *Rebecca Leaving Her Parents' Home* (in the Narodowe Museum in Gdansk),[2] of the event intervening between the *Meeting* and the *Reception.* The Gdansk sheet is signed on the verso, and is somewhat more elaborate than this drawing. In this drawing, Eeckhout, perhaps inspired by the Oriental splendor of some of Rembrandt's vast vaulted interiors, has taken a little liberty with the biblical account, for the two young people did not meet in front of a palatial building like this but rather outside of Abraham's settlement, in the fields, where Isaac had gone at dusk to meditate. Then "Isaac brought her into his mother Sarah's tent, and took Rebecca, and she became his wife; and he loved her..." (Genesis xxiv: 67). Eeckhout's is a small liberty, justified by the effect of Abraham's wealth conveyed by the background building, and by the contrast between the bustle of Eliezer's returning caravan and the tenderness with which Isaac greets his intended wife — he seems already to love her.

Although all the background activity and some of the details recall Rembrandt's paintings of the 1630's, when Eeckhout was his student, Sumowski dates this drawing to 1665-70. Comparison with Eeckhout's *King David and Uriah* (number 70) shows the subtle changes in his draughtsmanship as time passed and he evolved away from Rembrandt. Particularly notable is what Sumowski calls the artist's "cursory style" of the 1660's: that is, his tendency to be less specific in defining contours. Isaac's legs are comparatively sticklike, and the two turbaned figures (perhaps Abraham behind Isaac and Eliezer to the far left directing the disbanding of the caravan) stand out not only because their contours, like Isaac's, are so heavily laid on but also because these contours are firm and almost geometric in shape. The similarity of this draughtsmanship to that in Eeckhout's *Christ and the Woman Taken in Adultery*[3] in the Print Room at Copenhagen is striking. The Copenhagen drawing is close to a painting dated 1664 formerly in the Six Collection in Amsterdam; Sumowski dates the drawing correspondingly as ca. 1664.

1. Sumowski, 1979, vol. III, no. 637, p. 1384.
2. It is 134 x 193 mm., in pen and brown ink with black ink wash. See exhibition catalogue, *100 Finest Drawings from Polish Collections,* Heim Gallery, London, 1980, no. 25, ill. Sumowski dates it from the early 1640's, Gosieniecka from 1638-40.
3. Sumowski, 1979, vol. III, p. 1394.

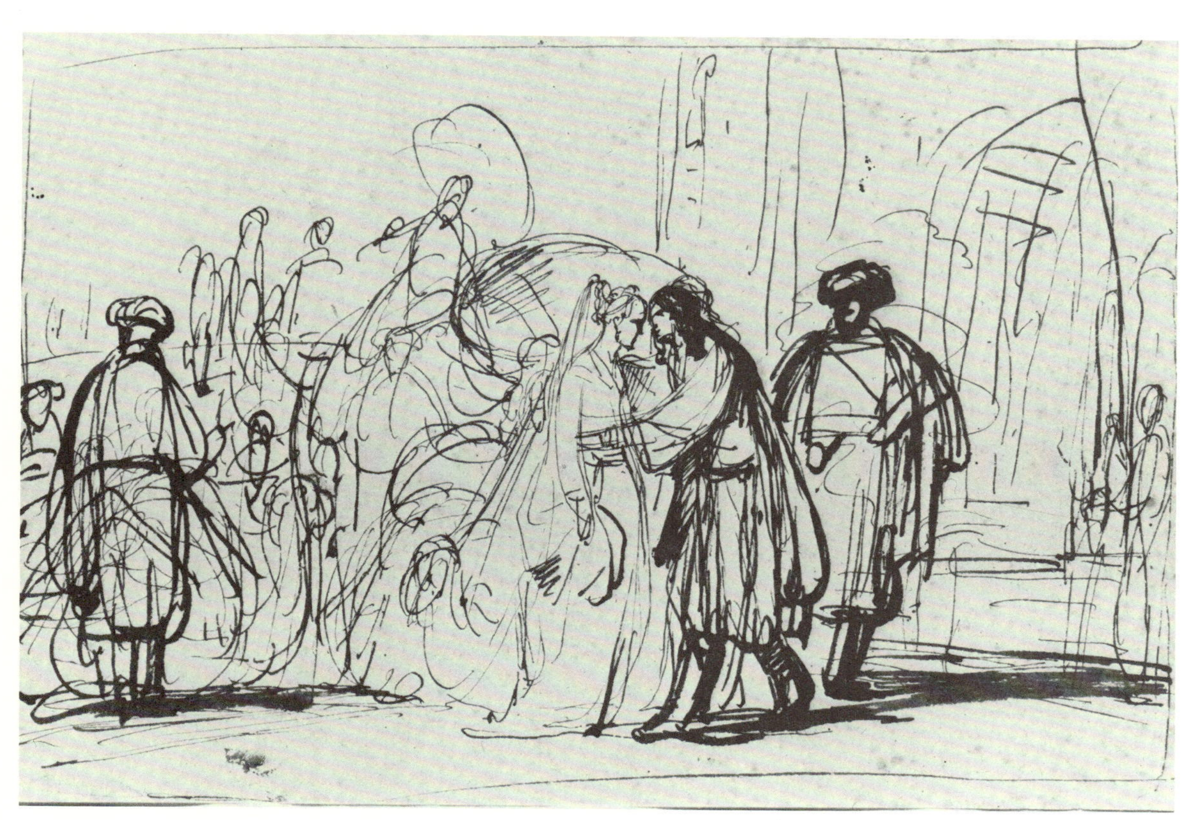

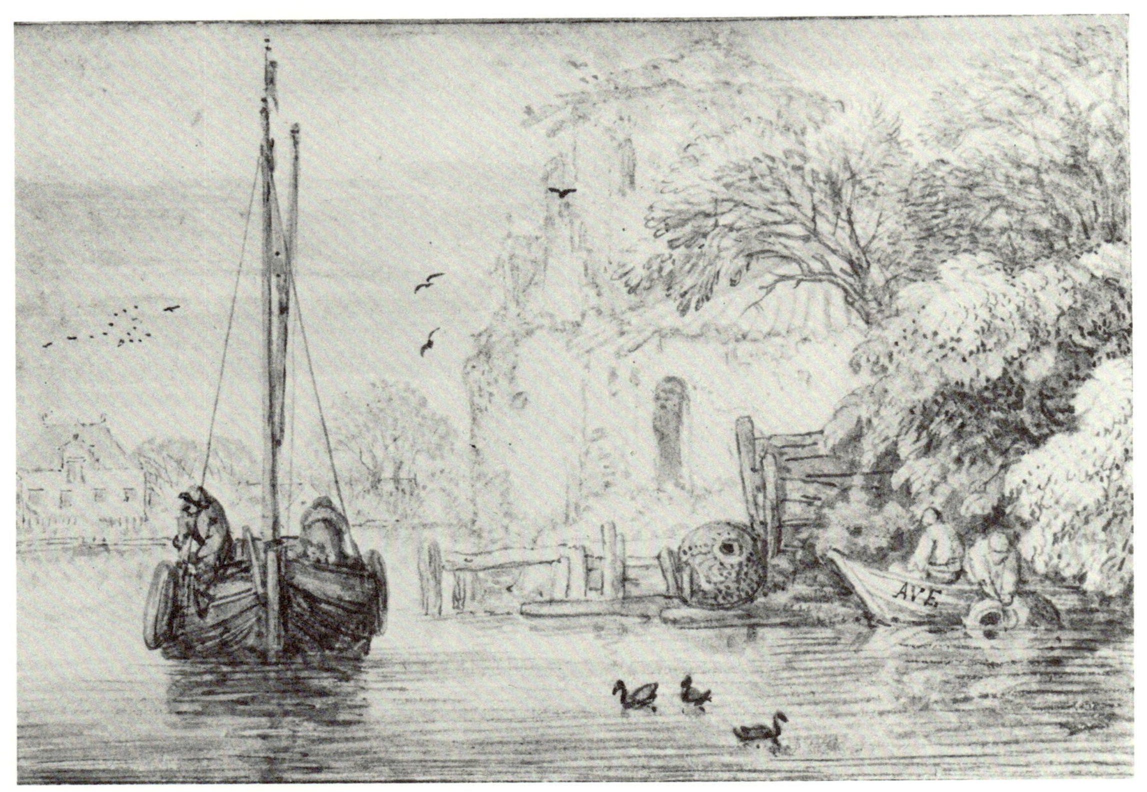
AVE

74.

ALLAERT VAN EVERDINGEN
(Alkmaar 1621 - Utrecht, Sweden, Norway, Haarlem - 1675 Amsterdam)

River Landscape with Two Boats

Pen and brown ink, brown and grey wash, over traces of black chalk; 102 x 150 mm.
Signed in pen and black ink with the artist's typical monogram *AVE* on bow of boat at lower right
Inscribed on verso: in chalk: *no. 35; Everdingen f2-10;* in graphite: *8-2 dessins; fu: 2-*
Provenance: N.D. Goldsmidt (L.1962); R. Burdon-Muller
Acquired 1972
Nancy D. Netzer in Oberhuber, 1977, no. 45, pp. 117-118
Literature: Colin Eisler, *Drawings of the Masters, Flemish and Dutch Drawings,* New York, 1963, pl. 78 incorrectly as at the Fogg Museum

Franklin Robinson[1] summarizes van Everdingen and his career as the "meeting-place of three generations and three aspects, of Seventeenth Century Dutch landscape [painting]." He was a pupil in Utrecht of Roelant Savery, whose Tyrolean mountain landscapes may well have inspired the work derived from van Everdingen's trip during 1640-44 to the Scandinavian wilderness. He studied also in Haarlem with the monochrome Impressionist Pieter de Molijn (1595-1661) who "transformed the Mannerist landscape into a more intimately naturalistic vision, closer to the Dutch countryside..." Finally, Everdingen's "melodramatic" Scandinavian views "bring him into contact with the third generation of landscape artists, notably Jacob van Ruysdael, whose work goes through a phase dominated by these towering visions of the overt power of nature."

As this drawing proves, neither van Everdingen's *oeuvre* nor his talent was limited to such cosmic imagery, although his fame is largely owing to his paintings of what the late eighteenth and early nineteenth century's connoisseurs would recognize as the "sublime," and he remained loyal to his Scandinavian subjects for the rest of his life. He did however have a secondary interest in Dutch marine subjects which, according to Davies, he painted from 1640 into the 1650's[2] followed by some "Netherlandish landscapes"[3] with which this drawing can be associated. The type might be described as river "painting." The mood is neither the excitement of the battle, the storm at sea nor the adventure of limitless horizons, but rather it is the contentment of tranquil daily life on Dutch inland waterways. A comparable drawing of the quays of a Dutch town, is in the British Museum[4]. Its unpretentiousness recalls Molijn's subjects, although without the drama of his diagonal compositions and weather effects; in both subject matter and mood, it seems close to the work of some of van Everdingen's contemporaries in the river-town of Dordrecht.

M.L. and A.M.

1. Robinson, 1977, pp. 65-66.
2. Alice Ingraham Davies, *Allart van Everdingen,* Garland Publishing Company, New York/London 1978, p. 64.
3. Davies, *op. cit.,* pp. 237 ff. Davies places only ten paintings in this classification.
4. Davies, *op. cit.,* p. 240, fig. 339.

75.

JAN GOEREE
(1670 Middelburg - Rome ? - 1731 Amsterdam)

The Death of Herod

Pen and brown ink, brown and grey wash, heightened with white, over red chalk; 130 x 202 mm.
Inscribed verso: ...*Actus 12 vs 20-23 het mheinde van Herods/Goeree/ no. 3968*
Provenance: Jhr. J. Goll van Frankenstein (L.2987)
Acquired 1983
Loaned by Lillian and Robert Fraker

Goeree was a student of Gerard de Lairesse (1641-1711), the author in 1707 of the *Groot Schilderboek* (the *Great Book of Painting*) and the leading history painter and exponent of the academic style in late seventeenth century Holland. Like his teacher, Goeree was skilled in fabricating complex scenes from history and literature, with highly studied and embellished settings. But rather than being a painter-theoretician like Lairesse, Goeree was primarily a book-illustrator, second in this art only to the father and son Jan and Caspar Luyken. Julius Held describes[1] him as "one of the most prodigious illustrators of Dutch books in the early years of the eighteenth century." Like other illustrators of his time, he worked on sacred and secular texts, and designed a number of intricate frontispieces. He may have visited Rome, but most of his life was spent in Amsterdam near his printers and publishers.

The subject matter of this drawing comes from Acts xii: 20-25, and describes how the wretched Herod, king of Judea and bane of the early Christian Church, came to his miserable end, a fate worthy of Greek tragedy. Receiving a delegation from a neighboring dependency, he appeared "arrayed in royal apparel, sat upon his thone and made an oration to them. And the people gave a shout, saying, it is the voice of a god and not of a man. And immediately the angel of the Lord smote him, because he gave not God the glory; and he was eaten of worms, and gave up the ghost." The Testament adds that the forces of virtue were then fully triumphant, and "...the word of God grew and multiplied." Goeree chose to represent the climactic moment, when the angel appears in the heavens to strike down the arrogant king in all his pomp before the assembled crowd. The details have been studied so lovingly and elaborated so painstakingly, as to lose much of the dramatic force that Rembrandt and his best followers would have given the subject. But Goeree's control is so sure that focus is maintained on the central protagonists, and whatever loss in drama there may be is compensated by the rich and exquisite particularization of the staging.

In 1700 Goeree provided the illustrations for the *Historie des Ouden en Nieuwen Testaments,* published in Amsterdam by Pieter Mortier, to which this drawing may be related.

1. Julius Held, "The Last of the Attic Nights: A Drawing by Jan Goeree," *MD* IX, 1971, p. 54.

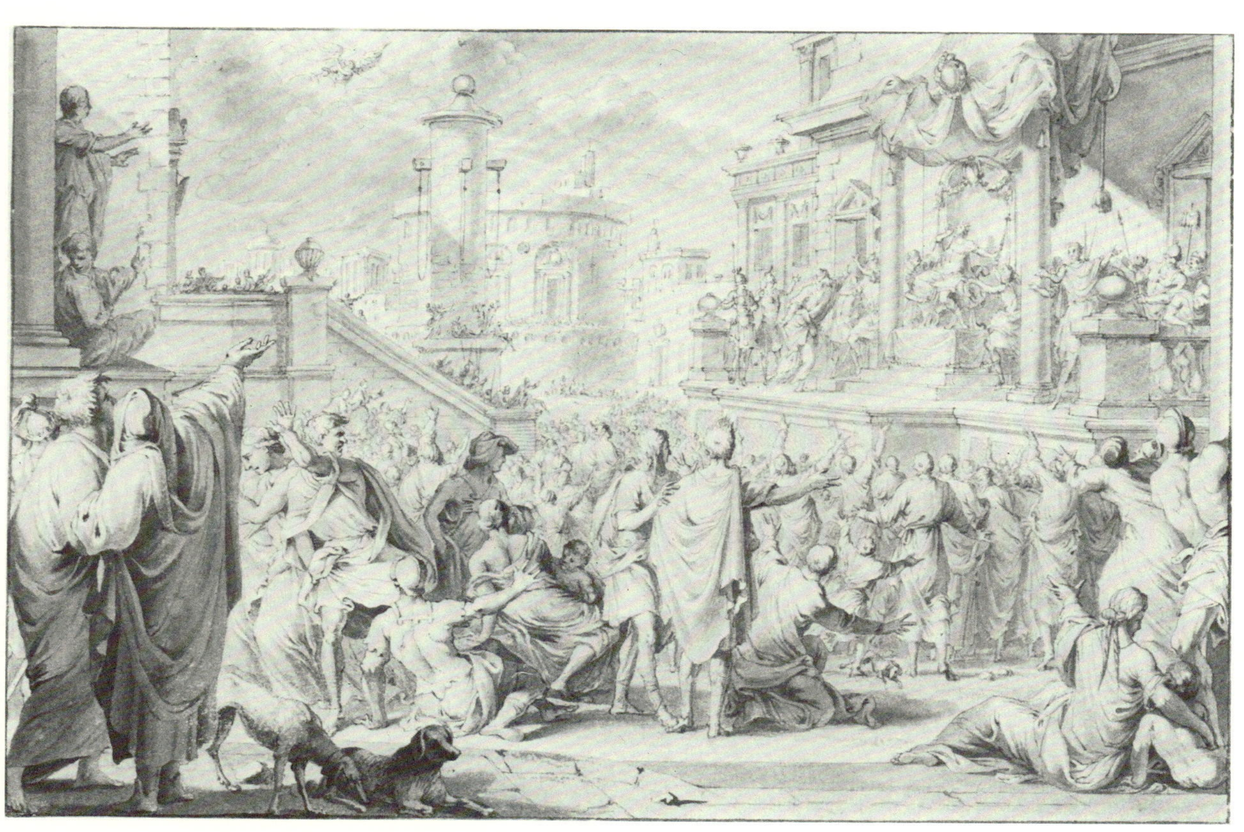

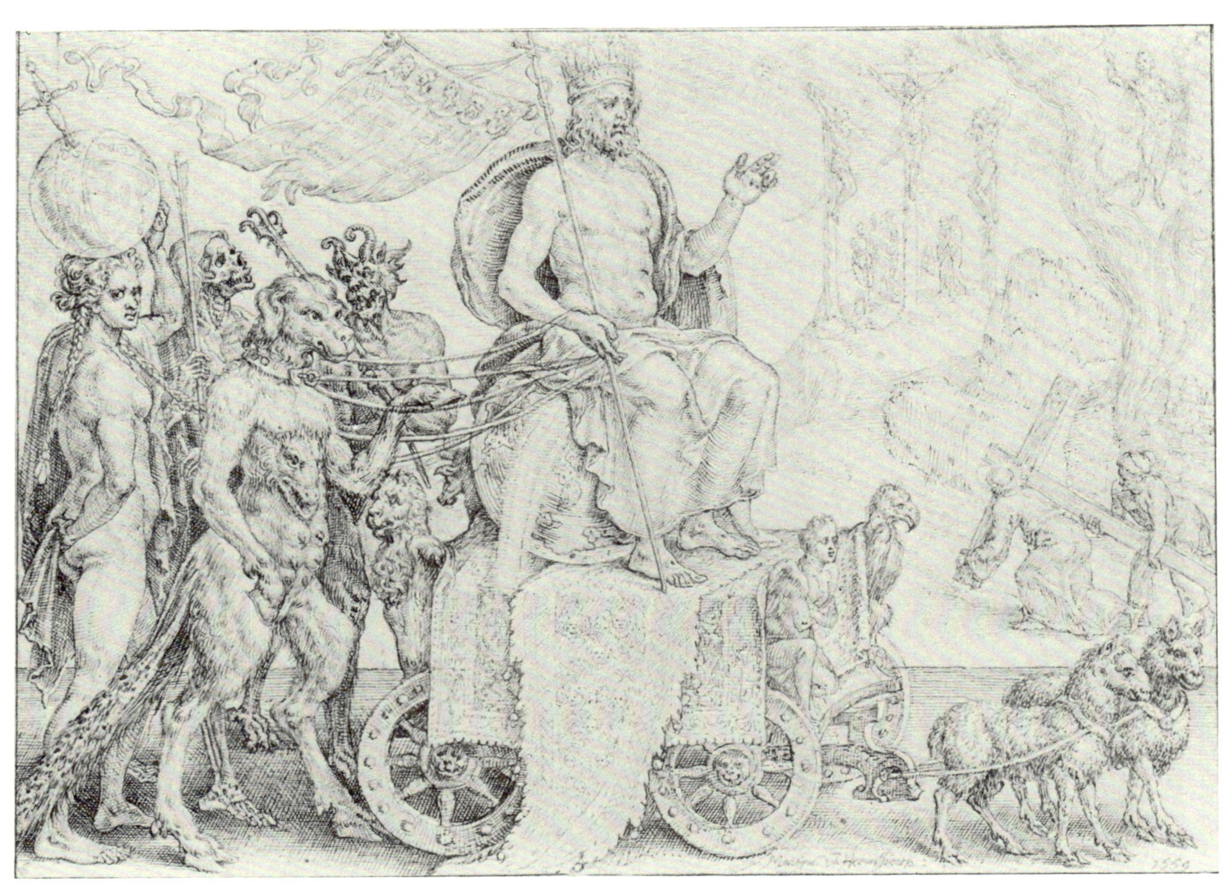

76.

MARTEN VAN HEEMSKERCK

(Heemskerck near Haarlem 1498 - Haarlem, Rome, Amsterdam - Haarlem 1574)

The Triumph of Christ

Pen and brown ink over traces of black chalk; incised for transfer; 184 x 260 mm.

Signed: recto, lower right edge: *Martinus va Heemskerck;* lower right corner: *1559*

Provenance: R. Freiherr von Kuhlmann; C.G. Boerner, Düsseldorf, 1972

Acquired 1972

Emily D. Bilski in Oberhuber, 1977, no. 48, pp. 123-4

Literature: C.G. Boerner, *50 Zeichnungen von 1850,* Düsseldorf, 1972, no. 28; Ilja M. Veldman, *Maarten van Heemskerck and Dutch Humanism in the Sixteenth Century,* Maarsen, 1977, p. 67, pl. 46; Rainald Grosshans, *Maerten van Heemskerck: Die Gemälde,* Berlin, 1980, no. 226, pl. 208; William Robinson in Deborah Johnson, 1983, p. 173 note 3

Copied: in the series of prints entitled *The Triumph of Christ* engraved by D.V. Coornhert and published by Hieronymus Cock (Hollstein, 1949 ff., vol. VIII, p. 240 nos. 120-27)

Loaned by Lillian Fraker

Heemskerck was a pupil in 1527 of Jan van Scorel (1495-1562) and apparently was infected by him with the passion for Rome and things Roman that was to be one of the dominating forces of his life and art. In 1532 he went to the Holy City for at least three and perhaps as many as five years. In the process of educating himself there, he provided us in his notebooks of sketches of what he saw, a precious record of the city's archaeology and appearance — including St. Peter's Basilica in the process of rebuilding. He settled in Haarlem in 1537 and remained there until his death, except for 1572-73 when the city was under siege by the Spanish army and he took refuge in Amsterdam. He was a fine painter, but was particularly active in designing prints of Christian moral subjects.

This drawing was preparatory in reverse for one in a cycle of eight engravings of 1559 entitled *The Triumph of Patience,* conceived as a moral analogy to the triumphal processions which victorious generals were awarded in ancient times. As Veldman points out,[1] if in the twentieth century this allegory and that of Heemskerck's other series seem arcane, in his century most of his subjects were well known, from various sources in contemporary literature. In this instance, he seems to have relied heavily on a book, *Zedekunst das is Wellevenskunste,* by his friend and collaborator, the humanist publisher Dirck Volkersz. Coornhert (1522-90), who also made the engravings. Six other of Heemskerck's preparatory drawings have survived, three in the Boymans van Beuningen Museum in Rotterdam, one in the Museum of the Rhode Island School of Design, and two in private collections. The first work in the sequence personifies Patience, accompanied by Hope and Longing, and triumphant over Fortune. The next six represent Isaac, Joseph, David, Job, Tobit and St. Stephen, each as exemplary of some moral strength. This drawing is preparatory for the last and climactic Triumph in the series. Christ, seated on the world globe borne by a chariot, triumps over the motley following throng consisting of a naked woman personifying the World, a skeletal Death carrying his lethal arrow, Sin with the dog's head of Envy and the Peacock's tail of Pride, and the horned and cloven-hoofed Devil. The cycle sequence represents the stages of man's progress toward the ultimate goal of divine mercy and deliverance from the World, Sin, Death and the Devil, through Christ, whose sacrifice in the crucifixion and whose resurrection[3] (on the right) gave man the possibility of hope for redemption and eternal life[4]. The sacrificial lambs drawing Christ's chariot appear also in the first of the series, as attributes of Patience, and thus draw the whole sequence together. A.L. and A.M.

1. Veldman, *op. cit.,* p. 56.
2. Bilski in Oberhuber, *op. cit.,* and Robinson in Johnson, *op. cit.,* no. 2, p. 173.
3. The resurrected Christ in an identical pose appears in a Heemskerck painting of ca. 1550 in the National Museum in Copenhagen.
4. The inscription on the print reads, in Veldman's translation from the Latin: "The almighty Christ, the only hope of mankind and the true life, was obedient to the eternal father unto death, the abominable death of the cross. Now we see him raised in triumph above heaven and above all name, now that Tartarus, the world, the devil, sin and the savage demons have been swept away."

77.

JAN VAN HUCHTENBURG
(Haarlem 1647 - Rome, Paris - 1733 Amsterdam)

Cavalry Skirmish

Brush drawing with grey wash; 195 x 317 mm.
Loaned by the Santa Barbara Museum of Art, gift of John and Alice Steiner

Huchtenburg was one of many seventeenth century artists like Salvator Rosa (number 37) who painted battle scenes, but he made them a specialty. Although he was born during the last year of the Thirty Years War, enough other conflicts continued throughout his lifetime to maintain his, and his clientele's, awareness of war as a constant reality. He was trained at home in Haarlem by Thomas Wijk (ca. 1616-77), who painted interior scenes but is remembered best for his beautifully atmospheric Italianate landscapes. Huchtenberg then went to Paris and studied with Adam Frans van der Meulen (1632-90), the leading painter of military subjects during the later years of the seventeenth century. A visit to Rome reinforced the attitudes Huchtenburg had learned from Wijk. Eventually he settled in Amsterdam, with a flourishing trade in battle-scenes like this one, both painted and drawn. He also painted portraits of military leaders, and various open-air scenes of hunting, riding schools, markets and the like — almost without exception including horses.

Huchtenburg's battle-scenes are usually similar to this drawing: assymetrical in composition with a cluster of trees on one side balanced by a distant view on the other. In the foreground is a cavalry skirmish, here (and usually) culminating in a rearing screaming horse. The skirmish provides the focus of this composition; in some others it is reduced to being a mere episode in a panoramic landscape, often subordinate to a vast military operation. Although the great general Prince Eugene of Savoy did employ Huchtenberg in 1708 to record his victories, the artist seems customarily to have depicted imaginary skirmishes.

Battle scenes had been of interest to painters since the beginning of the Renaissance in Italy. Some were political and chauvinistic, like Uccello's mid-15th century representations of Florentine victories or the pompous display at Versailles of the triumphs of Louis XIV more than two centuries later. A few, notably the series of prints entitled *Les Grandes Misères de la Guerre* by Jacques Callot, revealed the agony that was inflicted on soldiers and civilians alike. This drawing might be an example of a third tradition, of the "battle scene without a hero,"[1] that is, of battles as a genre, with unidentified soldiers fighting in unspecified wars. These costumes establish this conflict as contemporary; the point is neither historical nor simply descriptive, nor is it pathetic, although perhaps some compassion may be felt for the wounded men and the fallen horses. However Huchtenburg's battle-scenes of this sort seem instead to be basically a glorification of war's action, energy, excitement and even of its violence, like Rosa's scenes of the heroic "ideal of battle."

1. Fritz Saxl, "The Battle Scene without a Hero," *Journal of the Warburg and Courtauld Institutes,* III, 1939/40, pp. 70-87.

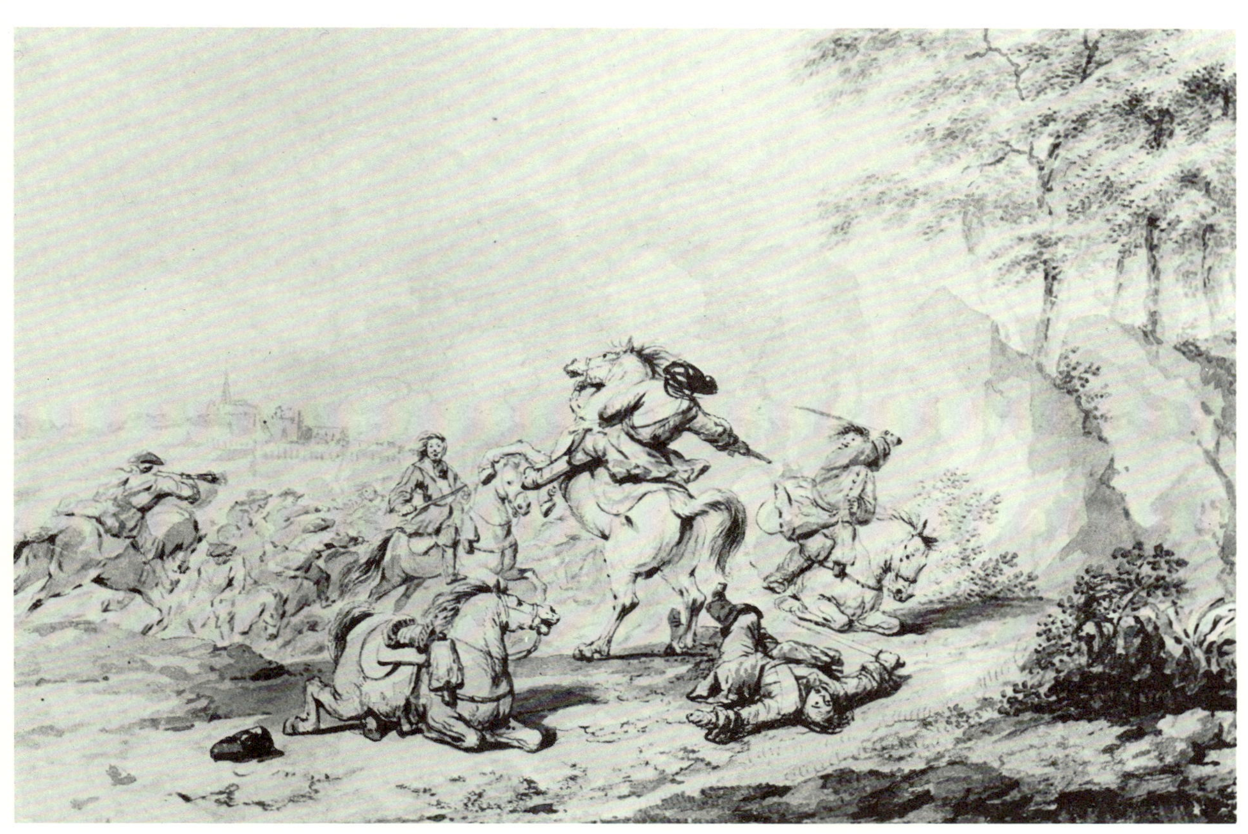

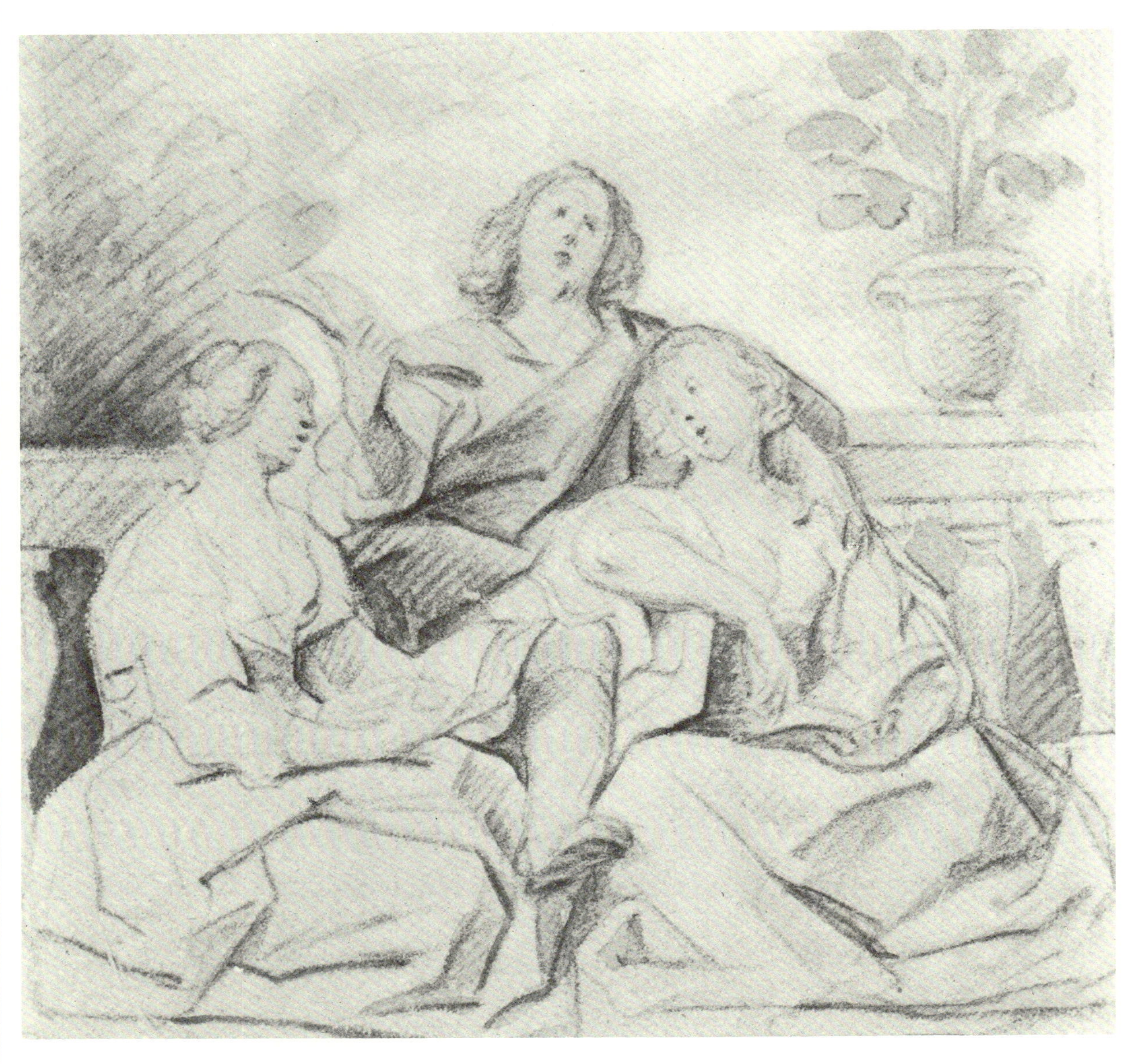

78.

JACOB JORDAENS
(Antwerp 1593 - 1678)

A Youth and Two Women Singing

Black chalk, brown wash, heightened with white on blue paper; 162 x 180 mm.
Acquired 1981

Two singing women and a young man sitting in front of a balustrade take part in what appears to be a *concert galant*. The pyramidal arrangement of the three protagonists dominates the composition. Apart from the balustrade, there is little development of three-dimensional space. The atmosphere of joy and light-hearted sensuality is somewhat contradicted by the abrupt delineation and the angularity of the drapery folds, characteristic of Jordaens' manner of drawing in the early 'forties. The forceful parallel hatching and the skillful integration of the figures, betray a master who was able to express the essential with a minimum of effort.

After the death of Rubens in 1640 and of Anthony van Dyck in 1641, Jordaens became the leading Flemish painter in Antwerp, his cherished town which he hardly left during his long career. His services were in demand not only by the upper clergy and the bourgeoisie but also by royal and aristocratic circles, including Charles I of England, Queen Christina of Sweden and Amalia van Solms, widow of Prince Frederick Henry of Nassau (see number 67). His studio was operating full time and commissions became more plentiful than ever.

From 1640 onwards drawing played an important role in Jordaens' studio practice, and his delineation tended to become increasingly automatic and his style tended to stabilize. Most of the 425 to 450 drawings attributed to him were executed during this period. Apart from Rubens, no other Flemish painter — not even Frans Floris — at any time organized his production on such a scale. As Jordaens' studio organization became more complicated, the nature and the style of his drawing altered as well. He no longer executed free sketches in pen, brush and bistre as he had up to 1620. Moreover, he gradually abandoned the technique of *trois crayons* that he had favored during the thirties. Instead, he developed a drawing routine based on the use of broken and angular shapes, and he executed compositional sketches for paintings and tapestries in watercolor and gouache over chalk. Figures were rendered in a schematic manner, often reduced to patterns.

The architectural setting, the angular delineation, and the medium in this charming drawing are characteristic of Jordaens' draughtsmanship between 1640 and 1645[1]. The exact purpose of the sketch is not known, but its architectural character encourages the assumption that, like a number of other drawings of groups in architectural settings, it was a *modello* for a wall painting. Wall decorations of this sort were executed in oil on canvas. Possibly, this sketch was intended for Jordaens' new house, which was completed structurally about 1641 but not decorated with paintings until some years later. Consequently, the drawing was probably executed by Jordaens himself ca. 1645, a proposal confirmed by Professor R.-A. d'Hulst[2]. H.V.M.

1. See Roger-A. d'Hulst, *Jordaens Drawings,* 4 vols., Brussels-London-New York, 1974, nos. A175, A219-A221, and A228.
2. In a personal letter 19 November 1984.

79.

PHILIPS KONINCK
(Amsterdam 1619 - Rotterdam - 1688 Amsterdam)

The Zaagmoelenpoort, Amsterdam

Pen and brown ink and wash over black chalk, with accents of red chalk and white; 143 x 293 mm.; retouched on center windmill, repairs on left edge and vertical tear through pond into sky
Inscribed in pen and brown ink, recto lower right corner: *Rembrandt;* verso: *Bij de Saagmolenspoort te Amsterdam*
Provenance: J.B. de Graff, 1820; George Clausen (L.539); J.P. Heseltine, Muller, Amsterdam, 27-28 May 1913, no. 134 pl. 16; Pieter Langerhuizen, Muller, Amsterdam, 29 April 1919, lot 252 as Rembrandt school; Seligman and Company, N.Y. 1925; Marie Sterner Collection, U.S.A.; H.E. ten Cate; B. Houthakker 1965
Acquired 1975
Cynthia Schneider in Oberhuber, 1977, no. 49, p. 127
Literature: Seligman and Co., *Original Drawings by the Old Masters,* New York, 1925, no. 41; Dirk Hannema, *Catalogue of the H.E. ten Cate Collection,* Rotterdam, 1955, no. 249; Bernard Houthakker Galleries, *Master Drawings,* Amsterdam, 1965, no. 36; Horst Gerson, *Philips Koninck,* Berlin, 1936, p. 65, no. Z1; Horst Gerson, *Philips Koninck,* new edition, Berlin 1980, p. 65, no. 1

Trained in Rotterdam by his older brother Jacob (1614/15 — after 1690), Phillips had arrived in Amsterdam by 1640, when he was married there. He may have been too old by that time[1] to have entered Rembrandt's studio as a pupil, although the nineteen year old Carel Fabritius did just that in 1641. In any case, Philips Koninck was certainly associated in some way with Rembrandt, if not as a student, then certainly as a friend, admirer and (to some extent) an imitator.

The paintings for which he is most admired are his panoramic landscapes. Unlike his predecessors who based theirs on fantasy, Koninck's landscapes give the impression of detailed observation — of the immense sweep of the Dutch plains under the shifting light of the sun, and of the changing structure of the volatile clouds piling up like ephemeral mountains within infinite skies. Although the space in this drawing is not so vast as these paintings, it corresponds in its sense of a flat expanse, as it does also in some details. It describes an actual place, identified as the area around the Zaagmoelenpoort (Sawmill Gate) on the western edge of the city both by the verso inscription, and by another drawing of the scene by Koninck's brother-in-law, Abraham Furnerius (1628-1668)[2]. The Furnerius sheet shows the same windmill and the same sharply foreshortened fence. Furthermore although this landscape is too circumscribed to be considered panoramic, nonetheless it does convey a sense of the sweep of the flat landscape, of the boundlessness of the heavy sky, and of the emotional quality of an overcast day. Koninck is indebted to Rembrandt not only for the means of evoking this mood, but also for the use of wash and the crisp draughtsmanship, features which are in keeping with the date of the 1650's suggested by Schneider. This drawing certainly is reminiscent of the comparable drawings of the 1650's by Rembrandt, such as the great *Het Molenje* in the Albertina.

Gerson expressed some reservations about the attribution, and Sumowski does not include it in his corpus, although it appears to be very similar to his 1521x, *The Polderhuis by the Boerenwetering,* in the Gemeentearchief in Amsterdam; Schneider reports that Seymour Slive accepts it. A.L. and A.M.

1. As Haak, 1984, p. 374 suggests.
2. Sumowski, 1979 ff., vol. IV, pl. 1020xx

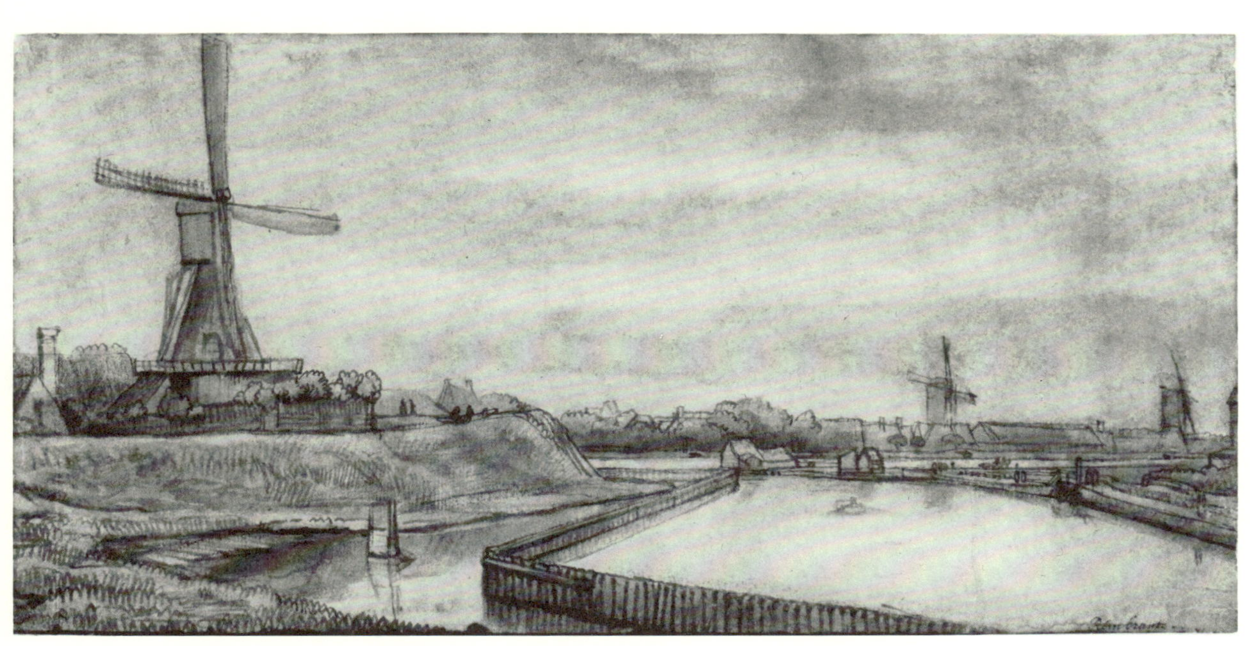

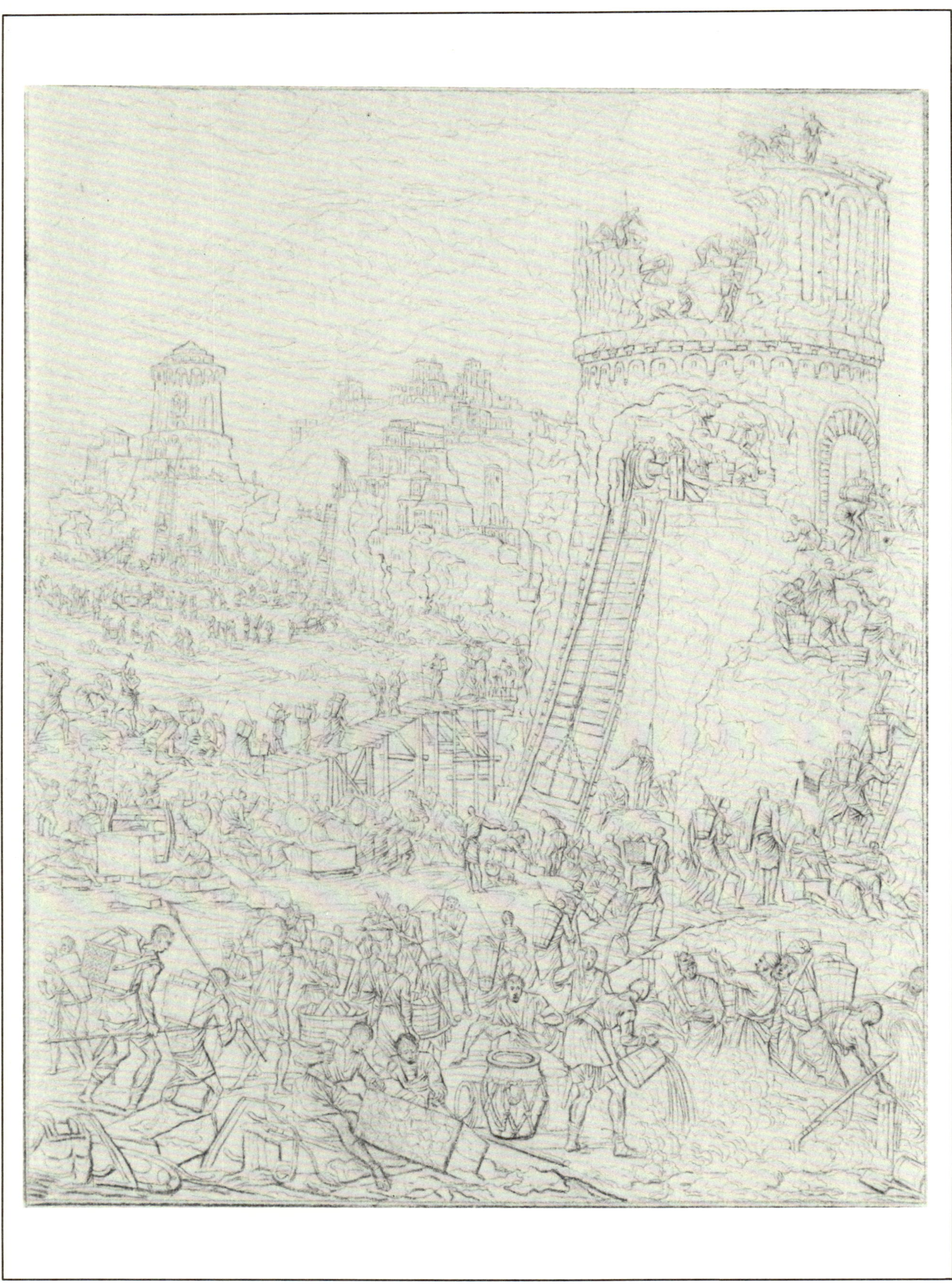

80.

FRANS LUYCKX
(Antwerp 1604 - Rome, Prague - 1668 Vienna)

Building of a Fortified Town

Red chalk; vertical and horizontal marks of a stylus; 188 x 153 mm.
Acquired 1973
Loaned by Lillian and Robert Fraker

Frans Luyckx (or Leux or von Luxenstein) became a master in the St. Luke's guild in Antwerp in 1620. From then until leaving for Rome in 1635, he was probably active in the Rubens workshop. In 1638 he became court painter to Emperor Ferdinand III in Prague and, under his successor Leopold William, continued his successful career from 1657 onwards in Vienna. He was much favored by the Emperor, who raised him to the peerage, whence his title of nobility von Luxenstein[1].

His juvenilia, inevitably under Rubens' influence, consist mainly of historical and New Testament themes. Perhaps because portraiture was much more lucrative and rewarding, he abandoned these soon after his first appointment as court painter, and devoted himself to portraying the imperial family, courtiers, generals and other personages. The major part of his *oeuvre* is divided among the museums of Prague, Vienna and Stockholm. Often repetitive in composition, his Viennese court style betrays Italian and Spanish influences[2].

This drawing is reminiscent of compositions of the *Building of the Tower of Babel* derivative from Pieter Bruegel the Elder (ca. 1525/30-1569), which Luyckx must already have known in his Antwerp days. A distant echo can be detected in Jan Luyken's drawing of the tower in the Boymans-van Beuningen Museum in Rotterdam[3]. The drawing's incised stylus marks indicate that it was intended for an engraving, perhaps as an illustration, although none derivative from it has been identified.

If this drawing is in fact by Frans Luyckx, it must have been executed no earlier than the late 1620's, and would therefore be clearly archaistic, reminiscent of the previous generation of painters of the Italo-Antwerp school, like Maarten de Vos (number 95) and Jan van der Straet alias Stradano. However it is tempting to think of a possible confusion of Luyckx' name with that of the engraver and art dealer Hans van Luyck, who was active in Amsterdam ca. 1580, and might be considered as an alternate author of the drawing.

The number of towers being built suggests that the drawing might be an imaginative conflation of the Tower of Babel theme with the rebuilding of the city walls in Rome, under the pontificate of Pope Urban VIII (1623-44). Luyckx' visit there coincided with Urban's advancement of the grandiose plans of his Counter Reformatory predecessor, Pope Sixtus V, when the Eternal City was increasingly established in the eyes as well as the minds of the faithful as the stronghold of True Faith. H.V.M.

1. Ernst Ebenstein, "Der Hofmaler Frans Luyckx," *Jahrbuch des Kunsthistorischen Sammlungen des Allerhöchsten Kaiserhauses,* XXVI, 1906-7, pp. 183-154.
2. Bernt, 1980, vol. II, pp. 37-8.
3. Bernt, 1980, vol. II, no. 376.

81.

NICOLAS MAES
(Dordrecht 1634 - 1693 Amsterdam)

Jacob Receiving Joseph's Blood-Stained Cloak (recto); Sketches of a *Bearded Man* and for a *Sacrifice of Isaac* (verso)

Pen and brown ink and wash over traces of red chalk (recto); pen and brown ink (verso); 220 x 302 mm.
Provenance: Carel E. Duits (L.533a)
Literature: Sumowski, 1979, vol. VIII, nos. 1767a (recto), 1765c (verso); William Robinson, "The Sacrifice of Isaac: an unpublished painting by Nicolas Maes," *Burl,* CXXVI, 1984, p. 534, fig. 2
Acquired 1985

Maes studied with some nobody at home in Dordrecht before going to Amsterdam in 1646[1] to enter Rembrandt's studio, where he was a contemporary of Eeckhout (numbers 70-71). He was back in Dordrecht in 1653, and stayed there until 1673 when he moved to Amsterdam for the rest of his life. Until about 1660 when he visited Jordaens in Antwerp, his work was sober and serious; genre and histories similar to those of such others of Rembrandt's circle as Barent Fabritius, and including Maes' most memorable and appealing paintings, perhaps, of poor, pious old women. But from 1660 onward, he turned increasingly to portraiture; probably the purpose of his move to Amsterdam was to put him in contact with the larger, richer clientele available in the larger city. And as time passed and Maes prospered, his portraits, becoming increasingly elegant and pretentious, lost the simple sincerity of his earlier work.

At least 150 of his drawings survive, all from the 1650's and contemporaneous with his religious paintings. Maes' drawings tend to resemble Rembrandt's more than his paintings, but they have distinctive features of their own. William Robinson[2] has described these features as "squat proportions..., mitten-like hands,...egg-shaped heads with highly schematicized features, and broad, often coarsely applied lines of the chalk and wash" — all of which can be recognized in the lively calligraphy of the recto. The drama of the confrontation between the son hesitantly holding out the bloody cloak and the thunderstruck old man may be worthy of the master, as may also be such details as the barking dog in the lower left corner and the heavy reinforcement in wash of the wall on the right; but the mannerisms are clearly the follower's.

Although few of Maes' drawings can be associated with his paintings, in this instance the verso sketch for the *Sacrifice of Isaac* does seem preparatory for a painting of the same subject in the collection of Dr. Alfred Bader in Milwaukee. Robinson[3] has dated the painting as 1655-58, which places at least the verso of the

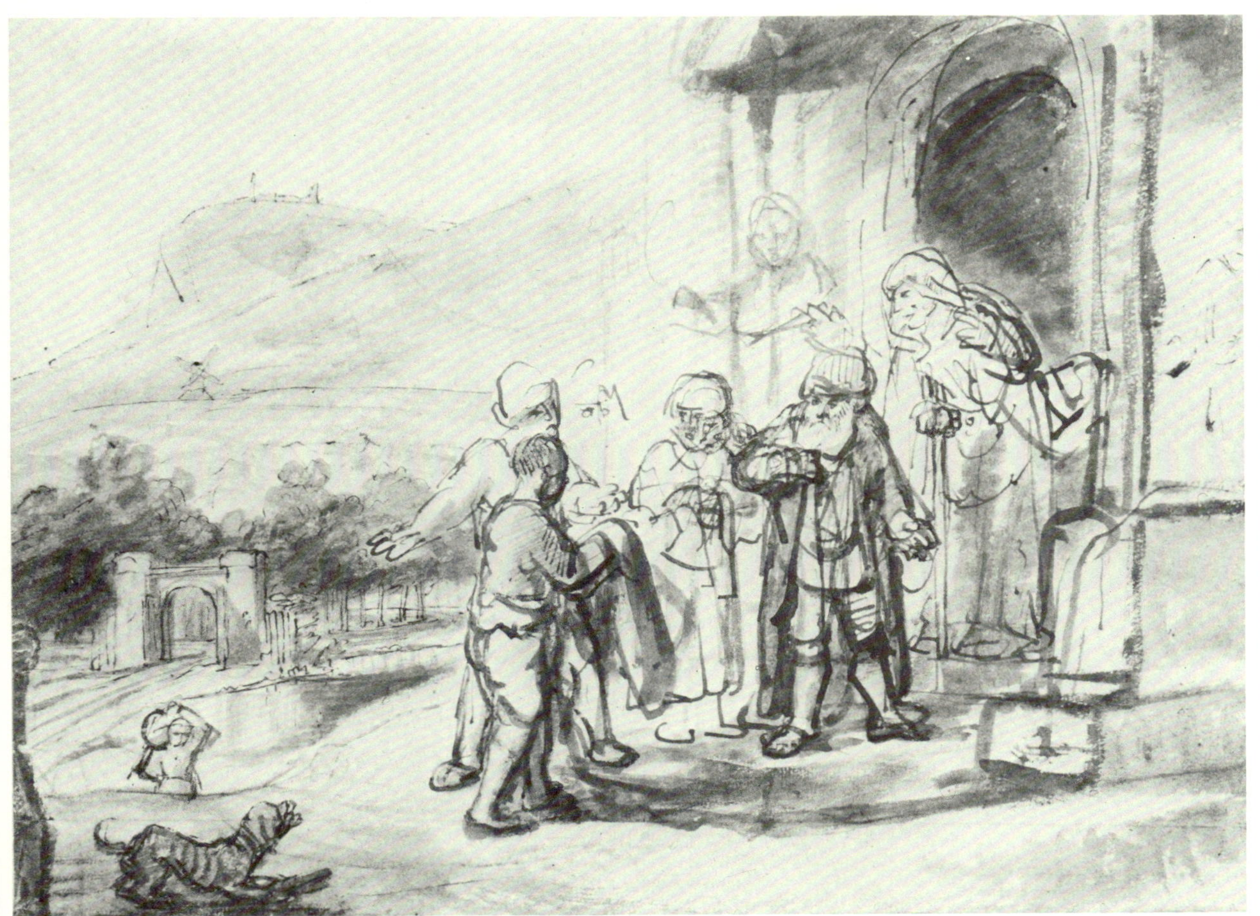
(recto)

drawing chronologically. Whether Maes drew the recto at the same time is questionable. Sumowski[4] associates it reasonably with a Maes drawing in the National Gallery, Edinburgh,[5] where Jacob is seated, but his face, and the pose of his old wife standing behind him, are almost identical. The date, of ca. 1653, suggested by Sumowski for the Edinburgh drawing, would place it in time with Maes' earliest signed and dated painting, the *Expulsion of Hagar* in the Metropolitan Museum[6].

1. According to Bernt, 1958, vol. II, no. 380
2. In Franklin Robinson, 1977, p. 78
3. William Robinson, *Burl, op. cit.,* p. 540
4. Sumowski, *op. cit.*
5. Sumowski, *op. cit.,* no. 1843x.
6. Published by John Walsh Jr., "The Earliest Dated Painting by Nicolas Maes," *Metropolitan Museum Journal,* VI, 1972, pp. 105-114

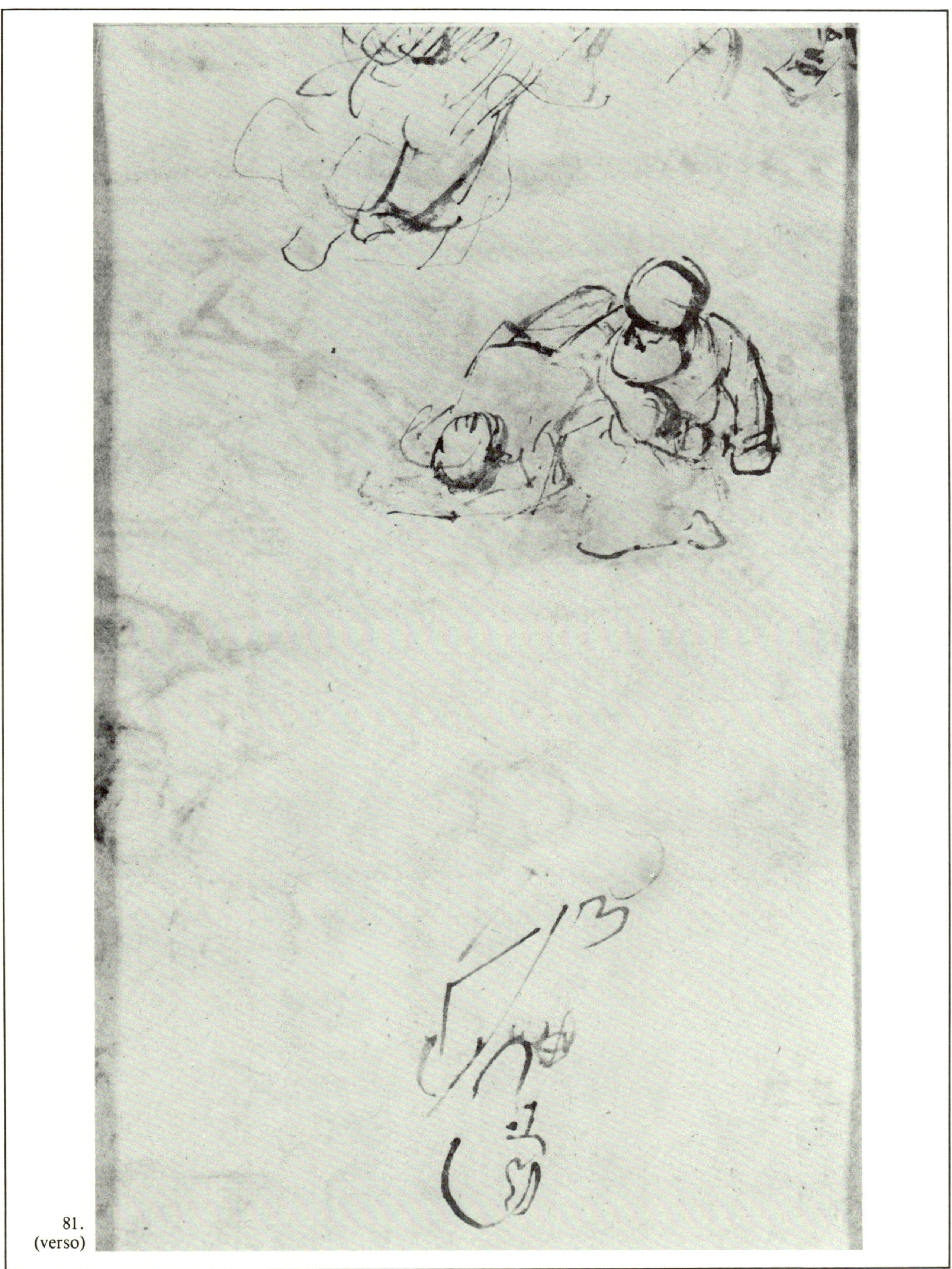

81.
(verso)

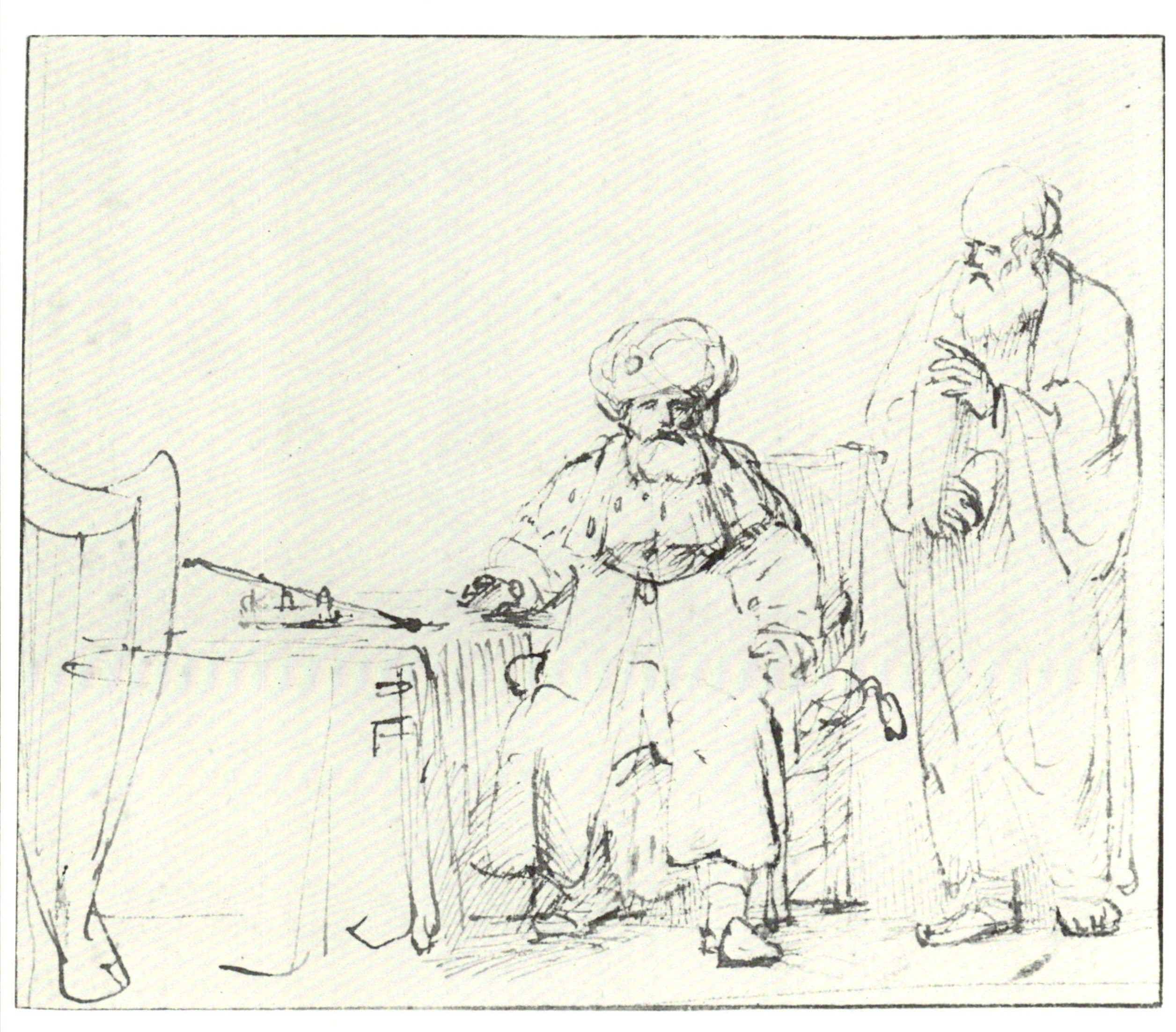

82.

REMBRANDT HARMENSZ VAN RIJN
(Leiden 1606 - Amsterdam 1669)

Nathan Admonishing David

Pen and brown ink; 126 x 149 mm.; Watermark: Churchill 1935, no. 355
Provenance: Valerius Rover (L2984a-c, L2034); Ploos van Amstel (L.3002-4, L.2034); sale, Amsterdam 3 March 1800, I, lot 15; J. Jacobsz de Vos (L. 1450): G. Schoffer; A.W.M. Mensing sale, Amsterdam 27-29 April 1937, lot 558; Frits Lugt; C.R. Rudolf
Acquired 1977
William W. Robinson in Oberhuber, 1977, no. 52, pp. 133-135
Exhibited: Royal Academy, London, 1953, no. 301; Arts Council, London, 1962, no. 1230
Literature: Wilhelm R. Valentiner, *Rembrandt. Des Meisters Handzeichnungen,* 2 vols., Stuttgart, 1925-1934, no. 166; Otto Benesch, *Rembrandt, Werk und Forschung,* Vienna, 1935, p. 51; exhibition catalogue, *Drawings by Old Masters,* Royal Academy of Arts, London, 1953, no. 301; Otto Benesch, The *Drawings of Rembrandt. A Critical and Chronological Catalogue,* 1st ed., 1954-57, vol. V, p. 268, no. 918, fig. 1129; exhibition catalogue, *Old Master Drawings from the Collection of Mr. C.R. Rudolf,* Arts Council, London, 1962, no. 123; Benesch, 1973, vol. V, no. 918, p. 256, fig. 1195; Marianne Bernhard, *Rembrandt: Handzeichnungen,* 2 vols., Munich, 1976, p. 470 (ill.)
Copied: etching (figures only) by Mathys Pool (1670-1732)[1]

The son of a miller, Rembrandt attended the University at Leiden briefly before beginning to study painting. He established a studio in Leiden in 1625 but moved in 1631/2 to Amsterdam where he stayed the rest of his life. At first he was phenomenally successful, had many commissions, married well, grew rich, and lived the life of a *grand seigneur.* His wife died in 1642, and gradually Rembrandt's success faded, although not to the extreme of misery of popular Romantic legend. Simultaneously his art gained in depth: his portraits became more sober, his religious, history and genre paintings less dramatic but more moving, and a greater insight into human nature and compassion for it infused his entire *oeuvre.* He was prolific not only in paintings but also in prints and drawings. Most of the leading Dutch history and portrait painters of the mid-seventeenth century spent some time as students in his studio during his years of success, including Bol (number 64), Doomer (number 68), van Dyck (number 69), van Eeckhout (numbers 72-73), and Koninck (number 79) in this exhibit.

Rembrandt often drew the same subject several times, working out its meaning in his own mind and devising various means of presenting it the most effectively. This drawing is the earliest of three representing the aged prophet Nathan rebuking King David.[2] Robinson has confirmed Benesch's dating of it as ca. 1652-3, the second in the series. To his observations can be added a recent discussion[3] of the possibility that one of the later drawings, in the Metropolitan Museum, may have been a study for a hypothetical companion painting of the controversial *Saul and David* in the Mauritshuis in the Hague, traditionally attributed to Rembrandt but recently thought by some to be by one of the pupils in his studio.[4] If this hypothesis is correct, it emphasizes the role of the Steiner drawing in the continuing evolution of Rembrandt's thought. For in the two later drawings, Nathan and David are both seated, as if Rembrandt had decided subtly to change their relationship, by reducing this haughty David's proud isolation.

Robinson's description of the moment represented here cannot be bettered: "...it allowed [Rembrandt] to capture the instant when the protagonist experiences a new state of awareness or an unexpected insight. The king's pained expression and the gesture of his right hand suggest that Rembrandt has chosen the moment where David suddenly recognizes the full significance of the prophet's words and becomes conscious of the gravity and the implications of his transgression."

This transgression, described in II Samuel xi, was in sequence to the event probably represented by Eeckhout in the earlier of his two drawings (number 72 above), David had sent the good soldier Uriah the Hittite into battle to be killed, after the king had seduced Uriah's beautiful wife Bathsheba. David then married Bathsheba, who bore him a son. But the Lord was "displeased...And [II Samuel xii] sent Nathan unto David." Nathan told him a touching parable of a rich man who robbed a poor man of his one possession, a "little ewe lamb which he had bought and nourished up...it did eat of his own meat, and drank of his own cup, and lay in his bosom, and was unto him as a daughter." Rembrandt chose in this drawing to show the moment of shocked enlightenment, when David in all his majesty is stunned to recognize the painful analogy between the unjust rich man and himself.

A.L. and A.M.

1. Alfred von Wurzbach, *Niederländisches Kunstler-Lexicon,* Vienna and Leipzig, vol. II, 1906, pp. 447, no. 6.
2. The fourth drawing mentioned by Robinson (in Oberhuber, *op. cit.*) of *David Receiving the News of Uriah's Death,* really is a different moment in the sequence of events.
3. Ary Bob de Vries, Magdi Toth-Ubbens, and W. Froentjes, *Rembrandt in the Mauritshuis,* Alphen aan de Rijn, 1978, p. 160; the drawing is Benesch, 1973, V, p. 274, no. 948.
4. Horst Gerson, *Rembrandt,* London, 1969, p. 602, rejected the attribution. So did Keith Roberts in his review of the Mauritshuis book (*Burl* CXXI, 1979, p. 125)

83.

ROELAND ROGHMAN
(Amsterdam 1627 - Italy (?) - Amsterdam 1692)

Wooded River Landscape

Brush and brown and grey wash, with accents of pen and brown ink, white; 452 x 322 mm.
Signed recto lower right in pen and brown ink: *Roelant Roghman*
Acquired 1976
Nancy D. Netzer in Oberhuber, 1977, no. 53, pp. 135-137
Loaned by Lori Steiner

Recent archival discoveries[1] have fixed Roghman's birthdate as thirty years later than Houbraken's 1597, and clarified the artist's associations. He may have been named after his uncle, Roelant Savery, and have been his student. Previously he was considered too old to have studied with Rembrandt, but now such an association although not proven is at least feasible; there seems no reason to doubt that he was, as Houbraken reports, a great friend of Rembrandt's, and of Gerbrand van den Eeckhout. The bravura draughtsmanship in some of his landscapes in fact has some affinity to that of Eeckhout's *Meeting of Isaac and Rebecca* (number 71).

Like his uncle, Roghman painted wilderness landscapes, although they are less fantastic, perhaps in response to a hypothetical trip to Italy during the 1640's. Haak[2] reasonably likens them to Salvator Rosa's. Roghman is most remembered, however, for his topographic drawings. Two hundred forty-one of them survive — of cities, towns, castles, windmills, peasant cottages, and notable sites throughout the Netherlands — done in black crayon and wash during 1646-7. Netzer notes that this drawing "is similar to these in...size, finished quality, application of washes and pen, and treatment of foliage..." and suggests that it is contemporary to them, rather than to a second series done in 1654. The delicacy with which it conveys Roghman's sense of the poetry of organic growth and structure, and the sensitivity of his touch, are comparable to Lucas van Uden's (number 89), different as the effects of the two drawings are.

1. W. Th. Kloek, "En *berglandschap* door Roelant Roghman," *Bulletin van het Rijksmuseum,* XXIII, no. 2, May 1975, pp. 100-101.
2. Haak, 1984, p. 375.

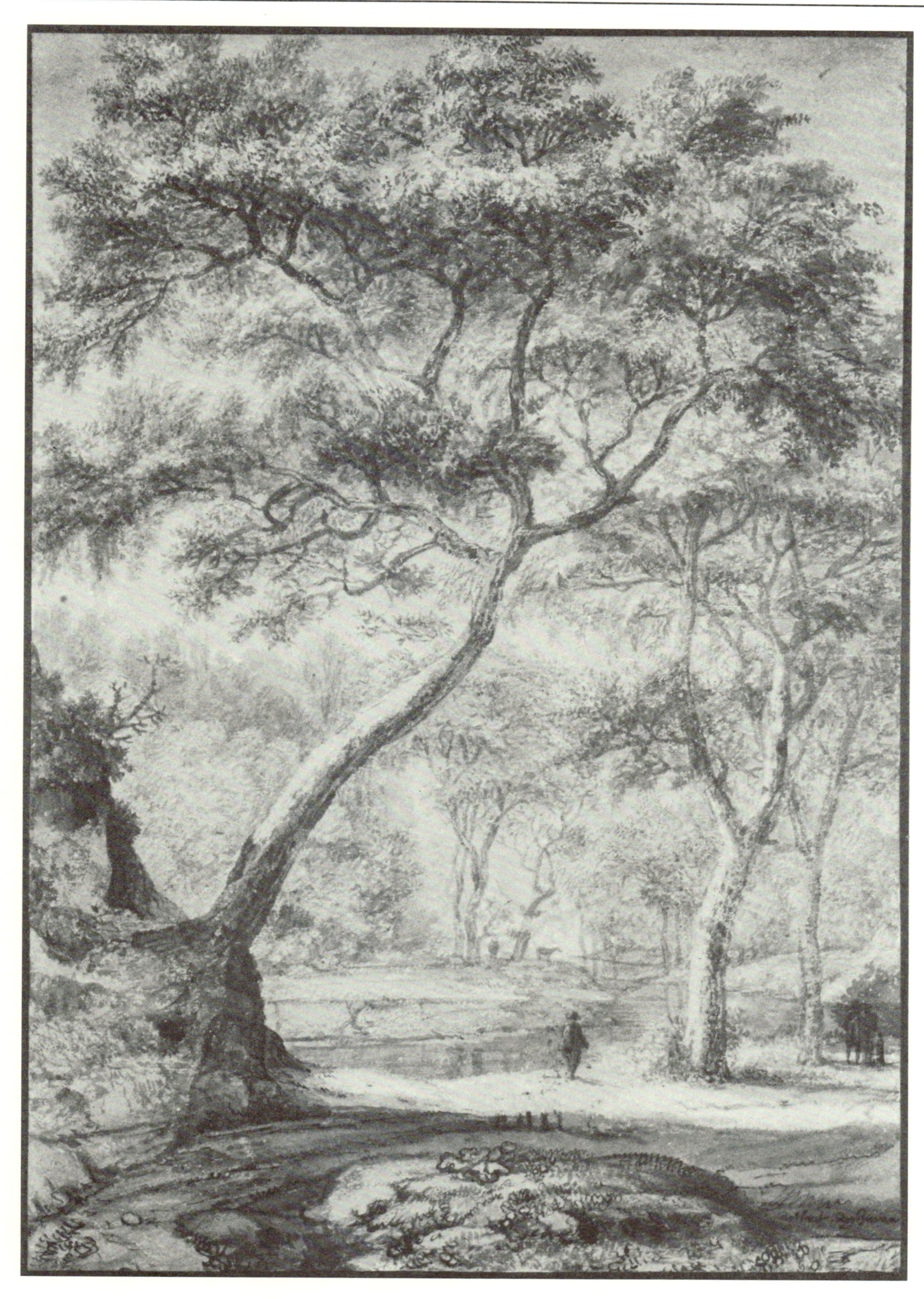

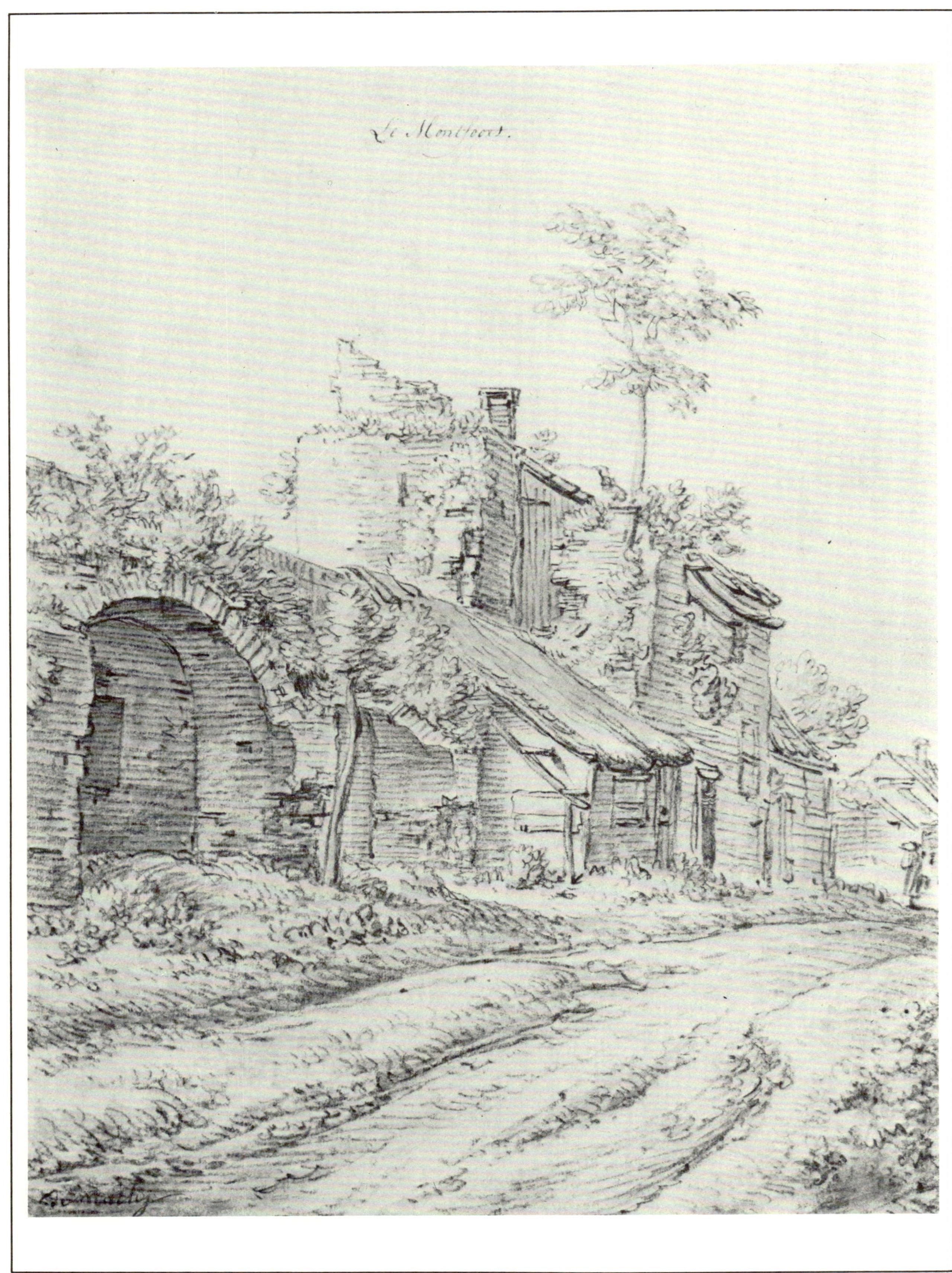

84.

HERMAN SAFTLEVEN
(Rotterdam 1609 - Rhineland - Utrecht 1685)

Landscape with the Ruins of Montfoort

Black chalk with brown wash; 365 x 292 mm.
Inscribed recto in brown ink (later hand): top center *te Montfort;* bottom left corner *de Marchy*
Provenance: Colnaghi's, London, 1965, no. 71; Bernard Houthakker, Amsterdam, 1965; Sotheby's, London, 13 December 1973, lot 118 (ill.)
Acquired 1979
Literature: Stampfle, 1979, p. 117; Wolfgang Schulz, *Herman Saftleven,* Berlin/New York, 1982, no. 621, pp. 295-6 as location unknown

Saftleven is reported to have studied with his brother Cornelis (1607-81), who was however more inclined to paint scenes of peasant life than landscapes. Herman himself began to paint landscapes primarily about 1638, and by 1650 had evolved his specialty, panoramas of high-banked rivers. They flow through minutely-detailed valleys into distant mists, presumably recreating the scenery he saw during his travels along the Moselle and the Rhine as far as Basle.

Perhaps this scene may recall some of the Italian ruins in the work of Bartolomeus Breenbergh (ca. 1599-ca. 1667) by whom Herman may have been influenced during the early 1640's. But it is closer to the tradition of Dutch realism than to Italianate Arcadian fantasy. The site is precisely identifiable not only by means of the inscription, but by another drawing, in the Morgan Library, of the same road and cluster of buildings seen from the opposite direction[1]. The Morgan Library drawing, in the same medium and about the same dimensions (345 x 293 mm.), is also inscribed — *te Montfoort* — and in a hand more closely resembling Saftleven's own[2].

Montfoort, on the Ijssel River about eight miles west southwest of Utrecht, "once was a nice little town. The walls built at the end of the 15th century were destroyed by the Spaniards in 1574... [and] the castle from the 12th century...by the French in 1672." Some fragmentary structures still survive.[3]

Saftleven was paid for some topographical views of Utrecht in 1648-9 (also in 1669) and quite possibly the two Montfoort drawings were done at that time. Many of his drawings of buildings in and around Utrecht survive, and a number are dated 1648 or thereabouts. The conception and composition of the Steiner drawing are much the same as those in a panel painting of a *Utrecht Winter Scene: the Plompe and de Beer Towers* in the Kassel Museum, which is signed and dated 1646[4]. The calligraphy seems very Dutch, with more than a trace of the influence of Jan van Goyen.

1. Stampfle, 1979, no. 87, p. 117
2. There are two other drawings of Montfoort by Herman Saftleven, both in Utrecht, one at the Centraalmuseum (no. 12710), the other at the Rijksarchief Topogr. Atlas; Schulz, *op. cit.,* p. 296, nos. 622 and 623 respectively.
3. This description is from Ann Zwollo's letter of 18 April 1983 to the Steiners.
4. See J. Niewstraten, "De Ontwikkeling van Herman Saftleven tot 1650," *Nederlands Kunsthistorisch Jaarboek,* XVI, 1965, pp. 81-117, and Schulz, *op. cit.,* no. 45, p. 137, pl. 19.

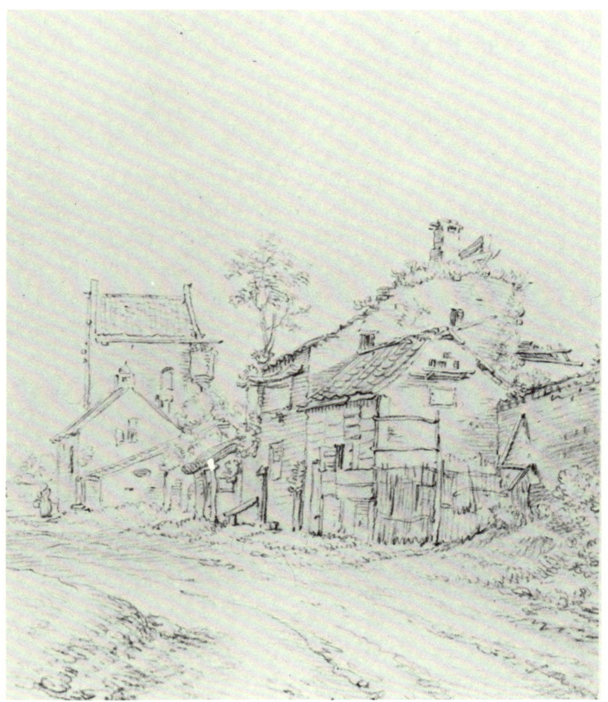

Herman Saftleven
Montfoort Landscape
Morgan Library

85.

PIETER STEVENS II (STEPHANI)
(Mechelen ca. 1567 - Rome, Naples - after 1624 Prague)

Huntsmen Fording a Stream in a Pine Forest

Pen and brown ink, colored chalks and washes, heightened with white on buff paper; 185 x 291 mm.
Inscribed: "R. Saveri" lower right corner
Provenance: Treowen Collection; Llanover House Sale, 26 June 1934, no. 977; Christie's London, 27 November 1973, lot no. 217; Gebroeders Douwes, Amsterdam, 1976, no. F255
Acquired 1981
Exhibited: Princeton, 1982; National Gallery, Washington, 1983; Carnegie Institute, Pittsburgh, 1983
Literature: Kaufmann, 1982, pp. 162-3, no. 59, fig. 59; review, *New York Times,* Arts and Leisure Section, 7 November 1982, p. 33
Loaned by Lillian and Robert Fraker

What little is known about Stevens' biography and *oeuvre* is owing to the research of Dr. An Zwollo of the Rijksbureau voor Kunst-historische Documentatie in the Hague,[1] who has confirmed the attribution of this drawing to him[2]. Stevens was the descendant of a family of artists in Mechelen, and was accepted as a master in Antwerp in 1589. Engravings by Gillis Sadeler and Hendrik Hondius after his work demonstrate that he went to Italy and visited Rome, Tivoli and Naples probably before 1594[3]. In that year he became court painter to Emperor Rudolf II in Prague where contemporaneously the landscapist Roelant Savery was employed, as well as Jan Bruegel, the fascinating perspectivist Hans Vredeman de Vries, and a number of other lesser Flemish painters. After Rudolf's death in 1612, Stevens remained in Prague. He served Prince Charles of Liechtenstein from 1620 to 1624. Presumably many of his paintings and drawings are hidden, waiting to be recognized among the *oeuvres* of Savery, Paul Bril and others.

Stevens is likely at some time to have had contact with the Frankenthaler school, a group of prolific Flemish landscape painters living in exile near Frankfurt, for his drawings show their influence. Perhaps he visited them en route to Rome ca. 1591-92. His greatest debt was to Roelant Savery, to whom this drawing was previously attributed. In 1604 Savery was called to Rudolf's imperial court in Prague and commissioned a series of views in the Alps and the Tyrol. His journey was complete by 1606, and it resulted in a series of landscape drawings including an album that belonged to Rembrandt in 1656, and is now in the Rijksprentenkabinett in Amsterdam.

This drawing's *motif* of a rocky landscape with pine trees is typical of Savery, as are the subtle yellow-green and blue washes. But these features are characteristic also of Stevens' landscapes, as are the delicate rendering of light and atmospheric effects and the sensitive botanical observation. There is little doubt that this drawing was executed in Tyrol or Bohemia, because it represents a mixed deciduous conifer forest, a forest type indigenous to Central Europe but not to Flanders. The Norway spruce (*Picea Abies*) can be easily recognized, whereas the tree in the right foreground is likely to be a winter oak (*Quercus Petreae*), also typical of the Tyrol-Bohemia area[4]. The dark color of the wild mountain-ash berry (*Sorbus Aucuparia*) in the left background — probably an impression of the dark red color of the scrub in autumn — and the spare foliage of the deciduous trees enhance the autumn atmosphere. The drawing can be assumed to have been made after 1606. Kaufmann suggests a date of "ca. 1610 or even later." H.V.M.

1. Published in a series of articles in the *Wiener Jahrbuch* (1968), *Oud Holland* (1969), *Umeni* (1970), and the *Leids Kunsthistorich Jaarboek* (1982)
2. In conversation with the Steiners in 1981
3. Matthias Winner, exhibition catalogue, *Zeichner sehen die Antike...1450-1800,* Staatliche Museen... Kupferstichkabinett, Berlin, 1967, no. 52, pp. 82-3
4. Marcel van Miegroet, *Van Bomen en Bossen,* 2 vols., Antwerp, 1976, vol. I, p. 237

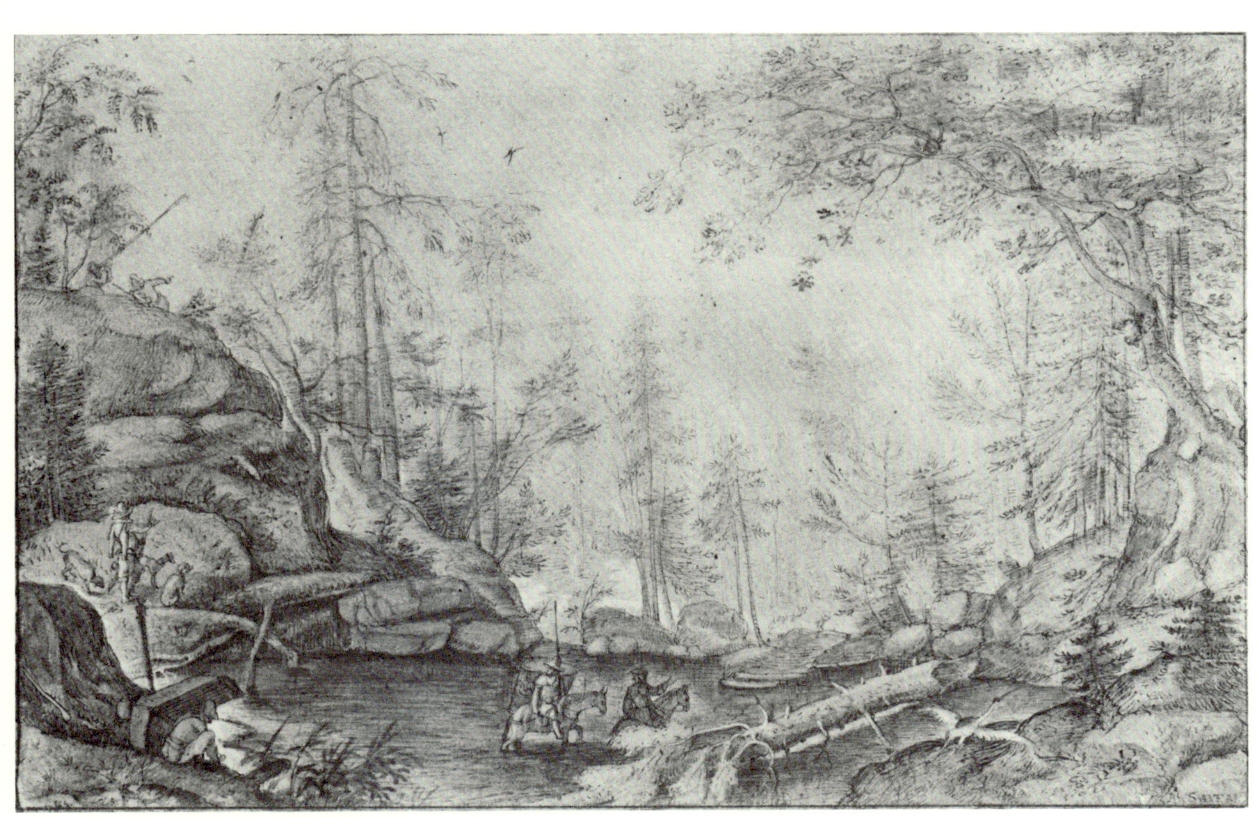

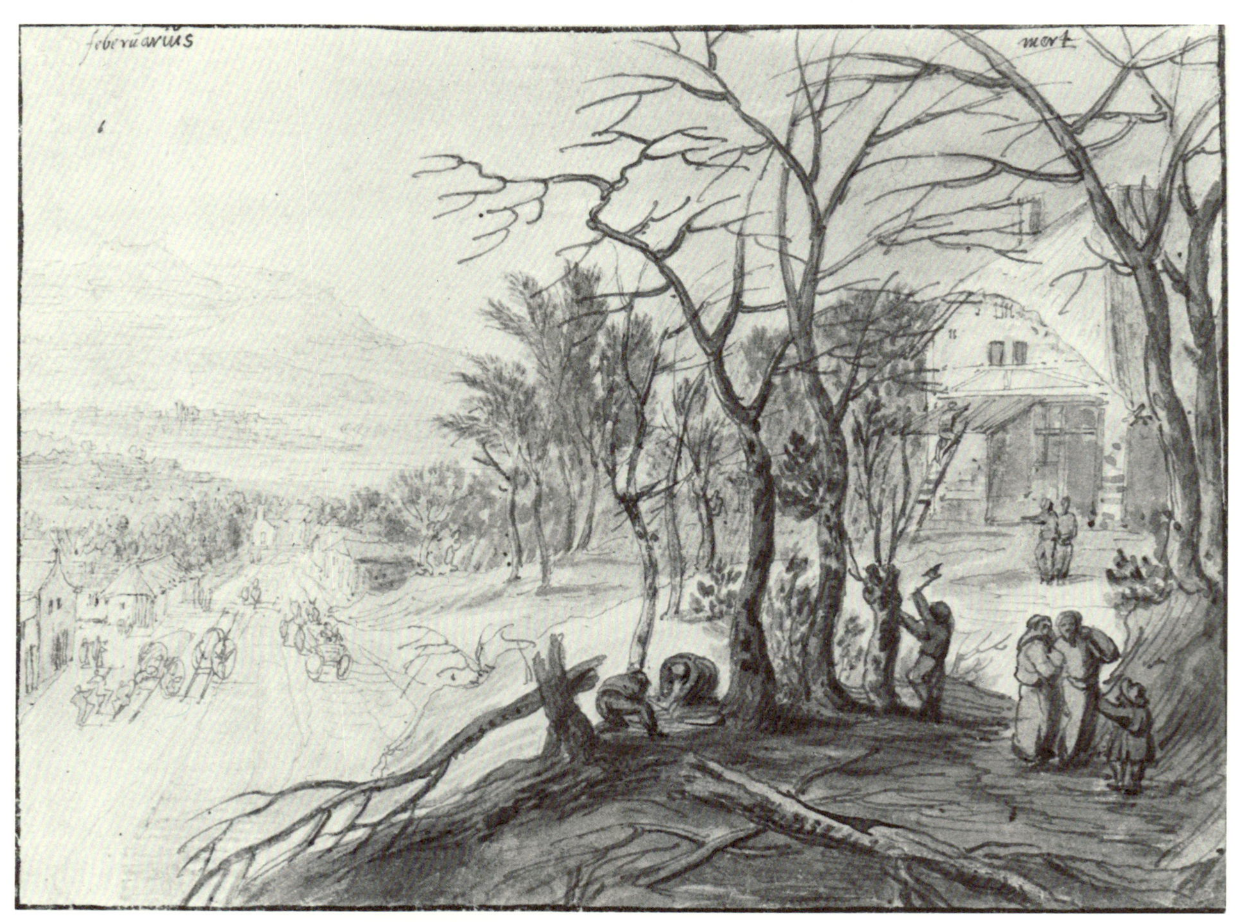
feberuarius
mert

86.

PIETER STEVENS (STEFANI) II

The Months February-March

Pen and brown ink over black chalk, watercolor; 148 x 203 mm.
Inscribed: *februarius* (February), upper left; *mert* (March), upper right
Acquired 1973

In the late 16th century, the representation of months and seasons was popular in Flemish painting. As in the calendar miniatures in Hours Books, each month or season was characterized both by human activities appropriate to the time of year and by the condition of the landscape and the weather. Frequently, also, drawings illustrating the months or the seasons were designed for engravers. As early as 1565, Pieter Bruegel had drawn *Spring* (now in the Albertina in Vienna), followed in 1568 by *Summer* (in the Kunsthalle, Hamburg). Bruegel's set, left unfinished at the time of his death in 1569, was completed by Hans Bol with compositions of *Autumn* and *Winter*. The suite of four was then engraved by Pieter van der Heyden (who signed the *Spring* plate with his monogram) and published in 1570 by Hieronymus Cock[1].

Stevens made drawings of both months and seasons. There is a *Winter* by him as well as *March, July* and *December,* all in the Albertina[2]; a *November* in the British Museum[3], *January* in Prague and *February* in Sacramento[4]. In the Steiner drawing, however, he rather surprisingly combined two months in a single sheet, as the inscriptions make clear. This is unusual; it was customary to represent a single month or a single season in each work, or to combine all four seasons in one image. Furthermore his choice of the two months represented here is even more surprising: he chose February and March, rather than a pair of months that would fit into a more normal bimestrial sequence beginning with January and February, continuing with March-April, May-June, and so forth. The explanation is simple, strange as it may seem in the 20th century: in Stevens' time, the year was conceived to begin not with January, but with Easter. So the division of the year into pairs of months did not begin with January at all, but rather, depending on the church calendar, either with March or (as in this instance) with April.

Quite apart from its inherent merit and the insight it provides into Stevens' career, this drawing is important for solving a problem in the *oeuvre* of Pieter Bruegel the Elder. For it can be recognized as a reflection, even a free copy, of Bruegel's painting in Vienna which is usually called *The Gloomy Day.* That is, the choice of months was not really Stevens' at all, but rather Bruegel's.

The *Gloomy Day* is also assumed to be one of a series, of which four other paintings are known: two in Vienna, the *Return of the Herd* and the popular *Hunters in the Snow; The Hay-Makers* in Prague; and the *Harvest* in the Metropolitan Museum in New York. The debate over whether Bruegel's suite was originally completed with only one other painting, now lost, or whether there are seven missing, seems now to be resolved. This drawing, clearly combining two months, indicates that each of Bruegel's paintings also was bimestrial, and therefore his suite was complete with just six. Furthermore, the peculiar combination of months in this sequence, proposed for Bruegel's paintings by de Tolnay years ago,[5] rather than in the January-February sequence, now seems justified.

Stevens could have seen Bruegel's paintings both in Antwerp where they are documented in 1565 and 1594, and in the court of the Emperor Rudolf II in Prague, where they remained at least until 1621. The presence of Pieter Bruegel's son Jan in Prague about 1604 may well have inspired Stevens to make this drawing, which might therefore be tentatively dated around 1604-5. This date is also proposed by Kaufmann for Stevens' drawing of *February* in Sacramento. One of two surviving drawings preparatory for a series of twelve month-engravings by Egidius Sadeler dated 1607, it is very similar in composition to the Steiner sheet.

Like Bruegel in his *Gloomy Day,* Stevens was not satisfied with showing only one characteristic of the month or one typical occupation. But more than any other single motif, the idea, the atmosphere, of the special phase of the year, is conveyed by the landscape itself. Pollarding of willows is most often shown in representations of February, although there are examples where the pruning of trees is also depicted as symbol for the month of March. The contrast between the barren trees in the foreground and the already foliated trees in the middle creates an internal tension and the landscape's symbolic connotation. H.V.M.

1. Hollstein, 1949-84, vol. IX, nos. 63-66
2. Benesch, 1928, vol. II, nos. 352-55
3. Arthur E. Popham, *Catalogue of Drawings by Dutch and Flemish Artists...In the British Museum,* London, 1932, p. 181, no. 3
4. Kaufmann, 1982, no. 58, pp. 160-161
5. Karl von Tolnai, "Studien zu den Gemalden P. Brueghels d. A," *Jahrbuch der Kunsthistorische Sammlung in Wien,* N.F., VIII, 1934, p. 125

87.

HERMAN VAN SWANEVELT
(Woerden 1600 - Paris, Rome - 1655 Paris)

River Landscape with Draughtsmen and Travellers

Pen and brown ink, grey wash; 173 x 277 mm.
Provenance: Ralph Willett; William Esdaile (L.2617) (from collector's mark on mount)
Acquired 1979
Literature: Hubert Damisch, "Claude: A Problem in Perspective," *Claude Lorrain 1600-1682: A Symposium,* Studies in the History of Art, National Gallery of Art, Washington, vol. XIV, p. 41, fig. 30

Swanevelt was an Italianate Dutch artist who spent little time in the Netherlands. Sometimes considered something of a clone of the great Claude Lorrain whose exact contempoarary he was, the reputation of his work has suffered by comparison to Claude's. As this beautiful drawing proves, he was in fact a very good artist, sensitive to the nuances of the Arcadian nature he both observed and created.

Born near Utrecht, he belonged to the first generation of the Dutch Italianates and is associated with the best of them, Jan Both. In Paris by 1623, Swanevelt went on to Rome in 1627, became a member of the Dutch artists' circle there, the *Schildersbent* or *Bentveughels* (the "Birds of a Feather"), and acquired the nickname of "The Hermit." After leaving Rome in the early 1640's, he settled in Paris where he was appointed Painter to the King in 1644. He remained there, making frequent trips home to Woerden. for the rest of his life.

Damisch has related this drawing to Claude not only in its lyricism but also, specifically, through Swanevelt's use of Claude's "angular perspective" where diagonal lines originating at each lower corner form a triangle "at the base of which the draftsman is located as if in the halo of the spotlight." In this drawing, there are two draughtsmen, in the lower left, with their portfolios tucked under their arms. One of them gestures toward the hill on the right, thus taking the role of the "artist as observer...in the same position in the picture as the 'witness' or the 'narrator' in relation to the *storia* in mythological or historical painting." These two artists stand at the fulcrum of a system of diagonals spreading to encompass the hill as it reaches from left to right across the image; the stream, from a focal point in the lower right corner, recedes diagonally in a counter direction. Thus Damisch sees the artist's gesture as "neither narrative or symbolic but strictly visual and topographical...based...on the opening of a perspective inside the [drawing] itself." Such a mechanistic analysis may seem to wreck pedantic and arid havoc with so directly appealing an image, but it is important in revealing the structure underlying Swanevelt's art as well as Claude's. Fresh and spontaneous as Swanevelt's observation and use of the medium are, nonetheless they are consciously constructive rather than simply descriptive.

Swanevelt's use of the wash seems equally purposeful. By manipulating the value of the surface areas to modulate from the light paper tone to the darkest wash, not only has he created effects of shifting sunlight and of luminous atmosphere but also he has reinforced recession into depth. The human figures, animals, and birds add to the animation of the scene almost as much as the sense of wind and of the sound of water; their smallness emphasizes the landscape's grandeur. But man is integral with nature rather than subservient to its majesty. There is a typical Dutch sense of serene contentment with life in this landscape. It opens up to a distant horizon; but it is bound together by the permeating light and unified in jubilant celebration of nature.

The date of this drawing is undetermined. But lacking the historical, mythological or religious episodes Swanevelt often introduced into his landscapes, and markedly spontaneous though carefully detailed as if made on the spot, it can perhaps be placed at the end of his long Italian sojourn, when he may have been closest to Jan Both, who left Rome in 1641. Although it is somewhat more atmospheric, it does correspond to a landscape in the Rijksmuseum in Amsterdam (inv. no. 2280A), which is signed and dated 1643.

M.L. and A.M.

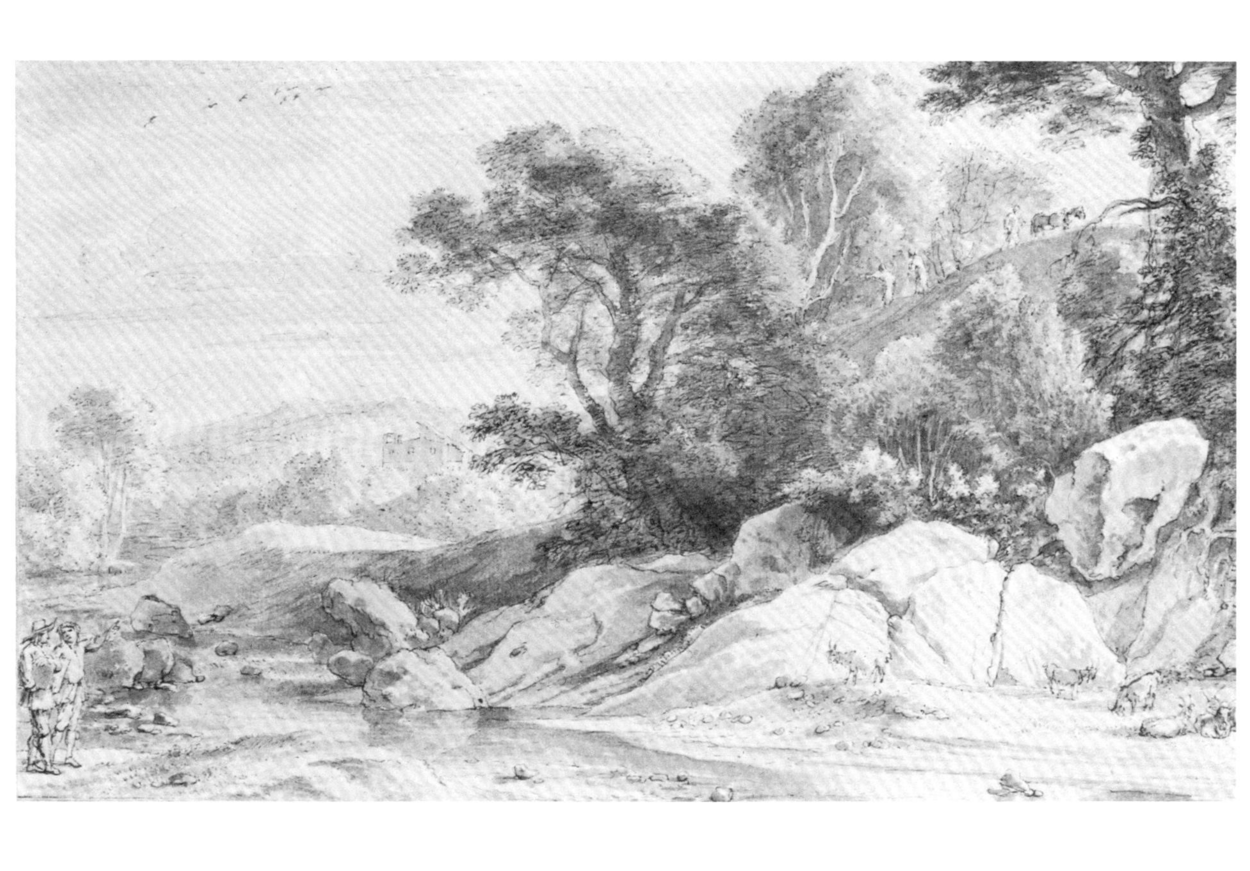

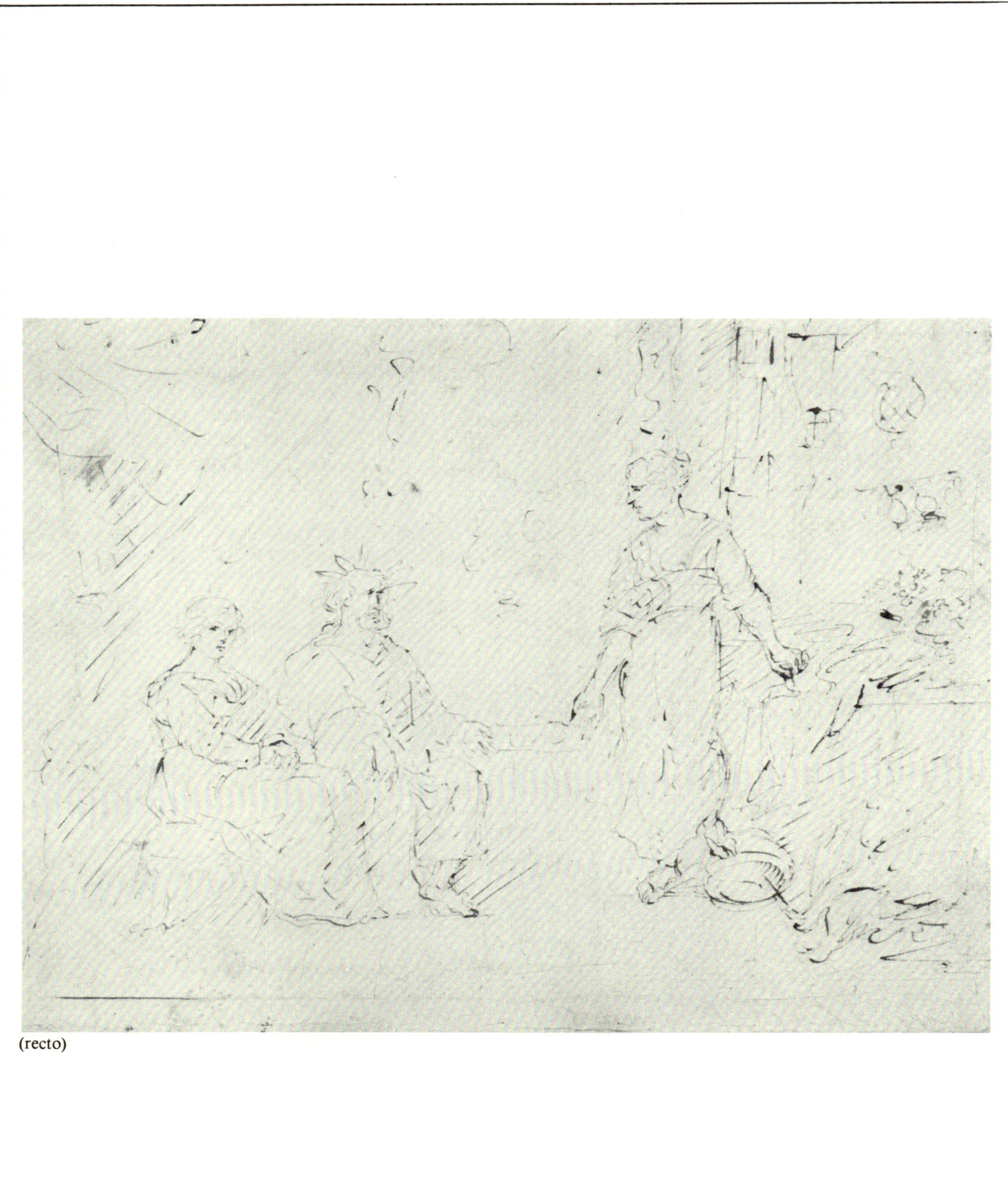

(recto)

88.

DAVID TENIERS THE YOUNGER
(Antwerp 1610 - 1690 Brussels)

Christ in the House of Martha and Mary (recto)
Feeding the Hungry (verso)

Pen and brown ink over black chalk (recto); red and black chalk (verso); 206 x 289 mm.
Acquired 1982, as Rubens School
Loaned by Lori Steiner

After training presumably in his father's workshop, Teniers entered the Antwerp Guild of St. Luke as a master in 1632-3. He was highly successful; he became Dean of the Guild in 1645 and moved to Brussels ca. 1650 to serve as court painter to the Archduke Leopold Wilhelm and to his successor as regent of the Southern Netherlands, Don Juan[1]. Teniers was also an art dealer.

The Biblical source for the recto of this drawing is Luke x: 38-42. Martha, patroness of busy housewives, is shown beside her kitchen. She symbolizes the active type, in contrast to her contemplative sister, Mary of Bethany, who is sitting at Christ's right. The active sister had taken the initiative in fetching Christ to their house when their brother Lazarus died. But now, as she chides her sister for sitting, apparently idly, listening to His words, Christ tells her that Mary is playing a necessary, indeed a better, part.

The seated Mary shows a striking resemblance to a similar figure in Rubens' drawing of *The Garden of Love* in the Metropolitan Museum (inv. no. 58.96.1; 58.96.2). Stance, position, coiffure, even the folds of the garment and the low bench, are almost identical in both drawings. Rubens' was made ca. 1632-3 as a model for a woodcut by Christoffel Jegher (Hollstein IX, p. 189) and is Rubens' second version of the theme; the first is the famous painting of ca. 1630-32 in the Prado. For the most part, Rubens kept his pen strokes sober and neat, so as to enable Jegher to follow his model line by line. The Steiner sheet, on the contrary, is drawn in Teniers' usual swift, nervous and sketchy style, with abundant loose parallel hatching. Teniers' manner of delineation was probably determined by the function of the drawing, as a *pensiero* for a painting, and presumably is analogous to his *Kitchen Interior* in the Louvre or similar kitchen scenes by Frans Snyders. The drawing may also be related to *Fifteen Scenes from the Life of Mary* painted by Teniers for Anna-Maria Bonnarens, wife of his son David Teniers III. These paintings, listed in the 1671 inventory of her collection, eventually passed to the Alte Pinakothek in Munich.

Mary's figure reoccurs in another *modello* for a woodcut *The Rest on the Flight into Egypt* in the National Museum at Posnan (Poland). Rubens painted such a canvas ca. 1632 and changed it ca. 1636. Obviously Teniers' sources for this composition were taken from

Rubens in the 'thirties at Antwerp. It may be therefore that Teniers copied his Mary of Bethany from a Rubens original, when both painters were still in Antwerp. After all, Rubens must have been close to Teniers, having been one of the guardians of Jan Bruegel's daughter Anna, and a witness at her marriage on 4 July 1637 to Teniers.

The drawing on the *verso*, of a man giving bread to a monk, was discovered in 1982 after the sheet was detached from the support. It is related to Teniers' paintings of the *Seven Acts of Mercy,* for one of which it was probably a *pensiero.* This composition — of a figure group in front of a building and behind a diagonally placed counter — reappears as a central theme in the paintings, incorporating the two acts of feeding the hungry and clothing the naked. It was probably an early version of the central group in the *Seven Acts of Mercy.* The obvious minor discrepancies between it and the painting indicate it was done before the painting and not afterwards.

David II painted at least seven versions of *The Seven Acts of Mercy,* several of which were reproduced by the famous French engraver Philippe Le Bas[2]. Teniers' best painted version is the one in the Louvre which was executed on copper and tentatively dated ca. 1660[3]. But the stylistic affinity between the recto and the verso of the drawing allows the assumption that Teniers executed the two sketches in the same period, in Antwerp and probably between 1633 and 1640. H.V.M.

1. Hans Vlieghe, "David Teniers II en het hof van aartshertog Leopold Wilhelm en Don Juan van Oostenrijk, 1647-1659," *Gentse Bijdragen tot de Kunstgeschiedenis,* XIX, 1961-6, pp. 23-49.
2. Jan Piet Balageer, "Bij het 17 de eeuwse schilderij fragment 'De Werken van Barmhartigheid' in de Koninklijke Musea voor Schone Kunsten van België te Brussel," *Bulletin Koninklijke Musea...,* 1909, pp. 141-8.
3. Jane P. Davidson, *David Teniers the Younger,* Boulder, Colorado, 1979, pp. 35-6 pl. 3.

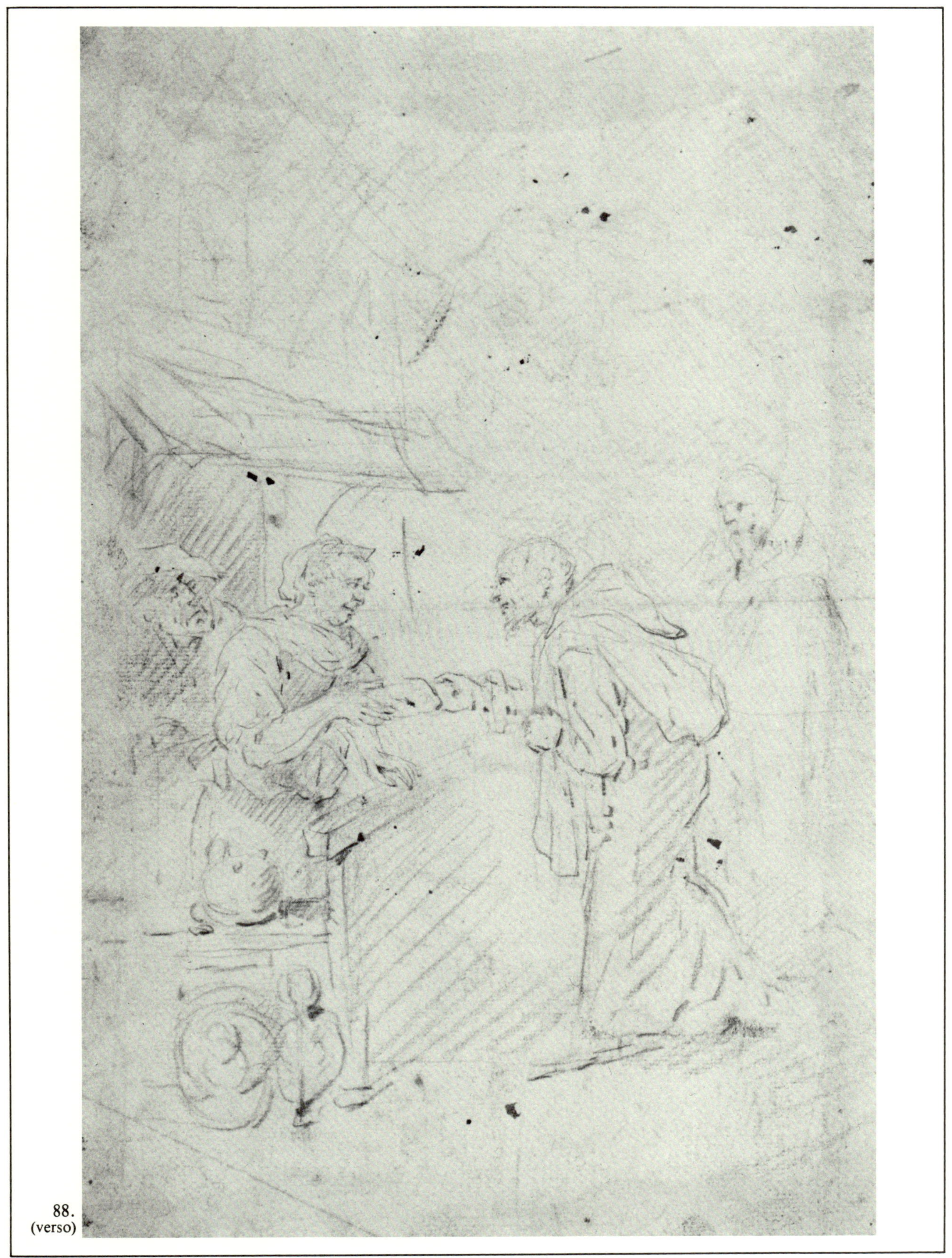

88.
(verso)

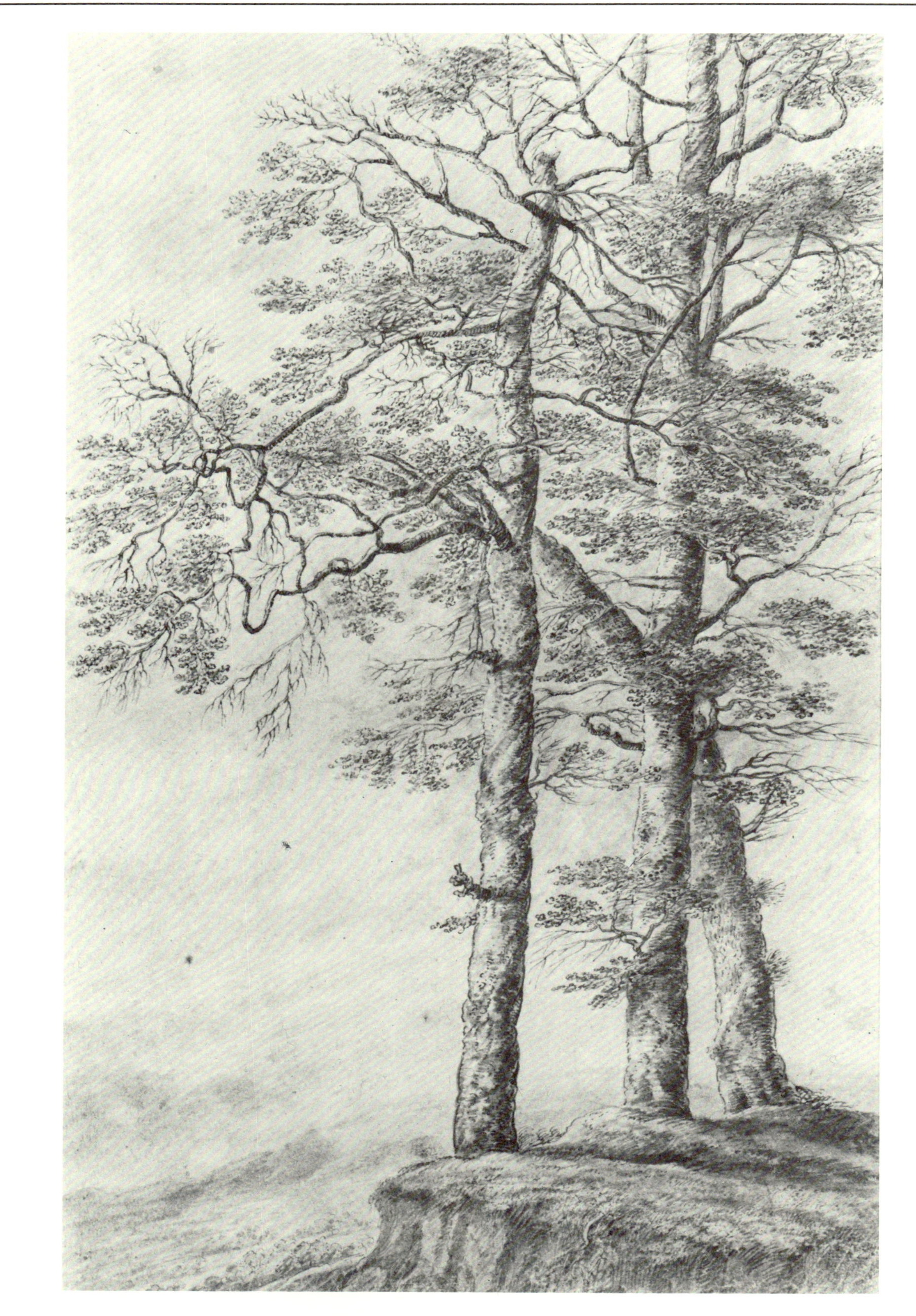

89.

LUCAS VAN UDEN
(Antwerp 1595 - Rhineland - Antwerp 1672/3)

Trees

Pen and brown ink, grey wash, watercolor over graphite; 347 x 225 mm.; horizontal fold diagonally across the center. Four corners made up
Inscribed verso in blue ballpoint ink: *26*; unidentifiable paraph
Provenance: Schaeffer Galleries, New York
Acquired 1972
Joseph A. Jozlin in Oberhuber, 1977, no. 58, pp. 145-147
Literature: Stephen M. Bailey, ''A preparatory drawing by Lucas van Uden,'' *MD* XIX, no. 4, 1981, pp. 441-2

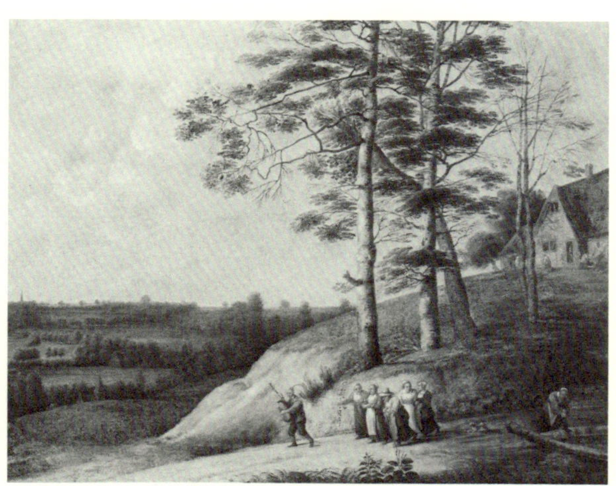

David Teniers the Younger
Landscape with Piper and Villagers before Cottages

Lucas van Uden probably studied with his father, Artus, but he is associated particularly with Rubens, whom he served as a landscape specialist during the 1620's[1]. He never recovered from the impact of the great man, and for the rest of his long and uneventful life continued to paint landscapes that often followed Rubens' formulas but rarely achieved his grandeur or recaptured his force.

His drawings, of which this is a typical example, are another matter. Perhaps sometimes made direct from nature, they are exceptionally sensitive, so that they not only describe the appearance of the natural world precisely but also perceptively create — or recreate — the effects of its processes. The result, in a drawing like this, is an extraordinary sense of vitality and organic growth brought up to, but just short of, anthropomorphism. It is tempting to see these three trees as standing in stalwart contrast to those in Roghman's graceful forest glade (number 83). Combined with van Uden's tactfully restrained use of the rich medium and his remarkably delicate touch, the total effect is comparable to Rembrandt's famous etching of the *Three Trees* of 1643, to which this drawing is almost contemporary. As Jozlin points out, it can be associated with a group inscribed by the artist himself with dates from 1640 to 1649.

Complete in itself and finished as this drawing seems to be, Bailey has shown that it is preparatory for a painting, *Landscape with Piper and Villagers before Cottages,* most recently seen in the New York art market[2]. The figures in the painting are attributed to David Teniers the Younger (number 88). Bailey points out that the trees are not so tall in the painting as in this drawing. He assumes that in adapting the drawing to the painting van Uden reduced their height to eliminate the stunted top of the closest of the trees.

1. According to Wolfgang Adler, *Jan Wildens: Der Landschaftsmitarbeiter des Rubens,* Fridingen, 1982, pp. 29-35. Jan Wildens was Rubens' landscape specialist from 1616 to 1620, when van Uden came into the atelier.
2. Christie's, 5 July 1985, lot 90.

90.

JACOB VAN DER ULFT
(Gorkum 1627 - Italy - Nordwijk 1689)

An Italian Landscape, perhaps the Monte Mario, Rome

Pen and brown ink, brown wash; 293 x 401 mm.
Watermark: WR below a Strasbourg lily
Signed (?): *Van der Ulft ft 1659*
Inscribed verso: *Art* [?] *Mario te sien nijt het cola dei 1659*
Provenance: E. Desperet (L.721); C.R. Rudolf
Acquired 1983

Van der Ulft was probably self-taught, although he was a loyal imitator of Jan de Bisschop (number 61) in Italianate landscapes like this, and he was so skilled as to be able to compose multi-figure compositions of processions and the like very ingeniously. Also, like Bisschop, he was upper class, serving as Mayor of Gorkum from 1660-1679; the implication is that as an artist he was to some extent a cultivated amateur rather than a professional artisan. Houbraken's report that van der Ulft never actually visited Italy is contradicted by the number of his landscapes of identifiable Italian sites, and the accuracy of their detail. However, at least as many of his Italianate works are apparently imaginary, like this one. Despite the inscription, these buildings are not those of the Monte Mario in the seventeenth century[1]. Instead they appear to be a composite of antique ruins — the closest building may be round or not, but its profile suggests the Temple of Minerva Medica in Rome; and the coffered vaulting of the next building back might be from the Baths of Maxentius, despite appearing to be flat rather than the remains of a barrel vault[2]. Similarly nostalgic architectural fancies are so frequent in van der Ulft's *oeuvre* as to encourage conjecture that he never did go to Rome.

However, this drawing's effect is certainly of sunny Italy. The strong play of light and shade, executed in fluid washes, creates a soft Spring-like atmosphere unifying the pictorial space and suggesting a shifting luminosity. The glow of the late afternoon sun enhances the nostalgic charm evoked by the ruins, the topography, and the pastoral settlement in the middle ground. This lyricism and such specific devices as the long areas of flowing wash reveal van der Ulft's indebtedness to Jan de Bisschop.

The figures of the men, and the dog, have been added over the washes on the foreground. They are awkwardly constructed and have little organic relation to the whole composition. So they seem to be added by a later hand, as the tricorne hats suggest[3]. M.L. and A.M.

1. Confirmed by Professor Norman Neuerberg in conversation.
2. These hypothetical identifications are the editor's.
3. As suggested by Dr. Franklin Robinson in a letter 6 November 1984.

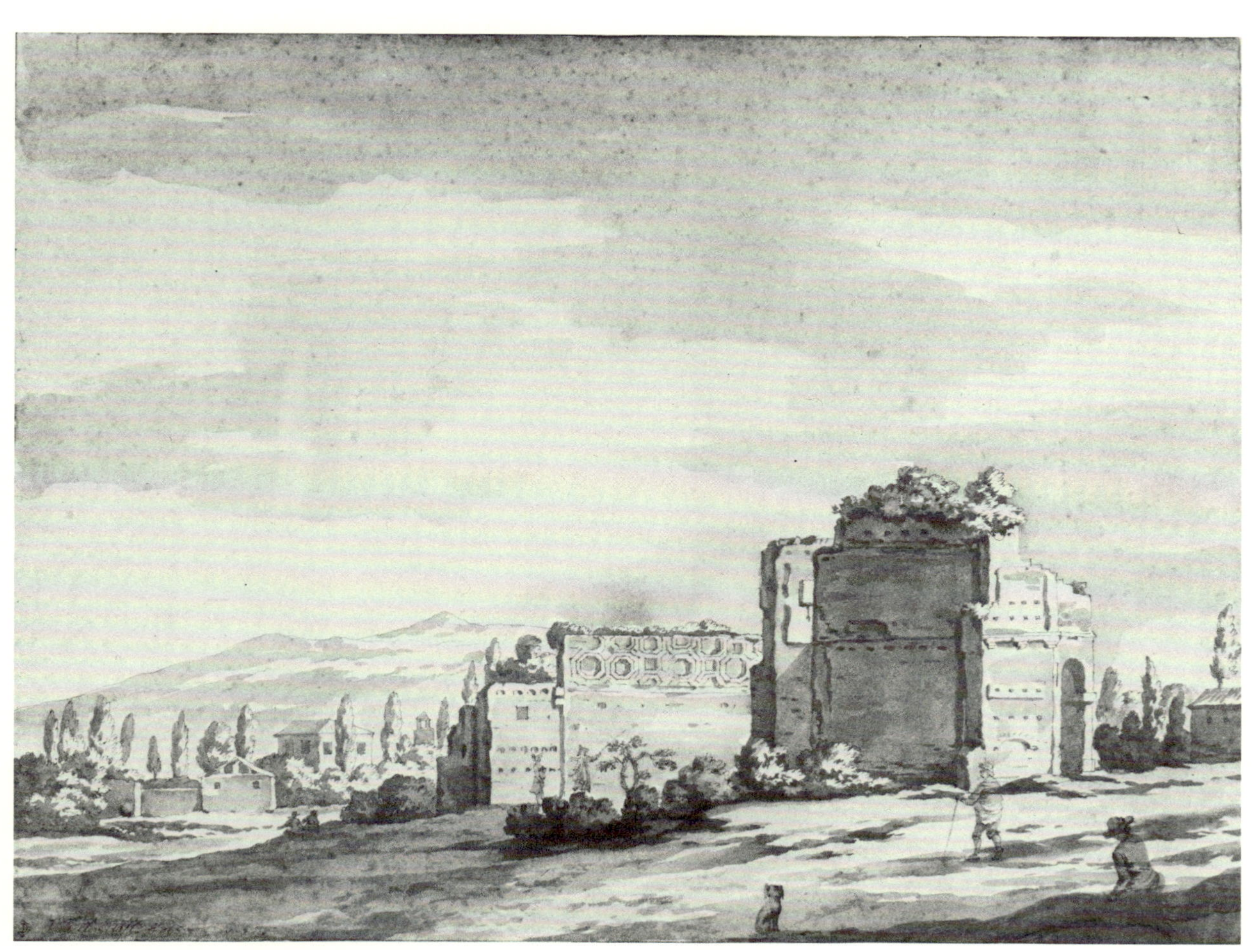

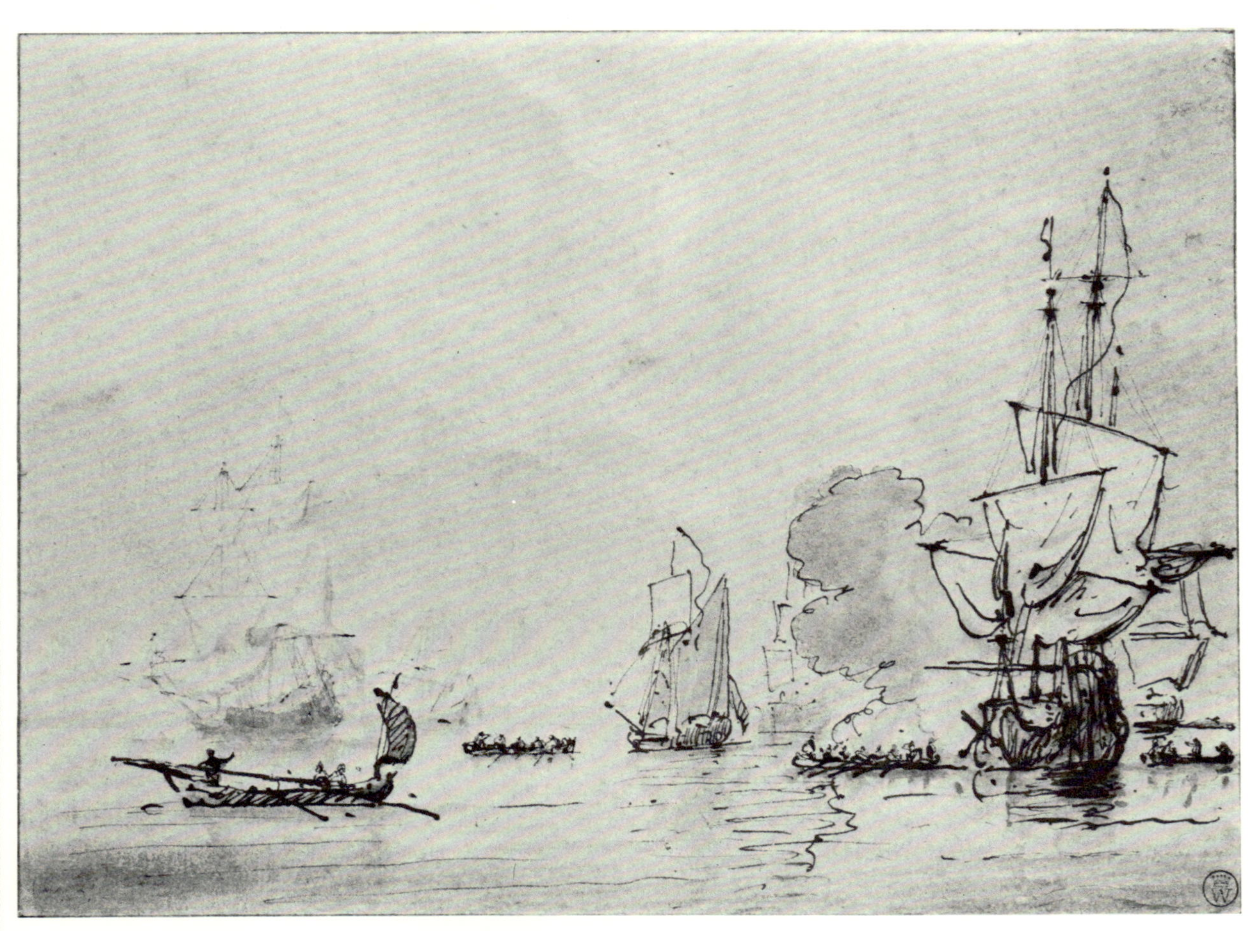

91.

WILLEM VAN DE VELDE THE YOUNGER
(Leiden 1633 - Amsterdam, Weesp, London - 1707 London)

Frigate at Anchor

Pen and brown ink with grey wash; 158 x 220 mm.
Provenance: Earl of Warwick (L.2000); J.P. Heseltine (L.1507); P. & D. Colnaghi, 1912; Robin Lehmann; P. & D. Colnaghi, 1972
Acquired 1972
Nancy D. Netzer in Oberhuber, 1977, pp. 147-9
Literature: *Original Master Drawings by Old Masters of the Dutch School in the Collection of J.P. Heseltine,* London, 1910, no. 34 (ill.); *Exhibition of Old Master Drawings,* P. & D. Colnaghi, London, 1972, no. 43

Willem van de Velde the Younger and his father (1611-93), of the same profession and name and therefore known as "The Elder," were inseparable, and much of their work is, too. Nonetheless the work of the son was the more admired and desired during their lifetimes, perhaps because he studied not only with his father but also with another marine painter, Simon de Vlieger (ca. 1600-53), and his *oeuvre* tended to be rather more consciously artistic and less painstakingly documentary. Among the many Dutch specialists in marine painting, the van de Veldes had their own subspecialty, which was marine-battle painting. The father was renowned for risking himself by actually participating in battles at sea rather than relying on informants' reports on them. The sketches he made, literally in the heat of battle, he took back to his studio and used as the basis for his peculiar preferred medium, which was drawing in pen and ink on an easel-scale canvas primed with white oil paint. There was plenty of opportunity for this specialty, because the Dutch were at war with the English during much of the decade from 1663. When the Dutch finally defeated the English-French alliance in 1672, the van de Veldes made their personal peace as well and moved to London, where they were highly successful for the rest of their lives.

Willem the Younger was not limited to battle-scenes only, as this drawing demonstrates. The mood is tranquil. The cannon shot implied by the smoke is not bellicose in intention but rather the announcement of the frigate's arrival or departure from port or a salute to honor a distinguished visitor. The nationalities of the ships can not be identified because no flags are legible. Van de Velde again and again repeated approximately this same composition with ships similar in structure and rigging. He varied the compositions by moving the ships around and adding or subtracting them like so many pieces on a chess board. The crisp delineation, the atmospheric wash, and the meticulous balance of his designs were invariable.

This drawing does closely resemble a signed painting recently in the New York art market,[1] which is more spacious. It has fewer boats but on the right shows an almost identical frigate, described as an English ship, and to its left is a similar and similarly rigged smaller boat. According to the scales catalogue, Michael Robinson dates the painting as ca. 1685. Netzer dates the drawing later, as around 1700 because of the medium, which is characteristic of this later time in van de Velde's career, and because of the use of the wash "for the most part to accentuate and fill out the penwork." Considering van de Velde's tendency to repeat himself and the greater spaciousness of the painting, its earlier date does not contradict her placement of the drawing.

M.L. and A.M.

1. Sotheby's, 17 July 1985, lot 94

92.

TOBIAS VERHAECHT
(Antwerp 1561 - Italy - Antwerp 1631)

Wooded Landscape with a Stag Hunt

Pen and brown ink, brown wash, over black chalk; 211 x 393 mm.
Inscribed in pen and ink *recto: Mattheus Brille*
Provenance: Sotheby's, London, 22 November 1974, lot 21 as Verhaecht; Yvonne Tan Bunzl as Lodewijk Toeput called Pozzoserrato
Acquired 1975
William W. Robinson in Oberhuber, 1977, no. 60, pp. 149-51

Verhaecht would be memorable, if for no other reason than having been Rubens' first teacher. Although his life spans the two centuries nearly equally, his style is that of the 16th century's fantastic mountain landscape which he continued into the 17th century, rather than adopting the new century's realistic landscape — exemplified in this exhibit, by the Fleming Lucas van Uden or by Herman van Swanevelt in Holland, who were born nearly two generations later than Verhaecht. His generation was that of two other Antwerp painters, Jan Bruegel the Elder, with whom he sometimes collaborated, and Joos de Momper (1564-1635) whose landscapes influenced Verhaecht. He also visited Italy, where he probably encountered Pozzoserrato (ca. 1550-1603/5), Momper's teacher, whose landscape drawings are so close to Verhaecht's as to have suggested the previous mistaken attribution of this sheet to him.

Robinson has dated this drawing to the 1580's, the time of Verhaecht's Italian sojourn, on the basis of its similarity to related works in the British Museum, Darmstadt and the Fogg Museum, which share "its looser execution and relatively spontaneous approach." In contrast is a group of later Alpine drawings of 1616-20 — in the Metropolitan Museum, the Hermitage, and the Kunsthalle in Hamburg — in which the "eccentric pen technique" with "short parallel or zigzag lines punctuated by innumerable dots lends [to them] an abstract, rigid quality...[and a] tight, abstracting style...characteristic of Verhaecht's mature years."

The calligraphic line in this drawing might be compared to high tension lines, electrifying the whole landscape with the excitement of the drawing's focus on the hunt's climactic moment — the kill of the stag.

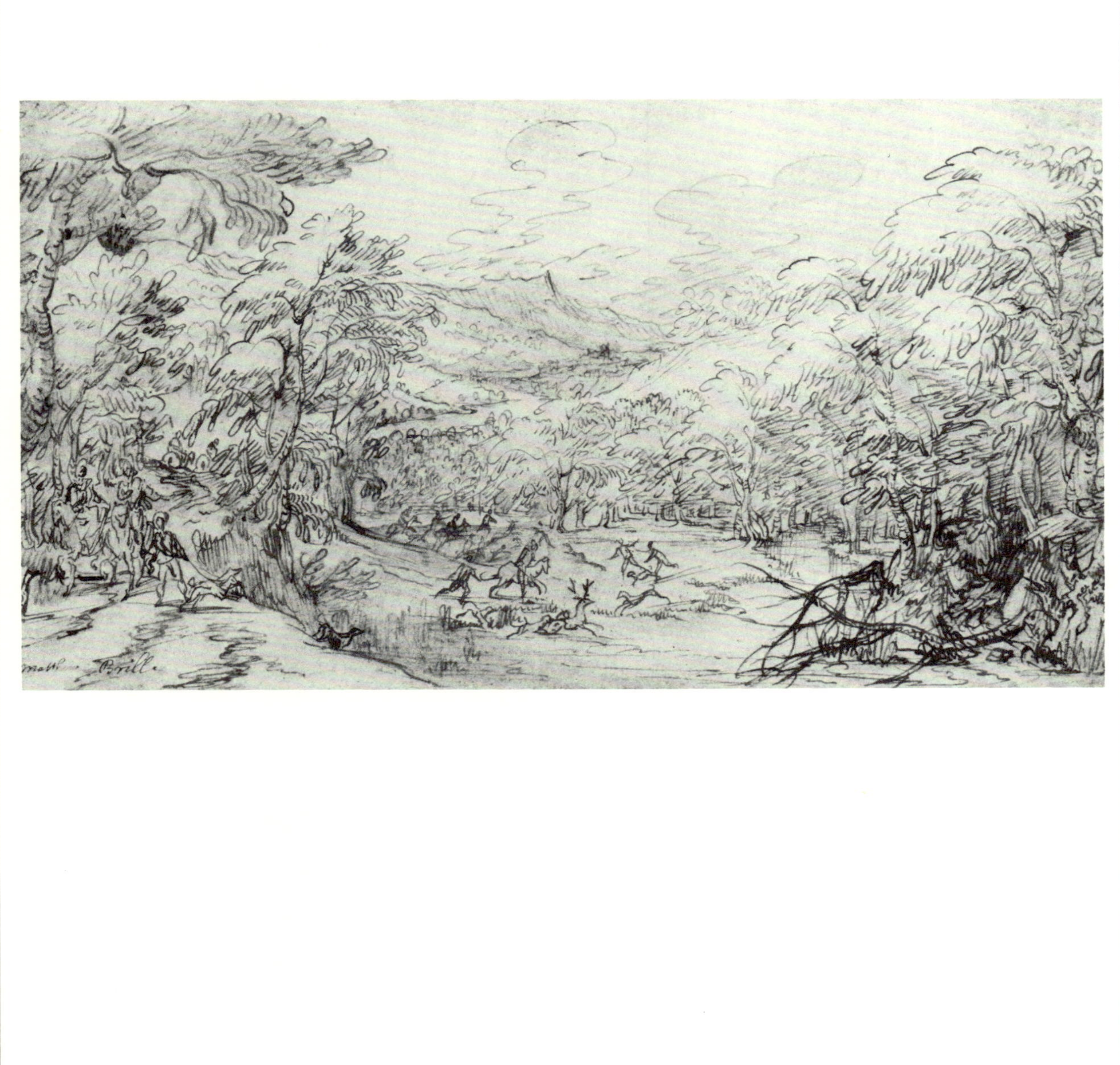
matth. Brill.

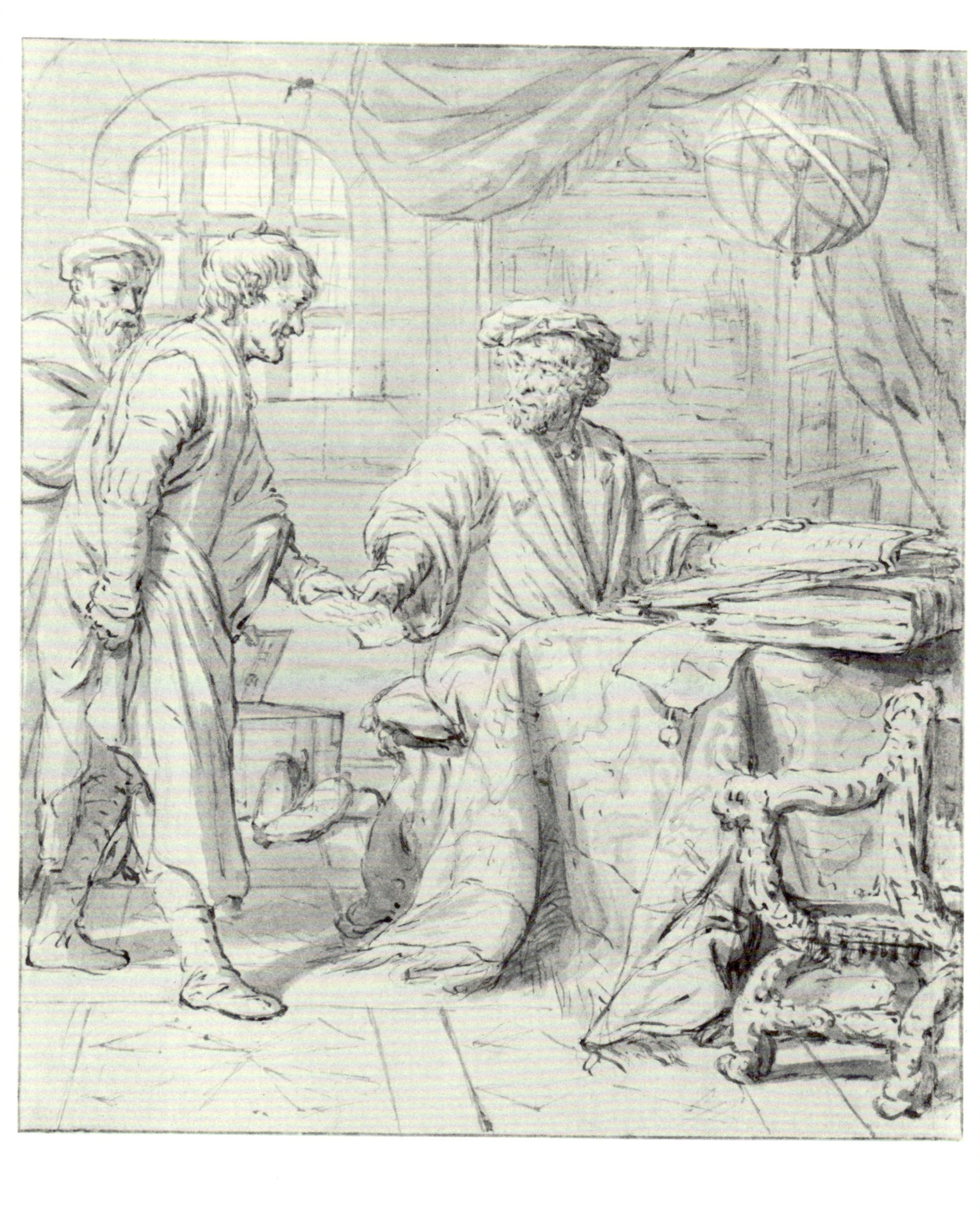

93.

JAN VERKOLJE
(Amsterdam 1650 - Delft 1693)

A Merchant in his Study (A Biblical Parable?)

Pen and brown ink, grey wash; 243 x 212 mm. including a strip 7 mm. wide added on the right
Signed (?) in pen and ink on verso, upper left corner: *Verkolje f.e.*
Inscribed in pen and ink on verso: *Verkolje/E.h.;* several graphite inscriptions of numbers and the word *Verkolje*
Provenance: Prince Cantacuzena
Acquired 1973

After studying briefly with Rembrandt's pupil Jan Lievens (1607-1674), Verkolje moved from Amsterdam to Delft in 1672, in time to encounter the city's greatest painter, Johannes Vermeer (1632-1675), who however by had apparently become relatively inactive[1]. Although some reminiscences of Vermeer's late works, the *Geographer* and the *Astronomer,* can perhaps be discovered in this composition and setting, Verkolje was mainly responsive to the more anecdotal art of such contempoaries as Gabriel Metsu, Caspar Netscher, and Gerard Ter Borch, which was less pristine than Vermeer's.

This drawing is characteristic of Verkolje's relaxed, unpretentious and genial artistic personality. The style, very distantly reminiscent of the early Rembrandt, is close to Verkolje's drawn portrait of the anatomist Reinier de Graf, who died in 1673[2]. Verkolje painted many other portraits and covered the usual range of seventeenth century Dutch figural interior painters, but he favored biblical and classical subjects lightly disguised in modern dress and setting. For instance, he painted scenes of courtship or in bordellos, justified as representing the prodigal son during his career as a libertine. It has therefore been suggested that this scene might represent the Parable of the Vineyard from Matthew xx, in which an employer pays off all the itinerant laborers in his vineyard with the same wage, ignoring the different lengths of time some of them have worked. The parable has two morals, neither universally appealing: "It is not lawful for me to do what I will with mine own?," (verse 15); and "...the last shall be first and the first last: for many may be called, but few chosen." (verse 16)

The central figures of a painting (in the Hermitage in Leningrad)[3] of the parable, signed and dated by Rembrandt in 1637, do anticipate in reverse the two principal figures in this drawing. But there is a problem: the biblical account has the master pay off his servants with one penny each, and the many contemporary images of the subject show not only money but a crowd. This master is evidently handing some kind of contract or document to his obsequious visitor. Furthermore under the two joined hands are rather shapeless objects that might be read as sabots or shoes, a traditional symbol for the making of a contract. So an alternate explanation for the subject may be more fitting: the parable of the talents (Matthew xxv: 14-30) in which the employer gave each of his servants a sum of money and rewarded those who invested their capital profitably and punished those who did not. In this interpretation, Verkolje's scene would represent the master either giving the servant his capital or rewarding one who had made it multiply.

Alternatively, the scene might represent the parable of the unjust steward (Matthew xviii: 23-27) at the moment when his creditor forgives him his debt. But that moment is less the point of the parable than the later moment when the creditor discovers that the steward has not been so generous to his own debtor. Finally, it is conceivable that the scene was taken from some event in contemporary theatre or literature or even from some aphorism.

Verkolje not only drew and painted, he also made prints, although none that is recorded represents a religious or even an obvious moralistic subject.

1. In 1668 Verkolje painted a portrait (in the Rijksmuseum, Amsterdam) of Vermeer's executor, the famous scientist Anthonie van Leeuwenhoek (1632-1723) and made a mezzotint (Le Bl 19) after it. See no. 73, exhibition catalogue, *The Orange and the Rose,* Victoria and Albert Museum, London, 1964, pp. 73-74.
2. Victoria and Albert Museum, *op. cit.,* no. 116, p. 52.
3. Abraham Bredius, *The Complete Edition of the Paintings of Rembrandt,* revised by Horst Gerson, London, 1969, no. 558.

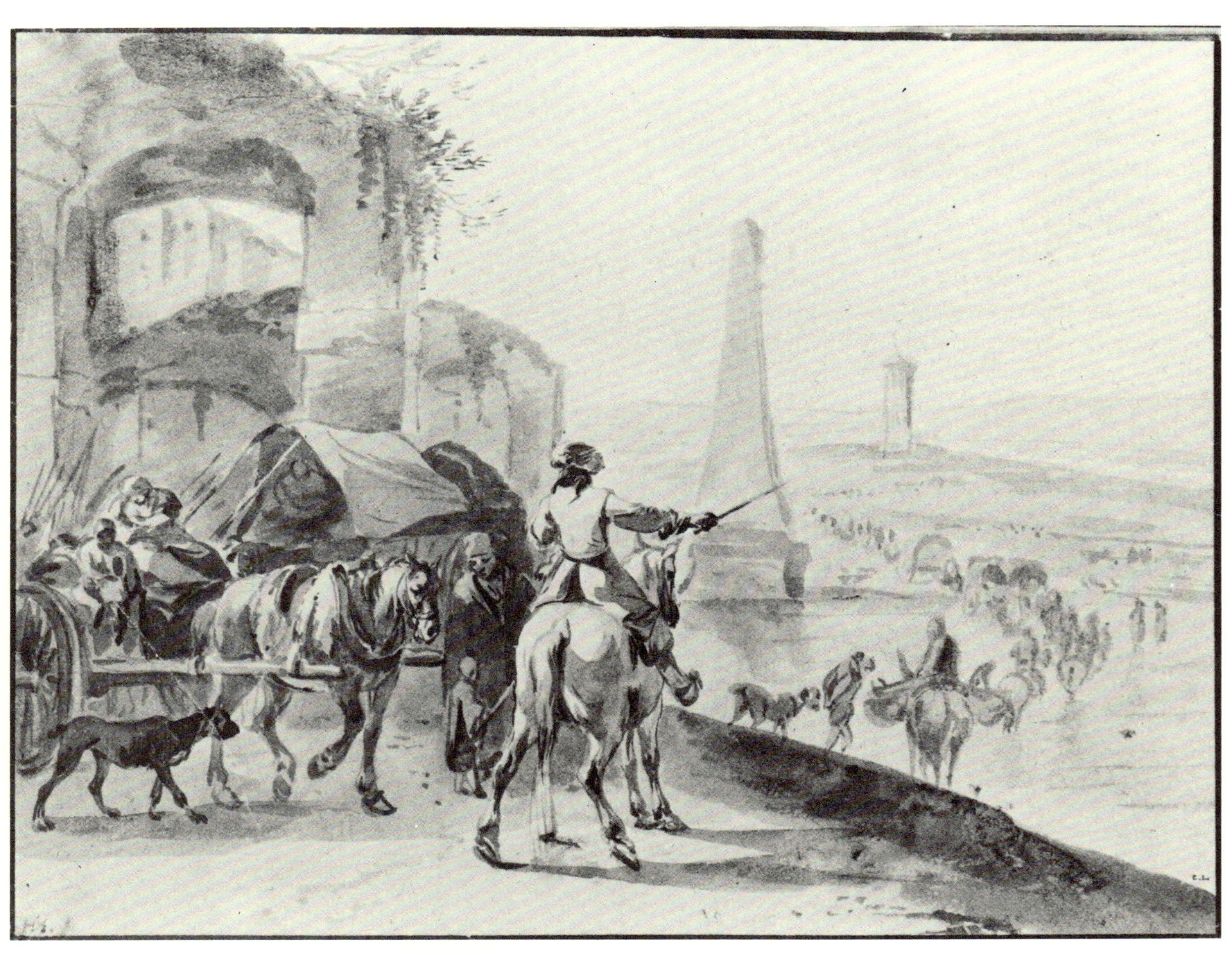

94.

HENDRICK VERSCHURING
(Gorchum 1627 - Italy - 1690 Dordrecht)

Fording a River

Grey and black wash on light grey paper; 182 x 245 mm.
Signed lower left corner with initials *HVS*
Provenance: Fairfax-Murray Collection (according to handwritten inscription on the back of the frame); Laporte (L.1170)
Acquired 1982

Verschuring, like a few other artists included in this exhibition — Jan de Bisschop, Jacob van der Ulft and perhaps Count Hendrick Goudt (numbers 61 and 90 and 98 respectively) — was a member of the ruling class, the son of the mayor of Leiden and, like his exact contemporary van der Ulft, eventually became mayor of Gorkum. But he was not an amateur, having studied for six years with Jan Both (ca. 1615-1652) described by Stechow[1] as "undoubtedly the leading master in [Dutch] Campagna landscape painting." Verschuring then spent eight years, from 1646 to 1654, in Italy, which he never forgot. His other passion seems to have been like Huchtenburg's for horses (see number 77). It brought him under the influence of the most famous Dutch horse-painter, Philips Wouwerman (1619-1668), and sometimes resulted in confusion of Verschuring's works with Huchtenburg's. Verschuring died by drowning at sea.

The ruins on the left foreground and the plump obelisk in the middle ground of this drawing seem evidently intended to establish the locale of this scene as Italian. But, like his master Both, Verschuring was less interested in classical remains in themselves than in the Italian setting. The bright atmospheric effect certainly is suggestive of a blazing hot summer day in the Roman Campagna. Possibly the caravan is one of those that regularly passed through the countryside to the North and South of Rome under armed protection against the bandits who flaunted their control of much of the area beyond the city walls. Apparently there is an armed squad on the left, concealed by the wagon in front, perhaps under the command of the gesturing equestrian in the center. However that may be, the drawing is obviously composed according to the Baroque diagonal formula, and presumably does not represent a specific incident at a specific time or place but is instead an imaginative adventure of the sort Verschuring and many similar artists often repeated. It is characteristic of Italianate Dutch art also in its use of washes more than line to construct the figures.

Verschuring's subjects range from violent battles, through peaceful landscapes to urban scenes of farriers, markets, busy piazzas — almost anything having to do with horses, and some not. He often dated his drawings as well as signed them. But after his return from Italy, his art seems not to have undergone notable change, remaining a dream of ordinary lives romanticized by the sunny sky and exotic setting of distant Italy.

1. Wolfgang Stechow, *Dutch Landscape Painting of the Seventeenth Century*, London, 1966, p. 154.

95.

MAARTEN DE VOS
(Antwerp 1532 - Rome, Florence, Venice - 1603 Antwerp)

Abduction of the Sabine Women

Pen and brown ink, brown wash; 279 x 332 mm.; vertical fold down the center
Provenance: Evans Collection 1940
Acquired 1983

Maarten De Vos was trained by his father, Pieter, and continued his studies in Florence, Rome and Venice, until 1558. The following year he qualified as a master in the Antwerp painters guild. He belonged to a generation of artists who were permeated by Italian art, known in Antwerp through engravings after Italian masters. In Italy, as a matter of course and like Heemskerck a generation earlier, he made many drawings; one of his Roman sketchbooks in the Rijksmuseum, Amsterdam, contains studies after works in the Vatican Belvedere, the Villa Madama, and the della Valle, Cesi and Farnese Collections. In 1572, De Vos founded a fraternity of local artists who had been in Italy. He and his followers were often called Romanists, a misnomer because their art was a mixture of Flemish tradition with Italianate stylization — a grand manner of Romano-Florentine origin colored by Venetian painting. De Vos' large-scale paintings — many made in the late 1580's and 1590's to replace altarpieces destroyed by the Iconoclasts in 1566 and 1580-81 — often give the impression of having been conceived as small and then inflated.

This drawing clearly reveals De Vos' passion for Rome. It represents an unfortunate legendary encounter between the Latin founders of Rome and their Sabine neighbors, whose women the Romans abducted. The composition hints of a debt to Taddeo Zuccaro, to such drawings as the battle scene (in the Uffizi, inv. no. 632F) preparatory for the frescoed *Battle of Charles V against the Lutherans* in the Sala dei Fasti of 1563-6 in the Palazzo Farnese in Rome[1]. The Zuccaro drawing was done after De Vos' visit to Rome, but can nonetheless be considered exemplary of the average artistic production in Rome at the time. De Vos' style, conception, and composition were determined by the same Italianate characteristics which he assimilated during his *Wanderjahre* in Italy. In accordance with both styles and theme, the background in the *Abduction of the Sabine Women* contains obvious references to Rome, such as the dome of St. Peter's, the Castel Sant'Angelo and the two columns of Trajan and Marcus Aurelius.

The compositional scheme of the Steiner sheet reflects Frans Floris' style, with reminiscences also of Tintoretto's, especially in the striking diagonals, the twisted poses and the flights of perspective. Several signed and dated drawings that De Vos made in the 'eighties show the same characteristics, among others those designed for engravings, such as the series *Thesaurus sacrarum Historiarum veteris Testamenti,* published by G. De Jode in 1585[2]. In fact, many of De Vos' drawings for engravings, for the most part hastily outlined and washed, have come down to us.

The only known painted version of the theme that has been attributed to De Vos, in the Kereszteny Museum at Esztergom, is now generally considered as the work of a follower, possibly Hendrik van Balen[3]. Presumably, this drawing was executed around 1585 and served as a *modello* for an engraving. H.V.M.

1. Gere, 1969, pp. 122, 143, cat no. 39, fig. 166.
2. Karel G. Boon, *Netherlandish Drawings of the Fifteenth and Sixteenth Centuries,* The Hague, 1978, pp. 172-3, nos. 468-9.
3. Armin Zweite, *Maarten de Vos als Maler: Ein Beitrag zur Geschichte der Antwerpener Malerei in der Zweiter Hälfte des 16. Jahrhunderts,* (Ph.D. dissertation, Göttigen, 1974), Berlin, 1980, p. 360

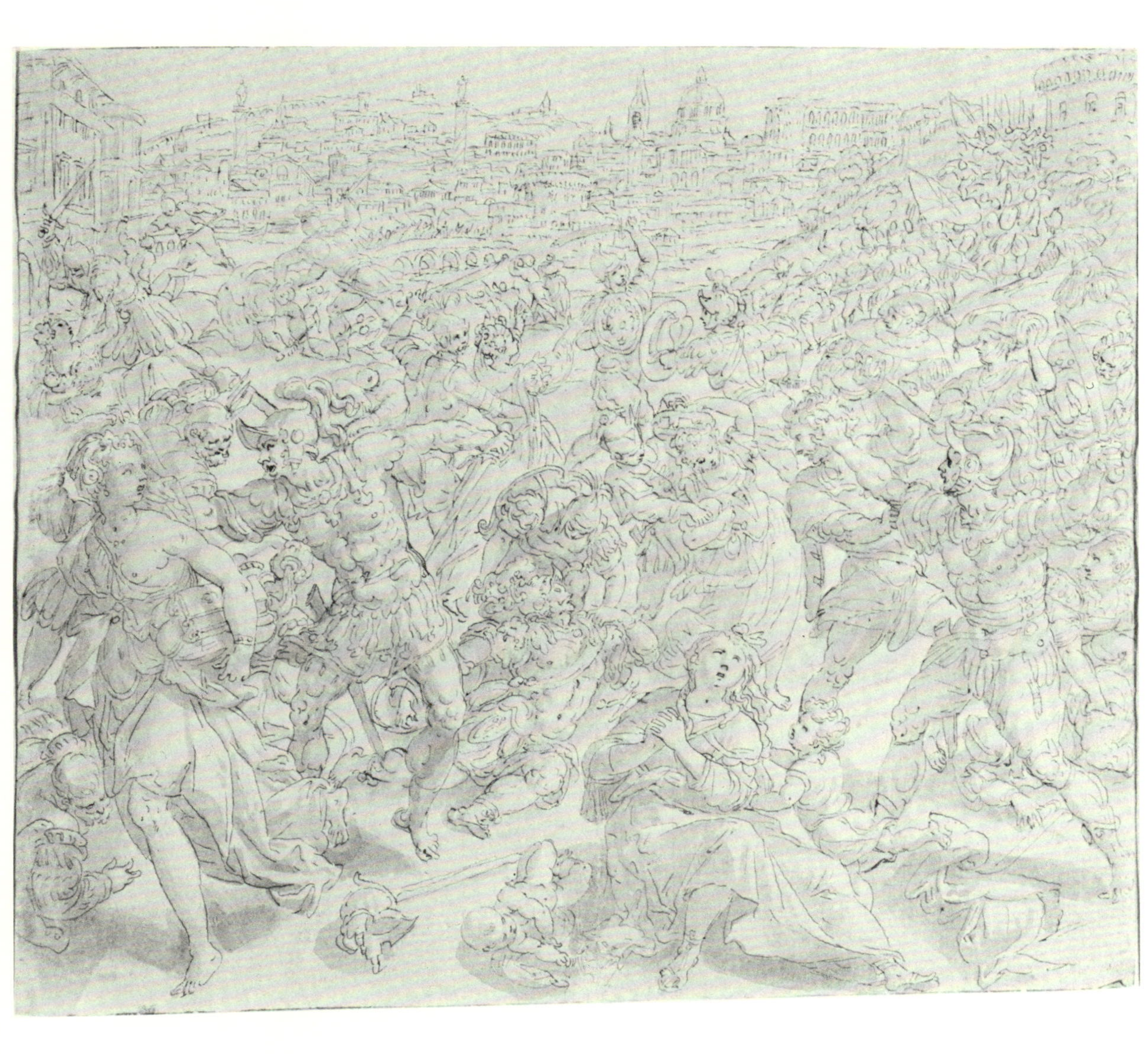

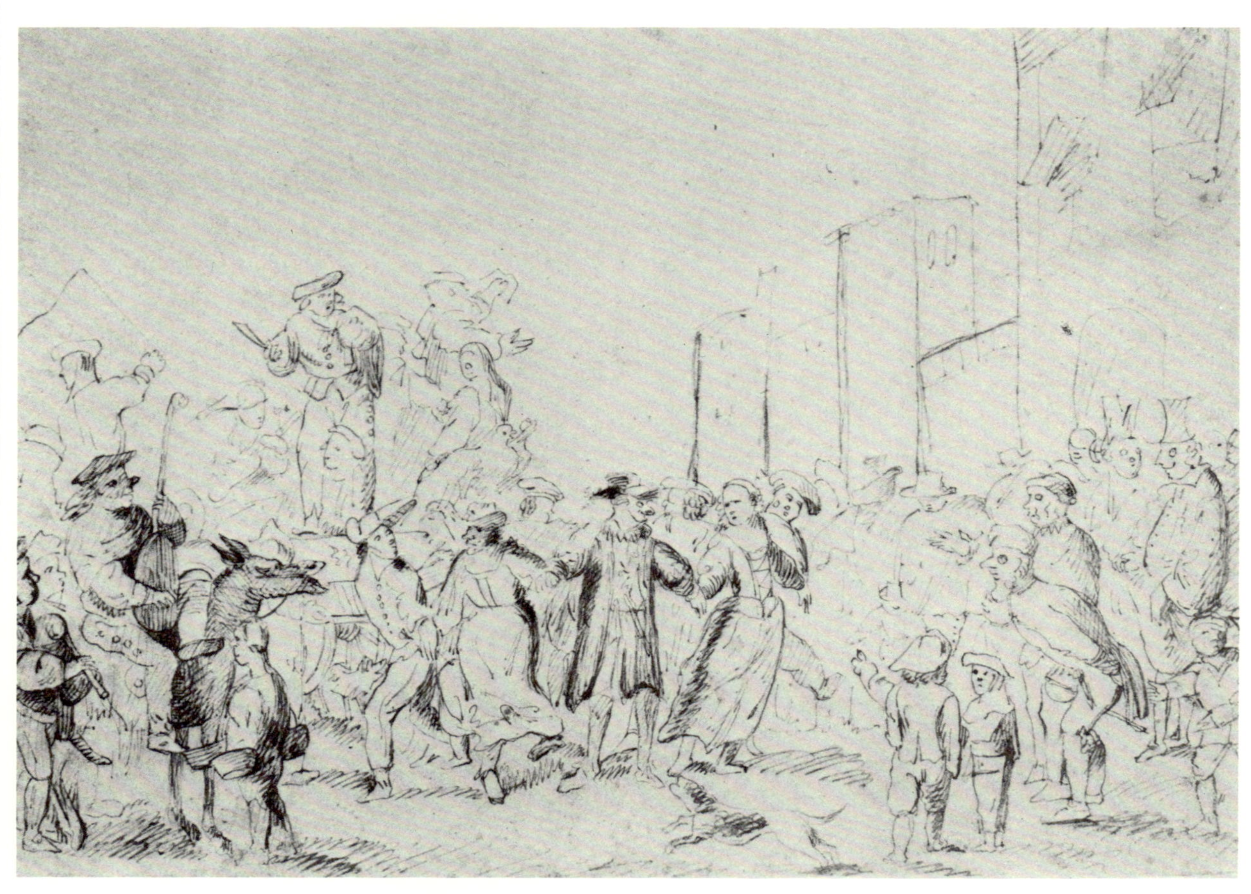

96.

CORNELIS DE WAEL
(Antwerp 1592 - Genoa - 1667 Rome)

Carnival

Pen and brown ink on tan paper; 199 x 292 mm.
Inscribed verso in pen and ink, an old hand: *Vinne, Vincent van der, geb. zu Harlem 1629, gest. 1702, Schueler von Franz Halz, Hinterliesz drei Soehne [...]*
Provenance: unidentified collector's mark, lower middle recto
Acquired 1973

The Flemish chronicler Cornelis de Bie[1] said that de Wael excelled in small historical pictures of battles on land and sea, and particularly, in scenes of military life. In an engraving by Wenzel Hollar in 1646 of the portrait of Cornelis and Lucas de Wael, after the well known painting by Anthony Van Dyck, Cornelis is appropriately described as "Omnigenum praecipue conflictuum representator..."[2].

After his training in his father's workshop in Antwerp, he left for Italy in 1610, and sometime after 1613 settled in Genoa with his brother Lucas. Lucas, who had been a student of their uncle, Jan Bruegel the Elder, stayed in Genoa only until 1628. Cornelis felt comfortable in this Italian harbor city, trained many painters there, and received numerous visiting Flemings, among them his youthful friend Anthony van Dyck. He prospered as a painter, engraver and art dealer and in 1642 became a citizen of Genoa. During the mature years of his life, he devoted his talent to representing scenes of local society. However, his quest for fame and fortune eventually drove him to Rome. There he lived with his nephew, the painter Anton de Wael, from 1656 until his death in 1667.

Many of his drawings are in the Cabinet des Dessins of the Louvre, some in the Albertina in Vienna or French private collections, and one of his sketchbooks, containing fifty-three drawings of soldiers and battle scenes, is in the British Museum[3].

This *Carnival* is conceived and carried out in a characteristically swift, playful style. Although more sketchy and volatile than usual, it is akin to a drawn *Dance Scene* in Berlin[4]. Both style and theme also recall a similarly drawn *Italian Market Scene* in the Yale University Art Gallery and a *Market Scene,* probably a copy, in the Staatliche Graphische Sammlung in Munich[5].

Carnival, traditionally held before the Lenten season, was popular in Italy, and it still is. This nominally religious feast had its roots in the ancient Roman *Hilaria.* On March 25, people remembered the resurrection of Attis, who, according to a Phrygian legend, died after castration. People disguised themselves during the festivities honoring Saturn or Bacchus (among others), a tradition that has survived until this very day. Basically a feast of joy (hence the name *Hilaria*), it was characterized by a sense of freedom and liberty. Frequently, roles were reversed and the rich played poor, whereas the poor pretended to be rich[6]. Like any ritual based on ancient traditions, dance and music played crucial roles in the celebration.

De Wael convincingly evoked the essence of this festivity, with men and women dancing in the center of the composition to the music of stringed instruments and (in the left foreground) a bagpipe. They are entertained by a troupe of performers on a wagon in the left middle ground while, at the right, some burghers watch the merry company underneath their city walls. Although it can not be determined whether these are the walls of Rome or Genoa, the relatively light dresses of the participants and the bare-footed children might place the scene in the warmer, more southern city. If this supposition is correct, it explains the vague reminiscences of Pieter van Laer and the Roman *Bentveughels,* and establishes this drawing as a work of about 1660.

The attribution to De Wael was first suggested by Dr. An Zwollo[7]. H.V.M.

1. Hollstein, 1949-84, ix, p. 72.
2. Cornelis de Bie, *Het gulden cabinet van de Edele Vrye Schilderkonst..*, Antwerp, 1662 (reprint by Davaco Soest NL, 1971), p. 229.
3. Bernt, 1980, vol. V, no. 669.
4. Wolfgant Wegner, *Die Niederländischen Handzeichnungen des 15.-18. Jahrhunderts,* Berlin, 1973, p. 144, no. 1046, fig. 130.
5. Haverkamp Begemann and Logan, 1970, p. 335, no. 629
6. Exhibition catalogue, *La Masque dans la tradition européenne,* Binche, 1975, pp. 199-204.
7. Letter to the Steiners dated 12 December 1974.

97.

ANTHONIE WATERLOO
(Lille ca. 1609 - Utrecht, Leeuwarden, Amsterdam -1690 Utrecht)

Church Apse Seen Through the Snowy Branches of a Tree

Grey wash with black chalk on blue paper; 309 x 191 mm.; vertical crease on the left
Acquired 1979

Waterloo's life is not particularly well documented. He is believed to have been self-trained, although he is also thought to have been associated with the members of the Vaillant family who were like him natives of Lille in the Southern Netherlands (now France). Waterloo lived in Utrecht, Leeuwarden and Amsterdam, was an art dealer as well as an artist, and traveled extensively in the Netherlands, Northern Germany, and the Alps, drawing as he went[1]. He did paint, but his drawings were generally preferred not only in his own time but also in the eighteenth century, particularly in Germany where they were influential. He also made as many as 150 etchings.

His works range in size from small to large, and his technique varies equally, although it is usually a combination of pen and ink, colored chalks and washes[2]. He can be classified as a forest-painter because most of his landscapes portray woodlands and vistas into or through them; many also include villas, castles, or a church. Some reflect the styles of Roeland Roghman or of Lucas van Uden.

This sheet is less refined in detail than either of their drawings (numbers 82 and 90), in part at least because it is a snowy winter scene and the dominant tree has lost all its leaves. Its tapering branches, set aginst a cold winter sky, create a filigree through which the church apse is visible. Summary as Waterloo's handling of this tree is, nonetheless he has managed the articulation of twigs to branches and branches to limbs so knowingly that the structure is convincingly organic. Although permeated by gentle light, the scene is as densely atmospheric as if the fresh snow were still falling; and the outlines of the mass of the building and the bridge are dim and softened. Only the church suggests any human presence, and that as shelter against the cold and perhaps against the anthropomorphic effect of the bold strokes defining the reach of the tree. A drawing in the Louvre[3] of buildings and bare trees in the snow is similar in composition and in romantic interpretation.

A winter scene without buildings[4] in the Frans Lugt Collection at the Institut Néerlandais in Paris (inv. no. 3463) carries the same dim misty effect and quiet mood even farther. Also on blue paper in chalk and wash, like the Steiner drawing it is spontaneous and loose without fine lines or specific details, and irresistibly suggestive of nature's qualities. The poetic, almost impressionistic, effect of both the Lugt and Steiner drawings places them late in the artist's career. M.L.

1. See for example, Lotte and Wolf Stubbe, *Um 1660 auf Reisen gezeichnet Anthonie Waterloo,* Hamburg 1983, with a number of photographs paired with Waterloo's drawings.
2. Robinson, 1977, p. 53.
3. Lugt, 1949-50, vol. II, no. 884.
4. Bernt, 1958, vol. II, no. 672.

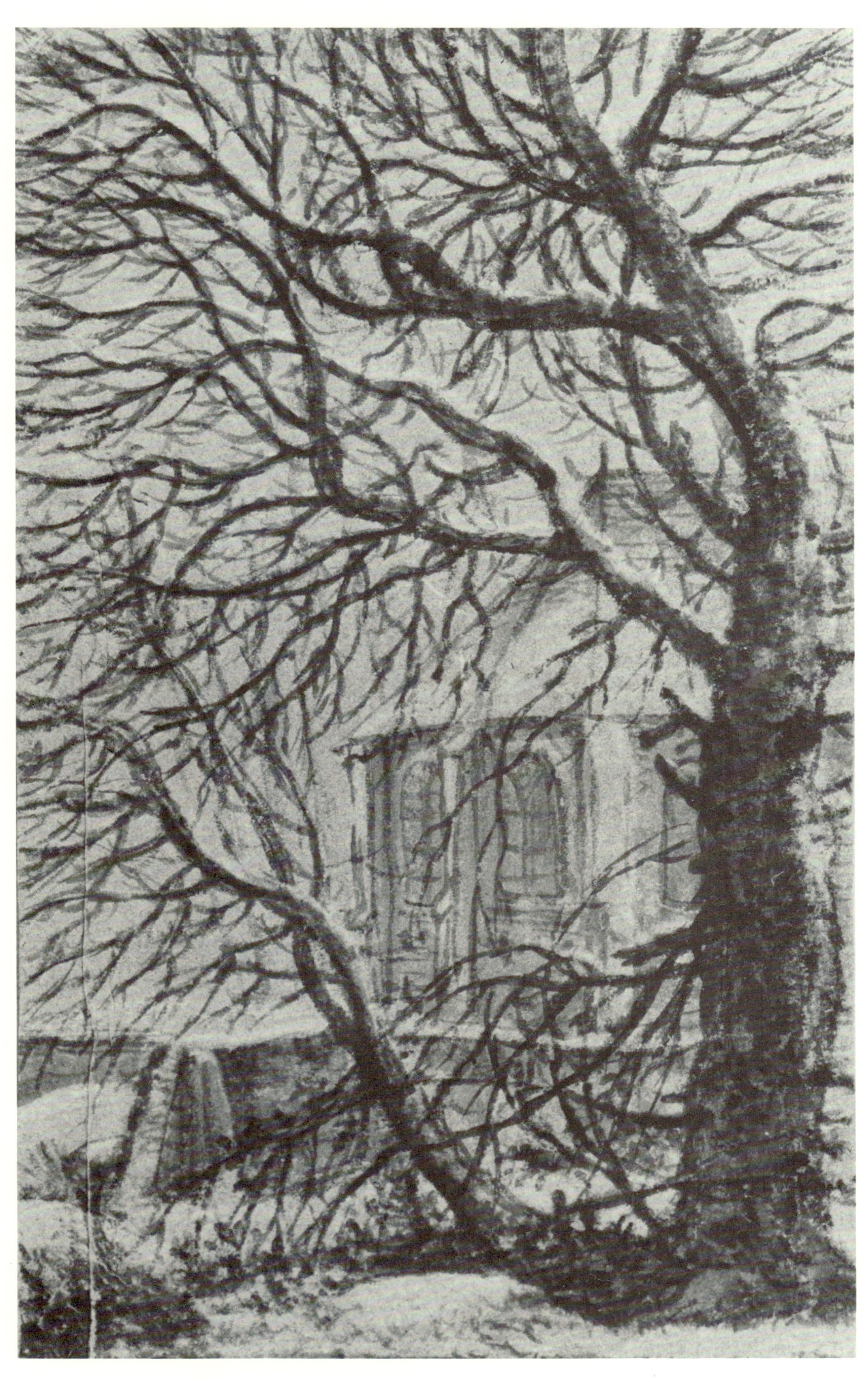

Other Drawings

98.

CIRCLE OF ADAM ELSHEIMER
(Frankfurt a/M. 1578 - Venice - 1610 Rome)

The Liberation of St. Peter

Pen and brown ink, brown wash over black chalk; left bottom corner made up; 164 x 201 mm.
Provenance: Rev. Dr. H. Wellesley, according to a note on the mount (L.1384); Victor Koch, Sotheby's, 29 June 1949, lot no. 69, as Elsheimer
Acquired 1980
Literature: Hans Möhle, *Die Zeichnungen Adam Elsheimers,* Berlin, 1966, p. 185, no. D 33, pl. 66

Elsheimer's life was short and his paintings small, but he was very influential, particularly on the artists in Rome during the decade before his death. His drawings are highly controversial. When Bode first rehabilitated the artist in the 1880s, he accepted over 300 as autograph[1]. The subtraction of copies and imitations by other artists gradually reduced this number, until Hans Möhle arrived at just under seventy[2]. He gave this *Liberation of St. Peter* to an Italian master of ca. 1630, presumably relating it to a *Liberation of St. Peter* attributed to Carlo Saraceni in the Staatsgalerie in Stuttgart. No painted version by Elsheimer has been discovered.

The drawing is closely related to a picture-within-a-picture, represented in the painting of *The Shop of Jan Snellinck* in the Museum at Brussels[3], dated by inscription 1621 and attributed to Hieronymus Francken II. The composition is also echoed in a picture formerly in Lord Elgin's Collection,[4] which traditionally was given to Elsheimer, but may very well be by David Teniers I. The similarities between the Steiner drawing and the picture-within-a-picture in the Francken panel point to a common source and make an attribution to Elsheimer tempting. But he is unlikely to have painted this lost version himself, for the simple reason that he usually painted on very small sheets of copper, and *The Liberation of St. Peter* in the Francken panel is too large for a genuine Elsheimer. Possibly the composition did originate in Elsheimer's shop. A description in the catalogue of the Fratacolla Collection sale in Amsterdam on 26 April 1813, fits it neatly: Lot no. 13, a painted panel, with almost the same dimensions as this drawing.

Perhaps David Teniers the Elder, who studied with Elsheimer between 1600 and 1606 in Rome, was the draughtsman. Nor should Jan Pynas or even Pieter Lastman be excluded a priori. The likeliest candidate, however, is Count Hendrick Goudt (1573-1648). A rich Dutch engraver, who lived with Elsheimer in Rome between 1606 and 1610, Goudt is an enigmatic figure. He seems to have played the dual role of pupil and patron; according to Sandrart,[5] he even provided the wherewithal to keep the Elsheimer household going until he lost patience and had Elsheimer thrown into debtor's prison. The unfortunate master died soon after his release, apparently reconciled with and nursed by Goudt. Perhaps this *Liberation of St. Peter* alludes to this unfortunate episode; less romantic is our present notion that Goudt not only collected, copied and imitated his master, but also forged Elsheimer drawings.

This drawing represents the moment when the angel, freeing St. Peter from prison, leads him past King Herod's sleeping guards (Acts xxi: 1-11). The scene contains features characteristic of both Elsheimer's and Goudt's drawing styles. The nervous handling of the pen, the awkward figure types and the delicately applied watercolor suggest Elsheimer. On the other hand, the pronounced accents on St. Peter's contours, the controlled parallel hatching in the shadows of his cloak, and the uncertain anatomy, are generally considered hallmarks of Goudt. But without more data on the intricate relation between Elsheimer, Goudt, and the other members of the studio, the drawing can only be attributed to Elsheimer's workshop, possibly between 1605 and 1610. H.V.M.

1. Wilhelm von Bode, *Studien zur Geschichte der hollandische Malerei,* Braunschweig, 1883.
2. Heinrich Weizsacker, *Adam Elsheimer, der Maler von Frankfurt,* vol. II, edited by Hans Möhle, Berlin, 1952, p. 231.
3. S. Speth-Holterhoff, *Les peintres Flamands de cabinets d'amateurs au XVII siècle,* Brussels, 1957, pp. 63-5, fig. 7.
4. Elgin sale, Christie's, London, 27 June 1958, lot 49 ill.
5. Joachim von Sandrart, *Teutsche Academie...,* Nuremburg, 1675 (edition of A.R. Peltzer, Munich, 1925)

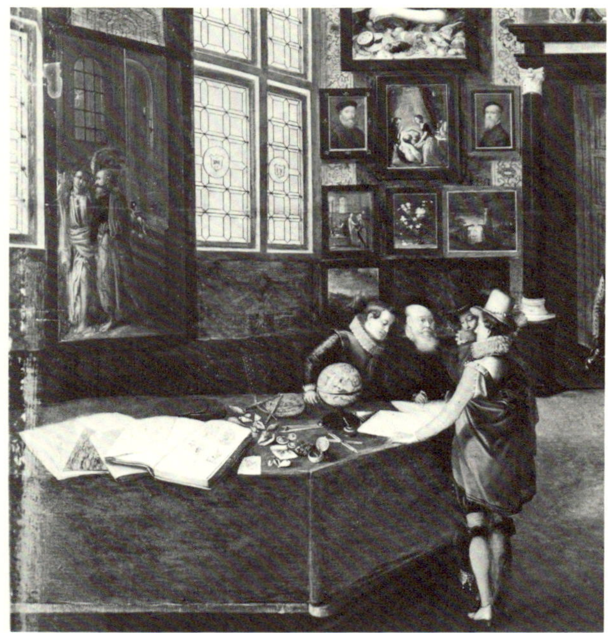

Hieronymous Francken the Second
The Shop of Jan Snellinck
Musée des Beaux-Arts, Brussels

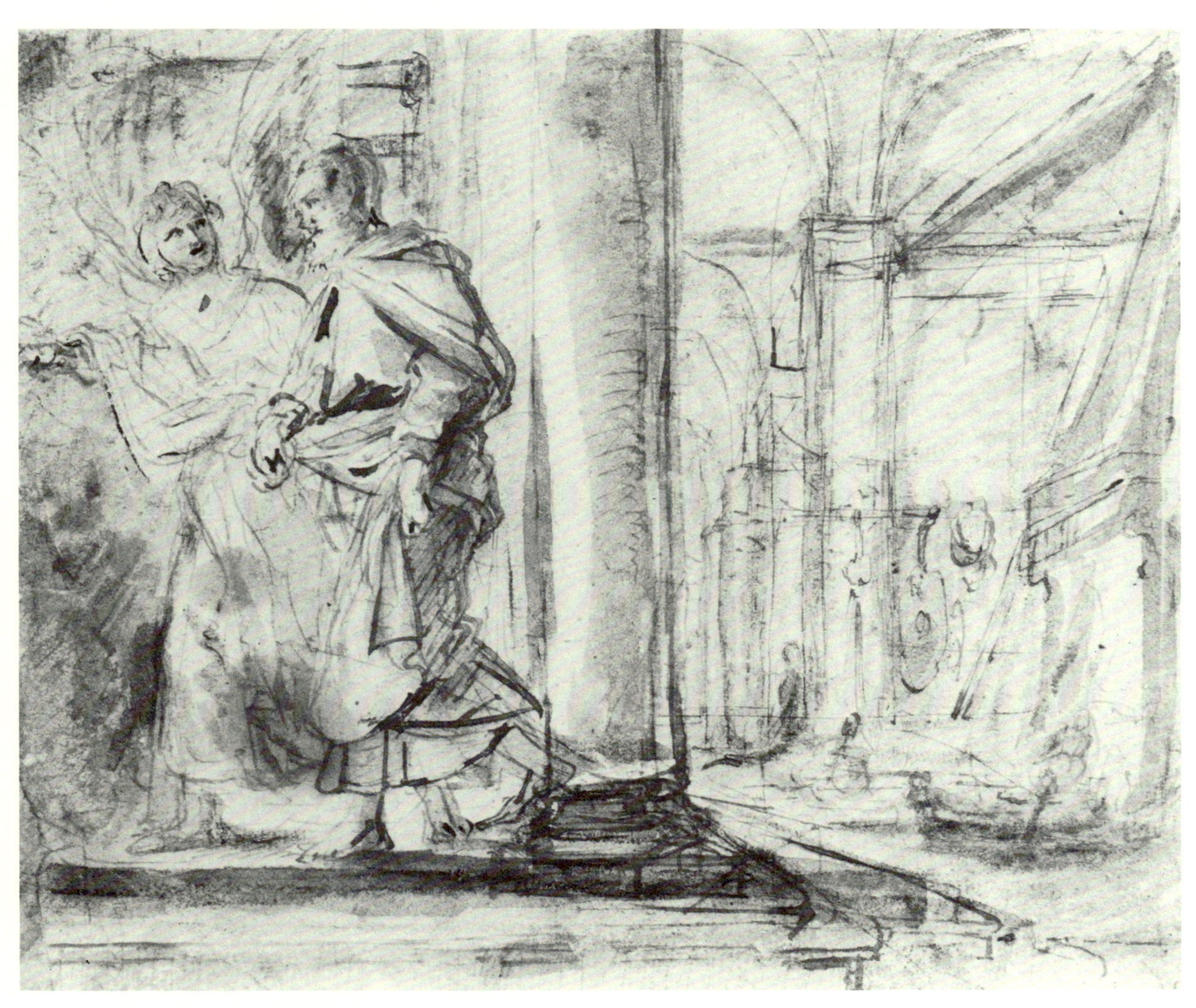

99.

CIRCLE OF URS GRAF
(Solothurn c. 1485 - Basle, Strasbourg, Zurich, Italy -Basle[?] 1527/28)

A Flagbearer: The Swiss Canton of Underwalden

Brush drawing in white on dark red-tinted paper; 144 x 102 mm.
Provenance: Albertina, Vienna; Archduke Friedrich Hapsburg; August Laube und Sohn, Zurich
Acquired 1972

Graf, who was a goldsmith and graphic artist rather than a painter, has had a bad press, perhaps deservedly — the Murrays in the *Dictionary of Art and Artists* describe him as "a vile man who frequently went off as a mercenary soldier...his drawings of the life of these brutes have a morbid fascination" (1976 edition, p. 198). This fascination may have been fatal for the artist; at least it has been suggested that he died while participating in the Sack of Rome in 1527. In any case, he was very well-traveled, although from the time of his marriage in 1511, he seems to have made Basle his headquarters.

The subject of this drawing is not vile, nor does he seem to be a brute. He is instead one of eight standard-bearers in a series of preparatory drawings of 1521 for white line woodcuts of the flags of the Swiss cantons. The flag in this drawing is blank; in the woodcut it bears the appropriate heraldic devices, identified as Underwalden[1] in central Switzerland on the Lake of Luzern. The woodcut is signed with Graf's usual VG monogram and bears the date 1521. In fact, although only eight drawings appear to be known, there are sixteen woodcuts[2].

This and the other seven drawings were in the Albertina in Vienna until the end of the Hapsburg empire, when they were turned over to the Archduke Friedrich as his personal property and he sold them. Another, for Zurich, is in an American private collection[3].

1. Hollstein, 1949-84, vol. XI, no. 33, p. 58
2. Hollstein, *op. cit.*, nos.29-44, pp. 58
3. Exhibition catalogue, *Princeton Alumni Collections: Works on Paper,* Princeton University Art Museum, 1981.

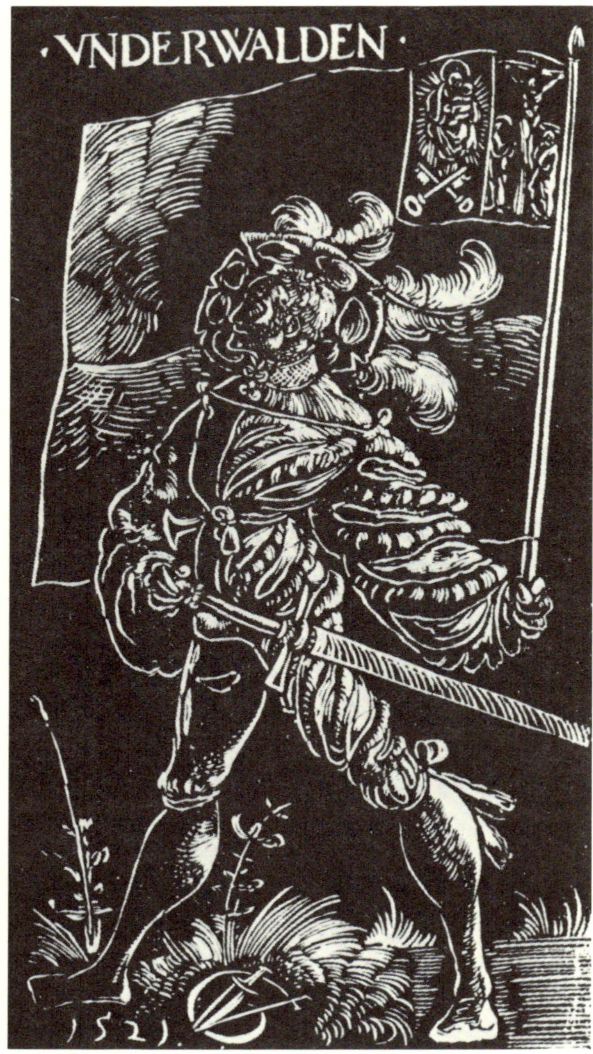

Urs Graf
Underwalden Flag-Bearer

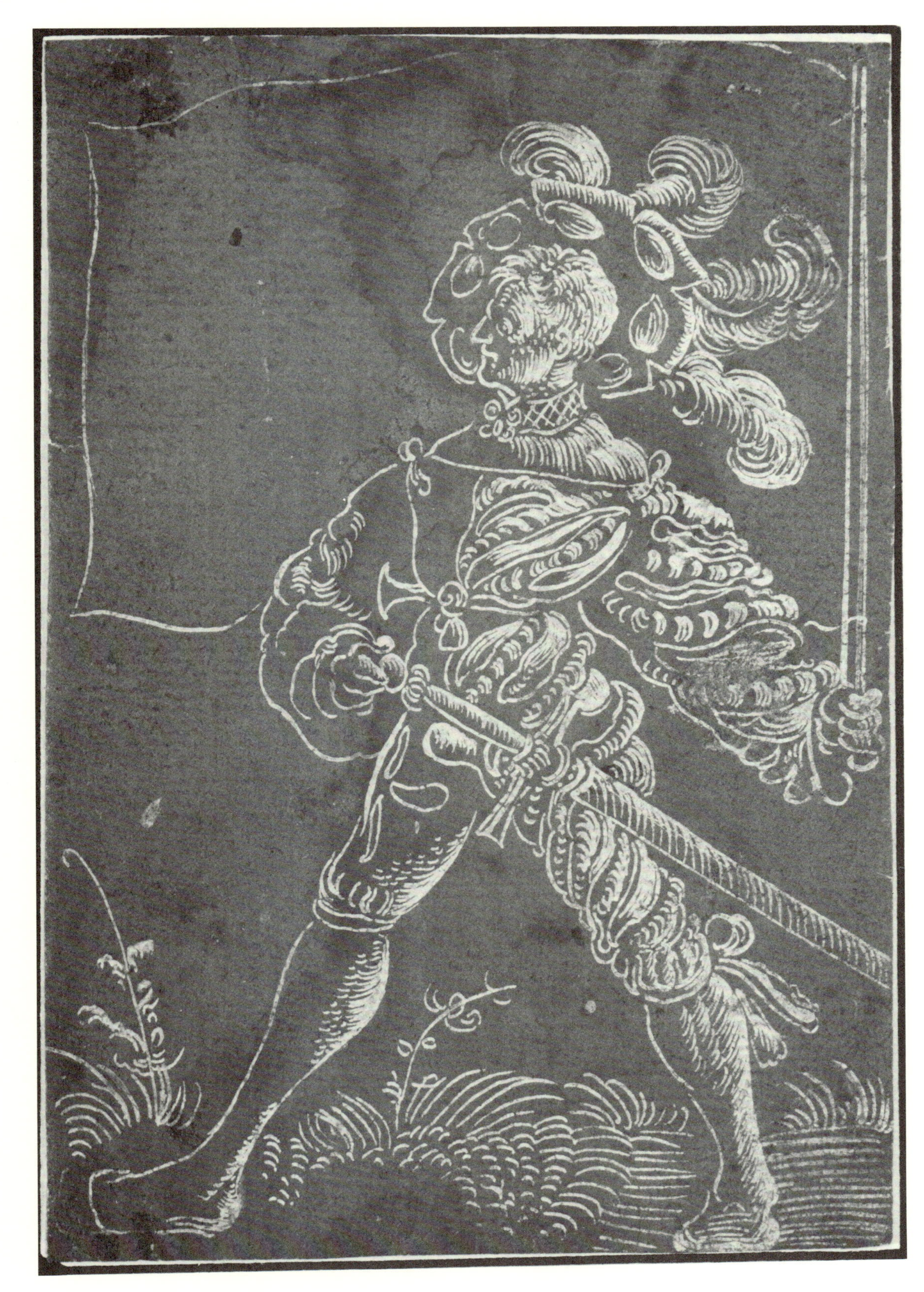

100.

JUSEPE DE RIBERA
(Jativa near Valencia 1591 - North Italy, Rome - 1652 Naples)

Blind Friar Led by a Man

Black chalk and brown wash; 189 x 140 mm.; laid down
Inscription: illegible letters and numbers in pen and ink showing through from the *verso*
Acquired 1973
Literature: Craig Felton with William C. Jordan, exhibition catalogue, *Jusepe de Ribera, lo Spagnoletto 1591-1652,* Fort Worth, 1982, p. 83, fig. 95

Ribera, though born and trained in Spain, spent all of his adult life in Italy. He went there as a young man, probably first to Naples, then visiting north Italy and Rome, and finally establishing himself permanently in Naples by 1616. His first training, presumably in the Spanish realist tradition, redisposed him to the profound sympathy toward Caravaggio's manner that is evident in his earliest known works. It may also explain his inclination throughout his career to bring the classical gods and heroes down to earth, and his occasional inclination to represent harrowing acts of unspeakable cruelty. Already in the 1620's, however, he began to respond to the gentler forms, subjects and attitudes of the successors of the Carracci. He became the leading painter in Naples, where he profited from generous patronage, not only locally from the succession of Spanish viceroys and from others, but also abroad, particularly in Spain.

Two hunched men with dour faces drag their feet across this sheet. Apparently the taller man, with a staff in one hand and a rosary in the other, is blind and is being guided by his companion, whose shoulder he grips. His habit appears to be Franciscan but because he has a beard, forbidden to Franciscans by an order of 1547, he may be a member of one of the minor medicant orders. The likeliest possibility is the Capuchins, founded in 1599. Like this man, they wore a habit with a pointed cowl, sandals and beards[1]. Perhaps it is not mere coincidence that Ribera had numerous commissions in the Capuchin monastery-church of San Martino overlooking Naples from the central hills above the city.

The guide is as shabby as his master, and his stooped posture suggests that he has been pressed into this service for quite a while. Probably, as Jonathan Brown has suggested,[2] the drawing is a study from life rather than from Ribera's imagination. He drew other genre scenes of this sort, with a similar lack of background and accessory detail that Brown observes "imparts an unreal quality to humdrum activities." It calls to mind also Ribera's many paintings of blind philosophers and sages in rags[3].

The combination in the drawing of chalk, rather than pen and ink, with wash is rare, not to say unique in Ribera's oeuvre. The masterful, quavering delineation places the drawing toward the end of Ribera's life, when Brown has suggested[4] that ill health caused this characteristic palsied line, effective as it is in rendering the ragged clothing and uncertain progress of the two men. These spasmodic lines and swiftly applied wash occur in other late drawings by Ribera, like the pen and ink and wash *Adoration of the Shepherds*[5] in the Metropolitan Museum (inventory number 68.64). R.R.

1. F.L. Cross, editor, *The Oxford Dictionary of the Christian Church.* 2d ed., Oxford, 1974, pp. 237-8, 532-3.
2. Felton, *op. cit.,* p. 83.
3. Delphine Fitz Darby, "Ribera and the Blind Men," *AB* XXXIX, 1957, pp. 195-217; "Ribera and the Wise Men." *AB* XLIV, 1962, pp. 279-307.
4. Jonathan Brown, exhibition catalogue, *Jusepe de Ribera: Prints and Drawings,* Princeton, 1973, p. 177.
5. Brown, *op. cit.,* p. 174, pl. 60.

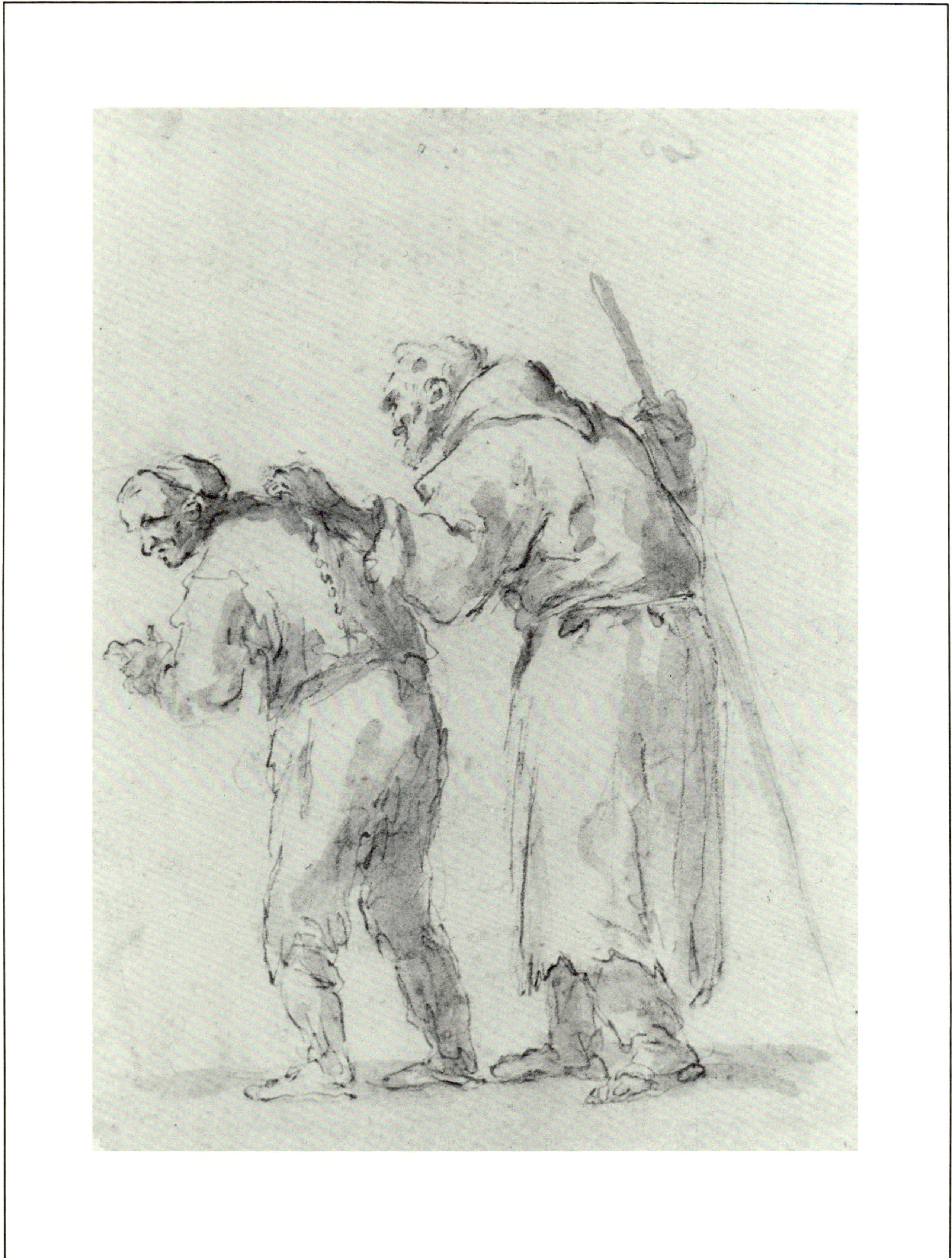

101.

THOMAS ROWLANDSON
(London 1756/7 - Paris - 1827 London)

The Game of Nine Pins

Pen and grey ink, watercolor; 158 x 242 mm.
Inscribed recto lower left corner, pen and grey ink:
GAME AT NINE PINS
Acquired 1981
Loaned by Lori Steiner

Rowlandson's birthdate is uncertain. His father, a bankrupt cloth merchant, died in 1764 and Rowlandson was then brought up by an aunt, who sent him to a proper grammar school before he went to study art at the Royal Academy in 1772. He first exhibited at the Academy in 1775. He made several trips to Paris, visited the Netherlands, Germany, and probably Italy but continued to live in London. There he and his prints, many published by Rudolph Ackermann in books, were much appreciated. His drawings were hardly less admired, so much so that as many as 10,000 may exist, enough to defeat even the most intrepid cataloguer[1].

Rowlandson is remembered primarily as a caricaturist, in the tradition of Ghezzi (number 22) and his predecessors, and of course in continuity with the great William Hogarth (1696-1764). But his range was greater: he did many landscape drawings, and if his pen often slipped into parody, nonetheless much of his *oeuvre* is more social documentation than simply caricature. His art might be described as the rowdy, not to say vulgar, reverse of his younger contemporary Jane Austen's more genteel coin; Wark has used the phrase "picturesque genre."

This drawing is certainly comic and caricatural, with its repeated details of lechery, particularly among more or less grotesque couples. But not all the couples are lascivious; nor are all of the women complacent, jolly and gross and all of the men leering importunate gnomes. The focus on the bowler and the concentration with which he marshalls his powers for a strike establishes Rowlandson as a sympathetic observer. The mood is uninhibited. But it is appreciative of sport and of the harmless pleasure it provides both participant and spectator. Basically Rowlandson's attitude is cheerful, uncritical, even admiring. If there is more than a touch of caricature it seems less likely to be moralistically imposed on the members of the crowd than simply description of how they look and behave during a sunny Sunday afternoon on the village green.

The slightly diagonal composition is more effective dramatically than Rowlandson's usual frieze. Comparison with other sports drawings, for instance the *Boxing Match* or the *Prize Fight* at the Huntington Collection,[2] suggests a date around 1800 or a little later, when Rowlandson favored scenes of fairs and the like. The game being played here, ninepins, was later outlawed for the very carousing that is evident here. But the law-makers were outwitted by the players; they simply added another pin, to make the different game of tenpins, which was legal.

1. To quote Robert R. Wark, *Drawings by Thomas Rowlandson in the Huntington Collection,* San Marino, 1976, p. 1.
2. Wark, *op. cit.,* respectively no. 125, p. 61 and no. 143, p. 65.

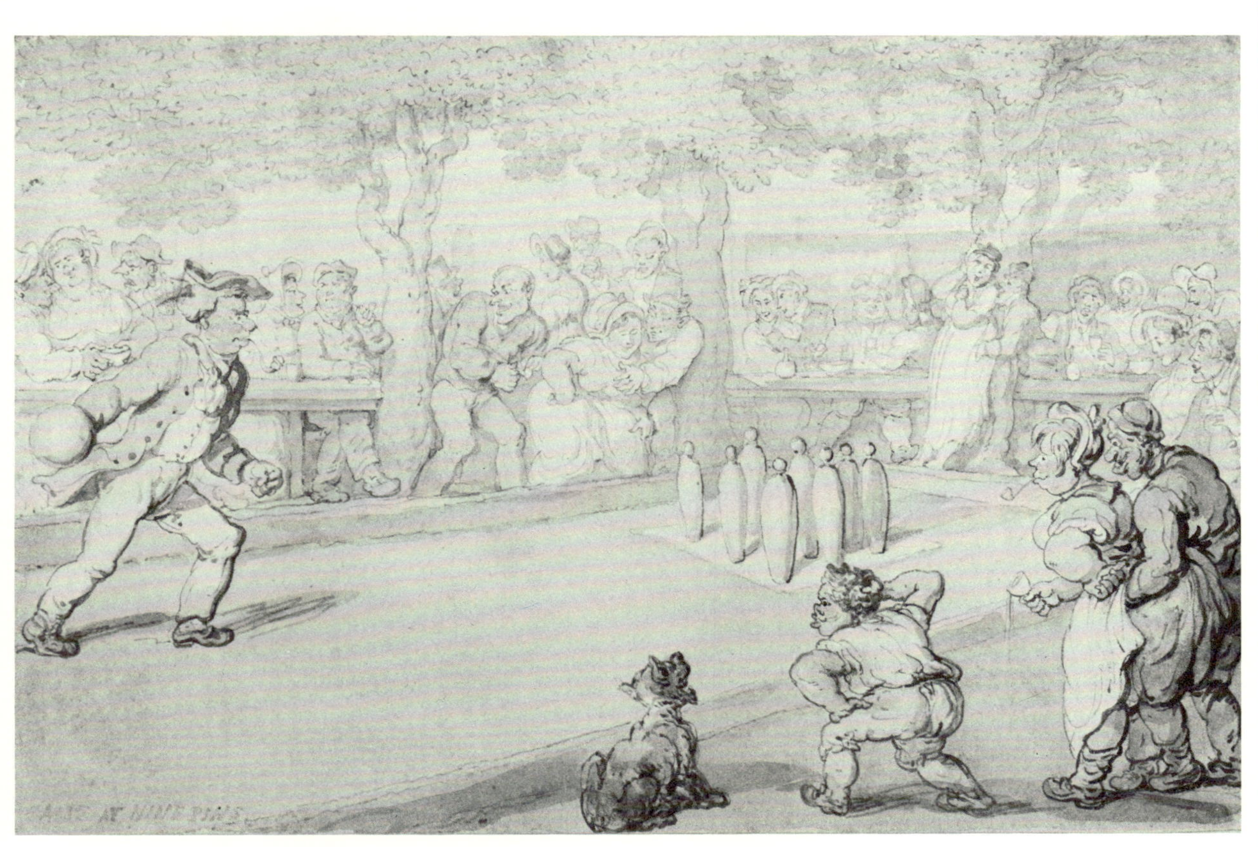
AT NINE PINS

Frequently Cited Works

Jacob Bean. *17th Century Italian Drawings in the Metropolitan Museum of Art.* New York, 1979.

Otto Benesch. *Die Zeichnungen der Niederländischen Schulen des XV. und XVI. Jahrhunderts.* Vienna, 1928.

________________. *The Drawings of Rembrandt. Complete Edition in Six Volumes.* Enlarged and edited by Eva Benesch. New York, 1973.

Walther Bernt. *Die Niederländischen Zeichner des 17. Jahrhunderts.* 2 vols. Munich, 1958.

________________. *Die Niederländischen Maler und Zeichner des 17 Jahrhunderts.* Five vols. Munich, 1979-80.

Giuliano Briganti. *Pietro da Cortona o della pittura barocca.* Florence, 1962.

Richard Cocke. *Pier Francesco Mola.* Oxford, 1972.

Correspondance des directeurs de l'Académie de France à Rome. Rome, 1901.

John A. Gere. *Taddeo Zuccaro: His Development Studied in His Drawings.* London, 1969.

John A. Gere and Philip Pouncey. *Italian Drawings in the Department of Prints and Drawings in the British Museum, c. 1550 to c. 1640,* 2 vols., London, 1983.

Felton Gibbons. *Catalogue of Italian Drawings in the Art Museum, Princeton University.* 2 vols. Princeton, 1977.

Bob Haak. *The Golden Age: Dutch painters of the seventeenth century.* Translated from the Dutch and edited by Elizabeth Willems-Treeman. New York, 1984.

Detlev Baron von Hadeln. *The Drawings of G.B. Tiepolo.* New York, 1970.

E. Haverkamp Begemann and A.M. Logan. *European Drawings and Watercolors in the Yale University Art Gallery 1500 1900.* 2 vols. New Haven, 1970.

F.W. Hollstein. *Dutch and Flemish Etchings, Engravings and Woodcuts, ca. 1450-1700.* Amsterdam, 1949-84.

Arnold Houbraken. *Grosse Schonburgh der Niederländischen Maler und Malerinnen.* edited by Alfred von Würzbach. Osnabrück, 1970.

Deborah Johnson. *Old Master Drawings from the Museum of Art, Rhode Island School of Design.* Providence, 1983.

Thomas D. Kaufmann. *Drawings from the Holy Roman Empire, 1540-1680.* Princeton, 1982.

Frits Lugt. *Les Marques de Collections de Dessins et d'Estampes.* Amsterdam, 1921.

Metropolitan Museum of Art. *Roman Artists of the 17th Century, Drawings and Prints.* New York, 1976.

Konrad Oberhuber. *Disegni di Tiziano e della sua cerchia.* Venice, 1976.

________________. *Renaissance and Baroque Drawings from the Collections of John and Alice Steiner.* Cambridge, 1977.

________________. *Renaissance and Baroque Drawings from the Collections of John and Alice Steiner; Addenda to the Catalogue.* Cambridge, 1978.

L. Réau. *Iconographie de l'Art Chrétien.* 6 vols. Paris, 1955-59.

Franklin Robinson. *Seventeenth Century Dutch Drawings from American Collections.* Washington D.C., 1977.

James Byam Shaw. *The Drawings of Domenico Tiepolo.* Boston, 1962.

Felice Stampfle. *Rubens and Rembrandt in Their Century: Flemish and Dutch Drawings of the 17th Century from the Pierpont Morgan Library.* Paris, 1979.

Wolfgang Stechow. *Dutch Mannerism, Apogee and Epilogue.* Poughskeepsie, 1970.

Werner Sumowski. *Drawings of the Rembrandt School.* New York, 1979-85.

Giorgio Vasari. *Lives of the most eminent painters, sculptors and architects* (translated by Gaston Duc De Vere; introduction by Kenneth Clark). New York, 1979.

PHOTO CREDITS

p.21 - Jacopo da Empoli, *Baptism of the Spanish Prince,* - Ashmolean Museum, Oxford

p.36 - Luca Cambiaso, *The Sacrifice to Leto,* Palazzo Lercari, Genoa

p.39 - Domenico Campagnola, *Isaac and Jacob,* Uffizi, Florence

p.42 - Annibale Carracci, *Allegorical Figure Leaning on a Column,* Louvre

p.49 - Pietro da Cortona, *Adoration of the Shepherds,* Villa Chigi, Castel Fusano, Ostia

p.50 - Donato Creti, *Madonna in Glory with Saints,* Sanctuario della Beata Vergino, di San Luca, Villani

p.55 - Jacopo da Empoli, *Saint Francis of Paola,* Stanza del Borgo, Milan

P.64 - Anonymous Italian, *Allegory,* Biblioteca Reale, Turin

p.84 - Perino del Vaga, *Saint George and the Dragon,* Museum of Fine Arts, Budapest

p.94 - Giovanni Battista dellla Rovere, *The Appointment of the Blessed Allessandro Sauli as General of the Barnabites,* Barnabite Church, Milan

p.132 - Hubert Robert, *Ruins of the Colosseum,* Musée des Beaux-Arts, Besançon

p.154 - Abraham van Bloemaert, *Crucifixion,* Roman Catholic Church, Scheveningen

p.197 - Herman Saftleven, *Montfoort Landscape,* Morgan Library

p.209 - David Teniers the Younger, *Landscape with Piper and Villagers before Cottages*

p.229 - Hieronymous Francker the Second, *The Shop of Jan Snellinck,* Musée des Beaux-Arts, Brussels

p.230 - Urs Graf, *Underwalden Flag-Bearer*

SANTA BARBARA MUSEUM OF ART

MUSEUM STAFF

ADMINISTRATION

Richard V. West, *Director*
Carl B. Vance, *Deputy Director; Director, Endowment Campaign*
Shelley S. Ruston, *Assistant Director, Publications and Programs*
Elizabeth Bradley, *Executive Secretary to the Director*
Peggy Stevens, *Administrative Assistant to the Deputy Director*
Joan Enasko, *Endowment and Campaign Executive Assistant*
Libby Mc Collum, *Publications and Programs Assistant*
Arlene Klobucher and Marilyn Skiöld, *Receptionists*

CURATORIAL

Robert Henning, Jr., *Chief Curator*
Barry M. Heisler, *Curator of Collections*
Merrily Peebles, *Curator of Exhibitions*
Susan Shin-tsu Tai, *Curator of Oriental Art**
Timothy Hearsum, *Curator of Photography**
Richard Hubbard, *Designer*
Frances Warr, *Curatorial Secretary*
Holly Wilson, *Curatorial Intern*

COLLECTIONS MANAGEMENT

Elaine Poulos Dietsch, *Registrar*
Elaine Cobos, *Assistant Registrar*
Silvia Tyndall, *Prints and Drawings Preparator**

EDUCATION

Ron Crozier, *Librarian*
Pamela Hoeft, *Museum Educator*
Lesley King-Wrightson and Connie Zaun
Assistant Librarian/Slide Librarian
Frances Thorpe, *Education Assistant*

DEVELOPMENT AND MEMBERSHIP

Wilbur Kenneth Cox, *Director of Planned Giving*
Virginia Cochran, *Director of Grants and Public Relations*
Mary McDonald, *Manager of Membership Services*
Kathy O'Leary, *Events and Volunteer Coordinator**
Kimberly G. Edgar, *Development Assistant*
Anita Masi, *Grants and Public Relations Assistant*
Sharon Slade, *Development Secretary*

BUSINESS OFFICE

Gale Poyorena, *Controller*
Kelly Cretti, *Accounting Clerk I*
Su-Ching Lin, *Accounting Clerk II*

TREASURE SALE AND CLOTHES GALLERY

Nancye Andriesse, *Manager*
Katherine Wollman and Letha Lovett, *Assistant Managers**

BOOKSTORE

Penny Mast, *Manager*

MAINTENANCE AND INSTALLATION

Dean Dawson, *Building Superintendent*
Jerry Travis, *Building Technician I*
John A. Coplin, *Building Technician I*
Eugene Brundin, *Building Technician II*
Dane Goodman, *Building Technician I*

SECURITY

Larry Larson, *Chief of Security*
William Andrews, *Deputy Chief of Security*
Noel Assayech, *Security Control*
Guards: David Brown, Walter Hildbrand, Ross Andrews*, David Barnes*, Steven Bissell*, Randall Fowler*, Phil Liddicoat*, Jerry Major*, Reuben Paris*, Jon Riddle*, Ann Skiöld*, Mike Woxell*, Brad Wright*

*Denotes part-time employment

ENDOWMENT BENEFACTORS

The Santa Barbara Museum of Art gratefully acknowledges the generous patronage of those who have established major perpetual trusts and endowments for general Museum purposes.

Trusts:

The Ina Therese Campbell Trust
The Preston and Sterling Morton Fund
The Sophie P. Morton Fund

Endowment Funds:

The William J. Jr., and Thirza G. Joyce Fund
The David Edgar Park Memorial Fund
The Education Endowment Fund

In addition, various special needs of the Museum have been generously provided for by donors who have established or contributed to major funds or endowments for special purposes, including endowments for future operations in the expanded Museum.

Quasi-Endowment Funds:

The Charles and Mildred Bloom Memorial Fund
The Elizabeth A. Chalifoux Fund for the Museum Collection
The Exhibitions Endowment Fund
The Wright Saltus Ludington Fund
The Alice Keck Park Foundation Fund
The Alice Keck Park Testamentary Fund

Community Treasure Endowment Campaign Fund:

Major contributors to this fund for endowing the expanded Museum include the following:

Dr. and Mrs. A. E. Amorteguy
Mr. and Mrs. Richard Reed Armstrong
Atlantic Richfield Foundation
Mr. and Mrs. Richard Bergen
Mr. and Mrs. Barry Berkus
Mr. and Mrs. C. Allan Braun through Braun Foundation
The Capital Group
Mr. and Mrs. J. Hewes Crispin
Mr. and Mrs. Eugene Davidson
Mr. and Mrs. Willard G. DeGroot
Carroll Donner Estate
Mrs. Robert B. Eichholz
Mr. Reginald M. Faletti
Mr. and Mrs. James Hansen
Jones Brothers Construction Corporation
Mrs. William H. Joyce, Jr.
Florence L. Lamb Estate
Mr. and Mrs. Jon Lovelace
Mr. and Mrs. Arthur A. Milligan
Dan Murphy Foundation
National Endowment for the Arts
Alice Keck Park Estate
Mrs. Charles Partridge
Mrs. Dorothy T. Peck-Flynn
Mr. and Mrs. Hugh Petersen
Santa Barbara Bank & Trust
Security Pacific Foundation
Mr. and Mrs. Robert K. Straus
Hammett and Thayer Memorial Fund
Times Mirror Foundation
Mr. and Mrs. Robert Vaillancourt
Mrs. Edward R. Valentine